THE DARKER NATIONS

ALSO BY VIJAY PRASHAD

Everybody Was Kung Fu Fighting: Afro-Asian Connections and the Myth of Cultural Purity

Fat Cats and Running Dogs: The Enron Stage of Capitalism

The Karma of Brown Folk

Keeping Up with the Dow Joneses: Debt, Prison, Workfare

The Darker Nations

A People's History
of the Third World

A NEW PRESS PEOPLE'S HISTORY

VIJAY PRASHAD

Series Editor
Howard Zinn

THE NEW PRESS

NEW YORK
LONDON

Requests for permission to reproduce selections from this book should be mailed to:
Permissions Department, The New Press, 38 Greene Street,
New York, NY 10013.

Grateful acknowledgment is made to the following for permission to reprint the following
previously published material:

"The Dictators" and a section of "Recabarren" by Pablo Neruda from *Canto General*, translated by
Jack Schmitt. Copyright © 1991 by The Regents of the University of California. Reprinted with
permission of University of California Press.

"A Call to Arms" and "Someone Who Is Not Like Anyone" by Forugh Farrokhzad from
A Lonely Woman: Forugh Farrokhzad and Her Poetry by Michael C. Hillman.
Copyright © 1987. Reprinted with permission of Lynne Rienner Publishers.

Published in the United States by The New Press, New York, 2008
Distributed by W.W. Norton & Company, Inc., New York

LIBRARY OF CONGRESS CATALOGING-IN-PUBLICATION DATA
Prashad, Vijay.
The darker nations : a people's history of the third world / Vijay Prashad.
p.   cm.—(A New Press People's history)
Includes bibliographical references and index.
ISBN 978-1-56584-785-9 (hc.)
ISBN 978-1-59558-342-0 (pbk.)
1. Developing countries—History.   I. Title.
D883.P74   2007
909'.09724–dc22
2006020908

The New Press was established in 1990 as a not-for-profit alternative to the large,
commercial publishing houses currently dominating the book publishing industry.
The New Press operates in the public interest rather than for private gain, and
is committed to publishing, in innovative ways, works of educational, cultural,
and community value that are often deemed insufficiently profitable.

www.thenewpress.com

Composition by Westchester Book Composition
This book was set in Fournier

Printed in the United States of America

4   6   8   10   9   7   5   3

FOR BELA MALIK

CONTENTS

Series Preface by Howard Zinn   ix

Acknowledgments   xi

Introduction   xv

Part 1: Quest

Paris   3

a concept conjured

Brussels   16

the 1928 League against Imperialism

Bandung   31

the 1955 Afro-Asian Conference

Cairo   51

the 1961 Afro-Asian Women's Conference

Buenos Aires   62

imagining an economy

Tehran   75

cultivating an imagination

Belgrade   95

the 1961 Non-Aligned Movement Conference

Havana   105

the 1966 Tricontinental Conference

Part 2: Pitfalls

Algiers 119

the perils of an authoritarian state

La Paz 134

released from the barracks

Bali 151

death of the Communists

Tawang 165

war most foul

Caracas 176

oil, the devil's excrement

Arusha 191

socialism in a hurry

Part 3: Assassinations

New Delhi 207

the obituary of the Third World

Kingston 224

IMF-led globalization

Singapore 245

the lure of the Asian Road

Mecca 260

when culture can be cruel

Conclusion 276

Notes 283

Index 349

SERIES PREFACE

Turning history on its head opens up whole new worlds of possibility. Once, historians looked only at society's upper crust: the leaders and others who made the headlines and whose words and deeds survived as historical truth. In our lifetimes, this has begun to change. Shifting history's lens from the upper rungs to the lower, we are learning more than ever about the masses of people who did the work that made society tick.

Not surprisingly, as the lens shifts the basic narratives change as well. The history of men and women of all classes, colors, and cultures reveals an astonishing degree of struggle and independent political action. Everyday people played complicated historical roles, and they developed highly sophisticated and often very different political ideas from the people who ruled them. Sometimes their accomplishments left tangible traces; other times, the traces are invisible but no less real. They left their mark on our institutions, our folkways and language, on our political habits and vocabulary. We are only now beginning to excavate this multifaceted history.

The New Press People's History Series roams far and wide through human history, revisiting old stories in new ways, and introducing altogether new accounts of the struggles of common people to make their own history. Taking the lives and viewpoints of common people as its point of departure, the series reexamines subjects as different as the American Revolution, the history of sports, the history of American art, the Mexican Revolution, and the rise of the Third World.

A people's history does more than add to the catalogue of what we already know. These books will shake up readers' understanding of the past—just as common people throughout history have shaken up their always changeable worlds.

Howard Zinn
Boston, 2000

ACKNOWLEDGMENTS

In 1981, during the summer, I wrote a short essay as a school project on the history of oil. My father introduced me to Anthony Sampson's *The Seven Sisters*, and to the complex history of the Organization of Petroleum Exporting Countries (OPEC), including the role of the Venezuelan and Saudi Arabian oil ministers who feature in this book. When my father died in 1999, I had already begun to think of this book, and we had briefly discussed its contours. As with all my other books, this one too is written in conversation with his spirit.

Andy Hsiao at The New Press unearthed this book, and edited it with care, wisdom, and grace. Sudhanva Deshpande at Leftword Books is my political mooring.

Ten years ago, Naeem Inayatullah gave me a copy of *Global Rift* by L.S. Stavrianos. The book allowed me to visualize the history of the Third World, although Stavrianos had a much longer story to tell (from the start of colonialism to the 1980s). My ambit is much briefer, but it could not have been without Naeem's gift.

Helpful librarians at Trinity College, the University of Massachusetts, the Hoover Institute, Singapore's National Archives, and the International Institute of Social History (Amsterdam) as well as the necessary labor of Professor Vatroslav Vekaric, editor of the *Review of International Affairs*, enabled me to assemble the materials necessary for this book. Friends here and there, including my sister Leela, provided me with the essential linguistic assistance (particularly to make my elementary European language skills come to life). Each snapshot, each section, is rooted in a city or a town. The book opens in Paris and ends in Mecca. I take advantage of this structure to tell the history of each city, of its country and its various movements. This kind of book relies greatly on secondary sources, and therefore on the hard and generous labors of generations of scholars. The length of the endnotes is an indication of how much I have borrowed from and owe them. For the lay reader, there might be too much detail; for the specialist, there will be too little. This is the risk of such a book.

Sarah Fan, Joel Ariaratnam, and Melissa Richards (all of The New Press), and Cindy Milstein, the copy editor, gave this book all the help it needed.

Several people took these ideas seriously before I knew they had any currency. The Labor/Community Strategy Center (notably, Eric Mann, Lian Hurst Mann, Tammy Bang Luu, and Manuel Criollo) not only invited me to Los Angeles to talk about these issues but also published my ideas in its *Ahora Now*. Greg Meyerson (of *Cultural Logic*) and I had a productive discussion during a trip to North Carolina A&T. Just Act (Rishi Awantramani, Josh Warren-White, and Steve Williams) provided a nice forum in San Francisco to debate the many left lines that cut through the darker nations. Betty Bayer afforded a more genteel podium at Hobart and William Smith College, where I got to deliver a Fisher Center Lecture and have valuable conversations on race and nationalism. Howard Winant's intellectual hospitality at the University of California at Santa Barbara is unmatched. Shiva Balaghi, Lisa Duggan, Andrew Ross, and Walter Johnson as well as Vivek Bald buoyed me with ideas and inspiration. Indira Ravindran gave me a push. At Trinity, I'm blessed to have Michael Niemann, Barbara Sicherman, Susan Pennybacker, Joan Hedrick, Johnny Williams, and Raymond Baker, all of whom know the world with clarity and compassion. Former students Toufic Haddad and Sai Madivala, among others, taught me with their wisdom and political commitments. Bill Strickland dropped the essential plumb line. Teo Ballvé, Shonali Bose, Amitava Kumar, Sunaina Maira, Gautam Premnath, Kasturi Ray, P. Sainath, and Rinku Sen give me my bearings. Mir Ali Raza gave me this line from Faiz (*Zindan Nama*, 1956), which reminds us of the hope in the twin projects of the Third World and socialism: "One day, this field will ripen for the bountiful harvest/Till then, we must toil in the field without rest."

In Delhi, I tried out these ideas thanks to Sudhanva Deshpande at the Oxford Book Store for a Leftword Books event. In Chennai, I tried out variations of the broad thesis at the Madras Bar Association (thanks to G. Chamki Raj and K. Subburam), All-India Women's Association (thanks to my sister Rani), the Indian School of Social Science (thanks to R. Vijayshankar), and the MS Swaminathan Research Foundation (thanks to K. Nagaraj, Rukmani, and Venkatesh Atreya). Shorter pieces that drew from the book appeared thanks to my editors at *Frontline* (N. Ram and R. Vijayshakar), ZNET (Mike Albert), *Counterpunch* (Alexander Cockburn and Jeffery St. Clair), and *Monthly Review* (John Bellamy Foster). The earliest version of this book was *War against the Planet: The Fifth Afghan War, Imperialism, and Other Assorted Fundamentalisms* (New Delhi: Leftword, 2002). Tom Fenton invited me to participate in a roundtable on the work of Peter Gowan for *Critical Asian Studies*, where I worked out some additional directions. Rachael Gillett and Paul Teodoulou of *Global Dialogue* opened their pages to some of this book's ideas. Salah D. Hassan (*CR: The New Centennial Review*) along with Naeem Inayatullah and Robin Riley (for their edited collection *Interrogating Imperialism* [Palgrave, 2006]) enabled Lisa Armstrong and myself to try out more elaborate versions of our analysis of women's rights in a national liberation framework. All this and more helped me craft the thesis and story that is *The Darker Nations*.

I wrote most of the book in Northampton, Massachusetts, which is such a terrific town. It would be so much less without the rigor of the *Valley War Bulletin* collective (Beth Adel, Diana Riddle, Fidelito Cortes, Jean Grossholtz, Jeff Napolitano, Jo Comerford, Lisa Armstrong, Megan Tady, Nerissa Balce, Phyllis Rodin, Sai Madivala, and Tim Scott). Larry Parnass owes me coffee. Catherine Carija is a solace. Michael, Mariangeles, and Kai: come back soon. Frances Crowe is an icon. Adare Place is a haven. Group B is paradise. So many dear friends, so little time.

My wise family gives me warmth and ideas. My mother and Rosy in Calcutta, sister in Madras, sister and brother in California, nieces and nephews in Arizona, California, Hyderabad, and Bangalore, the Bose-Pains in Los Angeles, the B207 nest made comfortable by the mashis, the new one in Chittaranjan Park, and the Armstrongs of California and Connecticut. The book would be nothing without the theoretical and political wisdom of Brinda Karat and Prakash Karat.

The Darker Nations is for Lisa, who gets it before I do. And for Zalia Maya and Rosa Maya, who know better.

INTRODUCTION

> The Third World today faces Europe like a colossal mass whose project should be to try to resolve the problems to which Europe has not been able to find the answers.
>
> —Frantz Fanon, *The Wretched of the Earth*, 1961[1]

The Third World was not a place. It was a project. During the seemingly interminable battles against colonialism, the peoples of Africa, Asia, and Latin America dreamed of a new world. They longed for dignity above all else, but also the basic necessities of life (land, peace, and freedom). They assembled their grievances and aspirations into various kinds of organizations, where their leadership then formulated a platform of demands. These leaders, whether India's Jawaharlal Nehru, Egypt's Gamal Abdel Nasser, Ghana's Kwame Nkrumah, or Cuba's Fidel Castro, met at a series of gatherings during the middle decades of the twentieth century. In Bandung (1955), Havana (1966), and elsewhere, these leaders crafted an ideology and a set of institutions to bear the hopes of their populations. The "Third World" comprised these hopes and the institutions produced to carry them forward.

From the rubble of World War II rose a bipolar Cold War that threatened the existence of humanity. Hair-triggers on nuclear weapons alongside heated debates about poverty, inequality, and freedom threatened even those who did not live under the U.S. or Soviet umbrellas. Both sides, as Nehru noted, pelted each other with arguments about peace. Almost unmolested by the devastation of the war, the United States used its advantages to rebuild the two sides of Eurasia and cage

Guinea-Bissau, September 1974: No Fist Is Big Enough to Hide the Sky. © ALAIN DEJEAN/SYGMA/CORBIS

in a battered Soviet Union. Phrases like "massive retaliation" and "brinkmanship" provided no comfort to the two-thirds of the world's people who had only recently won or were on the threshold of winning their independence from colonial rulers.

Thrown between these two major formations, the darker nations amassed as the Third World. Determined people struck out against colonialism to win their freedom. They demanded political equality on the world level. The main institution for this expression was the United Nations. From its inception in 1948, the United Nations played an enormous role for the bulk of the planet. Even if they did not earn permanent seats on the UN Security Council, the new states took advantage of the UN General Assembly to put forward their demands. The Afro-Asian meetings in Bandung and Cairo (1955 and 1961, respectively), the creation of the Non-Aligned Movement in Belgrade (1961), and the Tricontinental Conference in Havana rehearsed the major arguments within the Third World project so that they could take them in a concerted way to the main stage, the United Nations. In addition, the new states pushed the United Nations to create institutional platforms for their Third World agenda: the UN Conference on Trade and Development (UNCTAD) was the most important of these institutions, but it was not the only one. Through these institutions, aspects other than political equality came to the fore: the Third World project included

a demand for the redistribution of the world's resources, a more digni-
fied rate of return for the labor power of their people, and a shared acknowledgment of the heritage of science, technology, and culture.

In Bandung, the host Ahmed Sukarno offered this catechism for the
Third World:

> Let us not be bitter about the past, but let us keep our eyes firmly
> on the future. Let us remember that no blessing of God is so sweet
> as life and liberty. Let us remember that the stature of all mankind
> is diminished so long as nations or parts of nations are still unfree.
> Let us remember that the highest purpose of man is the liberation
> of man from his bonds of fear, his bonds of poverty, the libera-
> tion of man from the physical, spiritual and intellectual bonds
> which have for long stunted the development of humanity's ma-
> jority. And let us remember, Sisters and Brothers, that for the sake
> of all that, we Asians and Africans must be united.[2]

The idea of the Third World moved millions and created heroes.
Some of these were political figures like the three titans (Nasser, Nehru,
Sukarno), but also Vietnam's Nguyen Thi Binh and Ho Chi Minh, Algeria's Ben Bella, and South Africa's Nelson Mandela. The project also
provided the elements of a new imagination for its cultural workers—
people such as the poet Pablo Neruda, the singer Umm Kulthum, and
the painter Sudjana Kerton. The horizon produced by the Third World
enthused them, along with those who made history in their everyday
lives. The Third World project united these discordant comrades.

The Third World project came with a built-in flaw. The fight against
the colonial and imperial forces enforced a unity among various political parties and across social classes. Widely popular social movements
and political formations won freedom for the new nations, and then took
power. Once in power, the unity that had been preserved at all costs became a liability. The working class and the peasantry in many of these
movements had acceded to an alliance with the landlords and emergent
industrial elites. Once the new nation came into their hands, the people
believed, the new state would promote a socialist program. What they
got instead was a compromise ideology called Arab Socialism, African
Socialism, Sarvodaya, or NASAKOM that combined the promise of
equality with the maintenance of social hierarchy. Rather than provide
the means to create an entirely new society, these regimes protected the
elites among the old social classes while producing the elements of social welfare for the people. Once in power, the old social classes exerted

themselves, either through the offices of the military or the victorious people's party. In many places, the Communists were domesticated, outlawed, or massacred to maintain this discordant unity. In the first few decades of state construction, from the 1940s to the 1970s, consistent pressure from working people, the prestige of the national liberation party, and the planetary consensus over the use of the state to create demand constrained these dominant classes to some extent. They still took charge of the new states, but their desire for untrammeled profit was hampered by lingering patriotism or the type of political and economic regimes established by national liberation.

By the 1970s, the new nations were no longer new. Their failures were legion. Popular demands for land, bread, and peace had been ignored on behalf of the needs of the dominant classes. Internecine warfare, a failure to control the prices of primary commodities, an inability to overcome the suffocation of finance capital, and more led to a crisis in the budgets of much of the Third World. Borrowings from commercial banks could only come if the states agreed to "structural adjustment" packages from the International Monetary Fund (IMF) and the World Bank. The assassination of the Third World led to the desiccation of the capacity of the state to act on behalf of the population, an end to making the case for a new international economic order, and a disavowal of the goals of socialism. Dominant classes that had once been tethered to the Third World agenda now cut loose. They began to see themselves as elites, and not as part of a project—the patriotism of the bottom line overcame obligatory social solidarity. An upshot of this demise of the Third World agenda was the growth of forms of cultural nationalism in the darker nations. Atavisms of all kinds emerged to fill the space once taken up by various forms of socialism. Fundamentalist religion, race, and unreconstructed forms of class power emerged from under the wreckage of the Third World project.

The demise of the Third World has been catastrophic. People across the three continents continue to dream of something better, and many of them are organized into social movements or political parties. Their aspirations have a local voice. Beyond that, their hopes and dreams are unintelligible. During the middle decades of the twentieth century, the Third World agenda bore these beliefs from localities to national capitals and onward to the world stage. The institutions of the Third World amassed these ideas and nailed them to the doors of powerful buildings. The Third World project (the ideology and institutions) enabled the powerless to hold a dialogue with the powerful, and to try to hold them accountable. Today, there is no such vehicle for local dreams. *The Darker Nations* is written to remind us of that immense labor and its importance.

The account is not exhaustive but illustrative. *The Darker Nations* makes a broad argument about the nature of the Third World political project, and the causes and consequences of its decline. The world was bettered by the attempt to articulate a Third World agenda. Now it is impoverished for the lack of that motion.

Part 1
QUEST

PARIS

Among the darker nations, Paris is famous for two betrayals. The first came in 1801, when Napoléon Bonaparte sent General Victor Leclerc to crush the Haitian Revolution, itself inspired by the French Revolution. The French regime could not allow its lucrative Santo Domingo to go free, and would not allow the Haitian people to live within the realm of the Enlightenment's "Rights of Man." The Haitians nonetheless triumphed, and Haiti became the first modern colony to win its independence.[1]

The second betrayal came shortly after 1945, when a battered France, newly liberated by the Allies, sent its forces to suppress the Vietnamese, West Indians, and Africans who had once been its colonial subjects. Many of these regions had sent troops to fight for the liberation of France and indeed Europe, but they returned home empty-handed.[2] As a sleight of hand, the French government tried to maintain sovereignty over its colonies by repackaging them as "overseas territories." A people hungry for liberation did not want such measly hors d'oeuvres.

In 1955, Aimé Césaire, the Martinique-born philosopher and then-Communist activist, published his *Discourse on Colonialism*. Alioune Diop's celebrated publishing house, Presence Africaine, released the short manifesto as one more of its bold books intended both to create a dossier of the cultural wealth of Africa and its diaspora and to put European colonialism on notice for its brutality.[3]

In the opening pages of *Discourse*, Césaire writes, "*Europe is indefensible.*" "From the depths of slavery," millions of people "set themselves up

Belgrade, Yugoslavia, September 1961: Standing tall—presidents and prime ministers at the first meeting of the Non-Aligned Movement. From left: Nehru, Nkrumah, Nasser, Sukarno, Tito. COURTESY OF THE NEHRU MEMORIAL MUSEUM AND LIBRARY, NEW DELHI

as judges." The colonizer continues to brutalize the people in Vietnam, Madagascar, West Africa, the West Indies, and elsewhere, but the colonized now have the advantage. "They know their temporary 'masters' are lying. Therefore that their masters are weak."[4]

In 1945–46, thousands of French troops returned to the Red River delta in Indochina, and Ho Chi Minh and his comrades retreated to the highlands of the Viet Bac to regroup for an extended war of liberation. This war lasted for almost a decade. But the French had an ally in another ambivalent revolutionary. By 1952, the U.S. government had already begun to pay for almost two-thirds of the battered French military treasury's expenses. The French had to depart after their army suffered an embarrassing defeat from the poorly equipped but highly motivated Viet Minh at the garrison town of Dien Bien Phu (1954).

In 1945, meanwhile, the French paratroopers and air force used brutal force to disband the anticolonial Algerian Amis du Manifeste et de la Liberté (Friends of the Manifesto and Liberty), harass hundreds of thousands of people through the French policy of *ratonnades* (a rat hunt), and kill tens of thousands of Algerians. This massacre provoked the formation of the Front de Libération Nationale (FLN), which emerged in a spectacular assault on French positions in Algeria on All Saints' Day, November 1, 1954.

And again, in 1947, when the people of Madagascar demanded their freedom, formed the Mouvement Democratique de la Renovation Malagache, and rose in revolt, the French forces countered them with bloodthirsty violence and killed tens of thousands. The guerrilla war continued, until the French had to concede some power to the Malagasy people, but only after a decade of repression and deceit.

These are some of Césaire's examples, but there are more. Each instance pits a people fired up for freedom, even willing to submit themselves to suicide attacks (as in Vietnam and Algeria) or else suicidal advances against superior French military positions. The sacrifice of the colonized to secure their freedom terrified the French army and its political supervisors, just as it provided inspiration for others who had to fight for their own process of decolonization.

Why did the French forget *liberté, egalité, fraternité* when they went into the tropics? As Césaire noted, Albert Sarraut, the French minister of colonies in the 1920s, had written that France must not turn over the colonies to the nationalists in the name of "an alleged right to possess the land one occupies, and some sort of right to remain in fierce isolation, which would leave unutilized resources to lie forever idle in the hands of incompetents."[5] Sarraut followed John Locke's logic, as put forward in his 1689 treatise on government: "God gave the World to Men in Common; but since he gave it to them for their benefit, and the greatest Conveniences of Life they were capable to draw from it, it cannot be supposed he meant it should always remain common and uncultivated. He gave it to the use of the Industrious and Rational (and *Labour* was to be *his Title* to it;) not to the Fancy or Covetousness of the Quarrelsome and Contentious."[6] For Sarraut, those who *developed* the land had title to it, even as those without title would do the actual work on it. Since only Europeans could count as competent users of God's nature, only they could own it.

In 1922, Ho Chi Minh wrote a rejoinder in the French Communist press to the same Sarraut,

> We know very well that your affection for the natives of the colonies in general, and the Annamese [Vietnamese] in particular, is great. Under your proconsulate the Annamese people have

known true prosperity and real happiness, the happiness of seeing their country dotted all over with an increasing number of spirit and opium shops which, together with firing squads, prisons, "democracy," and all the improved apparatus of modern civilization, are combining to make the Annamese the most advanced of the Asians and the happiest of mortals. These acts of benevolence save us the trouble of recalling all the others, such as enforced recruitment and loans, bloody repressions, the dethronement and exile of kings, profanation of sacred places, etc.[7]

In Europe, the Holocaust gave pause to the idea that barbarity comes only from the darker races. In the aftermath of Auschwitz and Treblinka, Europe tried to blame Adolf Hitler as an insane individual or else the Nazis as a party with a warped ideology. In conference after conference, Europe's intellectuals bemoaned the insanity of the brutal massacre of Jews, Communists, Gypsies, and the disabled—but most of them remained silent about the ongoing violence in the tropics. Césaire invokes the barbarity of Western Europe and the United States, only to stop and warn us, "I am not talking about Hitler, or the prison guard, or the adventurer, but about the 'decent fellow' across the way; not about the member of the SS, or the gangster, but about the respectable bourgeoisie." The violence in the tropics is nothing if not "a sign that cruelty, mendacity, baseness, and corruption have sunk deep into the soul of the European bourgeoisie."[8]

Césaire's indictment of the European soul had company. Within France, a group of intellectuals had been repulsed by the horrors of both World War II and the ongoing war in Algeria. One such dissident voice belonged to Albert Sauvy. Sauvy had been a Resistance fighter, and after the war he began to write for *France-Observateur*, a paper that under the leadership of Sauvy's fellow Resistance veteran Claude Bourdet, became an organ of anticolonial thought. Bourdet himself wrote a scathing denunciation of the Algerian War. "Have we become the Gestapo in Algeria?" Bourdet asked.[9] The pages of *France-Observateur*, soon to be renamed *L'Observateur*, was home to anticolonial intellectuals like Michel Leiris and Claude Lévi-Strauss, who orbited around the antiracist activities of the UN Educational, Scientific, and Cultural Organization (UNESCO) House.[10]

In 1952, Sauvy, in the pages of *L'Observateur*, offered an evocative tripartite division of the planet into the First, Second, and Third Worlds.[11] When Sauvy wrote in the Parisian press, most people already understood what it meant to live in the First and Second Worlds. In March 1946, the former British premier Winston Churchill had declared that an "Iron Curtain" had descended across Europe, from the Baltic to the Adriatic, and it had divided the former allies into two distinct blocs. Churchill said this during a long speech in the United States, primus inter pares of the First World. This First World or the "West" was formed by states, notably the United States and those of Western Europe, that pledged themselves to partly regulated market capitalism and would, in 1949, form the North Atlantic Treaty Organization (NATO).

The Second World rejected market capitalism for socialist planning, and it generally worked in collusion with the largest socialist state, the USSR. "Warsaw, Berlin, Prague, Vienna, Budapest, Belgrade, Bucharest and Sofia: all these famous cities and the populations around them," Churchill told the students at Westminster College in Fulton, Missouri, "lie in what I must call the Soviet sphere, and all are subject, in one form or another, not only to Soviet influence but to a very high and in some cases increasing measure of control from Moscow."[12]

The First and Second Worlds fell out openly when U.S. president Harry S. Truman announced his support for the anticommunist forces in Turkey and Greece (1946), the Central Intelligence Agency (CIA) helped the conservatives defeat the popular Communists in the Italian and French elections of 1947, the USSR forced the Eastern European states into its orbit, and the animosity attained dramatic proportions during the First World's blockade of Berlin in June 1948. In this melee, an adviser to Truman (Bernard Baruch) used the term "Cold War" to describe the conflict, and a columnist (Walter Lippmann) made the phrase widely known.[13]

The Cold War defines how most people see the period from 1946 to the demise of the USSR in 1989–91; the East-West conflict, intensified by nuclear weapons, dominates the stage for this crucial fifty-year period.

The phrase "East-West conflict" distorts the history of the Cold War because it makes it seem as if the First and Second Worlds confronted each other in a condition of equality. In an insightful article from 1968, the Swedish sociologist Göran Therborn wrote, "*The Cold War was a fundamentally unequal conflict, that was presented and experienced on both sides as being equal.*"[14] The USSR and the United States portrayed each other as equivalent adversaries, although the former had an economic base that was far inferior to the latter. Despite the great advances of the Soviet regime in the development of the various republics, the USSR began its history with a battered feudal economy that was soon ravished by a civil war and, later, the ferocious assaults of the Nazi war machine. In 1941, both the United States and the USSR had populations of about 130 million, but whereas the United States lost upward of four hundred thousand troops in the war, the Soviets lost between twenty and thirty million troops and civilians.[15] The Great Patriotic War devastated the USSR's economy, population, and capacity to rebuild itself. Furthermore, the imperatives of rapid development tarnished the ideals of Soviet society since its population went into a severe program to build its productive base at the expense of most internal freedoms. The dominant classes in the First World used the shortages and repression in the USSR as an instructive tool to wield over the heads of their own working class, and so on both economic and political grounds the First World bore advantages over the Second. Regardless of the ideological commitment of the USSR to total equality and that of the United States to market equality only, the latter appeared to many in Europe and elsewhere as a more compelling model after World War II. For this reason, Therborn argues, "An unequal conflict fought as equal redoubles the inequality. The Cold War was a long penalization of socialism."[16] The concept of socialism had to pay the penalty for Soviet limitations.

But the First and Second Worlds only accounted for a third of the planet's people. What of the two-thirds who remained outside the East-West circles; what of those 2 billion people?

The First World saw them as poor, overly fecund, profligate, and worthless. Images of poverty in the formerly colonized world flooded the magazines and newspapers of the First World—not more so perhaps than in times past, but with a new emphasis. Now, these countries did not have the tutelage of their colonial masters but had to wallow in their inability to handle their resources and disasters. Images of natural calamities, famines, and droughts joined those of hordes of unkempt bodies flooding the First World's living rooms—where pity and revulsion toward the darker nations festered. Paul Ehrlich's 1968 *The Population Bomb* received such tremendous acclaim in the First World because its neo-Malthusian ideas had already become commonplace: that the reason for hunger in the world had more to do with overpopulation than with imperialism; that the survivors of colonialism had only themselves to blame for their starvation. The people of the colonies cannot save themselves, so they must be saved. The agencies of the First World could provide them with "family planning" or "birth control" technologies to break the Gordian knot of population growth, and they could offer them charitable aid. When "aid" came from the First World, it would not come without conditions. As the president of the World Bank, Eugene Black, wrote in 1960, "Economic aid should be the principle means by which the West maintains its political and economic dynamic in the underdeveloped world."[17] Contempt sometimes manifested itself in condescension. When the First World overly romanticized the darker nations as childlike or overly cultured, it did not see its people as human, fallible, contradictory, and historical.

When Asia and Africa had been under the direct colonial control of Europe, the colonizers spoke of the value of the regions, both for their resources and human labor. Amnesia rapidly set in within the First World, for those precious regions, even the Jewel in the Crown (India), became seen only as the sewer pit of humanity. Mother Teresa would soon get more positive airtime as the white savior of the dark hordes than would the self-directed projects of the Third World nationalist governments.[18] Any time one of the darker nations tried to exert its independence from the "political and economic dynamic" of the First World, military invasions and embargoes tried to strangle its capacity, and the media went along. For example, when a rebellion against British rule among the Kenyan Kikuyu went into high gear between 1952 and 1956, the British media trafficked in images of native savagery (several hundred thousand Kikuyu died in the "war"). The British policy sought to exterminate rather than contain the rebellion, and in the interim it energized the most vicious settler racism (the journalist Anthony Sampson recalled, "I heard it everywhere I went. How many Kukes [Kikuyu] had to be gotten rid of, how many Kukes did you wink today. [It was] almost like they were talking about big game hunting"). The concentration on the presumed savagery of the natives by the media provided an open season for the calculated violence of the imperial troops.[19]

But the First World also saw that zone of the world as prey for the Second World. To those who had recently attained political independence but had not yet harvested the fruits of opportunity and equality, the attraction of egalitarianism was great.[20] Certainly, Communism as an idea and the USSR as an inspiration held an important place in the imagination of the anticolonial movements from Indonesia to Cuba. Yet the Second World had an attitude toward the former colonies that in some ways mimicked that of the First World. For the founding conference of the Cominform held in Poland in 1947, the Soviets did not invite even one Communist Party from the former colonized world, and certainly not the Chinese Party. Nine parties, mainly from Eastern Europe,

heard Andrei Zhdanov report that the world had been divided into two
"camps," the "imperialist and antidemocratic camp," whose "fundamental leading force is the United States" with Great Britain and France
"as satellites of the United States," and the "anti-imperialist, democratic
camp," which "draws support from the working class and democratic
movement in all countries, from the fraternal Communist Parties, from
the national liberation movements in all colonial and dependent countries, and from the help of all the democratic and progressive forces
which exist in each country."[21] In his long speech, Zhdanov made only
this brief mention of national liberation movements. There was no mention of China in his entire report. For the "imperialist and antidemocratic camp," Zhdanov noted, "the leading role is taken by the Soviet
Union and its foreign policy."[22] The Soviets did not see the rest of the
planet as a storehouse of resources, but neither did they see it as filled
with people who had fought a strong anticolonial struggle and wanted
to *lead* their own movements, *craft* their own history. In answer to the
formation of NATO in 1949, the USSR had created the Warsaw Pact in
1955, a military agreement with Albania, Bulgaria, Czechoslovakia,
East Germany, Hungary, Poland, and Romania.

"Sadly," Sauvy wrote, the two major camps "struggled for possession
of the Third World." But Sauvy identified something critical from the
standpoint of the darker nations: that they should not be seen with pitiful
eyes, since they had not only struggled hard to dispatch their colonial
masters but had also begun to create a political platform for unity against
what the Ghanaian leader Kwame Nkrumah called "neocolonialism," or
domination by means other than territorial conquest. The "Third World"
was not prone, silent, and unable to speak before the powers. Indeed, at
the founding conferences of the United Nations (San Francisco, 1945) and
UNESCO (London, 1945), the delegates from the Third World held their
own. While there has been much-deserved attention to the role of Eleanor
Roosevelt for the drafting of the human rights agenda at the San Francisco
meeting, the historical record tends to underplay the crucial role played by
the twenty-nine Latin American states. Cuba sent thirty-year-old Guy
Pérez Cisneros as its representative, and he fought doggedly for an expansive interpretation of human rights, helped along the way by the Panaman-
ian delegation, which offered the decisive draft declarations on education,
work, health care, and social security.[23] In London, at the UNESCO
meeting, India's Rajkumari Amrit Kaur recognized that neither of the two
camps had an agenda that rose to the occasion of the Third World. Having gauged the sentiment of the Third World delegates, she called for

"true freedom," which meant a world in which "exploitation and injustice [would not] flourish side by side with pious expressions of good intentions and high-sounding policies."[24] The hypocrisy of "pious expressions" had already begun to infect the post–World War world, and dogged persistence from the Third World delegates to these conferences resulted in the creation of institutions for justice rather than declarations of intent.

Sauvy used the term Third World in a manner that resonated with how that part of the planet had already begun to act. His term, crucially, paid homage to the French Revolution, an important inspiration for the ongoing decolonization process. At the end of his article, Sauvy wrote that the "ignored, exploited, scorned Third World, like the Third Estate, demands to become something as well." In the ancien régime prior to 1789, the monarchy divided its counselors into the First Estate (clergy) and the Second Estate (aristocracy), with a Third Estate being for the bourgeoisie. During the tumult of the French Revolution, the Third Estate fashioned itself as the National Assembly, and invited the totality of the population to be sovereign over it. In the same way, the Third World would speak its mind, find the ground for unity, and take possession of the dynamic of world affairs. This was the enlightened promise of the Third World.

Sauvy's term Third World defined the political platform being constructed by the new nations in the formerly colonized regions of Africa and Asia. A central character in this story is Nehru, the prime minister of the Republic of India from 1947 to his death in 1964. When Sauvy's term came to his ears via his nationalist colleague Acharya Kripalani, Nehru heard it as "Third Force." He did not like the idea of force, because, as he told the Indian Parliament in 1957, force is measured by "armed strength, nuclear strength, ballistic strength, monetary strength," and since the countries that came together against the camp mentality did not have any of these, the only thing they could do was to "collect together." The countries that come together "may create moral pressures, but not a force. It will not make the slightest difference to the great military powers of today if the militarily weak countries band themselves together." Nevertheless, Nehru told the parliament in 1958, "it is right that countries of a like way of thinking should come together, should confer together, should jointly function in the United Nations or elsewhere."[25] The misheard term allowed Nehru to reiterate the main points of the Third World platform: political independence, nonviolent international relations, and the cultivation of the United Nations as the principle institution for planetary justice.

The struggles that produced Nehru had also incubated many of these ideas. Forged in the smithy of colonialism, the Indian freedom movement drew from the resistance of the peasants and workers, the revolutionary idealism of young people, and the smothered aspirations of the new professional classes. These social forces had tried violent terrorism and uprisings as well as the quiet solicitude of petitions. Neither armed struggle nor unctuous petitions dampened the confidence of colonialism. Rather, the turn to mass nonviolent struggle had commanded the field, and it is this experience of "moral force" (or *Satyagraha*, action on the basis of truth) that appealed to Nehru (as it did, among others, to Ghana's Convention People's Party as well as the South African Defiance Campaign of 1952). These anticolonial struggles that had adopted the broad approach of mass nonviolence had begun to converse with each other from as early as the 1927 League against Imperialism conference in Brussels. The delegates to that conference, like Nehru, confirmed their mutual antipathy to European-style cultural nationalism.[26]

If European nationalism took as a given that a people (who are perhaps a "race") need to be organized by a state so that their nation can come into its own, the anticolonial nationalists mostly argued that the people (who are often far too diverse to classify one way or another) need to be free of colonial rule. The formerly colonized people have at least one thing in common: they are colonized. Nehru, Sukarno, and others who had been pushed by similar social processes developed an alternative "national" theory. For them, the nation had to be constructed out of two elements: the history of their struggles against colonialism, and their program for the creation of justice. Whereas there were several limitations to their program, it was clear that few of the movements that moved toward the Third World agenda came with a theory of the nation that based itself wholly or even largely on racial or monocultural grounds (where they would have demanded, for instance, cultural assimilation).[27] Instead, they had an internationalist ethos, one that looked outward to other anticolonial nations as their fellows. The Third World form of nationalism is thus better understood as an *internationalist nationalism*.

Many of those who complain about the term's homogenization of the distinct histories of different regions miss the point. The conservative economist Lord Peter T. Bauer rejected the term Third World in his 1981 book of essays because he felt that it treated the world as a "uniform and stagnant mass devoid of distinctive character," and that it denied "those individuals and societies which comprise the Third World of their identity, character, personality and responsibility."[28]

Bauer entirely misconstrues Sauvy's term, and indeed the movement that fashioned the category into a political force. The category is an act of artifice for a global social movement that had only a short history behind it. Sociopolitical identities that are constructed outside sociopolitical movements are often unable to draw people to them—Third World as an idea could not have become common currency only from Sauvy's coinage or the First World media's use of it. The anticolonial nationalist movement produced a series of gatherings and a language of anticolonialism that elicited an emotional loyalty among its circle and beyond. This historical struggle made the identity of the Third World comprehensible and viable. The identity gained credence through trial and error, while participation and risk in the struggle produced the trust that gave the term social legitimacy.

Nehru, Sukarno, Nasser, and other leaders of the main social tendencies against colonialism who refused the camp mentality used other terms than the Third World to define themselves. They did not reject camps as such, only the dangerous camps available to them that did not promise much for their social constituencies, for the peoples of the darker nations. They spoke of themselves as the Non-Aligned Movement (NAM), the Group of 77 (G-77), or else with reference to the continents that formed the bulk of the colonized world (Africa, Asia, and Central and South America). These groups held conferences and produced joint action in the United Nations as well as at other international venues. Sauvy's notion of the Third World perfectly suited the way the unwieldy group operated: as the voice of the previously colonized that refused the bipolar division of the world, and sought to produce a world governed by peace and justice. The non-aligned states, the G-77, the Afro-Asian group, and others did not see themselves as united for cultural or economic reasons; they came together in a political movement against imperialism's legacy and its continuance.

To read the texts produced by the political project of the Third World can be gravely misleading. Most of the documents and speeches are triumphal, and few of them reveal the fissures and contradictions within the Third World. While this book will frequently use the words of leaders and institutions, it does not rely on them for its sense of the imagination and capacity of the Third World. The social forces that produced the Third World by the 1950s had a wider distribution than in any other modern political project of this scale. From peasant movements in India to rail workers in Senegal, from landless laborers in Indonesia to dissatisfied economists in Argentina—this is barely a sample.

A small, almost minuscule class became brokers between the massive social upsurge across the planet from the 1910s to the 1950s channeling that energy into the organizations they led. This group of leaders (whether India's Nehru or Indonesia's Sukarno, Mexico's Lázaro Cárdenas or Ghana's Nkrumah) elaborated a set of principles that both skewered the hypocrisy of imperial liberalism and promoted social change. On paper, the Third World gleamed. As the project met governance, it began to tarnish rapidly. One of the reasons for this is that the Third World failed to seriously undermine the deep roots of the landed and financial gentry in the social and political worlds that had been governed from above by imperial powers and their satraps. Without a genuine social revolution, the Third World leadership began to rely on the landed and merchant classes for its political power. Capillaries of power that provided legitimacy to the colonial rulers often transformed themselves into avenues for the delivery of votes in the new democratic dispensation. While this is broadly the case, one should not underestimate either the sheer magic of the individual franchise, which drew and continues to draw millions of people to the polls who often vote in unpredictable ways, or the opportunity provided for opposition political organizations to challenge local power and the national bourgeois leadership. Nevertheless, a major consequence of the lack of a social revolution was the persistence of various forms of hierarchy within the new nations. The inculcation of sexism, and the graded inequality of clan, caste, and tribe, inhibited the political project of the Third World. This is what the Palestinian historian Hisham Sharabi calls "neopatriarchy," where the Third World project, despite its commitment to modernity and modern state formation, "is in many ways no more than a modernized version of the traditional patriarchal sultanate."[29] The class character of the Third World leadership constrained its horizon, even as it inflamed the possibilities in its societies. The Third World, then, is not just the voice of the leaders or their political parties but also their opposition.

This story of the production of the Third World is not going to take us to antiquity or the devastation of the regions that become central to the concept. There is no brief here to tell the complete history of these regions or show that they are allied based on their underdevelopment. Certainly there are many social and economic, political and cultural features that are common to the many diverse countries of the Third World. But that is not my interest. We are going to follow the creation of the *political platform* from its first major meeting in Brussels at the League against Imperialism, then to Bandung, where twenty-nine Afro-

Asian countries gathered in 1955 to proclaim themselves outside the East-West divide. The formation of the Afro-Asian movement is an integral part of the story, because it is through the relations between the main non-aligned countries of these two continents that the Third World is constituted. We move to Cairo for a look at the Afro-Asian Women's Conference in 1961, not only to see the range of national liberation organizations created by the Bandung dynamic, but also to explore the place of women's rights on the platform of national liberation. We then head to Buenos Aires and Tehran to examine the economic and cultural agenda of the Third World, before we come finally to Belgrade. For it is in the Yugoslavian capital in 1961 that a number of states from across the planet gathered to form NAM, and pledge themselves to make the United Nations a serious force in world affairs. Finally, we rest in Havana, where the Cuban revolutions put the cult of the gun on the table. The Third World agenda hitherto had moved the spotlight away from insurgency movements against imperialism toward international treaties and agreements to give their regimes space for social development. The Cubans and others raised several questions. What about those places that still lingered in colonialism, and what about their armed struggle? Did the legislative strategy bear any fruit, or did the two main camps simply take the Third World for granted? Despite the fear of nuclear annihilation and the importance of a climb down from militant escalation, is there no room for armed action against obdurate powers? Or would such militancy be crushed by overwhelming force? The Cubans and others raised these important questions at about the time when the Third World dynamic was at its height, and it appeared that such a direction would bring more, rather than less, gains. The discussion about armed struggle at a NAM forum raises questions about the level of dissatisfaction in the Third World for the general failure of the movement to make gains against capitalism and militarism. This part sympathetically lays out the self-image of the Third World. We have to first understand it for what it was before I can lay out my critique of its internal failures.

BRUSSELS

Brussels is an unlikely place for the formation of the Third World. In February 1927, representatives of anti-imperialist organizations from across the planet gathered in the city for the first conference of the League against Imperialism. They came from warm climates to this cold city to discuss their mutual antipathy to colonialism and imperialism, and find a way out of their bondage. The young and the old, the African, the American, and the Asian, these representatives brought their decades of experience to one of Europe's most celebrated capitals to find an agenda in common. Amid snow and far from home, the project of the Third World began to take shape.

A visitor to the city at that time would normally take in the remarkable museums and the Palais Royal, a set of buildings gathered around the gorgeous Parc de Bruxelles that housed the royal families of Belgium. Leopold II, the second king of modern Belgium, had transformed the medieval city during his long reign (1865–1909) into a modern wonder—with wide roads, proper sewers, and a magnificent urban display that had been crafted for the Universal Exhibition of 1897. While the city celebrated the genuine architectural and artistic treasures of northwestern Europe, it did little to reveal the basis of its own immense wealth. In 1927, a visitor to Brussels would saunter through the Petit Sablon, a charming garden with forty-eight marble statues that represent the artisans of the city. For centuries the city had been known for its textiles, lace, and glassware, and it is this craft production that the city celebrated. But by 1927, the main source of wealth for Belgium and the city was not from the artisans but from Africa. It was Africa, particularly the Congo, that made Leopold II one of the richest people on the planet, and it enabled the Belgian economy to become the sixth largest in the world (after Great Britain, the United States, Germany, France, and Holland).

In 1878, Leopold II initiated the foundation of the Comité des Études du Haut Congo, a private firm financed by himself that went into central Africa in search of resources and profits. The U.S. explorer Henry Stanley took up an appointment from Leopold II, for whom Stanley helped subjugate the various chiefs of the Bantu. Leopold II, through the typical means of European colonialism, took possession of an area in the Congo that dwarfed his own kingdom. The Congo Free State, as Leopold II ironically fashioned it, was eighty times the size of Belgium. To settle tensions among the European powers over their African possessions, the German leader Otto von Bismarck convened the Berlin Conference in 1884–85. Here, fourteen European powers (including the United States) participated in the dismemberment of Africa. Leopold II became the sole owner of 2.3 million square kilometers of land.

The Congo Free State, as a private entity, had an ambivalent relationship with the Belgian elected government. Being a constitutional monarchy, Belgium had a parliament that, after the 1880s, began to seat socialists who were uneasy about colonialism. The parliament did not oversee the colony, and yet its riches provided the kingdom with much of its wealth. Although the Congo operations happened outside the scrutiny of the parliament, a substantial number of Belgians worked for the Congo Free State, and the reality of their jobs did not escape Belgian society. Leopold II set up the operations to extract the maximum profit, and over the course of the decades the Free State altered its policies several times to ensure its basic objective. The many different policies were united by a premise: as a 1923 manual put it, "The laziness of the colored races is a kind of genetic burden."[1] Violence was necessary to overcome this natural indolence. Therefore, the Free State's officials brutalized the people of the Congo, killing them mercilessly, and torturing those who could not or would not work. Leopold II's Free State set up the Force Publique, a militia designed to strike terror in the heart of the workforce. If a worker did not work hard, the officer would cut off their hand; one district official received 1,308 hands in one day from his subordinates. Fievez, an official of the Free State, noted of those who refused to collect rubber or else who did not meet their rubber quota, "I made war against them. One example was enough: a hundred heads cut off, and there have been plenty of supplies ever since. My goal is ultimately humanitarian. I killed a hundred people, but that allowed five hundred others to live."[2] Rape was routine, but so was the mutilation of the male and female genitalia in the presence of family members. To supply the emergent tire industry, Leopold II's Free State, therefore, sucked the life out of the rubber vines and murdered half the Congo's population in the process (between 1885 and 1908, the population declined from twenty million to ten million).

E.D. Morel, a Frenchman who worked for the English shipping line Elder Dempster, learned firsthand of the outrages in the Congo in the late 1890s. Until Morel began to make complaints to the Foreign Office in London, the only agency to expose the atrocities was the Aborigines Protection Society (founded in 1838 in London). Morel made contact with Roger Casement, an Irishman who worked in the Foreign Office, and Casement used the Anglo-Belgian rivalry to secure himself the task of investigating the Congo (he actually used the principle of *Civis Romanus Sum* to investigate misconduct against subjects of the British Crown—in this case, a few men from Sierra Leone who had entered Leopold's jails). Casement traveled the Congo and published his catalog of outrages in January 1904. The Congo Reform Association, the journalism of two U.S. Presbyterian ministers (the "Black Livingston" William Sheppard and William Morrison), Morel's own *Affairs of West Africa* (1902), Joseph Conrad's *Heart of Darkness* (1902), and finally Mark Twain's *King Leopold's Soliloquy* (1904)—these documented the barbarity of Brussels.

The Foreign Office in London wrote a tepid note critical of the Belgians, and Leopold II's reply rightly accused the British of hypocrisy: much of the policies followed by the Belgians in the Congo had been standard for the English elsewhere. Indeed, Casement found that British companies in the Putamayo region between Colombia and Peru followed the same kinds of barbarism, the U.S.-based United Fruit Company in Central America pillaged the dignity of the natives there, and in Portuguese Angola as well as French and German Cameroon, the companies used much the same kind of rubber plantation regime. When the Belgians formed the Free State, the first country to back them had been the United States, and the others lined up to congratulate Leopold II for his civilizing work in Africa's interior (when Leopold II founded the International African Association in 1876, he used rhetoric that could have come from any imperial capital: "To open to civilization the only part of our globe which it has not yet penetrated, to pierce the darkness which hangs over entire peoples, I dare say, a crusade worthy of this century of progress").[3] Belgium, after all, could claim to be a junior partner in the colonial enterprise. Between 1876 and 1915, a handful of European imperial states controlled a full quarter of the globe's land, with Great Britain and France in possession of far more than Germany, Belgium, Italy, and the states of the Iberian Peninsula (the United States directly controlled a small amount, but it held sway over all the Americas).

The Congo Reform Association, the U.S. and British governments, and most of the actors who participated in the condemnation of the Belgians remained silent on the brutality elsewhere. In fact, their criticism of the Congo enabled them to obscure their own role in the barbarity. As Adam Hochschild puts it, the Atlantic governments lined up behind the critique of Leopold II because it "did not involve British or American misdeeds, nor did it entail the diplomatic, trade or military consequences of taking on a major power like France or Germany."[4] The imperial powers made Leopold II the issue, at the same time as they buried the broader problem in which they had a hand: imperialism. In 1908, Leopold turned over the management of the Free State to the Belgian government, and the barbarism continued until the Belgians completed their rail system in 1914 that rationalized the removal of the Congo's minerals all the way to 1961 and beyond.[5]

The conveners of the 1927 League against Imperialism conference chose Brussels deliberately: they snubbed Europe's nose by holding an anti-imperialist conference in the capital of such brutality, and used Belgium's own international embarrassment as a vehicle to get permission to do so in the first place.[6] The organizers had initially hoped for Berlin, but the Weimar regime refused permission. Then they went to the government in Paris, but the French denied them on the grounds that the presence of the conference might stir up hope in the colonies. Belgium could not refuse the league, and Leopold II's successor Albert I held no brief one way or the other. The Belgian government had recently anointed Émile Vandervelde as its foreign minister, a job he held alongside his role as secretary of the Socialist Second International. The organizers made it clear that if Vandervelde turned down the league, it would reflect poorly on the Socialist Second International, whose reputation had already been tarnished by its failure to oppose World War I. Additionally, the organizers agreed to take the Belgian Congo off the table for the duration of the event, even though it came in for indirect criticism throughout.[7]

The event, covertly funded in part by the Communist International (and believed to be funded by the Kuomintang and the Mexican government of

Plutarco Elías Calles), took place in the Palais d'Egremont, one of those exaggerated palaces that dot the landscape of Brussels. Two hundred delegates came from thirty-seven states or colonized regions, and they represented 134 organizations. The delegates traveled from the major continents, some from within the heart of the imperialist states, and others from their periphery. They worked on resolutions about most acts of barbarity, from the tragedy of the Indian countryside to that of Jim Crow racism in the United States, from the growth of Italian fascism to the danger of Japanese intervention in Korea. The rich discussions and resolutions as well as the personal contact between delegates influenced many of those in attendance for a lifetime. At subsequent meetings, the delegates referred to the Brussels event as formative, as the bedrock for the creation of sympathy and solidarity across the borders of the colonized world.[8]

Two well-known Communist internationalists based in Berlin, Willi Münzenberg and Virendranath Chattopadhyaya, conceived of the conference and did much of the legwork for it. Regardless of the Comintern's vacillation over alliances with the national bourgeoisie, the general support given to national liberation movements across Asia and Africa by the Russian Communists is clear. In 1913, Vladimir Ilyich Lenin published a short piece in *Pravda* titled "Backward Europe and Advanced Asia," in which he noted, "Everywhere in Asia a mighty democratic movement is growing, spreading and gaining in strength. The bourgeoisie there is *as yet* siding with the people against reaction. *Hundreds* of millions of people are awakening to life, light and freedom." In response to this awakening, "all the commanders of Europe, all the European bourgeoisie are *in alliance* with all the forces of reaction and medievalism in China." In opposition to this alliance, "young Asia, that is, the hundreds of millions of Asian working people [have] a reliable ally in the proletariat of all civilized countries."[9] When the Soviets took control of Russia, they published and abrogated the secret treaties that the czar had made with the other European powers to divide up the darker nations among themselves.[10]

In early 1920, delegates from across the planet gathered in Moscow for the Second Congress of the Comintern, where they studied the condition of imperialism and debated the effectiveness of strategies to combat it. Two divergent lines grew out of the congress—whether to ally with the national bourgeoisie and treat nationalism as a transitional phase toward socialism, or reject the national bourgeoisie and forge an international working-class alliance for socialism against the illusions of nationality. Later that year, the Soviets hosted the First Congress of the Peoples of the East in Baku, where almost two thousand delegates from across Asia and elsewhere represented two dozen different peoples (from Persia, Bukhara, Turkey, and elsewhere); one of the notables was John Reed of the United States.[11] The delegates discussed the limitations of Soviet power in the lands outside Russia, and sent their criticisms to Moscow for consideration. But the main development from Baku was that the delegates went back to their homelands to found dozens of national Communist parties.[12]

Münzenberg and Chattopadhyaya did not choose the word *league* in the title of their new organization for nothing. The League against Imperialism was a direct attack on the League of Nations's preservation of imperialism in its mandate system. In April 1919, the Paris Peace Conference produced the League of Nations, which followed Woodrow Wilson's "Fourteen Points" even though the United States did not join the league. The "interests" of the colonized had to be curtailed, the Covenant of the League noted, because the colonized were "peoples not yet able to stand by themselves under the strenuous conditions of the modern world" (Article 22).[13] Instead of independence and the right to rule themselves, the league felt that "the best method of giving practical effect to [the principle of self-determination] is that the tutelage of such peoples should be entrusted to advanced nations who by reason of their resources, their experience, or their geographical position can best undertake this responsibility, and who are willing to accept it, and that this tutelage should be exercised by them as Mandatories on behalf of the League."[14] Self-determination did not mean the end to colonialism, but for the League of Nations it meant paternalistic imperialism.

Brussels scorned and repudiated Versailles.

The delegates in Brussels came from Communist and Socialist parties as well as radical nationalist movements. From South Africa came James La Guma and Josiah Gumeda (both of the South African Communist Party), from Algeria came Hadj-Ahmed Messali (founding member of the first group to call for Algeria's independence, Étoile Nord-Africain), from Indonesia came Sukarno, Mohammad Hatta, and Semaun (the first two from a newly founded nationalist party, and the latter from the Communist Party), from Palestine came Jamal al-Husayni and M. Erem (the former from the Arab National Congress of Palestine, and the latter from Poale Zion), from Iran came Ahmed Assadoff and Mortesa Alawi, and from India came Mohamed Barkatullah and Nehru (Nehru from the Indian National Congress, and Barkatullah from the Ghadar Party, founded in San Francisco in 1913). From China came the largest delegation, mainly from the Kuomintang, but also from its branches across Europe. From the Americas came civil libertarians like Roger Baldwin and activists like Richard Moore as well as major nationalist leaders like Víctor Raúl Haya de la Torre (Peru) and José Vasconcelias (Puerto Rico).

Albert Einstein became a patron of the organization, alongside the Swiss writer and Nobel Prize–winner Romain Rolland and the Chinese nationalist leader Madame Sun Yat-sen. Two years later, Nehru wrote in his autobiography, "There were also present at Brussels representatives from the national organizations of Java, Indo-China, Palestine, Syria, Egypt, Arabs from North Africa and American Negroes. Then there were many left-wing labor organizations represented; and several well-known men who had played a leading part in European labor struggles for a generation, were present. Communists were there also, and they took an important part in the proceedings; they came not as communists but as representatives of trade-unions or similar organizations." The Brussels Congress, Nehru commented, "helped me to understand some of the problems of colonial and dependent countries."[15]

The congress in Brussels called for the rights of the darker nations to rule themselves.[16] The connections made in Brussels served the organizations well, because now some began to coordinate their activities, while others used their affiliation with the league to publicize their efforts. While they planned to meet frequently, this did not happen for several reasons: the Comintern took a hard position against national liberation movements in 1927, with the view that these efforts would eventually betray the working class (the Comintern revised this line in 1935); distances and proscription made travel difficult for the leaders of the many revolutionary movements, several of whom spent years in jail in the interwar period; finally, the outbreak of World War II made any such gathering impossible, not only because of the dislocation of war, but also because the social revolutionary wave that broke across the world held the attention of the many organizations and their leaders.

Nevertheless, regional formations did gather after Brussels, and many of these provided the bedrock for the Third World. The movements represented at the 1927 meeting had worked to prepare the ground for this experiment in intraplanetary solidarity. The gathering in Brussels makes sense in light of that long history of engagement. I'll go from continent to continent to offer a short summary on what preceded Brussels.

In Brussels, Africa did not have a major voice, but its representatives did put its liberation on the map. Of course, the deal struck by the organizers of the conference and the Belgian government took the Congo off the table, and given that it remained one of the central issues in Africa, the silence was palpable. Yet the South African delegates' strongly worded statement against the regime there raised the question of a "native republic" free of white control.[17] The record shows contact between the delegates from across the continent, but nothing came of the meetings, perhaps because a leading light, Lamine Senghor of the Committee for the Defense of the Negro Race, died in a French prison shortly after the conference.[18] The Nigerian freedom fighter Nnamdi Azikiwe's 1937 *Renascent Africa* produced an image of the combined strength of a unified continent, and he joined with the Trinidadian radical George Padmore that very year to form the International African Service Bureau in London.[19] The real dynamic of African unity came at the Pan-African meetings that preceded and followed Brussels.

Driven by the force of the Trinidadian Henry Sylvester Williams, the first Pan-African Conference in London in 1900 drew people from across the Atlantic world, including the United States, the Caribbean, Europe, and Africa. Williams opened the proceedings with a stern criticism of British policy toward the Africans in the southern part of the continent. The African Association that Williams had founded in 1897 had pledged to "promote and protect the interests of all subjects claiming African descent, wholly or in part, in British colonies," for which reason he singled out South Africa and not the Congo or elsewhere.[20] Being in London, Williams felt that the British policy of colonialism should be challenged. Nevertheless, the 1900 meeting drafted a set of objectives for the Pan-African Congress that began with a much wider aim: "To secure to Africans throughout the world true civil and political rights." W.E.B. DuBois, the great American leader, laid out the charge for the delegates: "In the metropolis of the modern world, in this closing year of the nineteenth century, there has been assembled a congress of men and women of African blood, to deliberate solemnly upon the present situation and outlook of the darker races of mankind." For DuBois, these "darker races" included "the millions of black men in Africa, America, and the Islands of the Sea, not to speak of the brown and yellow myriads everywhere."[21] By 1945, at the fifth Pan-African Conference, DuBois would be a major leader, and would be surrounded by future leaders of the African continent and the Atlantic world, such as George Padmore, Kwame Nkrumah, and Jomo Kenyatta.[22] "If the

Western world is still determined to rule mankind by force," the 1945 conference declared, "then Africans as a last resort, may have to appeal to force in the effort to achieve freedom, even if force destroys them and the world." The demand for freedom came alongside the demand for socialism: "We condemn the monopoly of capital and the rule of private wealth and industry for profit alone. We welcome economic democracy as the only real democracy. Therefore we shall complain, appeal and we will make the world listen to the facts of our condition. We will fight every way we can for freedom, democracy and social betterment."[23] The theoretical concepts of Pan-Africanism and African independence gained material force during the continent-wide labor strikes in the 1940s—from Lagos in 1945 to Dar es Salaam in 1947, dockworkers slowed down the movement of goods, and joined the rail, post, telegraph, and factory workers as well as farm labor in a general strike against colonialism. These struggles produced organizations that were then marshaled by the Pan-Africanist and nationalist leaders who gave shape to an ideology.

When Ghana won its independence in 1957, Accra hosted the first Conference of African States, and then it became the home to the All-African People's Conference. The idea of "Africa" in this conference, and elsewhere in the movement, operated in a homologous manner to the idea of the Third World. What brought Africans together in these forums was not culture or language but, as Nkrumah put it, "a common interest in the independence of Africa." "Africans," he wrote, "have begun to think continentally," but not for cultural reasons.[24] What they sought was a "political union" on the African platform and the Third World one. Certainly, Nkrumah's "Africans" who had "begun to think continentally" referred to the political movements and their leaders, not necessarily to the vast masses whose own political ideas might not have been this cosmopolitan. At Accra, the leadership of the political movements recognized this and yet looked forward to the deepening of the idea of African unity across classes, across the continent.

If Africa has numerous languages and intertwined but separate histories, the same cannot be said of the Arabs of northern Africa and western Asia. Joined by language, the Arabs nonetheless suffered the costs of disunity. Ravaged by the Ottomans and the various European powers, the linguistic region that stretches from northwestern Africa to the borders of Iran has held sustained cultural contact but not political unity. Arab traders moved from one end to the other, and Muslims traveled from the two ends of the region to the Arabian Peninsula to perform hajj.

When the Ottoman Empire began to collapse, the peoples under its yoke mobilized for their freedom. The "Arab Revolt" on the Arabian Peninsula (1916–32), in Egypt (1918–19), in Iraq (1920–22), in Syria and Lebanon (1925–26), in Palestine (1936–37), and elsewhere united the Arab people not just against the Ottomans and others but also on behalf of a united Arab nation. In Brussels, the Syrian delegation took the lead, mainly because Syria had just been in the midst of a heated struggle against the League of Nations's mandate, here given to the French.[25] The Egyptians, the Syrians, the Lebanese, and the Palestinians forged a united front in Brussels, although individual members disagreed over the role of religion as well as that of Jews in Palestine (the Palestinian Communists wanted a united front of Jews and Arabs against the British—a position endorsed by the league).[26] The tumult in Palestine in the mid-1930s ended the hope of a Jewish-Arab alliance against the British, and hardened the xenophobia on both sides.

When the British approached the Arabs in 1942 to create a united organization against the Axis powers, they did not make a similar offer to the Jewish groups in Palestine, and so they further exacerbated the divide. Influenced by the British proposal, and the sentiment of unity that preceded it, in October 1944, representatives from Egypt, Jordan, Iraq, Lebanon, and Syria met in Alexandria to plan a unity conference for the next year. The main theme was to be the creation of a framework to address conflict peaceably, and develop economic and social ties within the region dominated by Arabic speakers. When these Arabic-speaking states met (along with Saudi Arabia and Yemen), they created the Arab League, to "strengthen the ties between the participant states, to coordinate their political programmes to such a way as to effect real collaboration between them, to preserve their independence and sovereignty, and to consider in a general way the affairs and interests of the Arab countries."[27] The first action of the league at its 1945 Cairo meeting was to condemn France's presence in Syria and Lebanon, and at its third session the following year, the league congratulated Syria, Lebanon, and Jordan for their independence. It also supported the Libyan struggle for independence, the Indonesian fight against the Dutch/English, and the Palestinian demand for the restoration of lands.[28]

The countries south of the great colossus of the United States did not form an independent association, for they had been yoked into a Pan-American Union with the United States from the first Inter-American Conference of 1889 (the name Pan-American Union came in 1910). "At periodic Pan-American conferences," the historian John Chasteen notes,

"U.S. secretaries of state promoted trade while Latin American representatives voiced dismay at U.S. interventions in the region. The unanimous protests came to a head at the Havana Conference of 1928."[29] At the Havana meeting, the Latin American states wanted to raise the prohibited topic: the political relations between states, and the military interventions by the United States into Latin America. In 1926, several thousand U.S. marines had invaded Nicaragua, to remain there until 1933. The United States wanted the Pan-American gathering to stay with talk of tariffs and trade, but the Latin Americans refused. The most vocal critics of U.S. imperialism and for Latin American unity did come to Brussels in 1928, where they came into contact with anti-imperialist forces from elsewhere. The most important presence from the region was Haya de la Torre of Peru, whose Alianza Popular Revolucionaria Americana (APRA, 1924) influenced radical nationalists from Mexico to Argentina.[30] "For me," said Haya de la Torre, "Latin America is the *Patria Grande*, of which each of its component states is an inseparable and interdependent part. I believe that the best patriotism for any Latin American with regard to the country of his birth is to sustain the inseparability of our states as members of a continental whole."[31] In Brussels, the target remained Europe, and even as the participants passed resolutions for the freedom of Puerto Rico and against U.S. imperialism in the Pacific Rim, there was little substantive exploration of the impact of U.S. imperialism in South America and elsewhere.[32]

The impact of populist nationalism across the continent, and the growth of political parties of the APRA variety, produced the first Congress of Democratic and Political Parties of America in October 1940. Representatives from Argentina, Bolivia, Brazil, Colombia, Ecuador, Mexico, Panama, Paraguay, Peru, Uruguay, and Venezuela gathered in Santiago, Chile, where they discussed issues of mutual interest— namely, the power of the great northern colossus—but they failed to make united headway particularly when many of the populist parties in these states came to power after 1944.[33] Instead, these powers continued to meet under the auspices of U.S.-dominated organizations, even as they persisted in their various forms of resistance. At the 1945 Chapultepec Conference in Mexico City, for example, the United States wanted to make European recovery a priority, another area of dispute with the Latin American states, which did not want to allow the open door for U.S. trade in the Americas to finance European reconstruction. These tensions within the American hemisphere became pronounced in the early United Nations, where 40 percent of the delegates came from

Latin America.[34] At Chapultepec, furthermore, the American republics announced "that all sovereign States are juridically equal among themselves," and "that every State has the right to the respect of its individuality and independence, on the part of the other members of the international community."[35] Such statements promoted the idea of independence for the Southern Cone, Central America, and the Caribbean.

The idea of Pan-Asianism emerged from two distinct political traditions. From the progressives, such as Nehru and Sun Yat-sen, came a desire for the union of the continent that had been rent by imperialism. Popular enthusiasm across Asia for Japan's 1904 defeat of Russia contributed to the sense that the continent's peoples should have close ties with each other. At the two Pan-Asian People's Conferences in Nagasaki (1926) and Shanghai (1927), the delegates from China and Korea held fast to the progressive notion of Pan-Asianism by demanding that the Japanese government abrogate its imperial pretensions. From Japanese reactionaries came the view that Asia should be ruled by the *Showa* (enlightened peace) monarchy of Hirohito rather than by the Europeans, or by the Asians themselves. Several secret societies, such as the Black Dragon and the Red Swastika, promoted the extension of Japan's 1910 conquest of Korea forward, toward Manchuria (1931) and Jehol (1933).

Japan's militarism, however, could not usurp all the space of Pan-Asianism, because the progressive side of it lingered, and became manifest after World War II. In March 1947, the liberation movements in Asia gathered in New Delhi to hold the Asian Relations Conference, where they pledged themselves to economic, political, and cultural cooperation between the nations. The gathering greeted the onset of liberation, and yet warned against "dollar imperialism." The Azerbaijanian delegate's proposal against racism was hailed. "The most important thing about the conference," Nehru told the press, "was that it was held."[36] The work done at this conference enabled Nehru to rapidly call a government-level Asian Conference once more to Delhi in 1949 to condemn the Dutch/British action in the newly founded state of Indonesia. Significantly, the 1949 conference decided to coordinate activities among the new Asian states within the United Nations.

These regional formations had a wide appreciation for the *universal* struggle against imperialism, for the need for coordination and consultation toward a just world. The best evidence for this is the enthusiasm with which each of these groups, and most of the countries within them, embraced the United Nations. It could be argued that one of the reasons for the success of the United Nations in its first three decades, unlike that of the League of Nations, is that the states of the Third World saw it as their platform. It was from the United Nations's mantle that the states of Africa, America, and Asia could articulate their Third World agenda. Whereas the league *was* a tool of imperialism and for the maintenance of peace within Europe, the United Nations became the property of justice for the formerly colonized world.[37] The Third World offered stiff resistance within the United Nations on the U.S. aggression in Korea as well as the French domination of Morocco and Tunisia. In both the Morocco and Tunisian resolutions, the African, Arab, and Asian states had crucial support from the eleven Latin American states.

The collaboration between the African, Arab, and Asian regional formations had a much greater intensity than the contacts they had with the Latin Americans. This was for several reasons. First, the Latin American states had attained formal independence from Spain and Portugal in the early nineteenth century so they did not share the contemporary experience of colonial domination. Most of Latin America, however, had come under the sway of either European or U.S. capital, and most of the governments had an antipathy to the empire of finance. In 1896, the founder of the Argentine Socialist Party, Juan Bautista Justo, thundered, "We have seen the Argentines reduced to the status of a British colony by means of economic penetration," and this was enabled by the Argentine oligarchy, the "sellers of their country."[38] Bautista Justo's statement entered the consciousness of many Latin Americans by its ceaseless repetition. The distinctions between the Americas and elsewhere in terms of their colonial heritage became less pronounced over time as both zones understood how global capital subjected them. Yet this did not lead to organizational ties before the Cold War.

Second, the Latin American states lived in an alternative imperial orbit. Their target was not Old Europe, but the New Yankee, and in this they differed greatly from most of Africa and Asia (except for the Philippines). Additionally, their colonial orbit gave them Spanish as their lingua franca (except for Brazil and the Dutch colonies), whereas most of the anticolonial leaders from Africa and Asia spoke English or French, and many of them met in their continental sojourns, whether in London, Paris, or Geneva. The worlds of the Latin Americans did not cross frequently with those of the Afro-Asians. So even if the Afro-Asian conferences from the 1920s onward referred to oppressions across the conjoined continents, that did not mean that the Latin Americans were any less internationalist or any more parochial; the strong ties forged in the 1950s and 1960s across continents shows that given the opportunity, many of them saw their struggles as part of an international, planetary crusade.

The legacy of the League against Imperialism is ambiguous. The major imperial powers knew that such a formation was dangerous, and they arrested many of the activists who attended it as soon as they returned to their homelands or else to any place where their colonial overlord bore jurisdiction. The colonial powers quickly tainted the league's work by intimating that it was nothing but a Communist front. Certainly, the Communists played a major role in the league, but they did not exhaust its range and the claim made on it by peoples who had little experience with Communism. The reproach of "communist" served to make the Communist movement almost omnipresent and divine in the eyes of many who had been taught to distrust the word of the colonial master and to see that any enemy of that master was an ally in the fight. For isolated struggles, the league was a crucial instrument of propaganda, an important medium to get the word out about massacres or protests as well as to coordinate solidarity work. The league also allowed inaccessible movements to make contact with others, so that those who fought the French in Indochina could remain in touch with those who fought the same French state in West Africa. In addition, incipient labor organizations affiliated to the league as a means to break out of their isolation.

The Soviets and the Comintern did squander much of the goodwill gained in the immediate aftermath of Brussels by their impulsive and distracting shifts in political line. During the league's foundation, the majority opinion of the Comintern was that the Communists should work in a broad front with national liberation movements. Because of this, the Kuomintang joined the Comintern to fund the conference, and both worked together for its success. Just after the Brussels meeting, however, the Kuomintang massacred more than five thousand Communists in Shanghai and elsewhere to prolong a civil war. That the Comintern had joined forces with the Kuomintang in Brussels is astounding, but in the nationalists' postconference violence lay the seeds of the league's destruction. This and other instances led the Comintern to denounce noncommunist national liberation forces, including Nehru, Roger Baldwin, and Hatta. The problem with the league's line was that it was inflexible—it chose to work with the Kuomintang before Shanghai, much to the chagrin of the Chinese Communists, and it chose to abandon its relationship with the Indian and Indonesian freedom movements even though these two did not have the kind of antipathy to the Left as the Kuomintang. In places such as India and Indonesia, anticolonial nationalism, even if led by a relatively weak national bourgeoisie, had become a powerful social force that could not be sidestepped.[39] The context of each setting, such as the internal class alignments, did not seem to bear on the Comintern's insistence on a homogeneous strategy for world revolution. Even as the league lost its footing in much of the colonized world, the Brussels meeting itself played an important role in the consolidation of the idea of the Third World.

Almost three decades after the Brussels conference, Sukarno, newly installed as the president of Indonesia, opened the Afro-Asian Conference held in Bandung, Indonesia. Within minutes of his address, Sukarno offered this assessment of the significance of Brussels:

> Only a few decades ago it was frequently necessary to travel to other countries and even other continents before the spokespersons of our people could confer. I recall in this connection the Conference of the "League Against Imperialism and Colonialism" which was held in Brussels almost thirty years ago. At that Conference many distinguished Delegates who are present here today met each other and found new strength in their fight for independence. But that was a meeting place thousands of miles away, amidst foreign people, in a foreign country, in a foreign continent. It was not assembled there by choice, but by necessity. Today the contrast is great. Our nations and countries are colonies no more. Now we are free, sovereign and independent. We are again masters in our own house. We do not need to go to other continents to confer.[40]

BANDUNG

In 1955, the island of Java bore the marks not only of its three-hundred-year colonial heritage but also its recent and victorious anticolonial struggle. The diverse island that is the heart of the Indonesia archipelago is home to a large number of coffee, tea, and quinine plantations—the main producers of wealth for the Dutch coffers. At one end, toward the west, sits the town of Bandung, the City of Flowers. Its tropical deco administrative buildings contrasted strongly with the shacks that housed its workforce, forming a cityscape of uneven hopes and aspirations. In the 1940s, the workers and peasants of the city and its hinterland rose in struggle alongside the *pemuda*, the youth activists. The cry of *Siaaaap* (Attention!) rang out in the streets of the city in opposition not only to the Japanese occupiers but also the British who had replaced them, and the Dutch who waited in the wings to reclaim the island. In March 1946, when it appeared as if the British would not allow the Indonesians their independence, half a million residents of Bandung abandoned the city en masse, as they set fire to warehouses, homes, and government offices.[1] This event produced an epic song:

Hello-Hello Bandung
The capital of Parahyangan [Province]
Hello-Hello Bandung
The city of remembrance.
For a long time,
I have not met you.

Bandung, Java, Indonesia, April 1955: Bandung's people greet the representatives to the Afro-Asian Conference. © BETTMANN/CORBIS

Now, you are a Sea of Fire.
Let's take over again, *Bung* [comrade].[2]

By 1955 the city had been repopulated, now largely by poor migrants who had been displaced by a rebellion led by the Darul Islam, an anticolonial force that had pledged to create an Islamic republic in Indonesia (it died out by the mid-1960s for lack of success).[3] And even repopulated, south Bandung remained scarred by the fire. The Indonesia government chose this city as the site for a meeting of twenty-nine representatives of newly sovereign Asian and African nations. This meeting brought Sauvy's concept to life. Of course, the April 1955 meeting did not create the Third World out of whole cloth. It simply made manifest tendencies such as the relatively common social conditions of the colonized states and the nationalist movements that each of these states produced. The Bandung Conference was, for the leaders of these nationalist movements, also the culmination of a process that began at the 1927 Brussels gathering of the League against Imperialism. All this is true, but what is still important about Bandung is that it allowed these leaders to meet together, celebrate the demise of formal colonialism, and pledge themselves to some measure of joint struggle against the forces of imperialism. Despite the infighting, debates, strategic postures, and sighs of annoyance, Bandung produced something: a belief that two-thirds of the world's people had the right to return to their own burned cities, cherish them, and rebuild them in their own image.

Taking the podium on the first day, Indonesia's president Sukarno welcomed the changes wrought by anticolonialism over Asia and Africa:

> Irresistible forces have swept the two continents. The mental, spiritual and political face of the whole world has been changed and the process is still not complete. There are new conditions, new concepts, new problems, new ideals abroad in the world. Hurricanes of national awakening and reawakening have swept over the land, shaking it, changing it, changing it for the better.[4]

A vast section of the world that had once bowed before the might of Europe now stood at the threshold of another destiny. Indeed, the freedom attained by the new nations seemed unimaginable just a few years ago. When Mohandas Karamchand Gandhi's Indian National Congress declared itself for Purna Swaraj or Complete Independence in 1929, many felt that the step had been premature, that neither would Britain allow such a caesura, nor could India survive on its own. Nevertheless, Nehru, then the president of the congress, the leading arm of the anticolonial struggle in India, told delegates gathered in Lahore in 1929, "We stand today for the fullest freedom of India. Today or tomorrow, we may not be strong enough to assert our will. We are very conscious of our weakness, and there is no boasting in us or pride of strength. But let no one, least of all England, mistake or underrate the meaning or strength of our resolve."[5] The resolve eventually came for India (and Pakistan) in 1947, as it came for Indonesia and Vietnam in 1945, the Philippines in 1946, Burma, Ceylon, Korea, and Malaysia in 1948, and China in 1949. In 1951, Ghana gained substantial independence (formally declared in 1957), the same year that Libya gained freedom from Italy to join Liberia, Ethiopia, and Egypt as Africa's independent states, while in 1956 the Sudan broke from its Anglo-Egyptian bondage (just as Ethiopia absorbed Eritrea). These are the countries that gathered at Bandung.

Little apart from their common colonial and anticolonial history united these nations. Sukarno, scion of a diverse people who lived across hundreds of dispersed islands, understood the limited basis for unity among those who came to Bandung. But if a nation-state could be made of Indonesia, why could a transnational unity not be fashioned out of the Bandung nations? "Conflict comes not from variety of skins, nor from variety of religion," Sukarno announced, "but from variety of desires." A unity of desire forged out of struggle and organized into a common platform could undermine the social differences. "We are united by a common detestation of colonialism in whatever form it appears. We are united by a common detestation of racialism. And we are united by a common determination to preserve and stabilize peace in the world."[6] These would be the elements for the Third World's unity.

Unity for the people of the Third World came from a political position against colonialism and imperialism, not from any intrinsic cultural or racial commonalities. If you fought against colonialism and stood against imperialism, then you were part of the Third World. Sukarno's views found common currency among most of the delegates to the Bandung meeting, whether of the Left (China), the center (India and Burma), or the Right (Turkey and the Philippines). When Sukarno argued that colonialism may have ended its formal phase, but that imperialism still lingered, he echoed the views of many of the Third World's leaders as well as its people, who suffered daily from "underdevelopment." Colonialism no longer came in sola topees but had "its modern dress, in the form of economic control, intellectual control. . . . It does not give up its loot easily." To eradicate it, Sukarno urged the delegates and their populations to stand united as a Third World against imperialism. But what can this Third World do, given that its "economic strength is dispersed and slight," and that without the "serried ranks of jet bombers," the Third World "cannot indulge in power politics"?[7] What is left for this Third World on a planet where the atom bomb and the dollar determined the course of human history? What is left for a region that contained two thousand million people?[8] "We can inject the voice of reason into world affairs. We can mobilize all the spiritual, all the moral, all the political strength of Asia and Africa on the side of peace."[9]

Sukarno's speech was the most powerful brief for Third World unity, which is why it is the best-known statement from the Bandung meeting.[10] Born in 1901, Sukarno came from the same social position as many of the important Third World leaders. From a family of lesser nobility, Sukarno's father became swept up in the fervor of patriotism. He renamed his son after a figure from the Sanskrit epic *Mahabharata*, Karna, who is known to be honest and fearless.[11] Sukarno studied in European institutions (in Surabaja and Bandung) and trained to be an engineer, but harbored an ambition for Indonesian independence. This combination of being from the petty nobility or the emergent middle class as well as open to the type of educational advantages of European colonialism produced a series of leaders such as Nehru, Sukarno, U Nu of Burma, and the large

number of *ilustrados* or "enlightened ones" of the Philippines.[12] As he
finished his engineering studies, Sukarno began to publish *Indonesia
Muda* (*Young Indonesia*), the journal of the Bandung Study Club. It was
in this periodical that he first articulated his vision of a united front between all the patriotic forces against European colonialism. In Indonesia,
the Marxists, the Islamists, and the nationalists formed the main opponents of Dutch rule, and Sukarno argued that all three must consider nationalism to be "as broad as the air" in a manner similar to the Congress
Party in India and the Kuomintang in China. As he described this vision,
the Communist Party (PKI) led a putsch, which failed and led to its repression. To take advantage of the energy produced by the PKI-led mass
revolt from late 1926 to early 1927, Sukarno and his circle founded the
Partai Nasional Indonesia (PNI).

The PNI, like the Congress Party and the Kuomintang, had a grab
bag ideology, rooted in an anticolonial ethos, but in favor of a vague nationalism that attracted all social classes. The middle class came on board
because many of them had been discriminated against in terms of administrative jobs and humiliated by the colonial hierarchy. Already veterans
in the struggle for justice, the working class and the peasantry would
gradually move to the PNI as it became central to the freedom struggle.
Unlike the Congress Party in India that had became a mass movement
by the 1920s through the creative campaigns led by Gandhi and unlike
the Vietnamese Communist Party whose mass base emerged through
diligent organizational work led by Ho Chi Minh, the PNI looked very
much like other urban, middle-class anticolonial organizations in places
as diverse as Peru and the Gold Coast—it developed out of an idea and
reflected the views of a narrow stratum, but its platform would soon be
adopted by many beyond its original circle. The educated youth would
do the most work for the PNI and the organizations that shared its class
origins. The Indonesian Youth Congress carried the struggle to the
masses and provided many of the foot soldiers of the "noncooperation"
struggle (a concept that Sukarno borrowed from Gandhi).[13]

Frustrated by Sukarno's actions, the Dutch administration arrested
him in 1931 and held him until the Japanese invasion of the archipelago
in 1942. When the Japanese took power, Sukarno worked with them,
but not as their shill; he used every opportunity he could get to promote nationalist ideas, so that as the historian George Kahin notes, his
speeches on the radio "were full of subtleties and double talk which generally passed over the head of the Japanese monitors but were meaningful to the population."[14] On August 17, 1945, two days after the Japanese

surrender, Sukarno (and his associate Hatta) declared independence for Indonesia—a move delayed by the entry of British troops who had come to restore the islands to the Dutch. Sukarno still had little mass base, and his declaration was sheer bravado. The Indonesian people backed him despite their shallow knowledge of his program, and he won. The fires of Bandung raged because people now believed that colonialism had ended. European rule no longer had any legitimacy. In 1949, Indonesia won its formal freedom.

Sukarno, like Nehru and other such nationalist leaders, came to the forefront of an upsurge against colonial power, without a clear agenda for the social development of their people. What was clear, however, was that they rode the wave produced by the actions of many small, local organizations—such as merchants forums, the PNI, religious organizations, and youth groups. Sukarno stood for freedom and justice, but not necessarily for a general revolution against the old social classes (such as the rural landed gentry, merchants, and others)—hence, the complicity of the Dutch and the PNI in the crackdown on the 1948 Communist rebellion in Madiun (which led to the execution and incarceration of scores of PKI cadre, and the suppression of the PKI in 1951–52, when the government arrested fifteen thousand party members).[15] Sukarno did put money into education and state industries, drawing some of the agenda from the Communists, who continued to recruit a mass party (by 1965, the PKI numbered three and a half million cadre and twenty million members in mass organizations). In 1965, at his last Independence Day ceremony before a U.S.-backed coup ejected him, Sukarno stated, "We are now fostering an anti-imperialist axis—the Jakarta-Phnom Penh-Hanoi-Peking-Pyongyang axis."[16] He had moved closer to the Communists than he would have imagined when he first entered politics.

But Sukarno did not represent all the voices in Bandung.

Communist China tore through the conference led by the ebullient personality of Zhou En-lai, whose legendary history and feverish attempts to befriend all had endeared him to most of the delegates.[17] Zhou had a vigorous schedule. Not only did Nehru guide him around and introduce him to those who already respected the Indian political leader but Zhou himself addressed as many sessions as possible and met almost all the delegates. Tea with the "centrists" Nehru and U Nu would be followed by tea with "rightists" such as Carlos Romulo of the Philippines and John Kotelawala of Ceylon (where Zhou met Afghanistan's Deputy Prime Minister and Foreign Minister Sardar Mohammed Naim). Finally,

Zhou and the Chinese delegation hosted a banquet attended by the major powers, but also the Arab states (represented by Crown Prince Faysal of Saudi Arabia, Seifel Islam Hassan of Yemen, Walid Salah of Jordan, Sami Solh of Lebanon, Mahmud Muntasser of Libya, and Ismail el Azhari of Sudan).

Zhou took a conciliatory tone toward the nationalist rhetoric of the conference and even begged those leaders who had a religious orientation to be tolerant toward his atheism.[18] The pacific approach by the Chinese delegation reflected the general Chinese Communist orientation toward foreign and domestic policy in that brief period from the 1940s until the early rumbles of the Cultural Revolution in the 1960s.[19] Right after 1949, when the Chinese Communists came to power, they cultivated a "democratic coalition" of peasants, workers, and intellectuals to strengthen and broaden their support and power base (Mao Tsetung encouraged the Communists on this line with the slogan "Don't hit out in too many directions").

If the Communists within China found alliances among the peasantry and some fractions of the middle class, they had a harder time on the international stage. The clash with the Soviet Union from the 1930s onward continued after 1949, and intensified after the death of Joseph Stalin in 1953. The Sino-Soviet divide isolated China on a world stage otherwise predisposed to shun Communists. The United States rattled its sabers across the Sea of China over Formosa (later Taiwan) and Korea. In late 1950, the Chinese government acted impetuously to defend the Korean people by sending its troops across the Yalu River into the conflict on the peninsula. The USSR had discouraged this, mainly because it had invested itself in détente with the First World. China rejected the "camp" divisions of the Cold War, and found itself isolated from its natural ally in the USSR, and later the Warsaw Pact. China was entirely encircled by hostile powers—the USSR to the north and west, and the U.S.-initiated military pacts on either end. In addition, there was no one to argue China's case at the United Nations because its seat was held by the government of Formosa. That the Chinese Communists resisted the idea that the darker nations should be divided into the spheres of influence of the two powers made it a principled ally of the Third World. China, it seemed to say, stood for independence and self-determination, not détente and division. Apart from principles alone, the Third World had something tangible to give China: however different in orientation, Bandung provided the terrain to end China's isolation from world opinion and support.

Of the twenty-nine states at the Bandung Conference, six important delegates had recently made military-economic arrangements with the United States and Britain. In 1954, Pakistan, the Philippines, and Thailand joined with New Zealand, Australia, France, Britain, and the United States to form the South East Asian Treaty Organization (SEATO, also known as the Manila Pact), while Iran, Iraq, Pakistan again, and Turkey joined with Britain and the United States to create the Central Treaty Organization (also known as the Baghdad Pact). At Bandung, the Pakistani, Thai, and Filipino delegates defended these pacts on the ground that they protected the "small or weak nations" from domestic and international Communism. As Romulo put it, "The empires of yesterday on which it used to be said the sun never set are departing one by one from Asia. What we fear now is the new empire of communism on which we know the sun never rises."[20] Mohammed Ali of Pakistan also defended the pacts on the basis of the "right to self-defense, exercised singly or collectively" because of what he called "new and more invidious forms of imperialism that masquerade in the guise of 'liberation.' "[21] The two major papers on the two sides of the Atlantic, the *New York Times* and the London *Times*, gave the speeches of Ali, Romulo, and Kotelawala a great deal of space. The U.S. paper cheered these three leaders, and found it "gratifying to the West to hear a strong championship of liberty of thought and action," and see them put colonialism "into the right perspective," which is to move the blame from European and U.S. imperialism to communism.[22]

The pro–First World states at Bandung shared at least one thing in common: they were ruled by weak national bourgeoisies that had militant mass movements within which threatened their own legitimacy and power. The Filipino regime of Manuel Roxas and later Ramon Magsaysay, under whom Romulo served, was challenged by the Huk Rebellion of 1946–54, a mass uprising that took up arms against the new government and its U.S. backers. With arms from Truman, Magsaysay's military dispatched the rebels just before the powers gathered in Manila to sign the SEATO treaty.[23] Thailand had reason to fear a Communist rebellion, for its own undemocratic regime had been challenged from within and its region had been rocked by a popular Communist insurgency in Malaysia that ran from 1948 to 1960, only to be suppressed by an aggressive British carpet-bombing campaign.[24] In 1951, the three-year-old Pakistani Communist Party joined with anti-imperialist officers in a failed coup that led to the party's suppression (by 1954, it moved underground). Iraq and Iran, too, had strong left parties that offered an alternative to the landed leadership which had taken power after the collapse of the Ottoman Empire in the region. Indeed, Iraq at this time had the largest Communist Party in the Arab lands. This pressure conjoined with the USSR to the north led many of these regimes to seek shelter under the military umbrella of the United States.

The blocs had much more than a military function because they worked to transform the social and political system of the states that yoked their destiny to the United States.[25] The "security zone" created by the United States gave many of these states a security guarantee from Washington, DC, for a price: the creation of U.S. military bases in these countries, and the opening up of their markets to U.S. firms. As the U.S. journalist I.F. Stone observed, "Pax Americana is the internationalism of Standard Oil, Chase Manhattan, and the Pentagon."[26] By this analysis, the independence of the newly liberated parts of the world was being curtailed not just by the military alliances but more important by the further integration of places like the Philippines, Pakistan, and Turkey into the economic plans of the First World's global corporations as well as the dynamic of "free market" capitalism that benefited these economic behemoths.

When Romulo gave the Weil Lecture on American Citizenship at the University of North Carolina, and when he wrote in the *New York Times Magazine*, shortly after Bandung, he used both forums to offer a stern rebuke of U.S. economic policy. There is a Marshall Plan for Europe, he told his audience in Chapel Hill, but only "chicken feed" for Asia. "What is worse," he stated in the *Times*, "it comes with the accompaniment of senatorial lectures on how we must be grateful and how imperative it is for us to realize the advantages of the American way of life. And so on. Must Asia and Africa be content with crumbs and must we be told what a great favor is being conferred on us?"[27] Not only does the U.S. government provide meager aid, and not only does it favor its global corporations to ride rampant on the Third World, but it disfigures the global agricultural markets with its "dumping of American surplus products in Asia, such as rice." This has "done irreparable harm to surplus-rice producing countries like Thailand."[28] Even allies like the Philippines could not easily stomach the economic arrangements of Pax Americana.

The heart of the Third World was in the hands of Sukarno, Nehru, U Nu, and Nasser. All four of them chided their colleagues for their formal association with the two major powers; they spoke against pacts and allegiances that divided the world into the toxic Cold War. On

September 29, 1954, Nehru had explained his position on military pacts at length before the Indian house of the people. India had been invited to join the Manila Pact, yet it had refused principally because the Indian government felt that the military pact was not so much a defensive treaty but a way for the major powers to exercise their influence. Why are Britain and the United States part of the "defensive area" of Southeast Asia, Nehru asked? It is not because they are part of the region but because they want to use SEATO to exercise their influence on the domestic and international relations of the pact countries. The "Manila Treaty is inclined dangerously in the direction of the spheres of influence to be exercised by powerful countries. After all, it is the big and powerful countries that will decide matters and not the two or three weak and small Asian countries that may be allied to them."[29] At Bandung, Nehru bore the brunt of the objections from more than half the delegates whose countries had joined one or more pacts. He soldiered on, joined by the Burmese, the Indonesians, the Egyptians, the Syrians, the Cambodians, the North Vietnamese, the Laotians, and the representatives of the Gold Coast and Yemen. "I submit to you," he told the political committee at Bandung, "every pact has brought insecurity and not security to the countries which have entered into them. They have brought the danger of atomic bombs and the rest of it nearer to them than would have been the case otherwise."[30]

Not only were there at least three different centers of opinion at Bandung but there were also areas of Africa and Asia that had not been invited to the conference. As the publisher of the *New York Times* noted, "The meeting is not truly regional. Australia and New Zealand are, for example, more intimately concerned with its problems than is the Gold Coast. Nationalist China, the two Koreas, Israel and South Africa have been excluded."[31] The same paper had no problem with the involvement of the United States and Britain in the regional pacts centered around Manila and Baghdad, perhaps because these two states already had a presumptive global role, whereas the darker nations should aspire to nothing more than a strictly local ambit. Kotelawala offered the pithiest reason for the exclusion of the republic of South Africa: "I can't go there. Why in the devil should I invite them?"[32] Apartheid disqualified South Africa's government from fellowship with the nascent Third World. Israel suffered the same fate as Formosa because both had the reputation of being too beholden to the colonial powers and insufficiently driven by the dynamic of anticolonialism.[33] Nevertheless, other pro-American states did get invited to and participated fully in

Bandung: Ceylon (Sri Lanka), Iran, Iraq, Japan, Jordan, Pakistan, the Philippines, Saudi Arabia, and South Vietnam. Bandung also left out the two Koreas, which had recently been in conflict, and all the Soviet Central Asian republics and Outer Mongolia, because they had an intimate relationship with Moscow.

What did Bandung accomplish? At Bandung, the representatives of the formerly colonized countries signaled their refusal to take orders from their former colonial masters; they demonstrated their ability to discuss international problems and offer combined notes on them. In this regard, Bandung did create the format for what would eventually become the Afro-Asian and then Afro-Asian–Latin American group in the United Nations. A fragment of this group (twelve Arab-Asian states) offered their first such feint at the United Nations during the 1949 debate over the state of the Italian empire, and then, in force in December 1950, to insist that the major powers (particularly the United States) agree to a ceasefire in Korea.[34] Nehru, in the Indian Parliament after Bandung, underscored the importance of the United Nations after the conference: "We believe that from Bandung our great organization, the United Nations, has derived strength. This means in turn that Asia and Africa must play an increasing role in the conduct and destiny of the world organization."[35] The final communiqué at Bandung demanded that the United Nations admit all those formerly colonized states, such as Libya and Vietnam, then denied admission into its body ("For effective cooperation for world peace, membership in the United Nations should be universal").[36] The creation of this UN bloc over time would be the most important accomplishment of Bandung—notably because this bloc would, alongside the socialist one, be the bulwark against "dollar imperialism" and offer an alternative model for development.

Bandung is best remembered, among those who have any memory of it, as one of the milestones of the peace movement. Whatever the orientation of the states, they agreed that world peace required disarmament. During Europe's domestic era of relative peace (1815–1914), the part of the planet under its control grew from a third to 85 percent, and Europe's military technology exerted itself on much of this newly conquered terrain. From the 1856 bombardment of Canton by British forces to the 1913 Spanish aerial bombardment of Morocco, the colonized world already knew what the weapons of mass destruction could do. The colonized also knew how such weapons cultivated a detached sadism among those who had their fingers on the trigger. English author R.P. Hearne, who had written a children's book called *The Romance of the Airplane*, wrote in *Airships in Peace and War* (1910), "In savage lands the moral effect of such an instrument of war [the air bomber] is impossible to conceive. The appearance of the airship would strike terror into the tribes," for these planes can deliver "sharp, severe and terrible punishment," and save "the awful waste of life occasioned to white troops by expeditionary work."[37] Hearne's thoughts are not idle, for aerial bombardment had become standard policy whether by the Italians in North Africa, the British in India and Iraq, the Americans in Nicaragua, or the Spanish in the Basque country or Morocco.

The racist disregard for human life occasioned a long discussion at Bandung on disarmament. In the conference communiqué, the delegates argued that the Third World had to seize the reins of the horses of the apocalypse. The Third World had a "duty toward humanity and civilization to proclaim their support for disarmament."[38] As the nuclear powers dithered over talks, the Third World called on the United Nations to insist on dialogue and the creation of a regime to monitor arms control. The Disarmament Sub-Committee of the United Nations had been formed as a result of Indian (and Third World) initiative in the General Assembly in 1953, to "lift from the peoples of the world [the] burden and [the] fear [of annihilation], and thus to liberate new energies and resources for positive programmes of reconstruction and development."[39] When the United Nations finally created the International Atomic Energy Agency (IAEA) in 1957, its charter followed that of the final communiqué at Bandung, which asked the powers to "bring about the regulation, limitation, control and reduction of all armed forces and armaments, including the prohibition of the production, experimentation and use of all weapons of mass destruction, and to establish effective international controls to this end."[40] The IAEA, in other words, is a child of Bandung.[41]

None of the flamboyance of the delegates on nuclear war is exaggerated. The United States had tested nuclear devices in 1945, and used them on two Japanese cities; the USSR had tested them in 1949, and the United Kingdom had done so in 1952. Besides that, the use of massive aerial bombardment over Japan and Germany as well as elsewhere had created a world marked by the expectation of eventual annihilation. The Bandung states not only confessed to being outgunned in any future conflict but also pleaded for the sanity of disarmament. The 1952 UN Disarmament Commission did not allay many fears, because most people knew that the United States came to the table to undermine Soviet claims, that the First World had no desire to cut back on its military prowess; indeed, in November of that year, the United States exploded its first thermonuclear device and further accelerated the arms race.[42]

That did not stop the Third World, which, led by India, proposed a four-point plan for disarmament to the United Nations in 1956. As a first step, the two major nuclear powers (the United States and the USSR) would have to suspend their experimental explosions. Second, the two powers should dismantle a few bombs to begin a process of total disarmament of nuclear weapons. The two powers should then come to the UN General Assembly and publicly declare their renunciation of nuclear weapons. Finally, all countries must publish their military budgets so as to have transparency in this great waste of social labor.

The struggle against colonialism had been both bloody and brutal, and the people of the Bandung states had lost lives even as they gained homelands. They knew the cost of war as much as anyone else, but more important, they had experienced the power of nonviolence to help shape the world. The obvious leader here was India, where the freedom movement had been shaped since the mid-1910s by ahimsa, mass nonviolent civil disobedience. Even those who had once taken to the bomb, such as the revolutionary Bhagat Singh, came to realize the power of nonviolence, as in his 1930 statement, "Use of force justifiable when resorted to as a matter of terrible necessity. Non-violence as policy indispensable for all mass movements."[43] That India and Ghana, among others, could emerge out of colonialism by the use of nonviolence had an impact at Bandung—although the Third World had not yet been fully marked by the development of the armed nationalist movements in Algeria and Cuba, both of which were liberated by the gun. Until Bandung, at any rate, nonviolence had a prestige, and for Nehru to propagate the "Five Principles of Peaceful Co-Existence" had a gravity that might not have been allowed by the Bandung powers without India's ability to exert pain and social costs on the British Empire.

The Third World, however, remained vulnerable on at least two counts. The Bandung states continued to hoard weapons—a fact that led many to charge them with hypocrisy. Both India and Pakistan had already embarked on a catastrophic arms race after their first war in 1947–48. Regional conflicts and invasions by imperialist powers (such as the Anglo-French-Israeli assault on Egypt in 1956) made the need for "defense" second nature in these states. While the Bandung states made various shades of a strategic decision to maintain armies, they proposed a planetary transformation in the way states dealt with each other—indeed, they demanded that the major powers take the lead to give teeth to the United Nations's role as peacemaker, to allow fellowship to be the basis for interstate relations rather than détente.[44] Second, one of the Bandung powers, China, had decided in 1955 (during the Taiwan Strait crisis) to develop nuclear weapons. Chairman Mao had once called nuclear weapons a "paper tiger," but now it seemed as if China wanted one of its own. The other Bandung states made many attempts to prevent China from its pact with the atom, but they failed. The pursuit went all the way to the eve of China's test explosion in 1964, as the delegates at the second Conference of Non-Aligned States in Cairo tried to "persuade China to desist from developing nuclear weapons."[45] The Chinese turn to the bomb and the persistence of conflict between the Bandung states significantly undermined the otherwise-strong moral challenge posed by the Third World to the radioactive Cold War.

Bandung's final communiqué did not open with disarmament or colonialism but with "economic cooperation." Amid the crucial points on bilateral trade and liaisons from one state to another, the points showed a determined effort by the Bandung states to stave off the imperialist pressure brought on them not so much by direct colonialism but by finance capital and the comparative advantages given to the First World by the legacy of colonialism. The communiqué called for the creation of a Special UN Fund for Economic Development (SUNFED) and for an International Finance Corporation to ensure the regulation of predatory capital flows. It envisaged the creation of a UN Permanent Advisory Commission on International Commodity Trade and encouraged its peers to diversify their export trade. Under colonial conditions, the darker nations had been reduced to being providers of raw materials and consumers of manufactured goods produced in Europe and the United States. The Bandung proposals called for the formerly colonized states to diversify their economic base, develop indigenous manufacturing capacity, and thereby break the colonial chain. SUNFED and the other UN bodies had been drafted with the view to enable these developments.

These moderate proposals came after a preamble written to settle any fears among international financiers that the Third World had "gone socialist," and yet, these proposals chilled the financial press in Europe and the United States. But even the most anticommunist among the Bandung delegates supported the idea of some autarky for the Third World from the immense power of the First World. When Romulo left the Bretton Woods Conference that set up the international financial system, he did so in anger at the manner in which the First World states "had already set themselves up to be the ones to decide what the economic pattern of the postwar world should be."[46] The near-universal acclaim for the formation of the UN Conference on Trade and Development (UNCTAD) in 1964 is evidence of the widespread agreement within the Third World on some anti-imperialist strategy for economic development.

The most powerful agreement at Bandung came over "cultural cooperation." The lack of agreement on the nature of the global political economy resulted in a weak combined position. Progressive nationalisms drew from the class interests of those who predominated in their various societies. What united these various classes, however, was a forthright condemnation of the indignity of imperialism's cultural chauvinism. The unity on this theme far exceeded that on the political economy. For the decade before Bandung, UNESCO had sponsored a crucial study of racism and racial attitudes in different cultural traditions. The work produced a series of important monographs, including works by the anthropologist Claude Lévi-Strauss and the psychologist Marie Jahoda. UNESCO's work had grown from the post-Holocaust insight that race is not only a biological fiction but that its mobilization in world history had torn people asunder. At Bandung, the twenty-nine new states condemned "racialism as a means of cultural suppression." Imperial racism, they argued, "not only prevents cultural cooperation but also suppresses the national cultures of the people."[47] Empires generally attempt to direct the cultural history of a people—to set one community against another (divide and rule), adopt one group as the leader above the rest, or else disdain the cultural traditions of a region and propose its substitution by the empire's own cultural traditions, at least for a select few. The Bandung twenty-nine demanded an end to this use of cultural richness for purposes of domination. But they went further, enjoining the world to learn about each other's cultures, to demand that the darker nations not only find out about European culture but that each of the twenty-nine and beyond learn about everyone's cultural history. The communiqué directed the countries toward "the acquisition of knowledge of each other's country, mutual cultural exchange, and exchange of information." This was not to be only in the arts but in all aspects of culture, including science and technology.[48]

From Belgrade to Tokyo, from Cairo to Dar es Salaam, politicians and intellectuals began to speak of the "Bandung Spirit." What they meant was simple: that the colonized world had now emerged to claim its space in world affairs, not just as an adjunct of the First or Second Worlds, but as a player in its own right. Furthermore, the Bandung

Spirit was a refusal of both economic subordination and cultural suppression—two of the major policies of imperialism. The audacity of Bandung produced its own image.

Nowhere was the impact felt strongest than in Moscow, among the newly installed leaders who took charge after the 1953 death of Stalin. Nikita Khrushchev and Nicolay Aleksandrovich Bulganin went on a major world tour, beginning in Yugoslavia, then going to India and Burma. Nehru and U Nu visited Moscow, and Nasser went to Yugoslavia—all this as the USSR increased its economic aid to the newly aggressive national bourgeois states of Africa and Asia. The visit of the Soviet leaders to Marshal Tito in Yugoslavia sent a signal that they had decided to change their tenor on the new nations.[49] Tito had already become close to many of the Bandung twenty-nine states, having visited India, Burma, Egypt, and Ethiopia. On Belgrade radio at the end of the conference, Tito offered his verdict: "The number of Asiatic and African countries participating in the conference, and the huge interest in the conference in Asia and Africa show that a crossroads of history has been reached in the sense that those peoples are determined to decide their own fate as far as possible."[50] Tito would soon join the main players in the Third World to help decide this fate. In the joint declaration of the Soviets and the Yugoslavians on June 2, 1955, they affirmed the concept of the Third World, welcomed the successful conclusion of the Bandung Conference, and noted that the conference had made a significant advance for the cause of world peace.[51] Finally, the USSR allowed its allies, such as the Czech government, to sell arms to the Egyptians, and it too consolidated economic ties with the Bandung states.

Dramatically, in 1956, the twentieth Congress of the Communist Party of the Soviet Union (CPSU) rejected its earlier two-camp theory of the world. The congress reiterated the position taken by Nehru and U Nu at Bandung, and by Nasser in Cairo. It noted that the camp theory provided a vision of the world that suggested that war was the only solution to the division, that across the abyss of the divide there could be no conversation and dialogue toward peace. For that reason, the congress adopted the notion of the "zone of peace," to include all states that pledged themselves to a reduction of force on behalf of a peace agenda. The congress included in the zone of peace the socialist Second World and what it called "uncommitted states"—that is, the non-aligned Third World.[52]

The Soviet motivations for this transformed role in world affairs are complex. Some argue that the new leadership of the CPSU had revised the previous commitment to the working class in the formerly colonized world and had now shifted its allegiance to the national bourgeoisie. The Soviet leadership, then, can be seen to be motivated by a desire to undo the postwar Soviet era of lax support for the nationalist movements, and therefore, the interest in expanding socialism by alliance rather than by social revolution. Others contend that the policy is motivated less by any general theory of world revolution, and more by the influence of the Chinese in the Third World. The USSR's shift occurred, by this logic, more in the context of the growing Sino-Soviet split than in any ideological congruence with the Third World's agenda.[53]

If the proof of the pudding is in the eating, then the Soviet adoption of the idea of "non-alignment," for whatever reason, tasted far better in the darker nations than the First World's disdain for it. The newly installed British government of Anthony Eden showed open hostility to what it termed "neutralism." Before Bandung, Eden, then foreign secretary, had urged his ambassadors in African and Asian countries that reviled Communism to send delegations to Indonesia with the purpose of putting up a show against the Chinese as well as to secure the formerly colonized world into a relationship with the First World.[54] Eden, who in 1938 had urged European powers to "effectively assert white-race authority in the Far East," projected Britain's hope for continued imperial power, even as it had already become an extension of the United States.[55] The Anglo-French invasion of Egypt in 1956 sealed the attitude of the Third World toward Britain, and even Ceylon (at Bandung, very pro–First World) joined the Burmese, Indonesians, and Indians in a November 12, 1956, condemnation of the assault.

The United States had an even more hostile attitude toward Bandung from the start. Indeed, when U.S. congressperson Adam Clayton Powell Jr. decided to attend the conference, the U.S. State Department not only tried to dissuade him but, as Powell told the press, advised him to "stay away from the U.S. Embassy and U.S. Ambassador Hugh S. Cummings Jr., because his association with the U.S. Embassy would give an official flavor to his presence." Twenty-four hours after Powell arrived in Indonesia, however, he was asked by the State Department to go to the embassy because, as Powell put it, otherwise "Communist propaganda would say that the U.S. State Department was discriminating against a member of Congress because he is a Negro." Powell refused to stay in the embassy, in protest. "This conference is not anti-white," Powell told a news conference, "but it was anti-American foreign policy and it could become an anti-white movement unless a narrow-minded and unskilled American foreign policy is revised." When he returned from Bandung, he could not get a meeting with the State Department, to which he had wanted to bring information about Saudi funds for rebels in North Africa.[56]

After Bandung, the U.S. foreign policy establishment took a strong position against what it called "neutralism." If a state decided to reject the two-camp approach of the United States and the USSR, then it was considered not to have a position of its own but to be neutral. In 1952, the U.S. planners had declared that neutralism was, according to Secretary of State Dean Acheson, "a shortcut to suicide," and as conflict broke out in the neutral world, the USSR might "force the maximum number of non-Communist countries to pursue a neutral policy and to deny their resources to the principle Western powers."[57] Ambassador Douglas MacArthur warned the United States that the Bandung Spirit might move Japan, a crucial geopolitical ally, to neutralism; the United States might lose its naval bases, and to prevent this, should treat Japan with more respect.[58] Following John Foster Dulles's trip to East Asia for a SEATO meeting in 1958, the National Security Council deliberated and created a policy on mainland Southeast Asia. The document had to admit that the states in the region valued their independence above all else. The U.S. government, it noted, should "respect each country's choice of national policy for preserving its independence, but make every effort to demonstrate the advantages of greater cooperation and closer alignment with the Free World, as well as the dangers of alignment with the Communist bloc." The United States must tie these states into interdependence with its own economy ("Provide flexible economic and technical assistance as necessary to attain U.S. objectives"), its cultural institutions ("Make a special, sustained effort to help educate an expanding number of technically competent, pro-Western civilian and military leaders"), and its military power ("Maintain, in the general area of the Far East, U.S. forces adequate to exert a deterrent influence against Communist aggression, in conformity with current basic national security policy").[59]

The Third World dominated Bandung—that is, those powers that sought to create a non-aligned space from which to critique both the camp mentality and the rush to war won the battle to define Bandung's legacy. Nasser, Nehru, and U Nu held the stage, not Romulo or Kotelawala. When U Nu traveled to Washington, DC, in 1955, he told the National Press Club that the UN Charter "is in effect one great mutual security pact." Like Sukarno, U Nu came from a patriotic family of some means who had been swept up in the early struggles against British rule in Burma. If Sukarno made an attempt to align Marxism and nationalism with Islam, U Nu spent his youth trying to develop a Buddhist-Communist-nationalist synthesis. In the late 1930s, U Nu wrote an article titled "I Am a Marxist," which asked, "How can people who starve and have to struggle from day to day for their very existence practice religion?" Such adverse conditions for Buddhism meant that "to help work for Marxism would be to repay our gratitude to Buddha for his suffering in all his aeons of existences for the benefit of mankind."[60] U Nu played a leading role in the Anti-Fascist Organization created in 1944 to fight the Japanese Occupation, and it, along with General Aung San's Burma National Army, became the vehicle for Burmese independence in 1948. A shaky relationship with the Burmese Communist Party, Communist China, and the U.S.-backed Kuomintang army that camped in large parts of Burma strengthened U Nu's belief in a third way apart from the two-camp division of the world. The United Nations, in which the Third World played a unique role, would not be neutral in conflicts but would actively oppose them. "A divided world stands in greater need of a common forum to discuss differences than a world united," U Nu said in Washington. For this reason, "I believe that if the United Nations did not exist today, the world would be working feverishly to establish it or something like it."[61] The Third World and its vehicle, the United Nations, would not be neutral but would be actively against the polarization of the world.

On September 24, 1996, the UN secretary general Boutros Boutros-Ghali addressed a commemorative meeting of NAM. The seed of this movement had been sown at Bandung, Boutros-Ghali noted. "At Bandung, the birth of non-alignment was an act of stunning, world-transfixing boldness. Freed from the shackles of colonial oppression, the non-aligned stepped onto the international stage, raising a new voice for all the world to hear. International politics were fundamentally and forever transformed." Boutros-Ghali's enthusiasm was anachronistic. It would probably have made sense in the late 1950s, but by the 1990s, the Bandung Spirit had withered and the United Nations was not what it could have been. The Bandung Spirit could have changed international politics, and it certainly made every attempt to do so, but as we shall see below, it did fail. Its failure, however, cannot be sought in its ideals alone.

A young socialist trained in Paris, Boutros-Ghali returned to Cairo in 1949 to teach at its main university, edit a business weekly (*al-Ahram Iktisadi*), write a book on Afro-Asian political solidarity in 1969, and struggle in his early years to move Nasser's Egypt toward justice and socialism.[62] When Boutros-Ghali lectured in the law faculty, Nasser returned from Bandung and announced that the conference was "one of the two most important events of modern history" (the other was atomic energy).[63] Nasser's enthusiasm for the Bandung Spirit was soured by the events of September 1955, when he linked Bandung to the Czech sales of arms to the Egyptians. For Nasser, the independence signaled at Bandung had to be protected by arms, an early perversion of the Third World agenda. Enthusiastically, Nasser wanted Bandung II to be held in Cairo, and even though it wasn't, Cairo became the favored destination for a host of Afro-Asian solidarity meetings, from the Economic Conference in 1958 to the Medical Conference in 1964. But most important for a movement that had begun to be represented by men, the Bandung dynamic hosted the Afro-Asian Women's Conference in Cairo in 1961.

CAIRO

Unlike Bandung, Cairo in the 1950s had the feeling of a defiant city on a war footing, ready to take on the First World with rhetoric or guns, if necessary. In 1952, a group of young officers in the Egyptian army seized power. Organized by Lieutenant Colonel Gamal Abdel Nasser, the Free Officers forced out a monarchy long tainted by corruption and subservience to European interests. The Free Officers represented all the major strains of Egyptian political life. There were old-school nationalists of the Wafd Party, members of the Muslim Brotherhood, Communists, and also aristocrats who had lost faith in King Farouk. The diversity was a testament to the organizational capacity of Nasser, who understood the necessity for broad unity in the fight against the monarchy. Most of the officers who joined and supported the coup came because it represented the aspirations of the "new middle class" of bureaucratic and technical workers. The ideology of Pan-Arabism and the secular Turkish lineage of Kemal Ataturk appealed to their ideas about Egyptian modernity. Initially, the officers had hoped to assassinate a slew of monarchists and paralyze the government. As Nasser drove away from a failed bid to kill General Hussein Sirri Amer, he heard "the sounds of screaming and wailing. I heard a woman crying, a child terrified, and a continuous, frightened call for help."[1] Rather than kill Amer, the officers had hit some innocents. "We dream of the glory of our nation," Nasser later wrote, "but which is the better way to bring it about—to eliminate those who should be eliminated, or to bring forward those who should be brought forward?"[2] The holstered gun alongside the mass rallies would become the preferred instrument of revolution.

Nasser took charge of the revolution and made from the many lineages that produced it the ideology of Arab Socialism. The United States and Europe did not reciprocate Egypt's request for assistance, so Nasser's government turned to the USSR and its allies. Nasser goaded the French further with his support for the Algerian FLN; indeed, Egypt became one of the FLN's principle supporters in its fight against French colonialism. The United States revoked its agreement to finance the Aswan Dam, and Nasser retaliated by seizing the Suez Canal, then owned by a French company.[3] In late 1956, an Anglo-French-Israeli expeditionary force landed in Suez to counter this, and the Egyptians fought back valiantly, only to be saved in the last instance by U.S., USSR, and Third World condemnations of the assault. The streets of Cairo overflowed with the voice of the diva of the East Umm Kulthum, singing *Misr Tatahaddath 'an Nafsiha* (Egypt Speaks of Herself) and *Misr allati fi khatiri wa-fi Dami* (Egypt, which is in my mind and in my blood), or else,

He taught us how to build glory.
So that we conquered the world.
Not through hope will the prize be obtained.
The world must be taken through struggle.

Nasser embodied the hopes of the Egyptians and the Arabs for several years after the coup of 1952, and when he returned from Bandung, he brought with him news that the world looked to Egypt for leadership against the barbarism of the Cold War. The Egyptian government opened its doors to the Afro-Asian solidarity organizations, especially by being the secretariat of numerous Afro-Asian and non-aligned institutions. Cairo became the headquarters of the movement, the host to a number of important conferences and conclaves, and the meeting place for Arab nationalists from across North Africa and West Asia.[4]

In late December 1957, Cairo hosted the Afro-Asian People's Solidarity Conference, the next major event after Bandung. Forty-five African and Asian countries sent their delegates—double the number at Bandung. While Bandung welcomed a diverse set of views, this conference took a partisan position against the First World—coming as it did just after Suez, and in the wake of the acerbic comments on decolonization by political leaders from Britain (Anthony Eden) and the United States (John Foster Dulles). Anwar es-Sadat, then Nasser's closest adviser, played host to the conference. In his welcome address, Sadat accepted the Bandung flame for Cairo. Delegates from newly liberated countries joined leaders of ongoing national liberation movements (notably from the world of the Portuguese colonies).

What also separated this conference from Bandung was the presence of women not only in the hall but also at the podium. One of the three plenary addresses came from the Gandhian Rameshwari Nehru, whose social reform work in India later earned her the Lenin Peace Prize (1961). The most remarkable figure at the conference, however, came from Egypt itself. Aisha Abdul-Rahman was born into a devout family from the Damietta Port region of northern Egypt in 1913. Her father taught at a local theological institute, while her great grandfather had been the grand imam of al-Azhar in the nineteenth century. With the encouragement of her mother and grandfather, Abdul-Rahman studied through correspondence courses (her father would not allow her to go to school). In 1929, through the mail, Abdul-Rahman earned the first teacher's qualification from al-Azhar University (women were only allowed on the campus in 1964). At age twenty-one, Abdul-Rahman enrolled in King Faud I (later Cairo) University, from which she earned a PhD in early Arabic literature. The university initially only allowed foreign women to attend a few classes, but thanks to a progressive rector, Ahmad Lutfi al-Sayyid, five women matriculated in 1929. Sohair al-Qalamawy, a pioneering Egyptian advocate for women's rights, was one of them.[5] She would soon be followed by Abdul-Rahman. Long before she earned her doctorate, Abdul-Rahman had become a household name among literate circles as a popular columnist for Egypt's leading newspaper, *Al-Ahram*. Pointed criticisms of both the monarchy and the Nasserite dictatorship came alongside several books on Arab women poets as well as her own poetry. Protected by her editor, Mohammad Heikal, Nasser's friend and ideological anchor, Abdul-Rahman continued to openly criticize elements of the state that bothered her.[6] In 1957, as both a journalist and a professor of Arabic and Islamic studies at Ain Shams University in Cairo, Abdul-Rahman offered one of the main speeches at the conference.

The history of national liberation movements, Abdul-Rahman pointed out, often ignores the central role played by women in them, and in the liberation of women by the struggle. "The renaissance of the Eastern woman has always coincided with liberation movements," for liberation from imperialism meant that "women were emancipated from the fetters of social slavery and escaped from moral death." Within the confines allowed by imperialism, "women remained the victim of ignorance, isolation and slavery." Since national liberation movements, for all their machismo and lack of appreciation for the role of women, still operate on the assumption that everyone has to be liberated, this conceit proves valuable to women who can take advantage of the opening to press for their social dignity and political rights. "The success of these revolutions depends on the liberation of the enslaved half, on rescuing women from paralysis, unemployment and inaction and eliminating the differences between the two halves of the nation—its men and women."[7]

Abdul-Rahman makes an underestimated point about the linkage between anticolonial nationalism and women's liberation.[8] There is nothing that stops the former from reproducing various patriarchal ideas. Yet most of the anticolonial movements relied on women, and several of them had put women's concerns on their freedom agenda. In 1919, Egyptian women of all classes took to the streets of Cairo to protest the British crackdown on demonstrations for a free Egypt. The women cut telephone wires and disrupted railway lines to stall the ability of the British troops who relied on them, and they attacked prisons to free their comrades. The British set aside their good manners and fired on the women radicals. Several of the women died, notably Shafika Mohamed, Hamida Khalil, Sayeda Hassan, Fahima Riad, Aisha Omar, and also, as the feminist writer Nawal El-Saadawi notes, the hundreds of poor women who "lost their lives without anybody being able to trace their names."[9]

During the major mass protests in India in 1905, 1909, 1919, 1920–21, and 1930–31, women held the streets.[10] Iran's constitutional movement saw women in public protest from 1907 to 1911, and again in 1919.[11] Much the same has been documented for women in China, Indo-China, Indonesia, Ghana, and South Africa.[12] These protests, and their contacts with women from other parts of the world, emboldened the bourgeois women to form organizations and exert themselves within the framework of national liberation.[13]

Well-heeled Egyptian women formed organizations for women's rights in the aftermath of these cross-class demonstrations. Huda Sha'rawi, from a family of wealth and political power (her father was the speaker of the House of Representatives), became the pioneer of the Egyptian women's movement. She founded the Egyptian Feminist Union in 1923, established the French-language periodical *L'Égyptienne*, and went to Rome for the 1924 International Conference of Women. Unveiled, Sha'rawi with her comrades Ceza Nabaraoui and Nabawiya Musa let European feminists know that Egyptian women came with a heritage (*turath*) from the Pharaonic era and early Islam that needed to be reclaimed. At the Rome conference, Sha'rawi reported that the European delegates wanted the Egyptians to be "romantic, ignorant heroines of the European novelists." The idea of the veil kept the real, living struggles of the Egyptians out of the European feminist mind, which "made them ignorant of everything about us." Yet the Egyptian woman, hidden in plain sight, understood European feminism because, as Sha'rawi remarked at the conference, "nothing is more similar to an Oriental woman than a Western woman."[14]

Many of the pioneers of the organized women's movement came from the old social classes that had either retained their aristocratic positions despite or in spite of the pressure from imperialism. A few of the leaders came from the new social classes that had been created by imperialism (military and civilian bureaucrats and merchants). Sha'rawi's husband, Ali, had been a founder of the Wafd Party, and her father, Sultan Pasha, was one of the richest landowners in Egypt. Abdul-Rahman's family had no such national pretensions, but she nonetheless came from a learned, relatively prosperous section. Women such as these drew their inspiration from the mass action against imperialism that enveloped them as well as from their interactions with European women (who were in the midst of their own suffrage campaign). While they found many allies among the European women, by and large the women of the colonized world experienced a patronizing dismissal. When confronted by the hesitancy of the International Alliance of Women in 1939, Ceza Nabaraoui wrote, "What did we demand? A little sympathy for the unfortunates who suffer in the East from the wrongs of imperialist policies." And what did they get? The International Alliance of Women proved "that their magnificent program addresses itself only to certain people of the West," and that they "alone deigned to enjoy liberty."[15] From the contradictions of their privileged locations, bourgeois women like Sha'rawi and Nabaraoui not only put the demand for the franchise on the table but they also created organizations whose subsequent history would move far from the salons and into the byways of small villages and towns.

As Sha'rawi and Nabaraoui fought to win the franchise for Egyptian women within the confines of the monarchy, in distant Latin America three women mirrored their work. Amalia Caballero de Castillo Ledón worked in the Alianza de Mujeres de México, Minerva Bernardino worked in the Accion Feminista Dominica, and Bertha Lutz worked for the Brazilian Federation for Feminine Progress. All of them came from the old social classes, and each pushed a fairly conservative agenda for women's emancipation. While they fought to get women the vote, these organizations and leaders settled for fairly patriarchal social definitions of family and marriage. The Alianza de Mujeres de México followed after the 1931 National Women's Congress of Workers and Peasants, which had demanded land rights, adult education, and equality for the sexes in unions. Nothing of the sort entered the Alianza de Mujeres, nor did it cross the minds of Accion Feminista or Feminine Progress.[16] Nonetheless, these three women insisted that the phrase "the equal rights of men and women" be inserted into the UN Charter based on the discussions at the 1945 Chapultepec gathering and the 1938 Lima Conference of Latin American states.[17] These Latin American delegates, moreover, pushed the United Nations to form the Commission on the Status of Women underneath the UN Economic and Social Commission.

In 1947, the Commission on the Status of Women adopted its guidelines: to "raise the status of women irrespective of nationality, race, language, or religion to equality of men in all fields of human enterprise; and to eliminate all discrimination against women in statutory law, legal maxims or rules, or in interpretations of customary law."[18] The guidelines meant nothing because they could not go into force.[19] It was not until 1967 that the UN Economic and Social Commission put forward the "Declaration on the Elimination of Discrimination against Women" for a vote to the UN General Assembly, all of this as a prelude to 1975 becoming the International Women's Year when Mexico City hosted the first UN conference on women.[20] Bourgeois feminism of the Alianza de Mujeres and Feminine Progress variety created a set of important international institutions and platforms that would be used later by women's rights activists aware of the deep inequality within the Third World. Such activists, who would populate the Afro-Asian meetings, did not emphasize gender struggles outside the broader struggle to create sovereign nations and working-class power within these nations.

Anticolonial nationalism drew from all sections of the oppressed population—men and women, working class and merchant—not only for demographic reasons but also because they had adopted the idea of equality. Few of the new states that had experienced anticolonial struggles had a problem with universal adult franchise. In Egypt, women briefly won the vote in the 1923 Constitution before the monarchy revoked their right to the ballot box. In 1952, after the Free Officers' Revolution, Nasser promised to reinstate the vote. The two main muftis took opposite positions on this, with the Grand Mufti Shakyh Hasanayn

Makhluf against it, and Shaykh Allam Nassar for it. In 1956, women won the vote again.[21] In the Wafd Party's early years in power, Nasser opposed its bourgeois nationalist anxiety with egalitarian democracy (including equality between men and women).[22] By the 1950s, women worked within the framework of the national liberation project because it appeared that it would be able to deliver the groundwork of the eventual liberation of women, notably, as Abdul-Rahman put it in 1957, for the "awakening of consciousness and the will to live."[23]

At the 1957 conference, the Afro-Asian Solidarity Organization created an Afro-Asian Federation for Women.[24] The federation subsequently hosted a conference in 1961, again in Cairo, attended by delegates from thirty-seven countries and movements.[25] At this first Afro-Asian Women's Conference, the delegates crafted a more coherent agenda for the struggles of women within the platform of the Third World. Few of the movements that gathered in Cairo in January 1961 saw themselves as Europe's misbegotten sisters, and fewer still felt that they had no title to the concept of the Third World. They came to insist that their female forebears had fought in the national liberation movements and so earned the right to craft the future. Karima El Said, deputy minister of education in the United Arab Republic, welcomed the delegates from thirty-seven states with this reminder, "The woman was a strong prop in these liberation movements, she struggled with the strugglers and she died with the martyrs."[26] In the longer general report to the conference, the writers detailed the efforts of women within national liberation movements, from Vietnam to India, from Algeria to South Africa. "In Afro-Asian countries where people are still suffering under the yoke of colonialism, women are actively participating in the struggle for complete national liberation and independence of their countries. They are convinced that this is the first step for their emancipation and will equip them to occupy their real place in society."[27] That is, participation in the anticolonial struggles would not only attack one of the impediments to the women's liberation agenda but the contribution itself would transform the relations between men and women in the movement and society.[28] Not only did women join the guerrilla wars in Algeria, Cuba, Guinea, Indonesia, Kenya, Korea, Oman, Venezuela, Vietnam, and elsewhere but they also helped supply the fighters, aided the injured, and in Egypt, India, Zanzibar, and elsewhere, dominated the street protests.

Imperialism made progress for women nearly impossible.[29] Even if women's movements did concentrate on various aspects of oppression, no women's organization could afford to ignore the anti-imperialist fight. The sisterhood of those who came to Cairo had been formed in struggle against imperialism, with the expectation that political rights within the independent nation would allow them to take the struggle further. Without political rights, all the other reforms would be meaningless. The state could promise equal education and equal wages, but if women had no political rights, how would they make sure these reforms were enacted and maintained?[30]

Even the brief history of independence had shown these women's rights activists that the national liberation state should not be left alone to be magnanimous in its gestures.[31] The new states had not been nirvana for women. Not only do the two Cairo conferences offer a list of prescriptions, a vision of equal rights for men and women, but within these lists is also an implicit critique of the new states for their failure to promulgate many of these policies. The list demands not only that the new states adopt the new international standards *for which they themselves fought*, such as in the International Labour Organization and other UN bodies, but that they actually implement them. The birth of the nation, Abdul-Rahman reminded the conference, was only "the first step of true solidarity."[32]

Every right that the women won was not itself the end of the struggle but helped build the power to further their demands. High on the Third World women's agenda was the stipulation that women must have choice over marriage: they must be able to dictate if they marry, when they marry, and to whom they marry. "Marriage should be based on the principle of the personal freedom of choice for the spouses concerned," agreed the delegates to the 1957 conference. If men and women have any problems in their relationship, the state should provide them with "marriage counseling and planned parenthood." To fight against the idea that marriage is simply about property or progeny, the conference demanded that "drastic measures should be taken to abolish polygamy." To offer women some freedom from the domestic sphere, "working women should be entitled to free medical care during pregnancy and childbirth, and to a suitable holiday with full pay during childbirth." Finally, it was argued, "the right of married women to work must be recognized and guaranteed."[33] Most of the policy demands were not simply for the betterment of everyday life; their purpose as well was to create the power for an engaged civil society that includes women.

Of the rights demanded by women to increase their political capacity, much is already familiar from the 1920s onward: cultural rights (the right to equal and free education being the principle one) and social rights (as listed in the previous paragraph).[34] A long section of the 1961 Cairo Recommendations on "Equality in the Economic Field" took the point further to argue that if women did not fight for and gain economic rights, they would not be able to be full political citizens. Modern citizenship meant that women should not have to rely on the family unit for their economic well-being but should be full economic partners within the family. The 1957 conference reiterated the slogan "equal pay for equal work," which reappeared four years later. The 1961 conference offered a detailed vision for feminist struggle in the economic arena, for the right of women to hold any job, gain promotion commensurate to their talents and not gender, have the right to their jobs regardless of pregnancy or convalescence, have vocational and technical training for all types of jobs, and have the right to join and lead trade unions. It demanded that contract work be abolished since such work is frequently done by women, without benefits and out of the clear light of legal regulation. For women agricultural workers, the recommendations called for the "equal distribution of land for those who till it and the guarantee of means of agricultural production."[35] Finally, the recommendations included women who do not work for a wage. For them, the conference had two recommendations: that the state try to reduce indirect (sales) taxes on consumer goods and so lighten the burden on household finances, and that the state find ways to give women income support without making them perform meaningless jobs.

Anticolonial nationalism, even in its reformist incarnations, worried about the woman question. An end to social oppression found its way on to the agenda of national liberation. At its most traditional, such an end looked like the modernization of patriarchy, with the new woman relegated to the domain of the home.[36] On the more progressive side of national liberation, one finds many who argued that cultural traditions had ossified under the impact of patriarchy and feudal relations, and any opportunity to redress this had been suffocated by imperialism's alliance with the old social classes, which benefited from misogyny and status. Women and men, in this model, had to struggle against conservative domesticity, and reconfigure what is to be the public space of the nation and the private domain of the family. As the report on social issues put it, women "participate in the struggle for independence of their countries and its maintenance so that they may be able to abolish all customs and traditions which are degradatory to the status of women."[37] Third World women's rights activists sought to reconfigure the nation in their interest; to them, in the struggle for justice, the nation was more inclusive than the family, and therefore it was within the horizon of anticolonial nationalism that they dreamed and acted.

Nasserism's relationship to gender relations shows how even a putatively progressive project is prone to conservatism. What advances came for Egyptian women in the Nasser era, writes political scientist Mervat Hatem, were in the guise of a "state feminism." The regime "produced women who were economically independent of their families, but dependent on the state for employment, important social services like education, health and day care, and political representation."[38] This state feminism opened up some space for women in the domain of politics and the economy (apart from the right to vote, the 1956 Constitution allowed all women the right to education and work). In 1957, two women, Aminah Shukri and Rawiyah 'Arriyah, won elections to the parliament. Yet the Nasser project remained constrained by social conservatism in terms of its attempt to undermine "personal status laws" and patriarchy. In 1955, the Nasserite regime eliminated the Sharia courts, yet the religious judges remained in newly constituted personal status courts. The weak vanguard within Nasserism remained the Ministry of Social Welfare (led by Hikmat Abu Zeid), which unsuccessfully tried to raise the question of personal laws in the National Assembly in 1958. In the context of state feminism, where some gains had been registered, Abdul-Rahman put her faith in the nation as a political vehicle for the struggle against monarchy, tradition, and empire. Two years after the Cairo conference, the Ministry of Social Welfare took up some of its topics in a conference on women and work, where the theme of women's economic independence (including in the arena of family planning) dominated. This was an outcome of Cairo, 1961.

More militant national liberation formations such as the African Party for the Independence of Guinea and Cape Verde (PAIGC) had problems other than that of a neopatriarchal state. They registered the hesitancy of their male comrades toward the reconstruction of the family as an institution. Liberation for women is good theoretically, they allowed, "but in *my* home? Never!"[39] Such attitudes did not faze fighters like Teodora Ignacia Gomes, who laid out the logic of women's rights in the national liberation frame:

> First of all, women must fight together with men against colonialism and all systems of exploitation. Secondly, and this is one of the most fundamental points, every woman must convince herself

that she can be free and that she has to be free. And that she is able
to do all things that men do in social and political life. And thirdly,
women must fight in order to convince men that she has naturally
the same rights as he has. But she must understand that the fundamental problem is not the contradiction between women and men,
but it is the system in which we are living.[40]

The progressive side of anticolonial national liberation not only
dreamed of equality but also tried to construct a program for equality
based on the history of economic exploitation and cultural suppression.
From Buenos Aires came the economist who stitched the economic critiques and anticipations into a doctrine, and it is to him and those who
gathered his ideas into action that I now turn.

BUENOS AIRES

In 1949, Raúl Prebisch wrote and circulated a paper titled "The Economic Development of Latin America and Its Principal Problems."[1] Prebisch, formerly undersecretary of finance in Argentina and then the first director general of Argentina's Central Bank, had been appointed to head the UN Economic Commission for Latin America (ECLA) in 1948. ECLA circulated the paper to continue a conversation among economists in the darker nations on the problem of "development." The paper traveled from Buenos Aires into many languages, and mimeographed copies of it found their way into the planning commissions of many of the new nations. The basic problem raised by the paper is elementary: how should the overwhelmingly impoverished Third World create economic policies geared toward the development of the totality of its population? After centuries of imperialism, the new nations had been left with economies that relied on the sale of raw material and the import of finished goods. This fundamental imbalance meant that countries like Argentina had to export vast amounts of raw materials at relatively low prices, whereas their import bills would be inflated with the high prices commanded by industrially manufactured goods. What would be the instrument to break out of this vise? That was the "principle problem" of Prebisch's paper.

ECLA and Prebisch had an answer, born out of the discrete experience of Latin America, notably its powerhouse of the time, Argentina. Until the early decades of the twentieth century, the dominant classes in Argentina held no brief for nation building. The oligarchs, the *haute portenos*, ran the country with an iron fist and held their own wealth in European banks (which meant that they preferred fiscal policies that favored Europe's currencies against Argentina's economic strength). This detachment of the elite fueled the growth of a socialist movement, led by Juan B. Justo and the trade unions, and it angered patriotic sections of the elite (such as Carlos Pellegrini, who carped, "We must strive resolutely for our financial independence").[2] Argentina's industrialization grew in the breach, when European and U.S. capital neglected the region for the period between the Depression of the 1930s and the wars of the 1940s.[3] As the Argentine minister of agriculture said in 1933, "The isolation in which we have been placed by a dislocated world obliges us to manufacture here what we can no longer buy in countries that buy from us."[4] British capital owned most of Argentina's railroads, and the Swiss, the United States, and the British owned almost half of its industries. The authoritarian populist Juan Perón bought the railroads from the British (despite the assessment of his adviser Miguel Miranda, "We do not propose to use our blocked funds in order to buy out-of-date equipment"), incorporated trade unions into the state, pushed ahead with industrialization (financed by the agricultural sector)—all the bedrock of his "non-aligned" El Tercera Position, the Third Position foreign policy from 1946 that resembled the formation of the Third World.[5] In 1947, Perón appealed to the economic nationalist tradition of Justo with his "Declaration of Economic Independence."[6] Import substitution and the use of foreign aid (including recycled Nazi gold) became useful as strategies for Argentina out of necessity rather than as foresight.[7] Prebisch, who otherwise detested Perón, drew from this experience when he went to work at ECLA.[8]

By the 1940s, it was obvious that the "core" of the world economy (the United States and a rebuilt Europe) had a technological advantage over the "periphery." The primary commodities produced in the periphery had a lower elasticity of demand than manufactured commodities: if raw material prices dropped, it would not mean an increase in demand for them. The core would be able to buy what it needed at lower prices, while the periphery would be unable to make up the difference in an increased volume of sales. Manufactured goods did not suffer from this problem for a variety of reasons. A combination of technological advantages, unionization, and the vagaries of the prices of primary products meant that the core enjoyed a sizable gain in the "terms of trade."[9] This line of argument forms the terrain of a field of study inaugurated in the late 1940s called "development economics."

From his experience and studies, Prebisch concluded that the new nations needed to move from the production of raw materials to that of manufactured goods. Such a strategy could be implemented through an infusion of capital investment (to create industry) or else the creative use of import-export legislation. Both these approaches should have attained global consensus, especially since both had precedents in the history of the United States and Europe. The United States and Europe at different times used tariffs and other legal mechanisms to protect and harness their domestic economies, and the United States began the Marshall Plan in 1947 to bring capital into war-ravaged Europe. Nevertheless, according to Prebisch's colleague H.W. Singer, the establishment economists in the United States and Europe as well as their leading politicians saw the development economists and the leaders of the Third World as "irresponsible wild men, radical utopians who could at most be entrusted with minor extensions and offshoots" of policy already decided by the First World–dominated institutions.[10]

Despite the contempt of the U.S.-European establishments, the lower levels of the United Nations attempted to build consensus among most policymakers on the problem of investment. In 1951, the United Nations released a report on the theme of capital investment, *Measures for the Economic Development of Under-Developed Countries*. The UN Department of Economic Affairs had wondered, along the grain of development economics, about the capacity of the new nations to break out of their poverty. Whereas most economists agreed that a modern economy required capital formation at about 10 percent of national income, that of the Third World did not even come close to half that percentage. The addition of foreign investment and aid did not make any appreciable difference. National savings and investment barely matched population growth, and with the hemorrhage of national resources toward an uneven world system, little remained for the population. Because of this, the report concluded, "How to increase the rate of capital formation is therefore a question of great urgency."[11] "The tragedy of investment," wrote the Polish economist Michal Kalecki, "is that it is useful."[12]

The report asked the most compelling question of the age: how can sufficient capital be harnessed to do the important work of reconstruction for economies battered not just by the world depression of the 1930s and the wars of the 1940s but by the centuries of colonial depredation? Would the new nations formed out of anticolonial movements be able to move ahead and create economic equality as they had already secured political equality? Would the new nations have a Marshall Plan, or would the powers only be interested in the regeneration of Europe's economy?

Europe, devastated by World War II, had received a dispensation of (mainly) U.S. money: from 1947 to 1953, the United States pumped $13 billion into Western Europe and raised its industrial plants to prewar levels (and in some cases, higher). Between 1948 and 1953, industrial production increased by over a third, and agricultural growth spiraled upward.[13] Nothing similar came the way of the formerly colonized world. Instead of such a vast transfer of wealth to the new nations, the policymakers in the United States and Western Europe held that modest aid and some technology transfer alongside minimal state intervention on the state and interstate level would help engender growth in the new nations.

The mainstream view in the field of economics and the halls of power within the United States and Western Europe held that development for the formerly colonized world would come through the precepts of "modernization theory." The problem of the colonized world was not so much its poverty but its traditionalism (including low levels of technological development). The traditional cultures needed to be cracked by political stability and the growth of science—both of which would be helped along by capital investment. Like the development economists, the modernization theorists also believed that an investment of about 10 percent of the national income would be necessary, in the words of W.W. Rostow, for a "traditional society" to achieve "takeoff" into modernity.[14] But where Rostow and the modernizationists differed from the development economists was in their assessment of where the money must come from, and what it must do. Largely, the investment would come from a modicum of foreign aid and a better use of national savings, which after a period of growth over some decades, would produce the level of national income for a takeoff into "maturity." The investment money, for Rostow, should go toward the commercialization of agriculture and the creation of transportation-communication networks. The rest of the economy had to be left outside the domain of state action.

Modernization theory typically put the onus for development on the cultures of the so-called traditional societies, and thereby excised the history of colonialism. This elegantly returned the emergence of capitalism to its pristine European setting, for like sociologist Max Weber, modernization theory contended that the darker world did not have the culture of frugality and thus willed itself into poverty. "The question of the motive forces in the expansion of capitalism," Weber wrote in 1904, "is not in the first instance a question of the origin of capital sums which were available for capitalistic use, but above all, of the development of the spirit of capitalism."[15] Capitalism, in précis, emerges in Europe because the Europeans crafted a special spirit that summoned wealth.[16] Such assertions irked intellectuals from the colonized world. Why is India poor, asked Dadabhai Naoroji? "It is not the pitiless operation of economic laws, but it is the thoughtless and pitiless action of the British policy; it is the pitiless eating of India's substance in India, and the further pitiless drain to England; in short, it is the pitiless perversion of economic laws by the sad bleeding to which India is subjected, that is destroying India."[17] The Third World bled to make Europe grow. Modernization theory avoided this, and rather sought to "Protestantize" the cultures of the world to seed capitalist culture.[18]

Against modernization theory, Prebisch and development economics in general started with the impact of colonial rule. Colonialism ravaged the world, and left more than half of it bereft of capital and with a surfeit of poverty. In 1500, the average per capita income in Europe ran only three times more than that in Africa and Asia, whereas in 1960, it was ten times greater. Colonial rule not only impoverished the darker nations but also appropriated wealth to produce the great leap forward for Europe and the United States. Prebisch, born in San Miguel de Tucumán in the northwest of Argentina, had an early education in both the plunder and the nationalist response to it. Of plunder, he would know of the mountain of Potosí, across the border in Bolivia, from where the Iberian colonialists drew incalculable amounts of silver.[19] The money entered Spain, but rapidly left to pay for the Crown's debts along with its imports from England, France, Holland, and Italy. The banks that held this currency boom nurtured the capital that went out to furnish the early factories of northwestern Europe.[20] Not only was San Miguel de Tucumán on the crossroads that joined Potosí to the rest of the southern cone, but also in 1816, it was the site where the nationalist forces convened a congress to declare the independence of Argentina. This declaration came partly because of the realization that the drain of wealth led to the distortion of the social goals of the people of South America, as it also led to the development of Europe.[21]

Since Europe and the United States benefited from colonial rule, they must bear responsibility for it. To be responsible should mean that the First World needed to provide outright grants to the Third World (what would later be called "reparations"). To ask the people of the Third World to sacrifice more toward development would be morally inappropriate. "The social tensions of our time," Prebisch wrote, "will often induce us to use an exaggerated proportion of resources in order to improve present consumption levels, or to make social investments for immediate welfare, at the expense of economic investments for future welfare. To give way to this pressure would defeat the social objective of [steadily] increasing the standard of living of the masses."[22] To fail to industrialize because of a lack of investment would be equally immoral because it would condemn parts of the world to stagnation, to socialized poverty. Indeed, some economists felt that the raw material producers should not industrialize because, as Prebisch put it, "if they were to do so, their lesser efficiency would result in their losing the conventional advantages of such exchange."[23] The idea of "comparative advantage" held that a country should specialize in the production of that which it can do best; or as David Ricardo put it in his 1817 tract, a country should not try to stimulate industry artificially, rather it should simply follow "the peculiar powers bestowed by nature."[24] In Ricardo's example, what makes the United States suited to grow corn and France suited to cultivate vines, and what makes England proficient in the manufacture of "hardware" or industrially produced goods? Is the argument for comparative advantage rooted in nature? Was England always the blessed isle of hardware? Or were the mercantilist policies and colonial extractions that preceded Ricardian "free trade" responsible for the creation of England's advantages?[25] The development economists rejected Ricardo's occlusion of colonialism, and the reliance on strategies that freed up the First World to donate aid rather than rethink its own financial and political dominance.[26]

Prebisch rejected the theory of comparative advantage, because he demonstrated that each region of the world could enjoy the fruits of modernity as much as the others. This did not mean that every region should produce everything for itself and therefore live in a state of pure autarky. On the contrary, trade is crucial because some regions have smaller markets than others, and raw materials and agricultural lands are not evenly distributed along national lines. But the basis of trade had to be altered. It could not be premised on the idea that some states are naturally good at being harvesters of low-value raw materials and others are naturally proficient at being producers of high-value-added finished products. The theory of comparative advantage, Prebisch claimed, stifles genuine economic development. And further, since modernization theory promotes the view that national income and investment capital must be raised from the export of raw materials, it will only entrap the new nations more deeply. As Prebisch and the development economists saw it, the import of manufactured goods and the export of cheap raw materials will continue to drain capital and fail to enable the conduct of technological improvements toward socioeconomic development. The cycle of dependency would intensify rather than break.

To counter this, Prebisch argued that raw material exporting states should create some mechanism to develop a domestic industry, and absent outright grants, the best approach would be legal-political. The new nations should use tariffs to make imports prohibitive (what became known as "import-substitution industrialization" or, in another guise, the "infant industry" thesis). Prices in the core remained high partly because of the *political* role of trade unions and industrial monopolies. The periphery needed its own political strategy, and this would have to be in the realm of interstate trade.

The darker world contributed greatly to the development of Europe, and based on this evidence, it is clear that the invisible hand is white. And the First World wanted it to remain white. Powerful nations, such as England and later the United States, foisted the rules of trade on the lesser peoples through an act of will rather than the laws of economics. The contempt of the First World's economists was palpable. John Maynard Keynes, for instance, complained to the English government about the invitations being sent out to the darker nations for the Bretton Woods Conference. Those that had been invited from Colombia to Venezuela, from Liberia to the Philippines, he noted, "clearly have nothing to contribute and will merely encumber the ground." For Keynes, this is "the most monstrous monkey-house assembled for years."[27] Only technocrats from the advanced industrial states should be allowed to formulate the rules, because otherwise those from the raw material providers would begin to make unbearable demands.

Indeed, this is just what happened at the UN Conference on Trade and Employment in Havana, Cuba, in 1948. At the preparatory conferences in Geneva and London, several of these formerly colonized states took leadership roles in the demand for the right of states to use tariffs as a mechanism to promote domestic industrialization. In Geneva, the powers allowed such tariffs only after permission had been obtained from the proposed International Trade Organization (ITO). The raw material producers returned to the fray in London, demanding that they be allowed to use tariffs, and once established, the ITO could examine them to see if they were unnecessary. They did not want to get advance permission for a policy that they saw as essential.

In Havana, the delegates from the darker nations drowned out the operatic expertise of the ennobled economists with "a chorus of denunciation," in the felicitous phrase of the U.S. delegation's head, Clair Wilcox. The delegates from the Third World pointed out that the Geneva draft only represented the opinions of the imperial powers, that it "held out no hope" for the rest of the world. The aggrieved delegates proposed eight hundred amendments, of which two hundred would have entirely sunk the ITO.[28] These nations denounced the 1947 creation of the General Agreement on Trade and Tariffs (GATT) in Geneva because it was restricted to the advanced industrial states. They objected to GATT's oversight of the economic rules, and demanded that they have the right to use preferential systems when it suited them. The chorus fell on deaf ears, as GATT remained and an ITO to work for the benefit of the peasant nations failed to emerge.

The question of preferential treatment in interstate trade, mainly the use of tariffs, continued to be a central instrument on the Third World economic agenda. It was the main economic plank out of Bandung.[29] The Third World states in the United Nations nurtured the theory and pushed it in every one of the forums. The argument for tariffs was as follows: The Third World states wanted to erect a discriminatory tariff regime to favor development. They wanted to allow their states to use tariffs against products from the industrial powers, just as they wanted the industrial powers to drop their various barriers to the entry of goods from the Third World. In other words, they implicitly accused the First World of a tariff policy that worked to its benefit, and now called for a reversal of the tariff mechanisms. Third World states should use tariffs and preferences strategically to block the import of those goods whose production could be promoted domestically. Tariffs would stimulate a domestic industry, and capital for industrialization could come from foreign aid or a better utilization of the domestic surplus. The point of industrialization was to increase the productivity of labor, whose end result was not simply an increased growth rate but a better standard of living for the masses. "Industrialization was not an end in itself," Prebisch wrote, "but the principle means at the disposal of those countries of obtaining a share of the benefits of technical progress and of progressively raising the standard of living of the masses."[30]

The issue of tariffs should actually be seen as subordinate to a more important point raised by the development economists and the Third World states, and this is the need to constitute a united Third World institutional framework to grapple with capitalism's uneven effects. To this end, Prebisch and the Third World states worked to create cartels of primary commodities, so that the producer nations could band together to get good prices for their products.[31] To stimulate trade across the Third World and create pricing mechanisms that were not determined by monopoly capitalism, the Third World states called for the "creation of conditions for the expansion of trade between countries at a similar level of development."[32] In 1961, Latin American, African, and Asian states created frameworks for common market arrangements in "a climate of mutual aid," as the Afro-Asian Organization for Economic Cooperation put it.[33] ECLA and the Oficinas de Estudios para la Colaboración Económica helped set the framework for the Latin American Free Trade Association (and in 1969, the Andean Pact); thirteen Francophone states created the Afro-Malagasy Union; Algeria, Ghana, Guinea, Mali, Morocco, and the United Arab Republic drew up the African Charter in Casablanca that same year to create a common market, the African Bank for Economic Development, and the African Payments Union; and the Afro-Asian Organization for Economic Cooperation called for the creation of an Afro-Asian common market. These initiatives sought to unite the economic and political power of the Third World to craft new forms of trade to ameliorate the effects of uneven imperialist exploitation.

The Third World states pushed for the creation of a UN institution to implement their agenda. If GATT had already become the instrument of the First World, the Third World wanted its own counter. The creation of the UNCTAD was just this instrument, with Prebisch as its first secretary general. One hundred and twenty countries attended the first conference in Geneva, and eventually seventy-seven of them joined together to form the G-77, a major bloc of the unwashed led by Prebisch within the United Nations and elsewhere. In Geneva, the G-77 called for increased exports into the First World's markets, better prices for raw materials, compensatory finance, and compensatory discrimination in tariffs.[34] The UNCTAD and its G-77 joined such formidable intellectual powerhouses as the UN Economic Development Administration (formed in 1949, and the brainchild of V.K.R.V. Rao, the chair of the UN Sub-Commission for Economic Development) and SUNFED (formed in 1953 as a "soft aid" delivery institution, one that gave grants for capital investment, which had no support from the First World).[35] These groups dedicated to the economic development of the Third World had allies in the UN Food and Agriculture Organization, and after 1966, the technical UN Development Program. The UNCTAD challenged the power of the First World's global corporations and its droit de seigneur on the products of the formerly colonized world.

At the United Nations in 1963, the Third World states pushed through a resolution for "more adequate financial resources at favorable terms" to facilitate the Prebisch agenda. This feint followed the broad demands formulated at Bandung, for the "investment of foreign capital" only if it came without strings, and could make "a valuable contribution" to the social and economic development of the new nations.[36] The pledges of disinterest were more honored in the breach than in the observance.

The First World took umbrage at the creation of the UNCTAD.[37] The U.S. government had set its sights on GATT, the IMF, and the World Bank as instruments of development. GATT allowed the First World to have an advantage in interstate trade, the IMF enabled First World banks to survive fiscal slumps in the debtor nations, and the World Bank engineered development that benefited monopoly corporations. The "economic hit men" went out to the darker nations, wrote reports that asked for highly technical development, engineered loans from First World banks for impoverished countries, drew in First World construction firms to build overcapacity infrastructure, and saddled the state with an economic debt that it tried to recover politically.[38] The UNCTAD drew the Third World states into the discussion, whereas GATT, the IMF, and the World Bank tended to keep them out, and preferred technocrats who would apply their recipes without discussion or negotiation.[39]

The First World pushed its own agenda for development, which included all the lineaments of modernization theory alongside "foreign aid." The U.S. government and its satellite nonprofit foundations offered funds for development, but with a carefully calibrated rate of return for the United States itself. The U.S. president of the World Bank, Eugene Black, quite forthrightly remarked, "Our foreign aid programs constitute a distinct benefit to American business. The three major benefits are (1) foreign aid provides a substantial and immediate market for United States goods and services, (2) foreign aid stimulates the development of new overseas markets for United States' companies, (3) foreign aid orients national economies toward a free enterprise system in which United States' firms can prosper."[40] The U.S. government, moreover, provided aid not only for economic purposes but also for the purchase of military hardware. In 1951, U.S. secretary of state Dean Acheson noted, "Economic and technical assistance must be sufficient to support the military programs and to deal with some of the fundamental problems of weakness where weapons alone are no defense."[41] Guns predominated over butter not because of any primordial blood lust in the tropics but because the principle providers of aid, the United States and

Europe, preferred such aid to bind new nations in military pacts. If their allies became banana republics, it had as much to do with the shipment of this weaponry as it did with any local culture of a strong leader.

The First World's foreign aid regime moved the USSR and the People's Republic of China into a cold war over aid.[42] If the one decided to assist a country in the formerly colonized world, the other would offer something as well. The Third World began to play one side against the other to get as much assistance as possible—a ploy that diverted attention from the system transformational agenda of the UNCTAD and the G-77. The USSR and China, however, did not have access to the massive financial armory at the disposal of the far richer First World. The USSR touted its success in the transformation of a mostly agricultural, feudal society of the czarist period to an industrialized superpower—all driven not by the market but by socialist planning. But World War II devastated the Soviet physical plant, and after the war, what wealth remained went into the reconstruction of the USSR and its newly constituted Warsaw Pact. When the First World moved into the business of foreign aid, the USSR despite its disadvantages could not be far behind.[43] Even though USSR aid for the Third World would only account for about 15 percent of Soviet foreign trade, much of the economic interactions with the formerly colonized world was in the form of barter, bilateral noncurrency exchanges, and industrial cooperation. The USSR also exchanged technological products (including weaponry) for raw materials and consumer goods—all without the burden of hard currency. The entry of the USSR into this arena put additional pressure on the United States and Europe, so that aid became part of the overall chess match between the USSR and the United States.[44]

This is not to say that the USSR and the United States had identical trade policies, only that their effects in the Third World were similar. Neither aid from the United States nor the USSR helped to undermine the structural problem identified by Prebisch: the terms of trade, and the dependency relationship this engendered. The USSR, within the Council for Mutual Economic Assistance (Comecon—made up of Cuba, Mongolia, Vietnam, and the USSR) provided aid and bought goods at reasonable prices. An informed study of trade conducted between the USSR and Eastern Europe through the auspices of the Council of Mutual Economic Assistance found that the USSR traded low-value raw materials and agricultural products for Eastern European machinery. In that case, Eastern Europe directed the trade, and the USSR played the part of the low-value exporter.[45] The "Soviet

Subsidy" was the uncomfortable reality for other parts of the Third World that adopted a socialist path (such as Cuba), although this subsidy did not come without its own constraints (such as a dependence on Soviet exports of a vast array of products).[46]

In 1957, the Russian-born U.S. Marxist Paul Baran published *The Political Economy of Growth*, in which he demonstrated the futility of foreign aid and the import-substitution industrialization strategy. "Far from serving as an engine of economic expansion, of technological progress and social change, the capitalist order in these countries has represented a framework for economic stagnation, for archaic technology and for social backwardness."[47] Most critics of Baran struck at his premise: that the Third World economies had developed to the stage of monopoly capitalism, and therefore, that aid would only strengthen the capitalist and not enable any social development. Debates raged in the radical journals over this theme, and it was the principal point of disagreement among revolutionaries. While Baran might have overstated his thesis and the role of monopoly capitalism within the darker nations, his critique of the reliance on the growth strategy was on point. The aid from outside (whether capitalist or socialist) purchased time for the dominant elites, who used that money to prevent necessary social transformation. A more substantial way for development would be the destruction of feudal social relations, and by the socialization of production. These parasitic elites acceded to the Prebisch logic in order to benefit their own class interests, rather than move their societies to socialism. The dominant classes in each of these societies purchased third-rate, out-of-date plants and machinery from the advanced industrial states, and paid top dollar for them. In Britain, for instance, firms that wanted to update their machinery (and entire factories) would sell them to their subsidiaries in places like India. They would then ship these rusty machines to India as new and update their own physical plants in the British Isles.[48] Indian industry, then, paid for some of the refurbished British physical plants in the 1950s. Such fraud occurred along the grain of import substitution.[49]

Many decades later, Prebisch recognized this major limitation in the Third World order: "We thought that an acceleration of the rate of growth would solve all problems. This was our great mistake." What was needed alongside growth were "changes in the social structure," indeed "a complete social transformation."[50] Of the various means for social transformation that sat high on the agenda, but low in terms of implementation, was land reform. At the United Nations, the Third

World states committed themselves to land reform on several occasions, but each time called for extended study and technical assistance from UN bodies such as the Food and Agriculture Organization.[51] From the December 1952 resolution to that of December 1960 and onward, the UN General Assembly called for further study and assistance, but little else. Within the United Nations there was often talk of land reform, and there was some discussion of the distorted or even corrupt use of the surplus, but hardly any concern given to it or the conflict among the different classes for use of the surplus (and for the surplus value drawn from the workers). The main problem was to raise capital for the Third World's development, and the Prebisch position also ignored or downplayed the fundamental role of financial capital over the world's economy. The structural problems of landlordism, domestic class struggles, and the better use of the economic surplus already produced within a national economy as well as the problem of the surplus value stolen from the workers in the normal course of capitalism, rarely came up for discussion at the United Nations. It had already become sufficient to be critical of the First World alone, which became a shield that protected the national bourgeoisie from criticism for its own lack of imagination and self-sacrifice. In other words, development theory and public policy emphasized economic growth as an end in itself without a built-in consideration for equity.

TEHRAN

One million dollars. That's all it took in 1953 for the CIA to overthrow a nationalist government. Langley's man in Tehran was Kermit "Kim" Roosevelt, the grandson of Teddy Roosevelt. Ordered to take out the democratically elected National Front government led by Muhammed Mosaddeq and restore the Shah of Iran, Roosevelt spread the cash and waited for it to do its magic. The army, the aristocrats, and other upwardly mobile class fragments went into action and overthrew a government that had stretched the imagination of the Iranian people. The Shah returned to stay until he was overthrown by a different kind of coup in 1979.

Mosaddeq had a long career in Iranian politics before the Iranian people called him to lead them in 1951. That year, the Iranian parliament, the *Majlis*, nationalized the country's oil industry (owned by the Anglo-Iranian Oil Company, where "Anglo" represented the English interests and "Iranian" simply referred to the place from which they drew the oil). When the prime minister, who had opposed the nationalization, was assassinated, the parliament turned to Mosaddeq to take it forward. The popularity of Mosaddeq and his National Front forced the Shah to accept the Oil Nationalization Act. Mosaddeq removed the English from the equation and founded the National Iranian Oil Company, the first nationalized oil firm in the oil lands (the Free Officers in Egypt took great inspiration from this action).

The British and U.S. governments flexed their muscles, the Shah refused to turn over the military to the parliament, and Mosaddeq resigned. People filled the streets: they came from all the political parties,

Tehran, Iran, February 1979: The Iranian Revolution—female Fedayin Communist fighters train in the use of armed combat at Tehran University. © ALAIN
KELER/SYGMA/CORBIS

and from among the country's intelligentsia. The Tudeh Party (heir to
the Communist Party founded in 1920) had a cadre of 25,000, while its
union federation boasted a membership of 335,000.[1] The influence of the
Tudeh angered the U.S. establishment, which offered the National Front
leader a choice: either crush the Communists, take U.S. aid and remain
in power, or else fall under Soviet-Communist influence. On May 2,
1953, Mosaddeq revealed the shallowness of his class, whose investment
in nationalism and national sovereignty only went as far as it would
guarantee its rule and luxury; he wrote a letter to President Dwight D.
Eisenhower, in which he cowered, "Please accept, Mr. President, the assurances of my highest consideration."[2] Afraid of the Soviets, Mosaddeq
crushed the Tudeh Party, thereby destroying the most organized defenders of Iranian sovereignty, and then fell before a coup engineered by the
CIA's representative and a far more reliable U.S. ally, the Shah.

The Shah exiled tens of thousands of National Party members and

Communists, and killed thousands of both. Tudeh, which means "masses," was reduced in size by brute force, as its members either went underground, into the Shah's jails, or else to Europe, where they reconstituted. The Tudeh was paralyzed by the coup. The USSR paid it little heed, preferring to make every concession to the Shah in hopes of pacifying a border state and gaining access to the oil—all this despite the close relationship between the United States and the Shah.[3]

Out of Tudeh came disaffected intellectuals, among whom numbered the best of Farsi letters. Enthused by the Mosaddeq moment, by the possibility of a socially just nationalism (guaranteed by the presence of a strong Tudeh Party), they had written manifestos and poems, short stories and diatribes. The cultural suffocation of imperialism and the feudal aristocracy had been lifted by the Mosaddeq moment, and even with the restoration of the Shah, this cultural productivity on the terrain of nationalism continued. The intellectuals and cultural workers who had been motivated by anticolonialism, antimonarchism, and the militancy of the Tudeh movement regrouped in the early 1950s into small organizations. One such was Niru-ye Sevum (the Third Force), led by Khalil Maleki, who had left Tudeh in 1947. Maleki prepared the ground for others to follow in the next few years. These people disparaged First World capitalism and Second World socialism. They took refuge briefly in Mosaddeq's National Front, even as they remained suspicious of the hesitancy and conservatism of the bourgeois party. They were essentially cultural workers who disliked equally the hierarchies of America's market economy as much as the arid monotony of the Khrushchev era socialist bureaucracy.[4] As artists, they longed for the space to let the spirit soar free, and neither of these options provided a way forward from the Shah.

The strong emphasis both on liberty and social justice attracted a wide following among an intelligentsia that had no loyalty to royalty, and little fealty to a political party that increasingly burdened itself with the foreign policy needs of the USSR. Maleki's journal carried imaginative discussions of the type of modernity envisaged by the Third World, by his Third Force. In 1955, one of his journals, *Nabard-e Zendegi*, ran a poem titled "Call to Arms" by Forugh Farrokhzad:

O Iranian woman, only you have remained,
In the bonds of cruelty and wretchedness and misfortune.
It is your warm embracing bosom that has nurtured
Prideful and pompous man.
It is your joyous smile that bestows

On his heart vigor and warmth.
For that person who is your creation
To be preferred and superior is shameful.
Woman, take action because a world
Awaits and beckons you.[5]

Filled with leaden speeches, economic discussions, and organizational matters, nationalist periodicals nevertheless made room for poems and stories, drawings and photographs. The "nation" had to be imagined as well as thought through politically, economically, and culturally. The imagination played an enormous role in the construction of the nation, its states, and of course the Third World itself. Stories of humiliation and hope, poems of despair and revolution—these form part of the massive output of the imagination that made its way into the texts of national liberation. Farrokhzad's verse is in that sense typical: there is the encomium to Iranian women for their buried labors, the condemnation of patriarchy for its rejection of women/mothers who have created the world, and a "call to arms" for women to birth a new kind of order. In these three moments—praise, condemnation, and war cry—there is the basic structure of the national liberation story. It charts out the past and demands an engagement with the future.

Farrokhzad's powerful verse inspired much discussion within Iran, and after her untimely death at the age of thirty-two, she became an icon for those who wanted to push the boundaries of modernity. The editor of *Nabard-e Zendegi* at the time was an eminence of Persian letters, and although he had differences with Farrokhzad, Jalal Al-e Ahmad cherished her work. Like Malecki, Al-e Ahmad had been in the Tudeh Party during its most productive phase (1944–48), and then, from 1951–53, he supported Mosaddeq's government. The return of the Shah, and Al-e Ahmad's outspoken criticism of the monarchy, earned him the leadership of the disaffected intelligentsia. Al-e Ahmad substituted the hopelessness of militant action in this period for the expansiveness of the imagination. He produced a remarkable corpus of short stories that counterposed the corruption and ruthlessness of the monarchy with the simple wisdom of folklore and the forgotten people of Iran.[6] He wrote a series of caustic novels about the "underdevelopment" of Iranian society and the feeling of hopelessness that confronted the intellectual; what must a teacher do, for instance, when the promise of education and cultural transfer is insufficient in such a hierarchical and unequal world?[7] This crisis for the teacher in an underdeveloped society (whose students have no shoes, for example) mirrors the principal contradiction for the Third World in the realm of culture: committed to the notion of an egalitarian society and culture, and yet within the context of immense inequality, how would the teacher come to terms with their position "above" that of their students? In the realm of the franchise and literacy, which I will develop further below, this problem arises as well: everyone must have the franchise regardless of their level of literacy, yet people need to be literate in order to enlarge their social and political selves.

It was far easier to concentrate on an all-points assault on cultural imperialism than to delve too long on the more pressing problem of expansive values and uneven realities. Al-e Ahmad, therefore, is best known not for the subtle way in which he raised important questions of cultural workers but for his 1961–62 screed against what his friend Ahmed Farid had called *Gharabzadegi* or "Occidentosis." Invited by the Iranian government to present a paper at the Congress on the Aim of Iranian Education, Al-e Ahmad offered a long manifesto on the collapse of the dignity of Asia, Africa, and Latin America before Europe's on-slaught. Not only had Europe managed to conquer, colonize, and re-shape the political economy of these continents but it had also been able to put them in cultural crisis. This crisis formed the topic of Al-e Ah-mad's vibrant critique.

From the "West," Al-e Ahmad argued, came the disease of Occiden-tosis. Europe said it was materially and morally superior: its material strength needed no résumé, and it had this great material advance on the basis of its moral and cultural inheritance. Europe had a Reformation, a Luther, the Enlightenment, the French Revolution, and the Industrial Revolution. The last followed from the chain that preceded it. If the rest of the world wanted to advance and attain industry, then it must also have a Reformation. Writers like Mexico's Octavio Paz concurred: "We never had a Kant, a Voltaire, a Diderot, or a Hume."[8] If Mexico had had such figures, and such movements, then it would not be in its relative poverty.

Al-e Ahmad knew that this was an inversion of the problem. A Refor-mation does not lead to the Industrial Revolution—indeed, to see cultural and economic history in such a way is to miss the theft of the wealth of the Americas for the glory of Europe, and the development of European lib-eralism in relationship to the degradation of the rights of the people in the colonies.[9] Along the grain of the ECLA view of underdevelopment, Al-e Ahmad described the world as being sundered between "two poles or extremes. . . . One pole is held by the sated—the wealthy, the powerful, the makers and exporters of manufacturers. The other pole is left to the hungry—the poor, the impotent, the importers and consumers. The beat of progress is in the ascending part of the world, and the pulse of stagnation is in the moribund part of the world."[10]

Although Iran had never been formerly colonized, it belonged with the hungry. Indeed, much of the world that stood at the pole of the hungry had remained nominally free during the era of colonialism. South America and some islands of the Caribbean won their political independence in the eighteenth century, and sections of Africa remained free, as did China and about half of India. Colonial conquest played only a part of the overall domination of the planet by European and U.S. imperialism. English oil firms (or at least an Englishman, William Knox D'Arcy) had dominated Iran's oil fields since 1901, and oil continued to be the major export from this large, nominally independent nation. Iran's government paid for the infrastructure to remove the oil, and earned a pittance from the oil company cartel. Not for nothing did Mosaddeq's struggle over oil earn him the affection of the masses.[11]

What the Iranian elite did with their small share of the oil profits baffled intellectuals like Al-e Ahmad. To the taste of these intellectuals, the elite (led by the aristocracy) imported meaningless commodities, including weaponry. Al-e Ahmad blamed the elite for this selfish consumption, but for him the lion's share of the fault rested with the imperialist system. "Once you have given economic and political control of your country to foreign concerns," Al-e Ahmad bemoaned, "they know what to sell you, or at least what not to sell you. Because they naturally seek to sell you their manufacturers in perpetuity, it is best that you remain forever in need of them, and God save the oil reserves. They take away the oil and give you whatever you want in return—from soup to nuts, even grain. This enforced trade even extends to cultural matters, to letters, to discourse."[12] The Iranian elite, like much of the parasitic elite in the postcolonial world, groomed their aesthetic sense around Europe's Sublime. Educational systems and the media as well as cultural purveyors did not *teach* the population about its own customs and traditions. Imperialism had sundered the organic relationship with these dynamics. The disruption of the links between the various classes resulted in the creation of an aesthetic and socioeconomic gulf. Al-e Ahmad's contribution to excise this gulf was his ethnographies, although these too are not without their attempt at the colonial preservation of heritages rather than the creation of a linkage between the rulers and the ruled.[13]

The general critique of cultural imperialism stays within a narrow ambit, because it is only the elite or the urban sections that have access to the symbolic and material items that enter the Third World (this has of course changed with the entry of television). Since the vast bulk cannot afford the actual cultural products of Carnaby Street and Madison Avenue, Hollywood and the Sorbonne, the problem of the import of these items is not necessarily a *mass* dilemma. What Al-e Ahmad rehearses is the conceptual problem, where people of the "East" continue to see themselves as lesser than the "West." The overwhelming military and industrial power of the "West" produces an immense hallucination that what it does is History and only what it does matters, whereas the rest of us are to remain in a cyclic stupor, in awe and paralysis.[14] It is this fact that Al-e Ahmad wanted the Third World to acknowledge.

Such a critique is not original to Al-e Ahmad. Most of the Third World produced cultural workers who came to the same conclusion, some in poetic anger, and others with abstract analysis. In the 1930s, at least two strands for the regeneration of the darker nations emerged: from the Francophone black Atlantic came the idea of *négritude*, which suggested that a new self had to be crafted out of the harshly dismissed cultural resources of Africa and a new self-confidence in being black in the world needed to drive one's visions; from Brazil, came the idea that social science would enable meaningful, positivistic economic development, which would engender a newly confident Brazilian personality.[15] By the 1950s, these two critical projects would by and large unite in the work of Third World cultural workers. In 1950, Aimé Césaire, one of the leading figures in the negritude movement, published his *Discourse on Colonialism*, which brought these two considerations into dialogue with each other. Most of these cultural workers had a career in and around their national Communist Party, which encouraged an aesthetic that did not depart from the material concerns of the masses. The economy and the imagination did not stray far from each other. Césaire, after all, was a leading figure in the French Communist Party by the mid-1940s, and even as he called for a spiritual regeneration of the postcolonial world, he nonetheless urged the economic development of the former colonies.

The contradictions and opportunities posed by these challenges from the 1930s emerged in relief at a 1956 conference hosted in Paris to promote the journal *Présence Africaine*. The most influential writers from the black Atlantic gathered to push these ideas around (they included Léopold Senghor, Césaire, Richard Wright, and Frantz Fanon). Alioune Diop, the founder and editor of *Présence Africaine*, welcomed the delegates: "If to the non-European mind the Bandung meeting has been the most important event since the end of the War, I venture to assert that this First International Congress of Black Writers and Artists will be regarded by our peoples as the second event of the decade."[16] The conference's central theme was that "culture" matters, and that an engagement with cultural development was central to the postcolonial project, even as there could be no such engagement without an assessment of the role of culture in economic underdevelopment.[17] The analysts insisted on the centrality of the cultural even when starvation peered over the horizon (after all, economic debates often relied on cultural stereotypes that needed to be expunged). Several presentations took the easy way out: they inverted the values of colonialism and plugged in various shades of nativism. Europe could be dismissed out of hand because the answers to Africa and elsewhere lay within their autochthonous traditions. It was this passive caricature of negritude that earned it scorn from the more radical thinkers (such as Fanon at the 1956 conference) and the militants (such as the anticolonial fighters from Portuguese-controlled Africa and elsewhere at the 1969 second conference held in Algiers).[18] Indigenous traditions could contribute to the solution, but most cultural workers agreed that they were insufficient against the problems posed by imperialism.

Most of the presentations, and indeed most of the cultural commentary from the Third World, walked a fine line between the reification of the divide between the colonizer and the colonized, and the treatment of it as dialectical. Even deft Césaire entertained the former route, before his analysis dragged him to the latter. Colonialism, Césaire pointed out, squelches the cultural confidence of the colonized. Colonizers denigrate the cultural world of the defeated, thereby impoverishing the idea of culture for everyone. The dynamic interaction of cultural forms and the vibrancy of culture itself were stopped by colonialism, which removed Europe's culture and cultural heritage onto a pedestal away from all influence and interaction. From this Archimedean point, Europe could judge and dissect other cultures. But the complex cultural forms of Europe and the darker nations would only be able to sit side by side, "juxtaposed but not harmonized." Cultural objects arrive and interact, but they do not inform each other. "Foreign elements are dumped on its soil, but remain foreign. White man's things! White man's manners! Things existing alongside the native but over which the native has no power." Water flush toilets, Rembrandt, movable type: these arrive, they are used, but they are not intertwined into the living culture of the colonized. The dichotomy stalls history; people stand before machines, they might even use them, yet they are unable to bring them into their lives.

The dichotomous view of culture produced the idea, Césaire noted, that anticolonial nationalism is dominated by "obscurantist forces priding themselves on reviving medieval ways of life and thought."[19] But would this be far from the truth, for chauvinisms of various kinds had begun to appear in the postcolonial world (for example, in 1972, Uganda's Idi Amin expelled Indians from the country—a policy that descended from the 1945 and 1949 anti-Indian riots in Kampala and Jinja; in 1969, Malaysia would experience terrible anti-Chinese riots—a result of chauvinist sentiments within the Malaysian freedom movement of the 1940s)? Short of chauvinism, there was also a cultural fantasy about those who remained traditional, untouched by modernity and therefore authentically national.[20] Diop, for instance, offered the conference an illustration: "The same Fulah shepherd whose knowledge of his local flora and fauna astonishes you by its accuracy, is likely to join with his companions in poetical jousts which afford a heartening spectacle. On top of this, he has a passionate sense of the history of his people, a lucid and well founded love of the heroes of his past, a solid knowledge of the classics of his culture and a natural familiarity with the conditions and economic laws which govern his existence."[21] This singular omnipresent shepherd is a dangerous fantasy. Communities that refused to abandon their ways outside the full-blown exercise of the market economy and the accoutrements of consumer society came in for a double dose of romanticism and ostracism. These "tribals" became objects of national fascination at the same time as their lands became areas for the predatory extraction of raw materials. Whether the Amazon region or southern Bihar, the Central American highlands or the Central African lowlands—nationalist regimes romanticized the tribals and dispossessed them (or else confined them into reservations euphemistically called national parks).[22] Cultural workers who operated with a dichotomous notion of culture did not conduct the necessary critique of colonial stereotypes. They often inhabited them, not to revile, but to celebrate. The tribals, or the rural peasants, would be a symbol of the nation, but they would not inhabit the nation. They remained outside it, either to be confined or else converted, but not to be considered as full citizens.

Césaire moved away from the antinomic quality of this analysis, even if only partially; for cultures, he said, are powerful and have "enough regenerative power to adapt themselves to the conditions of the modern world."[23] The British dumped tea on India after they could no longer absorb the Chinese exports; within a generation, tea became a staple drink of the subcontinent. The debates in Paris took place in French. These pedestrian examples show us that the dichotomies are not static, and that cultural worlds are alive to absorption, change, and dynamism. Nevertheless, one cannot make too much of culture's flexibility, because the high walls of privilege and power make some cultures *appear* dead. A civilization needs to "feel" alive, and it is this subjective liveliness that gives it "the power to *leave behind the past.*" Colonized societies come alive and thus are ready to be refashioned only in the throes of a major social upheaval, such as an anticolonial struggle. Césaire offers two examples of this, the first from Tunisia, where the new nationalist government nationalized Habu properties and abolished polygamy, and the second from India, where the new nationalist government shook the traditional status of women. In both cases, the colonial power did not take the side of justice, whereas the nationalist regime had begun to create cultural change.[24] To develop Césaire's formula of culture "juxtaposed but not harmonized," or else brought alive by struggle, let us look more closely at the three major social processes of the modern world (nationalism, democracy, and rationalism).

By and large, the Third World states rejected the idea of nationalism that emerged from Europe's history—where the various bourgeoisies constructed their nationalism to create discrete boundaries and markets around what they saw as common cultural markers, such as language, history, and race.[25] The Third World, from Indonesia to Guatemala, adopted the idea of multiplicity (Indonesia's motto is "*Bhinneka Tunggal Ika,*" or "Unity in Diversity," a pluralist approach to difference; Guatemala's solution lay in the promotion of *mestizaje,* or cultural hybridity—these are different approaches to multiplicity, which is not to say that they always accommodated their minority populations).[26] The new states adopted a multinational perspective, knowing full well that their countries were culturally diverse. This was a *practical* measure; many of the new states grew on culturally mixed societies that could not be easily homogenized. Certainly, most of them adopted one or two national languages, but they had to perforce acknowledge the existence and often support the persistence of multiple languages. Sometimes, the attempt to suppress one or more cultural communities led to separatist movements, such as among the Karen in Burma or the Ashanti in Ghana. The general trend, however, was to accept that one could not replicate what Kemal Ataturk had done in Turkey: to take complexity and enforce uniformity (indeed, the struggle by the Kurds within Turkey shows that even there the strategy failed).

The move to multinationalism was pragmatic, but also *principled*. At UNESCO's 1945 founding conference, the Cuban delegate Luis Perez spoke wistfully about national education policies based on a multinational ethos. "Diversity rather than uniformity should be encouraged," he said, "for it would be a disaster to the world to suppress differences and refreshing tendencies in matters of education."[27] Colonial regimes had attempted to divide their subject populations in order to better rule them; in India they crowned "princes" and elevated certain castes, in Iraq they promoted sheikhs, and in the Arab lands and Africa the colonial leaders tapped some tribal leaders and stoked tribal "instincts."[28] Against this, nationalist politicians and intellectuals found the historical basis for political pluralism in, for example, the identification of "composite cultures" and syncretism among the people's cultures.[29] That is, the multinational state would need to both *evoke* this historical dynamic of fellowship and *produce* it through the adoption of an official policy of diversity in religion (secularism), racialism (antiracism), and language (multilingualism). The multinational perspective questioned the racist claim that the darker nations could only be primordial, that blood and custom reduced the imagination of certain people. They could only be tied to kin and co-believer, not to a republican nationalism whose locus was both anticolonial and populist.

In this realm at least, Third World nationalist movements absorbed the idea of nationalism and digested it in accord with the rhythms and demands of their various histories. Fanon, who had learned about cultural regeneration in Algeria, developed the second strand of Césaire's cultural program in terms of the idea of nationalism. Like Césaire, Fanon argued that the period of nationalist struggle enabled a people to rethink the feudal forms legitimized by colonialism. These liberation struggles, as opposed to those for conquest, did not feel the need to justify themselves based on crude biological concepts. The colonial power tries to mobilize every racist idea to break down the morale of nationalism, but with each such attempt the imputed superiority of the colonizer wanes. The people, once held down, now determined the pace of change. "Those who were once immobile, the congenital cowards, those lazy beings who have always been made inferior, brace themselves and emerge bristling." The colonial ruler does not understand what has transpired. "The end of racism begins with this sudden failure to understand." Finally, the end of colonialism means that the "rigid, spasmic culture of the occupier is liberated," and it opens itself up to the culture of the colonized. "The two cultures can confront one another, enrich one another." Rather than turn inward, away from Europe or any others, Fanon contends, nationalist culture will explore other cultures as resources.[30] In the struggle lies liberation, or at least the process of national struggle gives energy to the national culture, which is now able to come alive and grow. Fanon overplays the lack of racism or the mobilization of biological notions in national liberation movements. National pride or patriotism often slid into the ugly language of racism or exclusion. But if what Fanon found is not a fundamental rule, it is at least a tendency.[31]

For its proponents, the notion of multinationalism was an idealist conceit. They hoped that people would respect each other (diversity), and that since their cultural worlds already overlapped, they would need to tolerate distinctions (composite culture). But more than that, the expectation of the national project was that the construction of markets and educational institutions would disallow differences to dominate social life. An overarching unity (a national identity) would supersede (but not subvert) the other social identities. Identification with the national project could be more important than the sedimented identities that one inherited. There was an unrecognized problem within this otherwise-valuable liberal project: it had a majoritarian cast. It is easy for the demographic majority in a society to ask for the suspension of identity, whose cultural features would anyway seep into the culture of the nation—for example, which religious holidays should be recognized by the state, which language should be promoted, or whose version of a contested history should be recounted. Culture is not a zero-sum game, and historians would be able to write contesting histories, so that this problem is not inherent to the construction of nations. For minority communities that already felt beleaguered, it was harder to voluntarily disregard the social significance of their identities. The multinational idea had a great attraction for them partly because it was *not* majoritarianism, yet it also posed problems because it had not come to terms with the accidental majoritarianism of national culture.

To produce or evoke the ethos of multinationalism, the nation-state had to assemble a history and an aesthetic. In most countries, the colonial rulers had already put together archives of their rule and what preceded them as well as museums and libraries that collected the material and symbolic record of native society. It was now the task of the nationalist intelligentsia to study these archives, add to them, and reinterpret them in a new light. Most of the new nations added a raft of institutions to formulate, craft, and disseminate the history, artistry, and indeed self-perception of the nation. India's Sahitya Akademi, Egypt's Public Authority for the Book, and Ghana's National Research Council exemplify the new nation's attempt to create major, decently funded national institutions for cultural development. The creation of the cultural canon came alongside its dissemination through mobile libraries, literacy campaigns, theater groups, motion picture vans, and the radio.

Canons had to be created, but what would be their temper? Given the broad commitment to multiplicity, the new nation had to protect the canon from chauvinism. It had to promote the idea of the composite culture or an inherent tendency toward syncretism. Of course, an element of defensiveness creeps into the narrative, which bodes ill for the liberal values that otherwise inform the enterprise. For instance, Césaire offers a brief summary of the contributions of the darker nations to humanity—"to wit, the invention of arithmetic and geometry by the Egyptians. To wit, the discovery of astronomy by the Assyrians. To wit, the birth of chemistry among the Arabs."[32] Despite the anxiety to demonstrate the value of the colonized world, one can still glimpse Césaire's catholicity, for he does not carry water only for the black Atlantic but also for the Arabs, the Assyrians, and others.

The national canon had to include the cultural practices and hopes of all the communities within a nation, and it had to include the cultural interconnections with the cultural worlds of other nation-states. At UNESCO's founding conference in 1945, the delegates agreed, "No longer must our children be taught to think in terms only of the glory of their own country; they must think of their country as being no more than a unit in and dedicated to the service of the larger whole of a world state."[33] At the 1958 Afro-Asian Peoples' Solidarity Conference, Chu Tu-Nan of China offered a report on cultural exchange, in which he detailed many of the connections between Africa and Asia, from the Egyptian-Mesopotamian contact in the ancient world to the early modern Chinese ships that traveled to Africa. He described the atrociously difficult transit of Buddhist and Arab rationalists, who traveled from the Mediterranean to Malaysia, from India to Japan. Then he spoke of the Silk Road, which "like a colorful ribbon bound together the cultural life of the Chinese and the Near and Middle East peoples." The cultural artery not only moved people and goods but also seeds and animals, flowers and fruits, ideas and dreams.[34]

At Bandung, the Third World's intellectuals and nationalist leaders wanted to restart this dynamic, but "not from any sense of exclusiveness or rivalry with other groups of nations and other civilizations and cultures." The motivation had to be the "age-old tradition of tolerance and universality," whose purpose would be to "enrich their own culture and would also help in the promotion of world peace and understanding."[35] The section under which this discussion took place was significantly called "Cultural Cooperation" not cultural purity or cultural presentation. To this end, the Afro-Asian nations held several conferences of Afro-Asian Writers (New Delhi, 1957; Tashkent, 1958; Cairo, 1962; and Beirut, 1967) and several Asian Film Weeks (the first in Beijing, 1957). Alongside these meetings, the writers published *Lotus*, the magazine of the Afro-Asian Writers' Movement, and selected one story a year for their Lotus Award.[36] In Latin America, the 1959 creation of the Casa de Las Americas in Havana under the stewardship of the Cuban revolutionary Haydée Santamaría provided a venue for Latin American artists similar to the Afro-Asian cultural conferences.

One of the ways forward, noted the Indian delegate to the UNESCO conference Rajkumari Amrit Kaur, was for the translation of books, both classic and modern, into every language. This desire to seek out cross-national appreciation for cultural heritages illustrates the best of Third World nationalism. A nation's culture had to be alive, and it had to be supplemented from other's cultural resources. Connections provided the oxygen for culture. India's Sahitya Akademi, for instance, not only translated novels from one Indian language into another but also translated novels and collections of short stories from elsewhere in the world.[37] There were some favorites around the Third World: Pablo Neruda's poems, Mulk Raj Anand's novels, and Lu Xun's short stories. The list of books that carried across languages has a decidedly masculine cast. Few of the innovative books by women found their translators until the 1970s: Magda Portal's *La Trampa* (Peru, 1954), Assia Djebar's *Le Soif* (Algeria, 1957), and Ding Ling's *The Sun Shines over the Sankan River* (China, 1947, which gained popularity in the Second World after it won the Stalin Prize). Portal not only wrote the wonderful *La Trampa* but was also the co-founder with Haya de la Torre of the APRA Party as well as the author of little-known socialist feminist tracts, such as *Hacia la mujer nueva* (*Toward a New Woman*) and *El Aprismo y la mujer* (*Women in the APRA Party*, 1933).[38] Al-e Ahmad's 1961 critique of cultural imperialism assaults Iranians for their concentration on "news of the Nobel Prize, of the new pope, of Françoise Sagan, the Cannes Film Festival, the latest Broadway play, the latest Hollywood film." But this criticism did not move inward. Instead, he asked, "What news do you see of our part of the world? Of the east in the broadest terms? Of India, Japan, China?"[39] And further, because his was not an involuted nationalism, he translated work from French and Russian letters into Farsi, including by authors such as Fyodor Mikhaylovich Dostoyevsky, Eugène Ionesco, André Gide, Jean-Paul Sartre, and Albert Camus. Al-e Ahmad also wrote elegiac descriptions of his travels to the United States, the Soviet Union, Saudi Arabia, and interestingly, Israel.

The Third World states incorporated the idea of nationalism quite effortlessly. They produced a novel rendition of national belonging, thereby enabling the idea of multinationalism to have an organic relationship with the new states. The absorption of democracy and literacy, two allied concepts, entered the social grammar of the Third World equally easily. On the ideological level, every Third World state adopted the idea of democracy as fundamental to itself (even antidemocratic states justified themselves with the language of democracy).[40] The claim of cultural backwardness justified colonial rule, so national movements typically argued for self-rule on the ground of cultural maturity.[41] The question of the franchise was therefore moot: everyone would get the vote, regardless of literacy and social status. Most new nations did not need a suffrage movement, because ipso facto the population would get to vote. Despite this, however, the question of the franchise (and liberal democracy in general) brought the issue of literacy front and center.

At the 1958 Cairo conference, the Sudanese delegate Mohamed Ahmed Mahgoub announced, "All individuals who have come of age [must] enjoy the right to elect and to be elected to parliament without any reservations."[42] People must have the vote despite their level of formal education, but the state must promote formal education in order to raise the cultural and political literacy of the population. The demand for the word, for literacy, came enveloped with the victory of the vote, the franchise. Illiteracy is not a function of the population's stupidity but its lack of opportunity. Education had to be provided. UNESCO and other international agencies maintained that literacy campaigns had to be coupled with mass campaigns for social justice.[43] People were motivated by campaigns that addressed their everyday grievances, and in these sorts of campaigns the new nations integrated the project of literacy. In other words, the articulation of democracy and literacy within this form of anticolonial nationalism was not simply about the franchise; it was always also (and sometimes only) about social development. In 1965, Tehran hosted the World Conference of Ministers of Education on the Eradication of Illiteracy, which pledged to continue the linkage between literacy campaigns and specific socioeconomic development projects.[44] That same year, under pressure from the advanced industrial states, UNESCO shifted its funding strategies from mass campaigns to more strictly educational training. Nevertheless, a combination of innovative strategies within the new nations and UNESCO's efforts dramatically reduced illiteracy across the planet; in 1950, according to UNESCO, two out of three men and one out of four women could read in any language, whereas in 1995, 80 percent of men and 70 percent of women entered the world of letters.

There was an additional imperative for education and literacy, which was the necessity recognized by most intellectuals like Al-e Ahmad and Césaire that their societies required a shy with the Enlightenment. Rationality and rationalism might have had roots in many societies, but Europe certainly had the most full-blown intellectual development along these lines. From the science of the self to the science of nature, European intellectual life had been suffused with skepticism for received truths (including religion), and had crafted both empirical and theoretical means to understand the world.[45] Al-e Ahmad and others recognized this, and they also knew that their own societies could not afford to ignore the emergence of rationalism in the world. In a defensive vein, many of them, including Césaire as we saw above, showed that the growth of rationalism in Europe had a lineage that stretched outward into the darker world (for example, there could be no mathematics without the Indian and Arab contribution; or that the Chinese independently invented explosives and many chemical processes). A crude rendition of this defensiveness contended that each cultural (and in this terrain, religious) world had its own science, so that there was an Islamic science, a Christian science, a Hindu science, and so forth.[46] Worse yet was the view that modern science was no more or less than ancient science (in other words, such a tendency invalidated progress). The Enlightenment challenged the Third World intelligentsia to engage with it, rather than whether to do so in the first place. Al-e Ahmad called this engagement *rushanfekri*, a way of the world that does not inculcate "blind obedience or fear of the supernatural" but instead insists that the social individual has the ability "to choose, to be free and responsible."[47]

In terms of scientific research and technology, the regimes in the new nations adopted the Enlightenment's scientific heritage without any discussion of its cultural implications. This was insufficient. "History has fated the world to fall prey to the machine," Al-e Ahmad noted, and so, the question to ask is, "how to encounter the machine and technology"?[48] What is the best way for the machine to enable rushanfekri, or enlightenment, in accordance with the cultural history of Iran or elsewhere? When Césaire spoke of the juxtaposition and not the harmony of European culture with native cultures, one could think of the machine. Al-e Ahmad warned, as many others did, that the machine was not neutral. Colonialism brought the machine into spaces whose own cultural history had not prepared them for this new device, and besides, the machine and mechanization had been one of the instruments of cultural transformation. A machine is imbued with cultural forms; the tractor, for example, changes the relationship of farmers to their fields, each other, and the place of the plough in their cosmological world. The tractor would not leave the other social relations unchanged. Does the tractor carry within it the cultural revolution of centuries past that transformed the European fields into factories, and dispensed with small farms in favor of large agro-businesses and reduced the family farmer into the farmhand?

Furthermore, an insufficient interrogation of the role of the culture of a place and scientific thought meant that there was little concern for local ecologies, with their capacity to produce certain crops and improve irrigation in particular ways. Local knowledge was the historical accumulation of wisdom about local terrains and capacities. That social hierarchies of caste and clan came along with these encyclopedias of locality did not mean that much could not be learned from these traditions for democratic production. Most of the new states also experimented with communal and nonindustrial means of organization—from the Gandhian self-sufficient villages to the Tanzanian Ujamma collectives, across the Third World regimes tried out different forms of socioeconomic and cultural organization that refused the machine in one way or another. These were, but for a few places, the exception or even, to the cynical, the showcase. They did raise important questions of sustainability and equity, of the rights of the citizen to progress over the right to progress over the citizen. The bulk of the social order inhabited the machine and grew around it, and often ignored these warnings.

Al-e Ahmad and his contemporaries (including Ali Shariati, who drew from Al-e Ahmad as much as Herbert Marcuse) could only say that the dilemma was what to do with the machine. After raising the question, Al-e Ahmad ended with a whimper: "The machine should naturally serve us as a trampoline, so that we may stand on it and jump all the farther by its rebound. One must have the machine, one must build it. But one must not remain in bondage to it; one must not fall into its snare. The machine is a means, not an end. The end is to abolish poverty and to put material and spiritual welfare within the reach of all."[49] In the next moment, Al-e Ahmad warned about the machine's capacity to regiment everyday life (what Shariati called "machinism"). "Conformity in the workplace," Al-e Ahmad wrote, "leads to conformity in the party and the union, and this itself leads to conformity in the barracks; that is, for the machines of war." The roots of fascist militarism lie in the assembly line, unless the way that the machine operates is decisively reconstructed.[50] If the machine dominates life, then culture is at its mercy, and everything will have to obey its commands. The machine must be domesticated, it must become part of the fabric of the dynamic culture of a place. To the capitalist and the modernization theorist, the Lebanese philosopher and president of the UN General Assembly Charles Malik once said, "Roads, dams, efficiency, and the smile of the rulers—that is all that matters; but spirit, freedom, joy, happiness, truth, man—that never enters the mind. A world of perfect technicians is the aim, not a world of human beings, let alone of beings divine."[51] To take control of culture, one had to take control of the machine, and to "develop" meant to do so both economically and culturally.

Nationalism, democracy, and rationalism: the root of the Third World intellectual's quandary was how to create a new self in the new nations. Each of their societies had ample resources to fill this self, but they also recognized the necessity to articulate a new relationship with the "West." Al-e Ahmad did not ask for the return to some pristine Iranian culture or even Islam as the solitary basis for the subjectivity of the new Iranian.[52] His affection for plebian Shiism meant that he sought a new Iranian personality in its cultural resources. In 1969, the year that Al-e Ahmad died (or was killed by the Shah's intelligence service, SAVAK), his wife, Simin Daneshvar, published a remarkable novel, *Savushun*.[53] Set in the 1940s, the novel traces the tale of Zari, a woman who fought against imperialism, agrarian inequalities, and family suffocation. The novel is named after a folkloric hero (from the *Shahnama*) who is betrayed by his people and killed by foreigners. That was one part of Daneshvar's reach into folklore; the other was in her search for national salvation. If the various social agents had been paralyzed by imperialism and autarky, Zari, like others, waited for the coming of a Mahdi, the last prophet. For people like Daneshvar and Al-e Ahmad, the new Mahdi would be a reconstructed people's movement. In 1966,

Forugh Farrokhzad evoked that longing in "Someone Who Is Not Like Anyone."

I've had a dream that someone is coming.
I've dreamt of a red star,
And my eyelids keep twitching
And my shoes keep snapping to attention
And I may go blind
If I'm lying.
I've dreamt of that red star
When I wasn't asleep,
Someone is coming,
Someone is coming,
Someone better.

Someone is coming,
Someone is coming,
Someone who in his heart is with us,
In his breathing is with us,
In his voice is with us,
Someone whose coming
Can't be stopped
And handcuffed and thrown in jail
Someone who's been born
Under Yahya's old clothes,
And day by day
Grows bigger and bigger,
Someone from the rain,
From the sound of rain splashing,
From among the whispering petunias,
Someone is coming from the sky
At Tupkhaneh Square on the night of the fireworks
To spread out the tablecloth
And divide up the bread
And pass out the Pepsi
And divide up Melli Park
And pass out the whooping cough syrup
And pass out the slips on registration day
And give everybody hospital waiting room numbers
And distribute the rubber boots

And pass out Fardin movie tickets
And give away Sayyed Javad's daughter's dresses
And give away whatever doesn't sell
And even give us our share.
I've had a dream.[54]

The tragedy of this beautiful hunger is that it displaces the *work* that needs to be done for the creation of this new Mahdi onto destiny or fate. In 1968, Tomás Gutiérrez Alea released his masterful *Memories of Underdevelopment*. In the movie, Sergio Corrieri Hernández played the part of a desolate bourgeois who, despite his sympathies to radicalism, has a hard time finding himself in the revolution. Such was the dilemma of Farrokhzad, Daneshvar, Al-e Ahmad, and others. Corrieri had no such trouble. He continued to act, but also worked for almost two decades in El Teatro Escambray, a rural theater ensemble. He reached the Central Committee of the Cuban Communist Party and took over international solidarity work, at the same time as he worked among young theater activists to forge a new way to be Cuban. Corrieri, too, longed for the coming of a Mahdi called revolution, and he put his life behind the attempt to construct that someone.

BELGRADE

Brijuni was the Third World's Yalta.

At the Yalta Conference, in February 1945, the original big three (Stalin, Roosevelt, and Churchill) colluded in the partition of Europe in anticipation of the fall of the Nazi war machine. Each of the major powers, the Allies agreed, would consolidate their "spheres of influence," whether over Poland (the USSR) or Greece (United States and the United Kingdom). The Yalta plot spilled over to the rest of the world, as it presaged an attitude among the big three that each nation-state on the planet had to line up behind one or the other of the blocs. Neutrality or non-alignment was unspeakable.

On Brijuni, a beautiful island in the north Adriatic Sea, the other big three (Nasser, Nehru, and Tito) gathered in mid-July 1956 to discuss the fallout from the spheres of influence concept and their own vision for a non-aligned force in opposition to the Yalta logic. At one time the glitterati of the Austro-Hungarian Empire retreated to Brijuni, but now it functioned as the conference site for the Federal Republic of Yugoslavia. Tito played host to his two friends, Nasser and Nehru. The trio spent three days in discussion, and also rested and got to know one another. They reviewed international developments, gauged the effects of the 1955 Bandung Conference, and began to formulate the agenda for the founding conference of what would become the NAM to be held in Belgrade in 1961. During this brief summit, the term "peaceful co-existence" was bandied about, as it had been for the past few years at summits across the Third World. Understood as a term for those countries that were unwilling to join one or the other of the superpowers in their blocs, peaceful co-existence had a broad appeal among the new rulers of the new nations. It had a negative meaning—as it referred to those states that did not want to ally with the USSR or the United States. It also had a positive meaning—as it indicated a principle for interstate relations that refused brute force in favor of mutual development. The rhetoric exceeded the policies. NAM produced all kinds of concepts (peaceful co-existence and active co-existence being examples). It wanted to base international relations on morals rather than in terms of power politics or national interest. This was the movement's challenge, and undoing.

For the Third World, peaceful co-existence would be the main concept for the organization of states in a nuclear world. Because of the overwhelming military power of NATO and the Warsaw Pact as well as financial capital, and because of the lack of genuine social reconstruction within their own states, most of the Third World leadership would adopt only the aura of the term. Peaceful co-existence allowed the new nations to squeeze out from under the weight of the bipolar world, but it would not necessarily lead to a reorganization of the states themselves or their own regional aspirations. The Atlantic powers denigrated the term from the 1940s onward, whereas the Soviets adopted it from 1955; this difference allowed the latter to gain some purchase at the expense of the former in the halls of the newly created NAM (but sometimes at the expense of the domestic Communist parties in the Third World). The practitioners of peaceful co-existence did not wish to threaten changes between states, so they moved their agenda to the forum of the United Nations. The United Nations and its democratization became the proximate goals of NAM, which had therefore abjured any attempt to overthrow, or even jujitsu, both superpowers. If Yalta presaged the division of the world, Brijuni and Belgrade augured the creation of an association that would seek more room for the darker nations—but not necessarily for the reconstruction of the world in their image.

All three leaders—Nasser, Nehru, and Tito—had earned their anticolonial spurs, but it was the host's personal antics that had greatly impressed the other two. Born in Croatia, Tito had worked as a trade unionist, fought in World War I, took part in the Bolshevik Revolution, fought in the Red Army, joined the Communist Party of Yugoslavia, led the Dimitrov Battalion in the Spanish Civil War, returned to Yugoslavia to fight a guerrilla war with his partisans against the fascists, and finally, in March 1945, became the premier of the federation of the socialist republics of Bosnia-Herzegovina, Croatia, Macedonia, Montenegro, Serbia, and Slovenia. By the Brijuni meeting he had already lived several lifetimes and more. With Nasser and Nehru, Tito was poised to start another, as the founder of NAM. By 1956, Yugoslavia had moved some distance from the USSR, and so even as it remained formally within the socialist camp, it did not see its future as a Soviet satellite.

Whereas when the Bolshevik Revolution took Russia out of World War I in an anti-imperialist flourish (the new government revealed the hidden imperialist correspondence of the European regimes), the Soviet state under Stalin had a much more cautious approach toward the new postcolonial states. The Soviet Union had been battered by the war. Its president, Mikhail Kalinin, warned the Communist Party in August 1945 that "the perils of capitalist encirclement [of the USSR] had not disappeared with Hitlerite Germany." From Kalinin's assessment, the USSR could neither afford to rest easy nor antagonize the hoards that gathered on its borders. In this vise, the USSR's principle leadership offered two contrary theses: that any entente between the United States and the USSR was "perfectly feasible" (as Stalin put it in December 1946), and that the United States and its allies were "rapacious imperialists" who were on the verge of defeat by the tide of socialism (as Andrei Zhdanov put it at the September 1947 founding conference of the Communist Information Bureau, the Cominform).[1] Zhdanov's two-camp theory privileged the national Communist parties at the same time as the USSR's commissars made arrangements with the bourgeois forces within the postcolonial states at the expense of the local Communists. This vacillation manifested itself in the ambiguity over the Soviet position regarding the Third World and peaceful co-existence. After the demise of Stalin, the new leadership led by Khrushchev and Bulganin adopted peaceful co-existence and pledged their support to the bourgeois nationalist regimes (often against the domestic Communists). The unclear situation suggested that the USSR seemed keener to push its own national interests than those of the national Communist parties to which it pledged verbal fealty.

Such, at any rate, had been Yugoslavia's experience. As Tito's partisans defeated the fascist forces, they welcomed the Red Army into Yugoslavia. Distrust over the behavior of the Red Army and a lack of support over the U.S.-UK invasion of Trieste (1945) drew the following assessment from Tito: "We have no wish to be dependent on anyone. We do not want to be small change; we do not want to be involved in any policy of spheres of influence."[2] Soviet aid packages that favored Moscow over Belgrade along with Stalin's reticence to allow a smooth federation of Yugoslavia and Bulgaria in 1947 led to the final Yugoslav Communist refusal to become a Soviet satellite in 1948. Thrown out of the Cominform, Yugoslavia joined the Italian Communist Party's view that each national party had to be independent of Moscow, even though it must have strong fraternal ties to the socialist bloc.[3] As the Soviets and the Yugoslavs clashed, U.S. airplanes violated Yugoslavia's airspace (twenty-one times in the first three months of 1948). Isolated, the Yugoslavs turned to the new postcolonial states for ideological and material help.[4]

A tour of India (1954–55) and Egypt (1955) enabled Tito to test the waters for some kind of nonsuperpower alliance.[5] Yugoslavian arms went to Egypt and Burma, and its UN votes went to the Congo and Angola—it used whatever it could to facilitate a relationship with the darker nations. Perhaps the best indication of this is in the Yugoslav ties with Algeria's FLN. In 1953–54, the Yugoslavian government made contact with the FLN in Cairo and began to funnel all kinds of assistance (including cover at the United Nations) from the inception of the FLN uprising in November 1954.[6]

If Yugoslavia found itself in the cold between the superpowers, so too did Egypt and India. Neither had any principled objection to the system championed by the United States and Europe; both Nehru and Nasser were personally enamored by the ideals of the USSR, but neither had any special predisposition to yoke their country to its stringent ideals and less-than-catholic foreign policy.[7] The United States and the European powers, however, alienated an otherwise-receptive Egypt and India. Secretary of State Dulles traveled to both Egypt and India in 1953. In South Asia, Dulles found Nehru "utterly impractical," whereas he enjoyed the "martial and religious qualities of the Pakistanis." Although Nehru's visit to the United States in 1949 had gone well, and although Nehru's regime had signed onto the UK-dominated Commonwealth that year, by the early 1950s it had become clear that India would not subordinate itself to U.S. interests. Dulles and the U.S. regime wanted to bind one or the other of the South Asian states into an alliance to isolate and encircle not only the USSR but also Communist China. When Nehru's India did not go along, Dulles signed on an eager Pakistan, whose General Ayub Khan inked an arms agreement with the United States—and this would culminate finally in the Baghdad Pact of 1955, an alliance of Iran, Iraq, Pakistan, Turkey, and the United Kingdom, brokered by the United States.[8]

In the Arab lands, Dulles failed to grasp the deep anti-British sentiment of the Nasser regime (and the bulk of the population). When he tried to impress on Nasser that the Soviets represented the real threat to Egyptian freedom, Nasser replied, "The population of Egypt would think crazy anybody saying this," because it was self-evident that the main problem was Britain. Dulles fumed to his superiors in Washington.[9] Peaceful co-existence and non-alignment had got his goat. Indeed, Dulles refused to use the latter term, favoring the word neutralism; since the term indicated that these states wanted to sit out the main conflict, Dulles felt that it was "an immoral and short-sighted conception."[10] His contempt notwithstanding, the leaders of the Third World admitted to haziness in their framework. While no one proposed that the Third World should deal with the conflict along the lines of Swiss neutralism, most of them worked hard to emphasize the need to both opt out of the bipolar conflict and yet find a way to move an alternative agenda; they did not adopt a passive hedgehog posture.[11] For Dulles, who had absorbed Zhdanov's two-camp theory, all this was academic. If a state did not subordinate itself to the interests of the United States and its global dispensation, then it had given itself over to the USSR and communism.

As Nasser and Nehru prepared to leave Brijuni, they heard news that the U.S. government had decided to cut its $200 million pledge to finance Egypt's $1.3 billion Aswan High Dam. The dam was crucial to Egyptian plans, as the Free Officers hoped that it would help the sluggish Egyptian agricultural sector, an area that needed immediate redress for the republic to retain the support of the fellahin, the peasantry. To gain investment funds, Nasser had tried to play the Atlantic powers against the Soviets.[12] Apart from these productive projects, Nasser also played off the two major blocs over arms sales. The United States had a less attractive offer: among its stringent restrictions, the U.S. government offered only certain kinds of arms, wanted them accompanied by a U.S. military assistance mission, and required that the U.S. arms aid be used to buy high-priced U.S. hardware (an elegant way to subsidize the U.S. weapons companies). All this being impossible for Egypt, Nasser bought weapons from Czechoslovakia. In addition, Nasser had refused to join the Baghdad Pact and pushed the English to remove their military base from Suez. Little wonder that Dulles despised the Nasserite regime.

"Our quarrel with Egypt," observed a Dulles aide, "is not that it is following a 'neutral' course in declining to align itself with either the East or West," which had been Dulles's own fixation. Rather, "Nasser is not guided by 'cold war' considerations but by his own vision of Egyptian preponderance first in the Arab world, next in Africa and then in the Moslem world as a whole."[13] The only primacy or preponderance that would be countenanced by the Dulles crew was that of the United States (in 1947, the State Department's policy planning staff wrote, "To seek less than preponderant power would be to opt for defeat. Preponderant power must be the object of U.S. policy").[14] "Those people," said Nehru of the U.S. government, "how arrogant they are." "This is not a withdrawal," Nasser responded. "It is an attack on the regime."[15] When Nasser arrived back in Cairo, he decided to raise the Aswan funds by the nationalization of the Suez Canal, itself a symbol of colonial abuse through the use of almost-free Egyptian labor to build the privately owned crucial waterway for the imperial powers. The canal's dues, Nasser felt, would raise enough capital to finance the Free Officers' schemes. When the Anglo-French-Israeli force invaded Egypt in retaliation, Tito and Nehru came to Egypt's aid. The objective conditions of the bipolar world and the subjective links between these three powers had been confirmed by the events of Aswan and Suez.

At the Brijuni conference, the three observed that the conditions in the world left them with few options and a great need for patience. The final communiqué noted that "as long as these fears and apprehensions dominate the world, no firm basis for peace can be established. At the same time, it is difficult to remove quickly these fears and apprehensions, and gradual steps will have to be taken for their elimination. Every such step helps in lessening tensions and is therefore to be welcomed."[16] One such gradual step would be to convene all like-minded new nations that wanted to go neither with the Soviets nor the Atlantic powers. They went to work.[17] In 1961, the other big three welcomed the representatives of twenty-two states from Africa, Asia, Latin America, and Europe to Belgrade to create NAM, an institution that grew in strength from conference to conference, within and without the United Nations, and lumbers on today.[18]

The nature of the regimes that participated in the NAM meeting reflects its limitations. With their pageantry came the monarchs, including Ethiopia's Emperor Haile Selassie and Cambodia's Prince Norodom Sihanouk. That they ruled autocratically over their populations seemed acceptable to the republics (India, after all, had joined the Commonwealth in 1948, and had accepted the titular role of the British monarch as its head). Among the republicans were heads of bourgeois nationalist parties, leaders of coups, and representatives of mass nationalist movements. Burma's U Nu and Algeria's Ben Youssef rubbed shoulders with Indonesia's Sukarno, Mali's Mobido Keita, and Ghana's Nkrumah, who in turn sat beside Sri Lanka's Srimavo Bandarnaike and Cuba's Osvaldo Dorticós Torrado. Many of these leaders (such as Nasser and Nehru) were popular in their home countries, and even as they had the authority from their various representative bodies (parliaments and cabinets), they had personalities that brooked no delegation.[19] They came to act, but they could not. This was a mixed crowd, and its sheer political diversity made an ideologically coherent and unified stance by NAM almost impossible.[20] NAM would remain a political platform, a sub–United Nations, but it would only be able to act in concert on two broad issues: to champion global nuclear disarmament, and to democratize the United Nations.

In August, two weeks before the Belgrade conference opened, the East Germans erected a wall through Berlin to prevent a brain drain (in 1960, almost three hundred dentists, seven hundred doctors, and three thousand engineers fled the German Democratic Republic for the First World). Troops moved, and populations anticipated bloodshed. The day before the conference opened, the USSR tested a fifty-megaton bomb ("Ivan"). U Nu warned NAM that the "two power blocs are prepared to risk a war over Berlin," and that this event, like so many others (such as the April 1961 Bay of Pigs invasion), might precipitate the final (nuclear) conflict.[21] The nuclear club had been joined by the British (1952) and the French (1960), and despite the existence of the IAEA (1957), the powers had little interest in restraint, only in nonproliferation. In 1954, Nehru had called for a formal test ban, but his suggestion was shunned. The Third World states had gone to the UN floor on several occasions to call for total disarmament, but to no avail. As recently as October 1, 1960, Ghana, India, Indonesia, the United Arab Republic, and Yugoslavia, the core nations of NAM, had put forward a UN resolution that urged the United States and the USSR to renew their suspended talks on nuclear matters. In June 1961, the two powers met in Vienna, but neither had the stomach to walk away from their nuclear arsenals.[22]

In Belgrade, one leader after another of the darker nations spoke against the logic of nuclearism. But their bombast recognized that they had little leverage on the four nuclear powers (who stood poised against each other on two sides, the Atlantic versus Moscow). All that remained was talk of the "great moral force" of NAM.[23] This analysis of the moral force of NAM in the bipolar world led to a straightforward political outcome: NAM dispatched four of its most senior representatives to Moscow and Washington. They carried an "Appeal for Peace" from NAM to end their obduracy and move toward eventual nuclear disarmament. Nehru and Nkrumah went east and Sukarno and Keita went west with the same letter (drafted by Nehru): "We feel convinced that devoted as both of you [Khrushchev and Kennedy] are to the world peace, your efforts through persistent negotiations will lead to a way out of the present impasse and enable the world and humanity to work and live for prosperity and peace."[24] The bluster of the conference was substituted by supplication. That both Moscow and Washington made empty promises in return provides a measure of the limited value of moral pleas in a nuclear age.

If a simple entreaty would be condescendingly accepted and shelved, then something other than that had to be attempted. The related path was to agitate for more democracy in the UN institutions, particularly in the all-powerful Security Council. Like most institutions, the United Nations bore the idiosyncratic marks of its history. At its formation, the Americas provided the largest membership because Africa and Asia then remained under Europe's thralldom. As African and Asian nations gained independence and membership in the United Nations, their presence did not automatically reshape the original rules and committee memberships. Far more important than these matters, however, was the question of the Security Council. The United States, the United Kingdom, the USSR, France, and the Republic of China (Formosa, later Taiwan) transferred their de facto power after World War II into de jure power within the United Nations.[25] They took their Security Council and Trusteeship Council seats in perpetuity, and dominated the leadership posts in the ancillary UN bodies. On the Security Council, only these powers had permanent seats with veto power over the decisions of the populous General Assembly.[26]

The structural disadvantage of the United Nations to the Third World could have led to cynicism about the value of the international body. In Belgrade, U Nu voiced this fear: "We think it would be a black day indeed for the world, and particularly for the smaller countries, if the United Nations were to suffer the fate of the League of Nations."[27] So why should the United Nations be saved, and why must the Third World give its energy to the democratization of the United Nations? In late 1948, Yugoslavia's Foreign Minister Edvard Kardelj wrote: "In spite of [the United Nations's] great weaknesses, this organization is nevertheless useful and can serve as a serious obstacle to those who are prepared for their own selfish aims to push mankind toward the catastrophe of a new world war."[28] The African, Asian, and Latin American states proffered draft resolutions to bring democracy to the United Nations in 1957, but it was not until 1959 and 1960 that the General Assembly heard debates on this theme. From Guinea to Pakistan, delegates reflected on the need for the United Nations to be awake to history, alter its structure as large numbers of new nations took their seats as sovereign powers, rethink its veto powers to the colonial and nuclear powers, and do so in the spirit of justice, not charity. In 1963, the darker nations proposed that the size of the Security Council and the Economic and Social Council should be expanded, with special regard for the representation of the two underrepresented areas of Africa and Asia (UN General Assembly Resolutions 1990 [XVIII], 1991 [XVIII], and 1992 [XVIII]). Resolution 1991 increased the *nonpermanent* members to ten with five from Africa and Asia, two from Latin America, one from Eastern Europe, and two from Western Europe; these would not have veto power. So while the NAM states tried to bring democracy to the United Nations, and even as they were able to expand the various organs and raise their voices about the cabal of states that dominate its process, they made little headway. The system, in a sense, had boxed them in. Nonetheless, the United Nations provided a crucial forum for the Third World to raise issues of colonial barbarity and use the General Assembly as the medium to broadcast previously hidden atrocities before the world.

Perhaps the best summary of the achievement of NAM within its first three years of existence comes from Amilcar Cabral, the leader of PAIGC. Cabral traveled to the second NAM in Cairo (1964), two years after his party, the PAIGC, had adopted the armed struggle against the Portuguese colonial regime. The PAIGC was not alone in this turn to guns. Further south, in Angola, the Movimento Popular de Libertação de Angola (MPLA) took up arms against the Portuguese, while a year later, the Frente de Libertaçâo de Moçambique (FRELIMO) began its guerrilla activities. NAM backed all three movements, with a 1964 pledge to "offer every type of support [to] the freedom fighters in territories under Portuguese colonialism."[29] Cabral acknowledged that while PAIGC's struggle is also the struggle "for peaceful co-existence and for peace," he made it clear that "to co-exist one must first of all exist, so the imperialists and the colonialists must be forced to retreat so that we can make a contribution to human civilization, based on the work, the dynamic personality and the culture of our peoples."[30] In his study of socialism and war, the major theorist of peaceful co-existence, Edvard Kardelj, made a distinction between the wars of the powerful and the wars of the weak. The former had to be condemned at all costs, while the latter could be defended in context. At all times, states had to be "in favor of peace in the abstract and against war in the abstract."[31] There is a difference between armed struggle to eject colonialism and the brinkmanship of nuclear warfare as well as the creation of a warfare state. The latter is a violation of peaceful co-existence, while the former is a necessity for it. Even NAM, therefore, could shill for the path of armed struggle.

NAM's principle strategic thrust was for the democratization of the United Nations and its re-creation into an instrument for justice. Cabral argued that the United Nations in the early 1960s was "a giant with its hands tied," and with its "structure renewed, its institutions democratized and its voice strengthened to include those hundreds of millions of human beings, it may fully serve the noble cause of freedom, fraternity, progress and happiness for mankind."[32] In early December 1964, Che Guevara took this message to the floor of the UN General Assembly: "We should like to wake up this Assembly. Imperialism wants to convert this meeting into a useless oratorical tournament instead of solving the serious problems of the world. We must prevent them from doing this. . . . As Marxists we maintain that peaceful co-existence does not include co-existence between exploiters and exploited, between oppressors and oppressed."[33] Few in the Third World would deny the words of Guevara, even if many of the elder politicians would urge a more moderate tone.[34] Indeed, after the second NAM conference in Cairo, the Third World experienced a period of oratorical inflation, notably at the Tricontinental Conference in Havana (1966). From the early 1960s to the late 1970s, the rhetorical denunciation of imperialism reached its apogee, even as the Third World began to lose its voice.

HAVANA

Between Bandung and Belgrade, a group of hardened revolutionaries went into the mountains of Cuba to put their military inexperience to the test. Led by the charismatic Fidel Castro, these national liberation fighters suffered early defeats and became almost entirely isolated from the main political parties in Havana. Their persistence, generosity toward those around them, and élan won them allies from among the bruised classes. From the Sierra Maestra, their good energy enthused students to attack the Presidential Palace in Havana, women's groups to fill Havana's streets with major demonstrations, and workers' organizations to hold a general strike against the regime of Fulgencio Batista, the U.S.-backed dictator and caretaker of Cuba's wealth for the Las Vegas– and Miami-based mafia. In winter 1958, two years after the insurgency began, the Batista regime evaporated. Batista left the island with his comrade, the gangster Meyer Lansky. Castro's small band entered Havana and took charge of the collapsed state.

The U.S. government was not pleased with this turn of events. Castro had lined up on the side of Third World nationalism. In his 1953 courtroom speech ("History Will Absolve Me"), Castro called on Cubans to fulfill their duty to revive the 1940 Constitution of Cuba. Pleas and legal challenges had not worked on Batista's regime. "We were taught," Castro said, "that liberty is not begged for but won with the blade of a machete." The United States had a poor track record with national liberation and anti-imperialist movements in Central America and the Caribbean. The armies and allies of the United States had been prone to oppose these movements, assassinate their leaders, and deliver arms to their monarchist or oligarchic opponents. Between 1900 and 1933, the U.S. military intervened to scuttle the national hopes of the people of Cuba (four times), the Dominican Republic (four times, including an eight-year occupation), Guatemala (once), Haiti (twice, including a nineteen-year occupation), Honduras (seven times), Nicaragua (twice), and Panama (six times). Most recently, in 1954, the U.S. government intervened to overthrow the democratically elected government of Jacobo Arbenz Guzmán in Guatemala. The new Guatemalan government had pledged itself to the national liberation program of extensive land reform and nationalization of the economy's commanding heights. Just before it could enact its agrarian reform and nationalize the Rockefeller-owned United Fruit Company, the U.S. Marines landed. Then, in 1959, when a right-wing coup brought François "Papa Doc" Duvalier to power in Haiti, the United States armed his Tonton Macoutes, who brought terror to the people.[1] The Castro government had every reason to be suspicious of their northern colossus.

A year into the Cuban Revolution, the U.S. president Eisenhower ordered his administration to start covert operations against Cuba. Castro did not know this, but he might have sensed it given Eisenhower's refusal to see him when he traveled to Washington, DC, to deliver a speech to the Association of Newspaper Editors in March 1959.[2] Fearful that Washington might do to Cuba what it had recently done to Guatemala, the Cubans went to Moscow in mid-1960 to secure a pledge that the USSR "will use all means at its disposal to prevent an armed intervention by the United States against Cuba."[3] Despite détente and peaceful co-existence, the reality of interventionism led the Cubans to take refuge in one of the two major camps. Threatened by the United States, Cuba went with the Soviets.

The Soviet nuclear umbrella had, however, not done anything to deter the U.S. military in Vietnam. In February 1965, the U.S. Air Force began to bomb North Vietnam, and between 1964–65, the U.S. administration had either assisted or given the green light for coups in Bolivia, Brazil, the Congo, Greece, and Indonesia. The Soviets could not prevent any of this. For Castro, part of the problem lay in the new doctrine that had been developed by the Third World project and adopted by the Soviets, the "strange concept of peaceful co-existence for some and war for others."[4] Castro expected NAM and the USSR to do something concrete for Vietnam as well as other colonized people. This expectation and impatience marks the political debates within the Third World from the mid-1960s until the late 1970s. It is in this period that armed struggle will be revived not only as a tactic of anticolonialism but significantly *as a strategy in itself.*

If China's Mao led a protracted armed struggle against the Japanese army and the armies of the old social classes of China, he did so because the concrete conditions demanded such a strategy. The Chinese line, as it was known, began to be lifted root and branch without much concern for the concrete conditions in China. The Cuban theory of the *foco* (insurrectionary center) and Fanon's theory of revolutionary violence as well as Lin Biao's theory of "people's war" all appealed to this impatience.[5] Militants and national liberation organizations in this period flooded the meetings of the Third World and demanded armed action against imperialism. They challenged the Soviet delegates and brushed aside any consideration of the limitations of popular anti-imperialist sentiment in the countries to be liberated by the gun. Some of the militants adopted the critique of the two-camps theory to suggest that both the United States and the USSR were imperialists, and the only force able to stand up to them was armed national liberation. The discrete reasons for the success of the Chinese and Cuban revolutions became less important than the mimicry of its method. That the Chinese took decades and the Cubans took a few years, and that the Chinese had to fight over an enormous landmass whereas the Cuban remit was an island, seemed irrelevant. The militants dismissed theory and debate in favor of the tactic of insurrection, with armed struggle as the means to seize and maintain power. Mass struggle and the central role of a party was not to distract the onward march of the revolutionary war.

The high point for the militants was a 1966 gathering, the First Solidarity Conference of the Peoples of Africa, Asia, and Latin America, held in Havana. The conference followed the lineage of Bandung and NAM meetings with two major differences. First, it drew together national liberation regimes and movements from all three continents (hence it was called the Tricontinental Conference).[6] Second, while there was broad agreement on the problems in the world, there were grave disagreements on the strategy to confront the world's predicaments.[7] Sensing a weakness for the progressive forces, some wanted to pursue the line of peaceful co-existence while they built the UN institutions. Others wanted to move immediately to militancy, to challenge imperialism on the battlefield and through small acts of revolutionary violence or terrorism. At the center of the debate was Vietnam. The discussion over how to provide genuine solidarity to Vietnam helped focus the more amorphous dispute over political strategy for the various liberation movements, for the Tricontinental and NAM.

By 1966, the war in Vietnam had become diabolical. Half a million U.S. troops could not break through the Vietnamese fighters, and the aerial bombardment created both grief and resilient opposition among the population. As a result of Vietnam, the Third World powers shed most of their illusions about the Atlantic powers. Of the main leadership at Bandung and Belgrade, Nehru was now dead, Sukarno had been overthrown by a U.S.-sponsored coup, U Nu was under house arrest in Rangoon, and Nasser suffocated the last remnants of democracy in Egypt. Those who had taken charge of the Third World dynamic, such as Castro, Algeria's Houari Boumédienne, Zambia's Kenneth Kaunda, and Jamaica's Michael Manley, had little patience with the First World. For them, its ideals had been compromised. Any supplication to the United States or its principle allies would be worthless.

At the Tricontinental, Castro thundered on about the war and the deplorable assaults, but "instead of gaining ground," he pointed out, the U.S. armies "have lost ground."[8] The extraordinary defiance of the Vietnamese shocked the Third World. It was one thing for a poorly armed guerrilla force to overthrow the Batista regime or combat the Portuguese colonial forces, but it was altogether a different matter for a peasant army to face the full frontal assault of the U.S. war machine. Nothing was more riveting for the 513 delegates from 83 groups across three continents than the presentations by Nguyen Van Tien of the National Liberation Front of South Vietnam and Tran Danh Tuyen of the government of North Vietnam. If Vietnam won, it would be a victory for national liberation globally.[9] The Tricontinental pledged its solidarity to the Vietnamese and looked forward to their victory.

Such pledges, however, can be empty. Guevara missed the Tricontinental. He had left Cuba for Africa, where he had begun to explore the possibility of joining the revolutionary movements in the Congo. In a letter to the Tricontinental, Che asked the hardest question of all: What is the value of solidarity when the imperialist guns were not challenged? "The solidarity of the progressive forces of the world towards the people of Vietnam today," he wrote, "is similar to the bitter irony of the plebeians coaxing on the gladiators in the Roman arena. It is not a matter of wishing success to the victims of aggression, but of sharing his fate; one must accompany him to his death or to victory."[10] To give genuine solidarity to the Vietnamese, Che argued, revolutionary forces across the three continents needed to create "a second, or a third Vietnam, or the second *and* third Vietnam of the world." As Neruda sang in 1967, "Who will erase the ruthlessness hidden in innocent blood?"

Che's fury eclipsed Neruda's elegy: "How close we could look into a bright future should two, three or many Vietnams flourish throughout the world with their share of deaths and their immense tragedies, their everyday heroism and their repeated blows against imperialism, impelled to disperse its forces under the sudden attack and the increasing hatred of all peoples of the world."[11] At the Havana meeting, Castro met with the Bolivian Communist Party chief Mario Monje, who agreed to host Che and support his attempt to create a Vietnam in Bolivia.[12] Che left Africa for Bolivia, began to organize a foco, but lost the support of Monje's Communist Party and therefore became isolated. His attempt to create a second Vietnam ended in his personal sacrifice in 1967 on behalf of anti-imperialism. Che's own failure did not invalidate his critique, though. Should solidarity cost something?

The USSR and China played a critical role in world affairs because they constrained the Atlantic powers' quest for primacy. The UN Security Council allowed the Soviets and the Chinese to threaten the veto or else condemn the actions of the Atlantic powers. What frustrated the Third World leaders was the lack of any other kind of response, and indeed sometimes a hostile reaction from the Soviets and the Chinese to the militancy in the Third World. Could the USSR threaten violence against the United States or else invade a U.S. ally so as to sue for peace in Southeast Asia? Since 1955, the Soviets had adopted the theory of peaceful coexistence. This meant that they could offer moral and material support to intensify the class struggle where they deemed it important, but they would not export revolution by the gun (the Soviets defended their 1956 invasion of Hungary as their revolutionary duty to assist Communist regimes that had been threatened by a counterrevolutionary coup).[13] Could China invade Taiwan to make the same point? The Chinese had already tried to do so in 1958, but they had to retreat when the United States sent along its nuclear-armed Seventh Fleet. For all its bluster about the export of world revolution, the Chinese could not afford to antagonize the United States and other Atlantic powers into a major conflict. In a 1964 statement on the Congo, Mao noted that each time the United States invaded a country, it would be advantageous for the world revolution. The United States had intervened in Vietnam, Laos, Cambodia, Cuba, Germany, Japan, Korea, and Latin America. "It plays the bully everywhere. U.S. imperialism has overreached itself. Wherever it commits aggression, it puts a new noose around its neck. It is besieged ring upon ring by the people of the whole world."[14] Imperialist powers had an inherent tendency to fight wars of conquest and subjugation, and as they did so, they would confront people's tenacious desire for liberty and independence. Despite the dispute between the Chinese and the Soviets, both followed the same policy of giving verbal and material support to their allies and the class struggle, without entering into interstate hostilities themselves.[15] Nuclear war had made direct warfare between the first two worlds impossible. It was now left to the nonnuclear powers to pin down imperialism's tentacles.

The NAM states and NAM itself did not have the means to join the Vietnam War. NAM could not send its armies to Hanoi, even as the Second NAM Conference in Cairo (1964) had stated that wars of national liberation are defensible, that they are the principal means to fulfill the "natural aspirations" of people being colonized by powers that were loath to transfer sovereignty, and that "the process of liberation is irresistible and irreversible."[16] NAM had supported the Algerian struggle in 1961, and it welcomed the victory of the Algerians in 1962. It also supported the main liberation movements in Portuguese Africa (Mozambique, Angola, and Cabo Verde).[17] It was enough to support wars of national liberation when these were far away and much harder to take a principled position on the armed overthrow of a recognized government. Many of the NAM states had already begun to experience armed struggle within. The dominant classes of these states held the reins of state power, and wielded it against their internal critics. It was far easier to bemoan U.S. interventions and the ailing Portuguese colonies than to validate the tactic of armed struggle, especially if such struggles had broken out within an NAM state.

Nehru and Sukarno had been ruthless against the Communist movements in their own countries, and they were incapable of a genuine challenge to finance capital. Like Nehru and Sukarno, Nkrumah of Ghana enjoyed the momentum of a successful freedom struggle and disliked any opposition. His Preventive Detention Act and use of the state apparatus against the rail workers in 1961 led inexorably to the creation of a one-party state in 1964 with Nkrumah as *Osagyefo* or Redeemer. Unlike Nehru and Sukarno, however, Nkrumah attempted to delink Ghana from the global capitalist economy and pursue his own version of African socialism. In 1965, Nkrumah published *Neocolonialism: The Last Stage of Imperialism*, a book that predicted his own demise. "A State in the grip of neo-colonialism," he noted, "is not master of its own destiny."[18] Nkrumah's popularity plummeted along with world cocoa prices, and in 1966, the CIA encouraged his opposition to conduct a coup against him. Nkrumah took refuge in Conakry, Guinea. While in

Guinea, Nkrumah studied the situation of the Third World and came to the conclusion that the only way to make a revolution given the bipolar world is by a protracted guerrilla struggle. Thus far, the Third World had used reasoned arguments to gain its ends. Appeals are not sufficient, Nkrumah asserted, even when these were eloquent. Success could only be "achieved by deeds," and while these deeds threatened total war, "it is often their absence which constitutes the threat to peace."[19]

"Time is running out," Nkrumah wrote in one of his manuals for revolutionary war. "We must act now. The freedom fighters already operating in many parts of Africa must no longer be allowed to bear the full brunt of a continental struggle against a continental enemy."[20] These were not deluded statements. In 1961, South Africa's Umkhonto we Sizwe began its violent career. In "Portuguese" Africa, the MPLA, the FRELIMO, and the PAIGC were in a full-scale war against a much-weakened colonial force. The Zimbabwe African People's Union (ZANU) and the South-West African People's Organization began guerrilla warfare in 1966. Nkrumah's vision of revolutionary war had become a reality in parts of Africa. He argued that all of Africa should join this struggle, not only to overthrow colonial rulers, but also as an instrument to radicalize the masses and create major social upheaval.

At the Tricontinental Nkrumah's comrade, Cabral of the PAIGC, opened his address with the statement, "We are not going to eliminate imperialism by shouting insults against it. For us, the best and worst shout against imperialism, whatever its form, is to take up arms and fight."[21] For Cabral, like Nkrumah, colonialism and neocolonialism are two forms of imperialism, both of which negate "the historical process of the dominated people by means of violent usurpation of the freedom of development of the national productive forces."[22] "If we accept the principle that the *liberation struggle is a revolution* and that it does not finish at the moment when the national flag is raised and the national anthem played, we will see that there is not, and cannot be, national liberation without the use of liberating violence by the nationalist forces, to answer the criminal violence of the agents of imperialism."[23] In 1956, Cabral founded the PAIGC, which worked through all legal channels against Portuguese rule. When the colonial forces massacred fifty dockworkers in 1959 at the Pijiguiti Docks at the Port of Bissau, the Guinean population went over to the PAIGC. The party did not move to the armed path until 1962, only after it had secured the majority of the population's support. The bloody war went on for a decade, and one of its victims was Cabral himself (shot by a disgruntled comrade). The PAIGC succeeded in 1974, as Portugal's junta fell apart. A flexible use of tactics based on a strategic anti-imperialist program drove the PAIGC. It had taken the legal route and had been able to conscript the bulk of the population to its side; only when it had this mass backing, and only when the dominant classes had begun to narrow its space for action, did it take to the gun. This is what distinguished the PAIGC from many of the other groups that used armed struggle, most of which had a more tragically symbolic approach to politics than a materialist one.[24]

The Tricontinental neither went out of its way to promote revolutionary wars or violent acts, nor did it condemn them outright. It did, however, offer its support for ongoing wars because, the final resolution contended, imperialists do not listen to exploited peoples, who "must resort to the most energetic forms of struggle, of which armed struggle is one of the highest stages, to achieve final victory."[25] This statement on behalf of armed struggle gave courage to people in the midst of major battles in "limited wars," but it did not lead to any dramatic increase of militancy within the Third World. After Algeria's victory in 1962 by armed struggle, the next major success came in 1974 when revolutionaries overthrew the dictatorial regime of Selassie. While the African continent began to wither under debt and policies enforced by the IMF, a popular movement in Ethiopia dispensed with the monarchy, enthroned a left-wing government, and immediately had to seek military assistance from Cuba and the USSR against a Saudi-U.S.-backed invasion by the armed forces of Somalia. Before the world could make sense of what happened in Addis Ababa, a progressive military junta overthrew the fascist dictatorship in Lisbon. Six African revolutionary movements took advantage of the turmoil in 1974 and declared independence (Angola, Mozambique, Guinea-Bissau, Cape Verde, São Tomé, and opportunistically, Zimbabwe).[26] After years of guerrilla war, aided by the Cubans in Angola, the revolutionaries had success by the gun. Yet the victory in these colonies came in large part because of the weakness of the Portuguese state, now shaken by internal political reforms and economic instability. The armed struggle in Africa, then, succeeded only in areas where the colonial oppressor had been severely weakened by other factors; the war did play an important, but not decisive, role in the process. The African success certainly emboldened revolutionary armed struggle across the globe. But the jewel in the crown of anticolonial armed struggle came in 1975, with the conclusion of the revolutionary wars in Southeast Asia (Vietnam, Laos, and Cambodia) against a considerable adversary, the United States. "Vietnam" and the national liberation armed struggle promoted at the Tricontinental encouraged revolutionary movements in South and Central America to confront the tyranny of their domestic elites and U.S. sponsors with the gun; Colombia, El Salvador, Guatemala, Nicaragua, Peru, and Uruguay, among others, held the torch for the armed path into the 1980s and beyond.[27]

A decade after the Tricontinental, in 1979, NAM convened in Havana for its Sixth Summit. Armed struggle had become less significant for the agenda of the Third World, with the victory of Vietnam over the United States and the defeat of the Portuguese in Africa. The Cubans had been active with their support in Africa, mainly for the anti-Portuguese struggles, but also in the Horn of Africa, and this continued despite the discomfiture of some states expressed at the 1978 meeting of the Organization of African Unity at Khartoum. The Chinese shift from militant confrontation with the United States to outright collaboration on foreign policy had also dulled the edge of international Maoism, not to speak of the military defeats faced by Maoists in India and elsewhere. Ninety-three countries attended the conference, where they heard the elder politician of the Third World, Tanzania's Julius Nyerere, offer a reminder that whereas NAM was "a progressive movement, it was not a movement of progressive states." In other words, the various NAM countries had their own agendas, their own sense of historical change, and their own strategies for social transformation. The internal development of these countries had something to do with the overall dynamic of NAM, but NAM's own agenda could not be reduced to that of its constituent states.[28] Nyerere called for the large tent approach to the Third World, to be less ideological at the gate, even as the meetings themselves could be a place to push each other to sharper positions. Better to hold discussions around concrete policy positions or else political programs than to oust people based on their insufficient revolutionary rhetoric. And Nyerere should know, being the leader of a movement that was not only eclectic but also innovative. Whatever the limitations of the Tanzanian struggle, and I'll go into that in the next chapter, few would deny its inventiveness.

Between the 1950s and the 1970s, the Third World formed a unique political force outside the atomic face-off between the United States–United Kingdom–France and the USSR. Filled with tactical and strategic disagreements on how to deal with colonialism and imperialism, the Third

World nonetheless had a core political program around the value of disarmament, national sovereignty, economic integrity, and cultural diversity.

At each meeting, the leaders and representatives of the Third World laid out theses for their struggles, but there was one thesis that rarely came up for discussion. At the Tricontinental, Cabral raised the notion, but could not get the delegates to address it at length. Cabral would have been the one to raise this point, having told his party cadre in 1965, "Hide nothing from the masses of our people. Tell no lies. Expose lies whenever they are told. Mask no difficulties, mistakes, failures. Claim no easy victories."[29] In Havana, Cabral said, "One form of struggle which we consider to be fundamental has not been explicitly mentioned in this program, although we are certain that it was present in the minds of those who drew up the program. We refer here to *the struggle against our own weaknesses*. . . . This battle is the expression of the internal contradictions in the economic, social, cultural (and therefore historical) reality of each of our countries. We are convinced that any national or social revolution which is not based on knowledge of this fundamental reality runs grave risk of being condemned to failure."[30] The Third World had immense internal weaknesses, which, Cabral apart, would not be addressed at the gatherings from Brussels to Havana. These weaknesses corroded the imagined community of the Third World, and eventually participated in the decimation of its agenda.

Who would have thought that by the mid-twentieth century the darker nations would gather in Cuba, once the playground of the plutocracy, to celebrate their will to struggle and their will to win? What an audacious thought: that those who had been fated to labor without want, now wanted to labor in their own image! By Havana, all the powers of the old empire had entered into a holy alliance to demolish the virus of anticolonial Third World nationalism; while John Bull and the Gaullists trembled at their fate in a world dominated by those they had once ruled, Uncle Sam lent his shoulders and wiles to keep things as close to the past as possible. On the other side of the Iron Curtain, the heirs of Uncle Joe saw promise in the movements of the Third World, and even while they offered assistance to them, they did so with every attempt to steer the ship of history, rather than to share the rudder. Direction was anathema to the darker nations, which had been told what to do for far too long. Time now to deliver oneself to the future.

For all the exhilaration, however, the constraints on the new nations were enormous. They began their independence period with immense fiscal burdens, even though they possessed considerable raw materials and other physical resources. Although they had populations with experience in all aspects of social life, the colonial educational systems had deprived them of scientific and technological talent (which they had to cultivate within a generation). Whereas the cultural worlds of the postcolonial nations had vast resources for the soul and spirit of people, the colonial matrix of inferiority and cultural division had a marked influence. Finally, that the leaders of the new Third World had to answer to entrenched old social classes meant that the horizon of social change was circumscribed. Cabral's "weakness" is in this, if not so much more, and it is to this weakness that I now turn.

Part 2
PITFALLS

ALGIERS

In July 1962, the Algerians evicted the French. The FLN came to power, and one of its founders, Ahmed Ben Bella, became the nation's president.

Ben Bella's road to power was not easy. Born on a modest farm in a small town on the Moroccan border, Ben Bella had an uneventful childhood. He joined the French army, fought valiantly in World War II (for which he was commended personally by General Charles de Gaulle), and returned to Algeria. On May 8, 1945, Armistice Day in Europe, the French forces massacred several thousand people who had gathered for a peaceful demonstration in the town of Sétif. This massacre drove Ben Bella into politics. After an attempt in the narrow electoral sphere, he took the armed road. Enthused by the nationalism of Messali Hadj (who had been at the 1927 Brussels meetings), Ben Bella joined Hadj's Mouvement pour le Triomphe des Libertés Démocratiques (MTLD). But impatient with its moderate tone, Ben Bella created the Organisation Spéciale, the armed wing of the MTLD. A few hasty actions led to Ben Bella's imprisonment. When he was released, he joined eight other hardened revolutionaries (at the average age of thirty-two) to create the FLN. None of the nine main leaders came from either wealth or extreme poverty, being mainly sons of artisans or from the middle class. Some were Arabs, others Kabyle (Berber). In 1954, as they met to discuss strategy, they heard that the French army had been defeated in Dien Bien Phu (Indo-China). This encouraged them, and on November 1, 1954, they called out their underground army to revolt. This was the opening salvo in the Algerian War of Independence.

Oran, Algeria, January 1964: The Revolution Is for the People—Algiers takes to the streets to defend President Ahmed Ben Bella. © BETTMANN/CORBIS

Armed action has the tendency to reduce ambiguity. There is no space for complex positions, because a war of liberation can have only two sides on a battlefield. Three months after the initial assault, colonial officials across Algeria noted a change in the popular mood and the emergence of a newly confident conversation about independence.[1]

The FLN's gambit succeeded politically, even if the military cost was enormous. During the course of the war, from 1954 to 1962, between three hundred thousand and a million people lost their lives. It was a heavy price to pay. All the factions within Algeria, even the liberals, lined up behind the FLN. They wanted freedom from French autocracy, and they were willing to subordinate themselves to the FLN and its military wing in order to get the French out. The factionalism within the Algerian liberation struggle was momentarily suspended. The FLN was a front, not a party, and it invited all Algerians to join. The Communist Party joined in 1955, as did the moderate liberals led by Ferhat Abbas. Abbas, who tried to ameliorate the FLN's armed line, told an interviewer, "My role, today, is to stand aside for the chiefs of the armed resistance. The methods that I have upheld for the last fifteen years—cooperation, discussion, persuasion—have shown themselves to be ineffective; this I recognize."[2] The FLN would brook no neutrality.[3]

The French responded brutally, and created the conditions for all forces to join the FLN. When the war entered the city of Algiers in October 1956, the trade union federation galvanized support for the militants of the Casbah, as did the previously vacillating Communist Party of Algeria. Included among these forces was a young doctor named Frantz Fanon. Born on the Caribbean island of Martinique, Fanon trained as a psychiatrist in France and went to work in an Algerian hospital. Already political, he now threw in his sympathies with the FLN. Before he left for Algeria, he published *Black Skin, White Masks* (1952), a searing diagnosis of racism's effect on the person of color. The book earned Fanon a place in the planetary discussion of racism and anticolonialism—for instance, at the 1956 *Présence Africaine* conference on black culture held in Paris. Fanon kept in touch with these currents while he worked as the head of psychiatry at Blida-Joinville Hospital in Algeria starting in 1953. Faced with the bodies of the victims of French colonialism, notably those who had been tortured, Fanon resigned from the hospital in 1956. "If psychiatry is the medical technique that aims to enable man no longer to be a stranger to his environment," Fanon wrote, "I owe it to myself to affirm that the Arab, permanently an alien in his own country, lives in a state of absolute depersonalization. The events in Algeria are the logical consequence of an abortive attempt to decerebralize a people."[4] Fanon documented the atrocities for the French media and the FLN's own *El Moudjahid*. Fanon's most influential book, *The Wretched of the Earth* (1961), came out just as he died. He was thirty-six.

The Wretched of the Earth is a collection of essays written by Fanon over the course of ten months (one of them was an address to the 1959 Second Congress of Black Artists and Writers in Rome). Already diagnosed with a fatal illness, Fanon dictated the book to his wife in haste; it was plagued with generalities and ill formulations, a lack of research as well as conceptual clarity. Nevertheless, it is filled with insights and fiery analysis. Sartre's preface sharpened the edges of an already-sharp set of arguments, and Sartre's comment that in Fanon's book "the Third World finds *itself* and speaks to *itself* through his voice," gave the document a magnified importance.[5] Fanon defended the right of national liberation movements to adopt armed struggle, as the movements would do at Havana's 1966 Tricontinental. His defense, however, was not on tactical or even strategic grounds; he maintained that violence is necessary to wrench a colonized society into freedom and reshape the subservience of the colonized so that they might truly be freed by the act of *taking* their freedom. This section, the first two chapters, has come to define Fanon's book. While it is no doubt of immense significance, it should not overshadow Fanon's chapter on the limitations of the national liberation project once it takes state power.

That chapter, "The Pitfalls of National Consciousness," was written before the FLN's victory. It was a cautionary note to Fanon's comrades. The disciplinary imperatives of an armed struggle, and the need to create a simple ideological and military battlefield, might leak into state construction and distort the egalitarian dynamic of national liberation. The Algerian people recognized that nothing could go forward without an energetic citizenry, and indeed in the areas under FLN control this self-management and collective planning had begun to manifest themselves. "In every *wilaya* [FLN district]," Fanon had written earlier, "cadastral plans are drawn up, school building plans studied, economic reconversions pursued."[6] Freedom would come in the combination of the spontaneous energy of the people and the disciplined channels of the government. A woman who fought hard in the struggle noted that the FLN already had a superior organization, and that the "enormous apparatus that our leaders have rapidly set up rests on solid and proven foundations such as the confidence, devotion, participation and even heroism of our civilian population." She looked forward to the opportunity for Algerian women as well as men to "take part in the rebuilding of our country."[7] But the FLN failed the legions of anticolonial supporters who wanted a role in the creation of a new Algeria. The FLN's charter did not fully support the energy of the people; it was keener to demobilize this enthusiasm. The Third World "nation" did not fully live up to its promise of radical democracy, where every person would be constituted by the state as a citizen, and where each citizen in turn would act through the state to construct a national society, economy, and culture. From India to Egypt, from Ghana to Indonesia—the great legions of the Third World drew their immense strength from popular mobilization, but none of these states enabled the people who created the platform for freedom to have an equal part in the project to build it. Of course, the construction of the new nation would require the labor of the people, but this work came with direction from above, and not with the co-equal participation of the people in the creation of the national plan or the division of the national surplus. The people had to act, not to lead but to take orders, and the state, the father figure, would protect its feminized subjects.[8]

The great flaws in the national liberation project came from the assumption that political power could be centralized in the state, that the national liberation party should dominate the state, and that the people could be *demobilized* after their contribution to the liberation struggle. National liberation movements like the FLN divided the movement into two categories: the people and the party, and it was the latter that would conduct the work for the former. There was little class analysis, and little acknowledgment that there would be classes antagonistic to the project of the Third World. The party of the working people, not simply the people, would need to create democratic structures not only to socialize production (which they attempted) but also to socialize decision making. Without the latter, the state would be vulnerable to the counterrevolution of the old social classes of property and the disgruntlement of those in whose name it ruled. Fanon identified this problem before the FLN came to power, and his insights help us navigate through one of the principle failures of the Third World project: the lack of effective socialized democracy.[9]

A hint of the problem came within months of the FLN capture of power. From July to September 1962, the FLN members fought among themselves. The people cried, *Baraket*, that's enough, but it was only when Colonel Houari Boumédienne entered Algiers and handed the reins of power to Ben Bella that the guns went quiet. Ben Bella centralized power. The 1963 Constitution of Algeria abolished all political parties except the FLN, and elevated the president of the FLN to the sole formulator of state policy. The energy of the Algerian Revolution would now be concentrated in the body of the president, who for the moment was Ben Bella. The 1964 Charter of Algiers defended the abolishment of parties other than the FLN. "The multiparty system allows all particular interests to organize into different pressure groups. It frustrates the general interest, that is, the workers' interest," and therefore, in the workers' name, there should only be one party, the "vanguard party."[10] In November 1962, the regime cracked down on the Communist Party of Algeria, which was otherwise in line with the socialist agenda of the FLN, and it soon went after the Parti de la Revolution Socialiste, headed by the former FLN leader Mohammed Boudiaf; the leadership of both parties languished in jail. The FLN whittled its own ranks to a hundred thousand "militants" who would "be the best what-ever they happen to be," said Ben Bella. "By 'best' I mean he who is the most dynamic, who has the greatest loyalty, who sets an example, who somehow has no other interest than the party."[11] When Ferhat Abbas was expelled from the FLN in 1963 after he objected to the lack of dis-cussion over the framing of the constitution, he told the parliament, "For me the Party [FLN] does not exist! The Party does not exist, and there are no other FLN militants than those in this Assembly, in the ad-ministration, in the army. The day when a party is democratically con-stituted, I will applaud with both hands."[12]

Since the constitution had already endowed the president with unac-countable powers, the power of the party essentially rested with its head, the president. The "loyalty" of the militants would then vest not simply with the party but with the president. There was no separation of powers, no oversight of the president from either the judiciary or the parliament, and little need to answer to anyone for appointments to the bureaucracy.[13] The president could rule by fiat, a structure that wel-comed a coup d'état because this alone could change the reins of gov-ernment in a society that had been substantially depoliticized. The question was not personal, because most scholars and FLN veterans agree that Ben Bella's character was not particularly given to the "cult of personality," nor was he ideologically predisposed to it.[14] When Ben Bella had Boudiaf arrested, one of his close FLN comrades, Hocine Ait Ahmed, led a protest in the National Assembly. While he agreed with the goals of the revolution, Ait Ahmed said, he felt that Ben Bella's state had reduced the nation to the "politics of *ʒaims* [clans]," or to the level of the old social classes. Little in the institutional framework of society had been altered, so Ait Ahmed went back to the Kabyle hills to lead an insurrection against the state. It should be said, however, that Ait Ahmed was himself unclear as to the relationship between the state and the party, and the state and the people. He sometimes called for a "revo-lutionary avant-garde party" and sometimes for a "multi-party sys-tem."[15] The problem had been identified (political centralization), but people like Ait Ahmed knew full well the power of imperialism to insin-uate itself into a weak civil society. This contradiction, rather than any diabolical intent, was often what led many Third World states into the reproduction of authoritarian state structures.

Ben Bella and the FLN centralized political power in order to social-ize production. That was the choice made by this regime and many other Third World states that leaned toward socialism. The FLN had to act rapidly, because the society it had inherited from the French had been devastated.[16] The seven-and-a-half-year war and the long period of colonial rule (1830–1962) had drained Algerian society. The FLN inherited the desiccated earth, still rich in nutrients and ability, but on the surface in ruins. Algeria's wealth had been siphoned off by the First World, and little remained. Few factories, few schools, and few hospitals—the emblems of modernity had been built around the colonial maintenance of "tradition." In this realm of necessity, the Third World had to craft its hopes. Of the twelve million Algerians, four and a half million lived in poverty, and two million had been locked in concentration camps, from which they went to abandoned herds and overgrown lands. As the French departed, so did the main bureaucratic staff, which meant that the state momentarily collapsed. The FLN had to rapidly take charge of the situation, create institutions that functioned, and help settle the massive dislocation that resulted from both colonialism and the anticolonial struggle. The task was not easy.

In March 1963, Ben Bella's government promulgated a set of laws known as the March Decrees. These had been created in consultation with a group of European and Arab Trotskyites (including the Egyptian Luftallah Solliman, the Moroccan Mohammed Tahiri, and the Algerian Mohammed Harbi) who favored worker self-management. The decrees declared any vacant property to be legitimate collective property, legalized worker self-management on farms and in factories, and forbade speculation. The workers had already seized the vacant factories, and the peasantry had already grabbed three million hectares of prime land left by the French colon farmers. The new government institutionalized the inventiveness of the workers and the farmers. So far so good, but then the state made some errors. Whereas it had written no role for the state in these new institutions, it also tried to cut out the main trade union federation, the two-hundred-thousand-strong Union Générale des Travailleurs Algériens (UGTA) that had led the factory takeover. Ben Bella wanted the UGTA to be "autonomous within the party," rather than an autonomous union, particularly because the FLN and the state were not yet strong enough to take on the UGTA politically.[17] The architects of the self-management schemes had good ideas, but they were not the ones to execute and oversee the self-management (*autogestion*) project. Ben Bella nominated his old comrade from the MTLD days, Ali Mahsas, to be the minister of agrarian reform. Mahsas was not an advocate of autogestion; he wanted the schemes to be under state control. In April 1963, Ben Bella's government announced another set of decrees that forced the farms to take credit from a state agency and market their products through that same agency. By January 1964, the factories had been placed under the control of the Ministry of National Economy.[18] The 1964 Charter of the Algerian Revolution adopted the contradictions: it hailed the need to nationalize the means of production, and argued that anything less than worker self-management was "bureaucratic formalism."[19]

The intellectuals who planned the autogestion scheme had not entirely considered the lack of political education. The FLN produced a major social change during the war, but it did not capitalize on it in peacetime. The attempt by the political commissars to subordinate all the independent institutions (such as the trade unions and all the political parties) into the state, and use the state as the institutional arm of the party, suffocated any attempt for social transformation. The Algerian peasantry was mobilized into the war, and suspended its various clan and ethnic divides in the service of the revolution. When it was demobilized, the opportunity for on-the-job political education needed for the creation of a new society lapsed. The peasants, observed a sympathetic book on the FLN, "have not proven as revolutionary as they were during the war of independence. They have not agitated to obtain an agrarian reform or to force the government to give more attention to their problems." Rather, the peasantry went back to their villages and into the social worlds from which they came. "The number of new mosques is just one indication that the peasants, after the interlude of the war, have returned to their old ways and values. . . . In the absence of any leadership from the party or the government, the peasants have fallen once again under the influence of the traditional authorities—*marabouts* [holy men], *imams* [Islamic prelates], and village chiefs and elders."[20] This was a major consequence of the lack of socialized democracy.[21] Groups like *al-Qiyam* (values), led by Hashemi Tidjani, would work on this terrain to create the social basis for the Islamic explosion that occurred in the 1980s.[22]

French rule did not create a sizable class of Algerians with developed technical expertise. Those who had joined the colonial state were not to be trusted by the FLN. And the FLN itself did not have sufficiently trained people to take over the management of complicated technical institutions. A lack of such personnel meant that the FLN relied on those among the petty bourgeoisie and bourgeoisie who did not flee to France in 1962. A census from April 1963 showed that French nationals and Algerians of the French colonial period held 43 percent of the planning and decision-making posts, whereas they held 77 percent of managerial posts.[23] In 1959, the state hired 63,000 civil servants, whereas by 1964 the state had 100,000 on its books.[24] The treasury leaked into the civil servant salaries: 2.9 billion dinars went to pay their salaries, while only 2.4 billion dinars went to economic development.[25] The state apparatus bloated, as did that of the military, and these became the primary source of demand in the Algerian economy (as the state nationalized more and more sections of the economy, this role intensified). The central role of the state and the insinuation of the bourgeoisie into its ranks led to the creation of a parasitic relation between the state and the bourgeoisie. The intimacy between the state and this dominant class (and in Algeria, certainly clans more than others) allowed the Central Bank and the Customs Office immense latitude. Their independence shows that whereas the national liberation state was able to clamp down on democracy for the working class and the peasantry, and speak in its name, it allowed the bourgeoisie and its institutions to have relative autonomy.

The national bourgeoisie did not capture the national liberation party, the FLN in this case, or even the new state. In the anticolonialist struggle, the party adopted the patina of being above class and standing for all the people. Because of this role, it attracted the working class and the peasantry as well as the class that worked in a bureaucratic capacity for the state, in addition to some elements of the mercantile and industrial class. Apart from some exceptions (such as India), the merchants and petty industrialists were not autonomous from the state; indeed they relied on it—either for government contracts, through licenses to operate their concerns, or else by the space created for them through the national state's tariff regime. National liberation parties that came to power without a well-honed class analysis opened themselves up to pressure from the newly confident mercantile and industrial classes, whose own position was greatly enhanced by the national liberation agenda for the domestic creation of industry, for the creation of a national economy. Although the national liberation party remained largely beholden to the bureaucratic-managerial-intellectual (sometimes military) elite, it did build close ties to the industrial class.[26] Import-substitution-type projects opened some space for institutional reform and social development projects, but in most cases they simply protected domestic industrialists who had no long-term commitment to the Third World agenda.

Some of the national liberation states, such as Algeria, pledged to follow a fairly radical social agenda—for land reform, and self-management in factories. The list of the reforms, however, is less important than the *character of governance*: would the state devolve power to the people, would it mobilize them into the acts of the state, or else would it demobilize the national liberation movement and promise to create change bureaucratically? If the latter, then the state would dictate to the people, who had dreamed while in the struggle of being partners in the national construction. When the national liberation state adopted "development" in a bureaucratic manner, it tended to mimic the approach of international agencies like the World Bank rather than the aspirations and hopes of the people who had empowered the new state in the first place. There was little discussion about how to bring the views of the peasantry, of men and women, of the outcast peoples, to the center of the national debate on priorities, nor about how to address differentials in relations of power between men and women, urban and rural folk, literate and illiterate people. The national liberation project had a tendency toward a naturalistic analysis of political rights: that if colonial power is removed, if the state is controlled by the national liberation forces, if these forces produce a decent economic model, then the people will be free.[27] The 1964 Charter of the Algerian Revolution anticipated this problem, as it warned the nation about the one-party direction. A single-party system could "lead to a petit-bourgeois dictatorship, or to the formation of a bureaucratic class that uses the state apparatus as an instrument to satisfy its personal interests, or finally to a regime of personal dictatorship that reduces the party to a simple political police." If during the period of armed struggle, the charter continued, it was acceptable to think of political unity, this "must be reconsidered in light of the objectives and perspectives of the socialist revolution. Such a union is now outdated."[28] Of course it was not revisited.

Algeria followed a tradition already established and defended in large parts of postcolonial Africa, whether ruled by governments of the "Right" or the "Left"—in Guinea (1958), Congo (1960), Ivory Coast (1961), Tanzania (1963), Malawi (1963), and Kenya (1964). The defenders of the "one-party state" argued that rival parties "have generally little interest for the great majority of the people." The idea of "national politics" is central to the national liberation view of the one-party state. To break the polity into factions would obviate the idea that the freedom struggle had united the people with one interest, to create a nation against imperialism. Classes and social divisions could not be allowed to disrupt the "fundamental unity of the nation." To allow rival parties might enable "a handful of individuals" to "put our nation in jeopardy, and reduce to ashes the effort of the millions."[29] To allow dissent might, in addition, open the door to influence by imperial forces, which will adopt proxies within the country to destabilize it. The one-party vision is one of fear of the people, fear that any devolution of power would lead to antinational activity or would cause fundamental dissension where there should be an assumed unity. Many national liberation politicians, having grown up with the belief that their party represented the entire population, denied the different and often mutually exclusive interests that rent the social fabric. Both the industrialists and the workers benefited from high tariffs to prevent the collapse of a domestic factory, but both did not benefit equally; the workers had to labor under a regime of exploitation that remained in place regardless of the tariff. When the national liberation movement sent its people home, it lost its immense power base. A state that acted bureaucratically on a population had a built-in tendency to rely on congealed, traditional sources of social power and control. Older forms of association returned to the fore, such as tribal and class loyalties. These power bases became indispensable for elections or the implementation of the state's development agenda. The national liberation state that came into being as the instrument of popular power now turned to the very agents who had often not supported it to enact its policies.

The problem of bureaucratization and the single party was a major topic of debate in Vietnam just as the Algerians won their freedom. At the 1961 Second Congress of the Vietnam Workers' Party, Ho Chi Minh warned his party and nation about the tendency toward bureaucratization and commandism, for the bureaucratic attitude "shows in fondness for red tape, divorce from the masses of the people and reluctance to learn the experiences of the masses," while commandism did not allow the people to "work on their own initiative and own accord and to use compulsion to do unexplained tasks."[30] In the darker nations, among Communists outside the pale, there is an extended literature based on the practical experience of what the Vietnamese called "collective mastery" ("*lam chu tap the*"). Che's lyrical essays on volunteerism and Communist morality come from and engendered the "work councils" (*consejos de trabajo*) that continue to be a feature of Cuban social life. Cabral's speeches on the duty of the Communist address the problem. Within a year of Guinea-Bissau's freedom from Portuguese rule, Cabral's government invited the renowned Brazilian educator Paolo Freire to visit the country, study its educational system, and provide assistance on a popular pedagogy for the creation of a nonbureaucratic society.[31] This was in the context of a country battered and devastated by war, and yet in search of the principle for a popular state. The resilience of the population strengthened the demand that the party not resort to commandism and bureaucratism but that it gradually create the mechanism for popular governance.[32] To set the task was one thing, but to be able to overcome the problem of technical skill and class hierarchy was another.

Because the national liberation state fails the population, Fanon wrote in 1961, "the masses [begin] to sulk; they turn away from this nation in which they have been given no place and begin to lose interest in it."[33] In Algeria, by contrast, some sections of the masses turned their ire against the regime. Ahmed Ait's Front of Socialist Forces attempted to assassinate Ben Bella on May 31, 1964. In June 1964 the UGTA, the main trade union, began to assert itself. Union workers struck on behalf of nationalization and against their limited role in statecraft. Strikes across the industrial spectrum paralyzed the country. The maneuvers by the workers and the newly militant UGTA as well as the onset of despondency among the people led Ben Bella and his core in the FLN to attempt a course correction. Ben Bella reached out to the UGTA at its Second Congress in March 1965; later, he patched up his relations with the Algerian Communists. The UGTA was entirely revitalized, and it was poised to play a major, democratizing role in Algerian society. Alongside it stood the Union Nationale des Femmes Algériennes, whose March 8 International Women's Day rally in 1965 drew ten thousand women, and the Jeunesse du Front du Libération Nationale, which had reached its peak of fifty thousand members after it began to organize in April 1964.[34] Ben Bella's autocratic interregnum seemed to be on the wane, as the social democratization implicit in the national liberation experiment seemed to be on the horizon. And then the army moved.

Houari Boumédienne, whose command over the army had given the presidency to Ben Bella in the first place, now revoked his trust. On June 19, 1965, just as Ben Bella received the Lenin Prize, the officers of the Algerian military broke into his house and placed him under arrest. Boumédienne took charge of the state, and the military became the main pillar of the regime. Although Boumédienne argued that he had taken power in reaction to Ben Bella's cult of personality, the reason that best explains this coup is the rapprochement between Ben Bella and the organized Left. The tendency toward socialized democracy went against the grain of the carefully wrought fabric of the Third World state. Boumédienne understood that Third World socialism, unlike Communism, could not afford to alienate the national bourgeoisie and the army. His liberation army that entered Algiers in 1962 was no longer in place in 1965. In the interim, it had absorbed the officer corps of the French Algerian army and had taken on the character of the national bourgeoisie. This new officer element had a strong influence in the events around the ejection of Ben Bella.[35]

Boumédienne continued most of the broad economic policies of the Ben Bella era: the nationalization of industry (particularly the oil sector, now consolidated into SONATRACH). Autogestion was entirely absorbed into the state structure, and industry earned priority over agriculture.[36] The military played a larger role in society, which meant that it also had a greater claim on the budget. This was all financed in the main by Algeria's substantial oil and natural gas reserves. These helped maintain a healthy treasury while oil and gas prices remained high. The state dominated society and ruled in the name of socialism. The class that dominated this state, however, as had been warned in the 1964 Charter, was the parasitic bourgeoisie (and its ancillary sector in the military). Boumédienne had a vision of a "solicitous" state that tended to the needs of a respectful and quiescent population. The state must extend its authority throughout society, Boumédienne believed, just as "the vascular system carries and breathes life into [the human body's] distant extremities." The regime's enemies were like "intruders who have penetrated the body of the revolution." They were an "excrescence," a "gangrene" that needed to be excised.[37] Boumédienne, therefore, cracked down on the Left, particularly the UGTA, which largely vanished, and the Communist Party.[38] In a sense, Boumédienne's was closer to the type of approach followed by most Third World states than that of Ben Bella.

Boumédienne's personality did not allow for aggrandizement, but he did adorn the state with the emblems of the freedom struggle. A cult of personality grew around the War of Independence and the FLN. The failed national liberation project, Fanon warned, asks "the people to fall back into the past, and to become drunk on the remembrance of the epoch which led up to independence."[39] Nostalgia is one means to prevent the total alienation of the population from the state. Nationalism is reduced to "grandiose buildings in the capital," marches and processions, immense statues to the leaders, and other such decorations to celebrate a struggle that is unfinished in the eyes of the population. If the European and North American states had a cenotaph in a strategic place to honor the unknown soldiers who died to protect the liberties of the republics, the anticolonial Third World states frequently honored the sacrifice of the untold millions in the struggle for liberation. Murals of the unnamed people, though, came in the context of large portraits and statues of the leaders of the national liberation parties. The leaders who stood in for the movements closely held the political capital from the liberation struggle. Failures by the leadership did not immediately lead to disillusion because, for all else, the popular association of these leaders with the audacity of national liberation allowed them a great deal of latitude. Nostalgia, then, had a political purpose, and it was not simply the wistful hope of a blind leadership or the naive hope of a betrayed population.

The character who promotes nostalgia, often the only one who can do so, is the hero of the national liberation struggle who has become the head of state. This leader "stands for moral power," the power of the struggle, but in doing so in the context of the betrayal of that struggle, "the leader pacifies the people."[40] Since this leader is now the fig leaf before the naked extractions conducted by the emergent wealthy, he becomes "the general president of that company of profiteers impatient for their return which constitutes the national bourgeoisie."[41] By the late 1960s, Algeria had moved from an attempt to create a socialist state to a state capitalist one, with a parasitic bourgeoisie confident beside the strong arms of the military.

If Ben Bella had confronted the army earlier, his regime might have lasted for less time. In the interim, the Algerian government did promote a considerable socialist agenda, some of which had to be followed by the military government of Boumédienne. Algeria continued to be a player in NAM, mainly because its own foreign policy kept it outside any arrangement with the United States and the USSR. In 1973, Algeria hosted the Fourth Non-Aligned Summit, the largest until then. At the summit, Boumédienne called for the construction of a New International Economic Order (NIEO). He argued that non-alignment must be given a new meaning, where economic liberation must be paramount and political questions should be secondary. Political rights within a nation can be subsumed as long as the rulers had an economic agenda that confronted capitalism. This view found few detractors, mainly because by the time of the summit in Algiers a number of Third World leaders arrived either in military fatigues or with military designations before their names. Without an insistence on popular mobilization, the state form adopted by the Third World could be best governed by the military. From the coup until the eventual demise of the oil-dependent growth, the military dominated the country (after Boumédienne's death, another soldier, Chadli Bendjedid, held office until 1992).

The demobilization of the population led almost inexorably within the Third World to military coups and military rule. Where the military did not overthrow the civilian government, the inability of states to break from colonial borders and other such dilemmas led to a strengthened military brass. More money to guns meant less to butter, and therefore to an impoverished agenda for the increase of the social wage, the improvement of agricultural and other social relations, and better prices for exported commodities. The main social agency that demanded this agenda within the constraints of the Third World regime remained the Communists, and it was the strengthened hand of the military that often exorcised the Left (helped out by the CIA and given a blind eye by the USSR). The broader story of these tragedies occupies us in this part, as we make our way from the military coup in La Paz, Bolivia, to the massacre of the Communists of the Indonesian archipelago, to the border war between India and China, and eventually to the reduction of the Third World's political and economic agenda into OPEC and the *ujamaa* villages of Tanzania. Neocolonial imperialism persisted, and the countries of the Third World remained in thrall to economic and political logics that disinherited most of them. The people wanted the formal trappings of freedom rather than flag independence (the Tanzanians called it *uhuru wa bendera*). They had to settle for mild reforms and nostalgia. Or else be "disappeared."

LA PAZ

In May 1963, at a conference of air force chiefs from throughout the Americas, a U.S. official rose to toast the Bolivian government: "Bolivian officials and military officers showed me priorities and necessities in the country immediately upon my arrival. Their intent is good and to be lauded. I believe that there is now greater awareness, greater acknowl-edgement, of the very important constructive role that is being played by the military in the development of Bolivia as well as the very great impor-tance they are playing in the control of subversive elements." Teodoro Moscono, the coordinator of the Alliance for Progress, the Kennedy ad-ministration's anticommunist regional umbrella, received hosannas in re-turn from General René Barrientos, a career Bolivian air force officer who had a close relationship with the U.S. military (as air attaché to the United States in the 1950s). Barrientos assured the U.S. military that Bolivia would work "under the Alliance for Progress and its civic action program to help secure internal stability and combat communism."[1]

The oddest thing about this interaction is that Barrientos officially represented the government of the Movimiento Nacionalista Revolu-cionario (MNR), the left revolutionary party that had been in power since its successful armed rebellion of 1952. What was a left-wing na-tionalist government doing in such proximity to the U.S. government at a time when the latter had pledged itself to the erasure of Communism in the world and the former had adopted a platform that was Communist but for the hammer and sickle?

Since the early Spanish invasion of South America until the present, the small country of Bolivia has been important to Europe. In the Spanish period, Bolivia operated as Europe's treasury. The Spanish captured the four-thousand-meter mountain of Potosí, and mined it for what seemed like its inexhaustible reserve of silver. Five hundred and fifty-seven concessions went out on the ninety-four veins of silver that the Spaniards uncovered. The rush of silver into Europe created the "price revolution of the 16th century."[2] By the mid-nineteenth century, the silver mines had been displaced in importance by the tin mines. A Bolivian, Simón Ituri Patiño became the "tin king," cultivated a tin oligarchy (La Rosca, or the Screw), moved to Europe, and governed the country through his representatives and the gun. The tin extracted from Patiño's mines left Bolivia for Liverpool, England, to be smelted in a facility substantially owned by Patiño, who profited enormously from start to finish.[3] Tin miners had little political role in a hundred years of "independent" Bolivia.[4]

In 1951, the decade-old MNR won a key election, but given that it directly threatened the power of La Rosca and its class allies, the military stepped in and revoked the election. A year later, the MNR returned to power in a popular coup, where the militias of the campesinos and tin miners overwhelmed the military and took charge of the country. The MNR's leader Víctor Paz Estenssoro became president and immediately put in place substantial reforms on behalf of the party's base, and therefore the majority of the population. Three months after it came to power, the MNR opened the suffrage to everyone, both men and women, literates and illiterates. Only 6.6 percent of the population (205,000) voted in the 1951 election, but by the time of the 1956 election more than 30 percent of the population (1,127,000) registered to exercise their newly won franchise. Even if women in the MNR could not break the back of Bolivian patriarchy, their organizations, the María Barzola Movement and the Comandos Femeninas, won a substantial victory for women with the franchise, far ahead of Brazil, Chile, Mexico, and Peru.[5] The franchise reform had effects long after the revolution of 1952's economic reforms had faded, and even during the military dictatorship from 1964 (considered even more illegitimate because people had once had the vote).

The two most substantial economic reforms were the nationalization of the tin mines and the land reforms. The MNR regime owed its power to the two social classes that worked these sectors: the miners and the campesinos. In October 1952, President Paz traveled to Siglo XX, the mine where the most militant workers of the Federacion Sindical de Trabajadores Mineros de Bolivia worked, to announce the nationalization of the tin resources. The move had a symbolic effect because Bolivia now seemed to reclaim its resources; the fact is that the quality of the tin had already begun to decline during the 1940s, no new source of tin had been found since 1927, and the Bolivian economy still had to export "raw" tin to be processed elsewhere. The nationalization alone showed that the MNR had the interests of the Bolivian people at heart, but it was an insufficient maneuver against the overwhelming dominance of external capital over the fate of the miners.

The second reform came in 1953, when the MNR conducted fairly extensive land redistribution on behalf of the landless labor, the campesinos. The 6 percent of the landowners who owned more than a thousand hectares, the hacendados, controlled 92 percent of the land, and they had not more than 1.5 percent of that land under cultivation.[6] This landed elite relied on brute force to get the mainly Amerindian labor to work. The MNR's Decree of Land Reform (August 3, 1953) confiscated large parts of the latifundias and transferred these to the *comunidades* (peasant communities) to be worked by the peasantry, who were mainly Amerindian. The best lands, the lands with the most capital-intensive agriculture, did not come into the communal pool, and therefore what the *comunidades* got was often substandard. Part of this occurred because the revolutionary regime did not incorporate the experienced leaders of the campesino, many of whom had been crucial not only to the revolution but also to the ferment in agricultural areas since the mid-1940s.[7]

Despite the drawbacks of the revolution, Bolivia in the early 1950s was in the same sort of social ferment as Algeria a decade later. For a few years, Bolivia trod a path unfamiliar to most Third World states, which is why it is especially important for consideration here. From 1952 until the late 1950s, the MNR attempted to dismantle the military and hand over the power of the gun to the militias of the campesinos, the tin miners, and the MNR's own *grupos de honor*. Its 1951 experience with the military led the MNR to shut down the Colegio Militar, dismiss a fifth of the officer corps, drastically cut the expenditure for the army (from 22 percent in 1952 to 7 percent in 1957), and even consider the complete elimination of the armed forces.[8] The lack of a central authority in Bolivia, or else the effective devolution of power to the people's organizations, led the U.S. State Department to note in 1957 that "the whole complex of lawlessness, combined with the government's apparent unwillingness or inability to control it, added up to a considerable degree of anarchy in the country."[9] The "anarchy" for the United States was popular democracy for the Bolivians.

The U.S. government did not intervene in Bolivia as it did with such ferocity in Guatemala, when its president, Jacobo Arbenz Guzmán, attempted to give a socialist shape to the relationship between the state and society.[10] The difference between Guatemala and Bolivia is perhaps in the role that U.S. firms played in the economy of each country. In Guatemala, the United Fruit Company owned vast tracts of land, and operated this land as an immense agricultural factory. The Arbenz government's land reform directly threatened United Fruit's holdings. In Bolivia, the U.S. firms did not own the tin mines. Since 1946, the U.S. firms bought half of Bolivia's tin, and a "swarm" of experts descended on the country that quickly became one large tin mine in the eyes of the U.S. government, which saw its Bolivian counterpart as a tin-pot government.[11] Bolivia's tin would come to the United States regardless of who owned the mines, although a genuinely socialized and nationalist structure might try to get a better rate for its core constituency, the miners. Nevertheless, there was no urgency to tackle the Bolivian reforms, because they did not affect the basic structure of U.S. dominance in the short term.

Rather than try to overthrow the MNR, the U.S. government began a two-step process to undermine the radicalism of the revolution. The two stages were encapsulated in President Kennedy's Alliance for Progress. In 1961, the Kennedy administration provided $20 billion to Central and South American states for economic development *and* military assistance. In March, Kennedy welcomed South and Central American leaders to the White House with a speech on the alliance, in which he noted, "The new generation of military leaders has shown an increasing awareness that armies cannot only defend their countries—they can, as we have learnt through our own Corps of Engineers, help to build them."[12] The U.S. government, in other words, saw the military as a stalwart institution for "development." The United States had already funneled large amounts of money into rebuilding the Bolivian army, and it soon increased the funds astronomically (from $1.4 million in 1962 to $4.1 million in 1963). An army leadership frustrated by the cutbacks and the overall demotion of its status in the country turned to the United States for assistance. In 1960, a senior general told the U.S. ambassador and military attaché that 90 percent of the officers and troops held strong anticommunist viewpoints.[13] The military put itself at the service of the U.S. government and awaited a green light for a coup.[14]

Indeed, when the Bolivian army, led by Barrientos, conducted its *golpe* (coup) in 1964, it was given substantial encouragement by the U.S.

attaché, Colonel Edward Fox (alternatively known as "Fox of the Andes" or "Zorro of the Andes"). While this is unimpeachable, what is often left out of the story is that the MNR had by the late 1950s already begun to build up the military and had ceased to rely on its central allies for popular support. President Paz came from the more conservative, albeit nationalist, side of the MNR—not the more socialist, miner-union side like his vice president, Juan Lechín. To crack down on the pro-Castro and procommunist element in the MNR, Paz began to dismantle the massive social movements and turn for support to the institutions of the old regime (the church and the military) as well as U.S. government aid funds. Paz's desire to concentrate power in the hands of his clique led to the departure of sections of the MNR and the alienation of the tin miners because of the removal of Lechín from his ticket for the 1964 election. By July 1962, Paz encouraged the military to crack down on the civilian militias, and by the end of the year, the renewed military had recovered ground against both the campesinos and the tin miners. The power base of the revolution was demobilized and disarmed. The MNR leadership's fear of the Left led it into the arms of the United States and the conservative social classes that fundamentally opposed the agenda of the Third World. The U.S. government did not alone fashion the coup of 1964; it gave international support to the generals whose power increased as a result of U.S. funds, and it eroded the compact between the social movements of the revolution and the government that had taken power in their name. The 1963 Panama meeting, therefore, was simply an indication of the coup that would come soon after.

The golpe of 1964 was well prepared by the Bolivian military and the U.S. government, and was facilitated by the ideological weakness of the Paz wing in the MNR, which was keener on order than on radical social change. The events in Bolivia replicated those elsewhere in the darker nations, from its neighbor Paraguay's 1954 coup led by General Alfredo Stroessner to the distant Thailand's 1957 coup led by Army Chief Sarit Tanarat. From the end of World War II to the early 1970s, one scholar estimates that at the most, two hundred coups took place in Africa and Asia as well as Central and South America.[15] In his prescient book, Fanon had warned about the structural role of the military in the former colonial nations: "Care must be taken to avoid turning the army into an autonomous body which sooner or later, finding itself idle and without any definite mission, will 'go into politics' and threaten the government. Drawing-room generals, by dint of haunting the corridors of government departments, come to dream of manifestoes."[16] Where every other institution had been battered by colonialism and neocolonialism, the military stood out as efficient and disciplined. The bureaucracy is often poorly trained and prone to corruption, whereas the political parties are frequently, even in South America, better at the struggle for freedom or the creation of manifestos than governance. In this situation, and with the general demobilization and disarmament of the population, the military is an obvious actor for social order.

Fanon has a prescription to prevent the golpe. "The only way to avoid this menace," he writes, "is to educate the army politically, in other words to nationalize it. In the same way another urgent task is to increase the militia."[17] Indeed, Third World states that did not disarm the population, and that created citizens' militias and retained the population in a general political mobilization, did not succumb to coups or easy intervention by imperialism. The classic case is revolutionary Cuba. Shortly after the Castro group took power in Cuba, the leadership of the revolution maintained the level of popular participation in revolutionary activities as part of the order of governance. To defend the nation, the Cuban government transformed the army, and supplemented it with the Milicias de Tropas Territoriales (the Territorial Militia), the National Revolutionary Militias, the various battalions of the regional militias (such as the Cienfuegos militia), the Association of Pioneer Rebels, the Ejécito Juvenil del Trabajo (the Youth Labor Army), and such smaller outfits like the Conrado Benitez Brigades and the Mariana Grajales Women's Platoon.[18] These militias not only provided crucial homeland defense during invasions such as the Bay of Pigs but also participated in agricultural operations (namely, the Ejécito Juvenil) and literacy campaigns (namely, the Benitez Brigades). Hours after the Cuban people routed the invasion at the Bay of Pigs in April 1961, Castro offered four hours of explanation on television: "Imperialism examines geography, analyzes the number of cannons, of planes, of tanks, the positions. The revolutionary examines the social composition of the population. The imperialists don't give a damn about how the population there thinks or feels."[19]

Following Cuba's example, Guinea mobilized sections of the population into civic brigades and popular militias (1966), Tanzania created the National Service (1964–66), and Libya created the Popular Resistance Force (1971). These militias worked against a military coup, but in some cases they also allowed the one-party state to suffocate any dissent in the population. This is a perennial problem with popular mobilization, when the organs of the people stifle dissent in civil society in the name of national progress or democracy. There is no easy solution to the problem of popular mobilization and dissent, particularly when the forces of imperialism are arrayed against national liberation—indeed, when they are pledged to overthrow the new nations. Can dissent be institutionalized, or is the space for dissent only to be produced by the attitude of the state? Dissent is a fundamental liberty, not only for its political utility (it does not alienate parts of the population), but also because dissent might carry useful suggestions and criticisms that are otherwise silenced by the echo chamber of government. Regimes that advocated popular mobilization did not pay sufficient attention to the importance of dissent, and even as they held progressive views they did not promote democratic institutions.[20]

Most new nations that demobilized and disarmed their populations fell prey to military intervention, often driven by imperialist pressure. The U.S. government, by the early 1950s, began to assume responsibility for corporate interests against the new nations' attempts to nationalize production. The U.S.-engineered coup in Iran (1953) is an early example of this planetary role for Washington, DC. Whereas the evidence of U.S. involvement is unclear in most of the coups in the Third World, the footprint of the CIA and the U.S. military intelligence has been clearly documented in the coups in the Dominican Republic (1963), Ecuador (1963), Brazil (1964), Indonesia (1965), Congo (1965), Greece (1967), Cambodia (1970), Bolivia again (1971), and most famously Chile (1973).[21] This is the short, uncontroversial list. Why would the U.S. government, the champion of democracy, initiate military regimes in places where these governments would resort to brutality against the nation? In 1959, the Pentagon commissioned the RAND Corporation, a nonprofit think tank, to do a study on the role of the military in the Third World, and this report helped President Eisenhower's Draper Committee formulate the agenda for the U.S. military assistance program. Both RAND and the Draper Committee agreed that the military in the tropics provided technical and bureaucratic skills for state construction, and that despite their shortcomings, the military in the "underdeveloped areas" should be supported by the U.S. government.[22]

Establishment intellectuals such as the political scientist Samuel P. Huntington created a subfield called "military modernization."[23] Huntington, who taught at Harvard University, was a regular consultant to the CIA during the 1960s, and in the circle of senior government figures such as McGeorge Bundy (also a Harvard professor who was Kennedy's and Johnson's special assistant on national security) and

Robert McNamara (secretary of defense). Huntington's 1968 *Political Order in a Changing Society* provided the best account of military modernization. Huntington played a central role in the Trilateral Commission. Founded in 1973 by representatives of the dominant classes of Asia, Europe, and North America, the Trilateral Commission was of the opinion that world elites must be "concerned more with the overall framework of order than with the management of every regional enterprise." Huntington co-authored its 1975 study, *The Crisis of Democracy.* While working for the Trilateral, Huntington advised the Brazilian military.[24] In the late 1970s, Huntington went on to be the coordinator of national security on the U.S. National Security Council. He has been close to power ever since. In his influential 1968 study on "political modernization," Huntington argued that liberal democracy in the tropics might "serve to perpetuate antiquated social structure."[25] The state needed to concentrate political power as a prelude to economic development, and so there was no better social institution to govern in these parts than the military.[26] Huntington's sophisticated analysis mirrored a 1962 policy document from the National Security Council: "A change brought about through force by non-communist elements may be preferable to prolonged deterioration of government effectiveness. It is U.S. policy, when it is in the U.S. interest, to make the local military and police advocates of democracy and agents for carrying forward the developmental process."[27] Counterinsurgency, coups, and support of the most brutal military dictators could be done not simply for reasons of corporate "stability" but for development, *for the sake of the people of the country now ruled by the military.*

Few will be able to defend this line of analysis in hindsight—the aftermath of Mobutu's Congo, Suharto's Indonesia, or Pinochet's Chile hardly validates the promise of military modernization. When Mobutu Sese Seko fled after over three decades of U.S.-backed power, he left behind a national debt of about $5 billion—a billion less than he had secreted in his accounts at various Swiss banks. Haji Mohammed Suharto, the bulwark of stability, looted the Indonesian treasury of perhaps as much as $35 billion during his three-decade rule.[28] Rather than modernization, we have "primitive accumulation" for a small circle of the ruler's family members. Few will be able to defend these dictators from the charge that they committed horrible acts of routine violation against individuals and the body politic. They did not use the institution of the army to create the basis for modern rights. To the contrary, they used the army to mutilate the population and rule by fear.

Ecuador and Guatemala offer two useful examples of the limitations of the Pentagon's theory of military modernization. In both cases, the Pentagon backed the military rulers. Since neither ruler could fully hew to the Pentagon's line without risk of complete alienation from the Ecuadorians and Guatemalans, they had to be deposed by an alternative ruler or else a constitutional movement from below that traduced the posture of the Pentagon's modernization attempts. In 1958, the "exuberant reactionary" General Miguel Ydígoras Fuentes gathered the reins to run Guatemala's military dictatorship. Ydígoras closely followed the dictates of the Alliance for Progress, created the Ley de Transformación Agraria that used the rhetoric of land reform to turn back the clock on the social experiments of the nationalist Arbenz regime, and did all that he could to insinuate the U.S. military into Guatemala's future plans (the country provided the base for the Bay of Pigs invasion). When popular uprisings broke out in March 1962, Ydígoras unleashed the U.S.-armed and trained Guatemalan military, and welcomed the establishment of a permanent U.S. base, staffed by troops from Puerto Rico and Mexico. With the growth of resistance against Ydígoras, however, the United States ditched him in 1963 for Colonel Enrique Peralta Azurdia.[29] Dictators come and go, but the form of dictatorship remained. Guatemala shows that none of the promises of military modernization, such as the creation of political institutions and the rule of law, had a high priority for the U.S. government.

The Ecuadorian story, like Guatemala, illustrates how despite rule by a military junta backed by the U.S. government, the people continued to fight and won a constitutional regime. In 1963, the newly installed military triumvirate banned "communism" to the great joy of the military's boosters, the local CIA station—the CIA speedily crafted a plan for national development and sent it to the Alliance for Progress to gain funds for the development promised by the theory of military modernization. A year later, the junta followed the logic of national liberation regimes and abolished the feudal land tenure system (*huasipungo*), but what they put in place did not benefit the largely Amerindian landless laborers. All this bore within it the promise of military modernization, except that the people would not bear to have their basic rights trampled for Washington's theory of social development in so-called underdeveloped areas.[30] The junta's anti-Communism meant that it went after the unions and the universities, both institutions with meaning to the people. When the junta tried to crack down on imports to stabilize the balance of payments, the merchants joined the students and the unions to send the army back to the barracks. A constitutional regime reemerged by 1968, and even as it failed to do much for the people of Ecuador (the country suffered another coup in 1970), the failure of the military to engage with the reality of people illustrated the fundamental gap in the military modernization thesis: that people wanted to participate in the creation of their society, not simply be spectators to the military's actions. The institutions that were not "in the U.S. interest," such as student and worker groups, played an important role in the social order and the people did not allow them to be dismantled.[31]

The conventional progressive literature on coups in the tropics tends to assume that the main actor here is the CIA or the United States, or else the USSR (whose hand in the coup tradition is actually remarkably limited). The darker nations are pawns on the board for the United States and the USSR to move about in their deadly game of planetary chess. Such a view assumes that the people have little role in the creation of their own history, that they are simply prone figures to be shuffled at the will of El Norte. Indeed, the CIA and U.S. governmental funds do play a considerable role not only in various coups but also in the political economy of the Third World in general. Yet there is more to the story than the interventions from outside. Each coup has its own reason, and it is hard to make a generalization based on some model of the Third World coup. A generalization without adherence to the specific details of each coup, or a succession of coups (such as the five in Ghana from 1966 to 1981), will not tell us much. To analyze a coup or a military intervention requires an assessment of the struggles within a society, of the class dynamics, the regional interactions, the history of ethnic strife, and other such relations. Those who act alongside the U.S. military, such as Bolivia's Barrientos or Indonesia's Suharto, are emblems of certain class fragments that have domestic reasons to *use* the U.S. government for their ends. They are not passive and guileless, simply misused by "Western imperialism." The Barrientoses, Mobutus, and Suhartos of the world, and those classes that they defend, are part of the ensemble of imperialism, even if as subcontractors.[32]

Huntington's 1968 book on the military and "changing societies" offers one theory to understand the persistence of coups in the tropics. Smartly, Huntington clashes with most conventional interpretations of the coup d'état by noting that "the most important causes of military intervention in politics is not military but political and reflect not the social and organizational characteristics of the military establishment but the political and institutional structure of the society."[33] The structure of social development then will be an indicator of the nature of the coup, Huntington contends, not that the coup is itself always reactionary or illiberal: "As society changes, so does the role of the military. In the world of the oligarchy, the soldier is a radical; in the middle-class world he is a participant and arbiter; as the mass society looms on the horizon he becomes the conservative guardian of the existing order."[34] For Huntington and much of the modernization theory school, the main agent of history is the middle class; a society with a middle class is thus optimum. Anything less smacks of monarchy, and anything more is Communism. The worst of all outcomes is Communism, and therefore at times oligarchies or even monarchies can be tolerated if it means that a middle class might eventually flourish. In the Third World of the 1950s and 1960s, Huntington points out, absolutism might be the way forward because "the primary need their countries face is the accumulation and concentration of power, not its dispersion."[35]

What is so significant about Huntington's analysis is that he sees a correlation between the character of military rule and the level of "mobilization of lower classes into politics."[36] The fear of the lower classes infected the U.S. establishment. At a speech before the American Society of Newspaper Editors in 1966, Defense Secretary Robert McNamara noted that the "sweeping surge of development, particularly across the whole southern half of the globe, has no parallel in history. It has turned traditionally listless areas of the world into seething cauldrons of change. . . . Given the certain connection between economic stagnation and the incidence of violence, the years that lie ahead for the nations in the southern half of the globe are pregnant with violence."[37] With this assessment of the darker nations, it is little wonder that the United States supported the military coups.

In 1970, after a decade of coups in Africa, the militant South African intellectual Ruth First published her monumental, and now forgotten, study on coups on the continent, *The Barrel of a Gun*. Having early in her life joined the resistance to apartheid in her native country, First went on to the front lines of the African National Congress and the Communist Party. Barred from politics several times by the government, First suffered in South Africa's jails, notably for 117 days in 1963.[38] In the midst of this struggle, including as a partisan in the violent underground along with Nelson Mandela and her husband Joe Slovo, First wrote a trenchant study of the suppression of South West Africa by the apartheid government.[39] Worn out, she fled to London for a brief exile, although she took the time to visit the rest of the African continent and assembled the materials for her work on the coup. What bothered First was that large parts of Africa north of the Limpopo had thrown off the yoke of colonialism only to fall prey to military dictatorships. Her book did not offer an analysis of the functional role of the military in the Third World, but what role the military played in the internal class dynamics of the new nations and how African nations could avoid the route of dictatorship. Unable to remain far from the struggle, First returned to Africa, to Mozambique, where a South African death squad killed her on August 17, 1982.[40]

One place where First would find common cause with Huntington is in the disregard both pay to the theory that coups are the form of politics for the less developed peoples—or that the coup is imprinted in the political personality of the culture of the darker nations. The literature on South and Central America often suggests that the caudillo is central to the region south of the Rio Grande because of the special machismo of "Latin" culture. Or else we hear that the Arabs, Africans, and tribal societies in general are unable to be democratic but eager for a leader.[41] Instead of such reductive arguments, First, like Huntington, offers a "general theory of power for newly independent states which explains why they are so vulnerable to army intervention in politics."[42] "The facility of coup logistics and the audacity and arrogance of the coup makers," she observes, "are equaled by the inanity of their aims, at least as many choose to state them."[43] The military rulers, schooled in hierarchical order and efficient action, are uncomfortable with the mess of politics, so they claim to stand above it. In fact, they cannot, and indeed, their posture to be above the political and rule in the name of the "nation" is almost identical to that of the national liberation party that creates a one-party state. "At the outset, it is enough for [the coup makers] to announce that they rule for the nation," writes First. "Power lies in the hands of those who control the means of violence. It lies in the barrel of a gun, fired or silent."[44]

How is the army able to conduct a coup so easily? Huntington's theory is that the "slow development" or lack of political institutions and the "rapid mobilization of new groups into politics" produces the coup.[45] Modernization leads to instability, which results in violence, which pulls the military into governance. First comes at the coup from the opposite angle. Coups occur not simply where new social classes have entered politics but where this politicization has been squelched or suppressed. In states where the national liberation movement has been demobilized or else where there has been no national liberation movement in recent memory, the coup occurs with much greater facility. Without popular organization and popular institutions, to conduct a coup means that an armed faction can take charge over another without much need to draw legitimacy from the masses of the population; a coup such as this, to borrow from Marx's description of "Asiatic states," leaves the "fundamental economic elements of society" and the bulk of the population "untouched by the storms which blow up in the cloudy regions of politics."[46]

Like Huntington, First acknowledges that there are a host of military coups that do not change anything substantial in the structure of social life but simply change the administration. These are "palace or political establishment revolutions, not social ones." Apart from these, there are other coups that are meaningful, where the army operates to defend the legacy of national liberation. Here the army acts as a "competitor for power." The officers "identify themselves with the government ushered in to office with independence," and so they are sentimentally and structurally predisposed to their rule regardless of their actions. The "founding fathers" are tolerated for their actions, and these political leaders cosset the senior military leadership in return. The junior, often younger officers do not have any such class and emotional loyalty, though. They "question the record of such government, and champion other aspirants." The success of the junior officers, First argues, is in their ability to "formulate alternative strategies and corresponding social instruments."[47] First's distinction in terms of the generation of officers is valid, although it ignores the importance of whether the country had a mass decolonization struggle or not. That, for the Third World, is a crucial variable. Drawing from First, and adding in the question of the mass struggle, I want to distinguish between at least two kinds of coups: the *generals' coups* and the *colonels' coups*.

All coups are structurally reactionary, because they adorn the military with the solitary role for social change and cast out the masses from an active role in the construction of a nation-state. Some coups are, however, more reactionary than others. Coups that are conducted in countries that have had either a national liberation struggle (to eject a colonial ruler) or an electoral victory against the oligarchs tend to be reactionary. The military frequently takes power to reverse the gains of national liberation, to thwart the agenda of the Third World. The generals often lead these coups, which is why I shall call them the generals' coups. The military in these countries make the argument that they must protect the patrimony of the nation from Communists or other left-wing forces who want to generate, to their mind, social disorder. To the rank and file, the generals say that the revolutionary government wanted to cut back on the role of the military in social life—a claim that is true in the early years of national construction in the Third World. The aggrieved military brass in Algeria (1965), Dahomey (1965), Ghana (1966), Togo (1967), Uganda (1971), and Chad (1975) overthrew the government with just this contention. Pakistan provides a useful example as well. In October 1958, General Ayub Khan dismissed the civilian leadership and purported to lead Pakistan into the modern age with land reforms. He pledged to stay in power for a short time to give stability to the nation. Ten years later, a massive social movement ejected him from office. Another general, Yahya Khan, took charge, and the rule of generals has continued until this day (now General Pervez Musharraf pledges that he is the main defense against fundamentalism, but only through repression and not popular mobilization). The main agenda of these coups is to roll back the social reforms of the Third World states, not to ensure that the monarchy returns (because almost none of the generals' coups are restorative), but so that the military leadership and the oligarchy can preserve their reign over society. General Augusto Pinochet's 1973 assault on Chile is a well-developed example of this type of coup.

Pinochet acted with the full permission of the U.S. government, and the blessings of the landed and industrial Chilean oligarchy.[48] The army killed about four thousand Chileans (including the socialist president Salvador Allende), destroyed the main political parties of the Left, exiled many of its leaders, and spread fear through the Dirección de Inteligencia Nacional. The World Bank and the InterAmerican Bank, among others, refused to grant Chile credit during Allende's experiments, and his social reform agenda had provoked the elite's anger. For this reason, the Christian Democrats who spoke for that elite welcomed Pinochet's coup. Pinochet promised to protect the privileges of the past for those whom Chile's poet Pablo Neruda called "a quadrille of nouveaux riches with coats of arms, with police and with prisons."[49] That Allende had nationalized the U.S.-owned firms of American Anaconda Copper, ITT, and Kennecott led Nixon to authorize $10 million to "make the economy scream."[50] When Pinochet came to power, the United States did its utmost to repair all frayed relations between the transnational firms and the Chilean bureaucracy. The telecommunications giant ITT had demanded $95 million as compensation from Allende. The Pinochet junta gave them $235 million. In 1975, Chile welcomed the economist Milton Friedman, who advocated "shock treatment" and austerity to increase growth rates. The general's coup of Pinochet restored the rule of the oligarchy and the transnational corporations, much to the satisfaction of the U.S. government.

For states where there is no national liberation movement, and where there is no hope for social reform, the coup d'état is often the means for aggrieved social classes within the military to assert the rule not so much of the military as for their social class. These are the colonels' coups. For the Third World, the modular form of this coup is the Egyptian overthrow of the monarchy in 1952.[51] Nominally led by General Mohamed Naguib, the revolution soon came into the hands of its architects, the Free Officers commanded by Colonel Nasser. In his first May Day speech (1963), Nasser laid out his vision of the 1952 revolution as "undertaken for the working people, for dissolving differences between classes, for establishing social justice, for the establishment of a healthy democratic life, for abolishing feudalism, for abolishing the monarchy and control of capital over government and for abolishing colonialism."[52] This, in sum, was the vision of Nasser's "Arab Socialism." Inspired by Egypt, younger officers in the Iraqi army formed the Free Officers Movement. Led by Brigadier 'Abd al-Karim Qasim and Colonel 'Abd al-Salam 'Arif, the Free Officers overthrew the Hashemite monarchy in 1958. Eleven years later, on the African continent, an adjutant of the Signal Corps, Colonel Muammar Qaddafi, overthrew the monarchy in another Free Officers coup in Libya, while Colonel Jaafar al-Nimeiri led the Free Officers to overcome the chaos that had befallen the political system in Sudan. Both Nimeiri's and Nasser's fathers worked as clerks in the postal service, and all four of these colonels came from families who had dirt under their fingernails. Qaddafi's purpose for the coup suits all of them, and indeed it speaks to the colonels and lower ranks across the Third World who conducted similar coups: "Our souls were in revolt against the backwardness enveloping our country and its land, whose best gifts and riches were being lost through plunder, and against the isolation imposed on our people in a vain attempt to hold it back from the path of the Arab people and from its greatest cause."[53] The latest variant of the colonels' coup comes from Colonel Hugo Chávez of Venezuela in 1999.[54]

The colonels' coups succumbed to their authoritarian roots in military culture. In Egypt, for example, Nasser moved against all opposition to his regime shortly after a foiled assassination attempt by the Ikhwan al-Muslimin (the Muslim Brotherhood) against him in 1954. Initially

Nasser sent his armed forces against the Muslim Brotherhood, but by 1955 he began to liquidate the United Revolutionary Front (a united front of the Muslim Brotherhood, the nationalist Wafd Party, and the Communists, created in February 1953). Nasser's attacks across the political spectrum weakened the space of politics to create what became in effect a military dictatorship. While Nasser's deputy, Anwar es-Sadat, continued to be the liaison with the Muslim Brotherhood, the Communists came in for especially brutal treatment—a crackdown in April 1957 demoralized the party, which effectively dissolved a few years later to refashion itself as a Nasserite ally when Nasser formed a close relationship with the USSR. Part of the reason for this difference of treatment was that the Muslim Brotherhood, by the 1950s, had a considerable mass following, whereas the Communist Party of Egypt had not grown at the same rate. It was easier to destroy, and given the pressure on it from the USSR, easier to render more pliable. Indeed, Nasser himself seemed quite cavalier about the Egyptian Communist Party; prior to his 1955 visit to the USSR, Nasser noted, "Nothing prevents us from strengthening our economic ties with Russia even if we arrest the Communists at home and put them on trial."[55] The crackdown on Communist parties in Iraq, Pakistan, and Sudan followed the Egyptian model, as all four states descended into the dark night of dictatorship.

Even if the colonel's coup comes with tremendous promise, it can only momentarily deliver the administrative apparatus to energetic officers. The soldiers, as First put it, "hold the ring while new internal power amalgams are arranged." The soldiers can do no permanent good. They can only postpone solutions.[56] As the national liberation state removes itself from popular mobilization, begins to cultivate the domestic elites in the name of national development, and perhaps opens itself to intervention by imperialism, it loses the élan of the national liberation struggle. In the worst case, the military intervenes to preserve the status quo or recover the past. In the best case, the military rejects the civilian administration to disrupt the cozy alliance of the revolutionary leaders, the domestic bourgeoisie, and imperialism. Nevertheless, the military in power, as First shows, regardless of its motivations, *freezes the political process and cuts down the ability of social movements to move the historical process in a progressive direction*. Nothing good comes from a military dictatorship.

While on the run from a Chilean government that he had condemned for its betrayal of its people in the 1940s, Neruda composed his *Cantos*

General. In its midst, he offered a lyrical passage titled "Los Dictadores" ("The Dictators"):

An odor lingers among the sugarcane:
A mixture of blood and body, a penetrating
Nauseous petal.
Between the coconut palms the graves are filled
Of demolished bones, of smothered grasps.
The delicate dictator talks
With wineglasses, collars, and gold braid.
The tiny palace shines like a wristwatch
And smart-gloved laughter
Occasionally drifts across the corridors
To join the dead voices
And freshly buried mouths.
The sob is hidden like a plant
Whose seed falls ceaselessly to the ground
And makes its great blind leaves grow without light.
Hatred has been formed scale by scale,
Coup by coup, in the terrible water of the swamp
With a snout full of clay and silence.[57]

BALI

Neruda's rage at the betrayal of popular aspirations came with a deep sense of hope that the people, organized by Communists and others, would prevail. When Communism arrived in the darker nations in the 1920s, it drew adherents who had been embittered by the failures of constitutional nationalism and revolutionary terrorism as well as empire. Intellectuals and peasants from their different places, but with equal intensity, took refuge in the new ideology, grafted it on to their various homespun versions of freedom and equality, and sewed red flags for their demonstrations. Repression followed as soon as they let out their flags. Empire knew immediately that Communism spelled its doom. It did not stop to negotiate with the Communists; it wanted only to annihilate them. Neruda sings of the formation of the Communist Party of Chile in the 1920s, of the foundation of the party by people like Luis Emilio Recabarren to the massacres of its members by the oligarchy. And then, in "Recabarren," Neruda explodes:

How much has happened since then,
How much blood upon blood,
How many struggles upon the earth.
Hours of splendid conquest,
Triumphs won drop by drop,
Bitter streets, defeated,
Zones dark as tunnels,
Razor-edged betrayals
That seemed to sever life,

Repressions armed with hatred,
Militarily crowned.

The earth seemed to give way.

But the struggle goes on.[1]

As Neruda hid from the authorities in the borderlands of Chile, across the Pacific Ocean, the Communists in Indonesia faced their first major bloodbath, in Madiun in eastern Java. Unhappy with the nationalist negotiations with the Dutch, the Indonesian Communist Party (PKI) urged a popular uprising against both the Dutch and the newly emergent bourgeoisie in Indonesia. Defeated in street battles in Surakanta, the PKI (and the Trotskyists) regrouped in Madiun, where they faced the full force of the military. The army killed many of the PKI's leaders, jailed about 36,000 people, and crushed the party into relative insignificance. The "adventure of 1948" ended swiftly. President Sukarno's rise to power came with the blood of the Communists on his hands. His fall, in 1965, would be accompanied by the murder of one or perhaps two million Communists and sympathizers.

Sukarno was not an adherent of Communism, and was discomforted by the creation of the PKI in 1920. Nevertheless, in 1926, he wrote an important book that gestured toward cooperation between Islam, Marxism, and nationalism, to Sukarno the three main resources for the Indonesian freedom movement.[2] In 1960, President Sukarno created an ideological framework for his nationalist party and the new national institutions: NASAKOM drew its inspiration from nationalism (NAS), religion (A, *agama*, the Sanskrit word for religion, which Sukarno deployed as a way to draw Hinduism, a major minority faith, into the web of Indonesia), and Communism (KOM). The agenda for national construction, Sukarno recognized, needed the PKI, which not only had a program worthy of Sukarno's project but also had an experienced and disciplined cadre. As Sukarno moved toward the Left, the PKI became a critical base for him.

In 1951, the PKI had sufficiently recovered from the adventure of 1948 to choose a group of young leaders to revitalize the party. Among the quartet of leaders stood Dipa Nusantara Aidit, who argued that the party could not have any influence if it did not grow. As a result, the PKI decided that its standards for membership should not be too celestial because "from a large quantity it is far more possible to achieve higher quality."[3] The PKI grew rapidly; by 1965, 3.5 million people were members of the party. To move into all aspects of Indonesian life, the PKI revived its mass organizations. By 1965, the youth group (Pemuda Rakyat) boasted a membership of 3 million, while the women's organization (Gerwani) had 1.5 million. Adding these members to those from the trade union federation (Sentral Organisasi Buruh), the cultural league (Lembaga Kebudayaan Rakyat), the peasant's front (Barisan Tani Indonesia), and the scholar's association (Himpunan Sarjana Indonesia), the party commanded the loyalty of more than 20 million Indonesians, in a country of 110 million. PKI had a substantial presence in the archipelago, with its greatest growth rate being on the island of Bali.[4]

Despite this massive growth, the PKI under Aidit did not make any move to take state power. The labor unions seized control of Dutch-owned firms in late 1957, but that was as far as they would go. In 1957–58, in Sumatra and Sulawesi, the military and the right wing joined together to create liberated areas and arrest PKI cadres. Instead of using this as an opportunity to crack down on the old social classes and the military, the PKI leadership put its faith in Sukarno. Aidit followed a well-hewed analysis among Marxists across the Third World: that a relatively nonindustrial society cannot have a proletarian revolution, and so the Communist Party must work alongside progressive sections of the bourgeoisie to create democratic capitalism. When the conditions of industry are more developed, the Communists can come to state power. This was the dominant position articulated by the Soviet Union and the Chinese, who gave support to Communist parties as long as they maintained an alliance with the progressive section of the national bourgeoisie. On the basis of this premise, Aidit articulated a four-part strategy: to enlarge the party and its mass organizations, constrain or win over the progressive sections of the national elite, "use" Sukarno's move to the Left, and neutralize the armed forces.[5] The PKI was able to both grow and make a connection with Sukarno, but it was not able to insinuate itself into the imagination of the national elite or make a crack in the armed forces.

The PKI developed cells of party members inside the armed forces. By 1955, about 30 percent of those in uniform leaned toward the PKI (mainly those from the ranks, not from the officer corps). In response to the Sumatra and Sulawesi rebellions (which were supported by the CIA), Sukarno declared martial law (from March 1957 to May 1963). By this means, he attempted to secure the officer corps to his side. He succeeded in bolstering the role of the army, which received $20 million from the U.S. government for an upgraded military assistance program.[6] The army regained its stature despite the PKI's efforts to send it back to the barracks.[7]

Irresolute, Sukarno brought Indonesia into the 1960s with a strong army and a strong Communist Party, with his own Guided Democracy experiment eager for the disciplined loyalty of the former and the economic program of the latter. Aidit's PKI realized that the growth of military power needed to be countered on the streets and in the *kampungs* (villages). In early May 1965, the politburo of the PKI called for the creation of "people's revolutionary mass actions from below" to bolster the "revolutionary mass actions by the bodies of the state from above." Aidit wanted to create a "fifth force" of armed workers and peasants. The party set up a training camp in Lubang Buaja for the PKI's youth wing. The armed defense of the NASAKOM had to be conducted by the PKI, or else the state would fall to the military and the old social classes.

In 1965, the year of living dangerously, the army pretended that this fifth force had begun a rebellion. It overthrew Sukarno and installed General Suharto. So far, little distinguishes the Indonesian case from that of most coups d'état in the bruised nations. But the direction of Indonesian history takes a nasty turn. In September 1959, Sukarno presciently told the PKI at its sixth congress, "You are my blood relatives, you are my brothers, and if you die, it is I who shall be the loser."[8] To invoke death was to have seen into the future, for Suharto's army unleashed all the anticommunist social forces, and itself, on to the PKI, its mass members, and its supporters, or else anyone who stood to the Left. Between 1965 and 1966, anywhere from one hundred thousand to two million people fell to their deaths before Suharto's New Order.[9] Aidit tried to flee to Yogyakarta, but he was caught and killed. The new regime dismissed the massacre as the anger of a population suppressed by Communism and Sukarno. Suharto dismissed all culpability and scoffed at any suggestion that his military had anything to do with the genocide.

The island of Bali lost about 8 percent of its population, or a hundred thousand people, in the assault on the PKI in 1965–66.[10] Bali is now thought of simply as a planetary tourist paradise, ruffled only by the bomb blasts of October 2002.[11] One can stroll about the island today with little sense that in December 1965, after they had sent many PKI to the grave in Java, the Resimen Para Komando Angkatan Darat (Army Paracommando Regiment) arrived on Bali to begin the slaughter. Near the Bali Beach Hotel, the commandos started to kill, as others shipped entire villages to anticommunist strongholds where murder had been streamlined.[12] The disappeared villages transformed the countryside, which later appeared "pockmarked with the blackened shells of former settlements."[13] In the village of Kesiman, the army and its allies killed five hundred people and jailed another three hundred out of a total population of four thousand. Asked about the event years later, the survivors remembered "the height of the terror as a time when the streets were littered with body parts, innards, and blood and the rivers were overrun with the stench of death."[14]

The actual massacre came at the hands of the army and the activists of the right-wing, mainly theocratic, political parties. They had lists of names of activists and organizers of the PKI and its affiliated organizations. They used these lists to gather the victims for execution. Although the U.S. and Australian governments neither instigated nor conducted the massacre, they encouraged the purge, fattened the lists of Communists for the army, funded the paracommandos, and supported the media effort to blame the entire genocide on the Communists.[15] Reports of the atrocities began to pile up in the document room of the U.S. embassy in Jakarta, with one summary going by telegram to the State Department at Foggy Bottom with this description of events in Aceh: "Moslem fervor in Atjeh apparently put all but few PKI out of action. Atjehnese have decapitated PKI and placed their heads on stakes along the road. Bodies of PKI victims reportedly thrown into rivers or seas as Atjehnese refuse to 'contaminate Atjeh soil.' " A few weeks later, the embassy reported, "The Army with the help of IP-KI [the League of Upholders of Indonesian Independence, a group integrally linked to the army] Youth organizations and other anti-communist elements has continued systematic drive to destroy PKI in northern Sumatra with wholesale killings reported." News came from Bali that with eighty thousand dead, there was "no end in sight." To minimize the role of the U.S.-backed army and New Order regime, the embassy noted, "Many of the killings that are taking place under a political cover are actually motivated by personal and clan vendettas."[16] The U.S. State Department acknowledged in the 1990s that its agents had given lists of PKI members to the New Order regime, and that it had done little to stop the violence.[17] The historian Geoffrey Robinson's assessment is that "even if it is not possible to establish definitively the extent of U.S. complicity, it can be demonstrated that U.S. policy contributed substantially to the seizure of power by the military under Suharto and to the massacre that ensued."[18] Robinson left out the Australian and British governments, both of which played significant roles in the liquidation of the PKI.[19]

The genocide produced little outrage from around the world. When it became clear what the army had begun to do in Java and Sumatra, the United Nations felt it more important to urge, in the abstract, "all Governments to make special efforts during the United Nations Development Decade to promote respect for and observance of human rights and fundamental freedoms."[20] Admittedly, Sukarno had removed Indonesia from the United Nations some months before the coup, but when Suharto applied for reentry in 1966, the General Assembly welcomed the dictator without any public condemnation. Pockets of the dedicated Left within Europe and the United States organized vigils and issued statements, but the mainstream media turned a blind eye. With a hundred thousand people held as political prisoners in the New Order, exiled leftist Carmel Budiardjo arrived in London and set up Tapol, an organization to help free these prisoners. Tapol worked with Bertrand Russell and his foundation to publicize the scale of the atrocity, but few listened.[21] The governments of the First World had already pledged themselves to criticize the USSR and "Communism" to the exclusion of all else; they would certainly not come to the defense of the Communists against a "factor of stability" who would soon become their great ally. Nobody collated the *Black Book of Anti-Communism*.

Moscow and Beijing remained mute. Since the 1920s, the USSR had an ambiguous relationship with Communist parties in the darker nations. On the one hand, the USSR had been the one state that gave enormous ideological, diplomatic, and material support to many independence struggles. The early Comintern meetings, the publication of all the imperialist treaties on colonial domination by the new government, the Baku Congress of 1920, the 1928 Brussels meeting of the League against Imperialism, and many other events and episodes signal the immense contribution the USSR had played to assist the growth of social and political struggle in the nascent Third World. The Comintern, from the early 1920s to 1935, urged Communists in the darker nations to keep some distance between their activity and that of the nationalist groups in their regions. In China, though, the Comintern pushed the Communists into an alliance with the nationalist Kuomintang that ended in the disastrous Kuomintang 1928 massacre of the Communists in Shanghai. The space allowed by the Comintern resulted in the creation of hundreds of Communist parties on the three continents, from Nicaragua to South Africa to Indonesia. In South America, the Communist parties that grew the fastest (in Argentina, Chile, and Uruguay) enveloped the Socialist parties and became heir to their organizational apparatus. Elsewhere, the

Communists had to start from scratch, often on terrain that had no industrial working class and only a limited history of socialist struggle (such as in Vietnam).

At the 1935 Seventh Comintern Congress, the Soviet Communists reacted to the development of fascism within Europe by telling Communist parties to work in a "popular front" with all patriotic social forces. The Comintern asked Communist parties to work in coalition with all other antifascist forces, in order to enlarge its ambit by working in tandem with other classes, including sections of the bourgeoisie. While the strategy of the Comintern developed out of the German Communist Party's failure to stop the Nazi rise to power in 1933, that experience now came to dominate the work of Communists in far different settings. Furthermore, as the USSR shifted its own international alliances, first with a pact with the Nazis in 1939, then in one with the Allies against the Nazis in 1941, the Communist parties in the periphery had to scurry to find reasons for their own turbulent swings. While the idea of a popular front (and a united front) played an important role in ameliorating the adventurism of the Communists of the 1920s, it did not necessarily lead the Communists in the darker nations to take the opportunity to expand their constituency. The parties made opportunistic alliances with the nationalist forces, often with the encouragement of Moscow, and they used this place as a way to wield rather than to build power. The USSR urged local Communist parties to go into hibernation or else make alliances with ghastly political forces in the name of unity often because these forces wanted to make an expedient link with the USSR against the depredations of imperialism. By the advent of the Cold War in the late 1940s, the class collaborationist line had substantially weakened the Communist parties in the Third World, and they became easy prey for attack by the CIA and the nationalist regimes.[22]

Within Moscow and Beijing, there was no theoretical unanimity on the question of alliances and revolution. Debates raged along many lines. One position argued that each society must first develop its domestic industry, and only then when its means of production are well established can its proletariat overcome the morally supine bourgeoisie. Such a view acknowledged that history must move in stages, and only after a given society had moved from the feudal stage to the capitalist one could a transition to socialism be possible. Another, counter opinion suggested that given the way the darker nations had been held in a situation of permanent dependence, it would be impossible for them to develop into capitalist societies. To hope that the national bourgeoisie would be capable of creating a capitalist society with the stake set against these new nations would be quixotic. Therefore the Communists had to seize power, delink the new state from international capital, and rush the country through the stages. In China, Liu Shao-ch'i articulated the "stagist" view, while Lin Biao took the "uninterrupted revolution" approach. Similar divides manifested themselves in Moscow and elsewhere.

Regardless of the debates, by the 1960s both Moscow and Beijing produced concepts that validated the Communist alliance with bourgeois democratic forces. In 1960, the USSR unveiled its concept, the national democratic state, which referred to those noncommunist national liberation states that emerged within the Third World. These states governed according to their own variant of socialism (Arab socialism, African socialism, NASAKOM).[23] Beijing proposed the theory of new democracy: a coalition of four classes (the proletariat, the peasantry, the petty bourgeoisie, and the domestic capitalists) would join together against imperialism to develop the country toward socialism. The Communist Party would lead these classes, which would develop capitalism to expedite growth rates and the transition to socialism.[24] Both Moscow and Beijing, therefore, guided the Communists in the darker nations to make allowances for the national bourgeoisie. They had to work in "national democratic fronts" and create the groundwork for a future socialist transition.[25]

The concepts of the national democratic state and new democracy allowed Moscow and Beijing to accept noncommunist regimes and national liberation movements as sufficient for the nonindustrial world. The conflict between Moscow and Beijing also added to their lack of scrupulousness when seeking alliances. The development of Communism became almost secondary to the promotion of national democratic fronts. Given this line of analysis, the USSR and the People's Republic of China gave perhaps more support to the national democratic leaders who preached socialism and had control of a state than to emergent Communist parties that had organized across the exploited classes and others into a movement to change the basis of social production. Nasser's Egypt, Qasim's Iraq, Boumédienne's Algeria, Indira Gandhi's India, Ne Win's Burma, Sékou Touré's Guinea, Ayub Khan's Pakistan, and Modibo Keita's Mali became part of the USSR's and the People's Republic of China's most favored states, even though most of these leaders suppressed their local Communist parties.

By the early 1960s, the three largest Communist parties (outside a Communist state) in Asia, Africa, and the Arab lands were the PKI of

Indonesia, Sudan's al-Hizb al-Shuyu'i al-Sudani (SCP), and the Iraqi Communist Party (ICP), respectively. These parties commanded the respect of a large section of their societies and controlled important people's organizations (including trade unions, women's leagues, and youth associations). Within a decade, these three parties would be devastated when the national bourgeoisie (with the assistance of the United States as well as a blind eye from Moscow and Beijing) would call the military out of the barracks to exterminate them. If the USSR and the People's Republic of China had taken a strong stand in any one of these instances, they might have given courage to Communists elsewhere to continue with their work. Instead, the silence scared Communists into alliances with political forces that wanted to use and then destroy them.

The Communists were useful. Sukarno needed the PKI for its program and cadre. When Brigadier Qasim overthrew the Iraqi monarchy (1958) and Colonel Jaafar al-Nimeiri rejected a corrupt military junta in Sudan (1969), both leaned on the strong Communist parties to extend their power. A military coup has little institutional basis for legitimacy—people might respect the individual leaders or their cliques for their honesty, and wish them well, but these leaders or cliques have only the institutions of the armed forces to help give the coup legitimacy. In addition, most military factions come to power without a detailed program because army personnel have little experience in politics. In the case of Iraq and Sudan, the leaders made alliances with the Communists both for their capacity to reach into the social worlds of the Iraqis and the Sudanese, but also to borrow from their established programs for social change. Qasim did not personally share the Communists' views, but he knew that his coup would languish without them. By 1958, all political parties had absorbed the social program of the ICP, a testament to its relevance and probity. Even the Baath, no friend to Communism, adopted elements of the ICP's program. When the ICP took advantage of the opening to revive its banned organizations such as the Peace Partisans, the League for the Defense of Women's Rights (*al-Rabita*), and the League of Iraqi Youth, the ICP grew to more than twenty-five thousand cadre members with an additional mass membership of a million (about a fifth of the total population of Iraq).[26]

The growth of the ICP and its social power terrified the dictatorship of Qasim. Shortly after Qasim came to power, the founder of the Baath, Michel 'Aflaq, visited Baghdad from Damascus to promote his party over the ICP. "We represent the Arab spirit against materialist Communism," he told the Iraqis. "Communism is western, and alien to everything

Arab."[27] The Baath had only three hundred members in Iraq, and would grow to only three thousand in the early 1960s. In May 1959, Husain ar-Radi, the ICP's first secretary, entered a politburo meeting and argued that the time had come for the party to make a move for power. He was outvoted. The Soviets had sent an envoy with a message not to provoke Qasim.[28] The Baath took the initiative; the United States backed it. The ICP defended the nationalist military regime when the Baath attempted a coup in October 1959. It quickly took charge of the Ministry of Defense and the communications network. Half a million Communists and their allies filled the streets. This terrified the colonels, who began to decimate the ICP, their only organized defenders. Qasim ignored the Baath, even after they attempted to assassinate him in late 1959 (led by the young Saddam Hussein). The Baath's way had been prepared, and it eventually captured the state in 1963.[29] The window to the future closed.

In 1968, Hussein came to power. The USSR became a major ally of Hussein, who cultivated a split in the battered ICP. As Hussein made an alliance with the USSR, a pro-Soviet faction of the ICP joined hands with him. The anti-Baath group, the ICP (Central Leadership) led by 'Aziz al-Hajj felt the wrath of the Baath's militia, the Jihaz Haneen. The USSR, meanwhile, provided Iraq with one of the five nuclear reactors that it built in the bruised nations, welcomed more students from Iraq than any other Third World state, and provided considerable military and industrial assistance in exchange for oil. The ICP that remained within the government enabled Iraq's 1972 friendship treaty with the USSR, but as Hussein increased his hold on the country he began a campaign against the ICP itself. In 1978, Hussein had the "loyal" party members arrested, executed many cadre, and used the ICP's suppression to send a strong message to his own Baath that all loyalty had to be to his regime, and not to an ideology or another party. Hussein's campaign against the ICP led to his enhanced stock among Washington policymakers, whose own alliance with him began in 1983. The remainder of the ICP's cadre either fled overseas or else remained within Iraq to continue the struggle, notably in the Kurdish regions (long a bastion of the Left). The Communists that remained in Iraq clandestinely fought on against the Baath and smuggled out documents on the atrocities against Iraqis by the Hussein regime.[30]

In Sudan, Nimeiri came to power on a Nasserite agenda, and he, like Qasim, could not rule without the SCP. After the coup he banned all political parties, but allowed the SCP to continue its activities. Founded in 1944, the SCP was the only political party with national standing because, unlike the sectarian and racialist parties, it recruited equally in the north and south, among Christians as well as Muslims. Nimeiri needed the SCP. In the typical formula, Nimeiri first went after his right flank. In 1970, he began an assault on the reactionary Umma Party led by Sadiq al-Mahdi. When that party had been substantially pacified, Nimeiri turned his attention to the SCP. The brutal repression of the SCP drove the Communists to attempt a coup of their own along with sympathetic army officers. The Nimeiri regime arrested the party leadership, executed most of them (including Abdel al-Khaliq Mahjub, Joseph Garang, and Ahmed El Sheikh), and urged their followers to "destroy anyone who claims there is a Sudanese Communist Party. Destroy this alleged Party."[31] When news of the events in Sudan reached the Soviet leadership, it tried to negotiate with the Nimeiri government, as well as with the Egyptians and the Libyans, for asylum to the SCP's leaders. Once rebuffed, it did not pursue the matter. It is not that Moscow felt nothing for its comrades in the tropics, but that the fortunes of the Communist parties in the Third World came second to the strategy mapped out by the USSR and the People's Republic of China. When the Nimeiri regime executed the SCP leaders despite the entreaty from the USSR, Moscow rewarded the dictator with economic and political treaties as well as a special honored place as a delegate to the Communist Party of the USSR's twenty-fourth Congress in late 1971. In Syria (1972) and Iraq (1973), the USSR brokered a deal to create national fronts so that the Communist parties in both countries would enter the government in a minority, indeed second-rank position and with few rights to conduct political organization.

The crackdown led many Communists to the gun. In Iraq, twelve militants including Khalid Ahmed Zaki of the Popular Front for Armed Struggle attempted a quixotic insurgency in the southern marshlands in 1968, only to be gunned down by the Iraqi army. They acted a decade too late, by which time ar-Radi's assessment had become anachronistic. The revolutionary moment had passed.[32] Zaki's move to the gun came as part of the general turn of many Communist parties toward Maoism. An elementary precept of Maoism was ignored by many of these movements: they did not consider whether they had built up sufficient mass support or if there was a sufficiently mobilized mass movement to join their small armed venture. In Congo's Kwilu region, Pierre Mulele, a minister in Lumumba's deposed government, took up arms against Mobutu's regime, but while his insurgency lasted a few years, it too failed to make any headway.[33] In India, in 1967, a breakaway group from the

Communist Party of India (Marxist), which had itself broken with the pro-Soviet Communist Party of India in 1964, began armed struggle in several parts of India, once more to suffer immense defeats. In Indonesia, the PKI conducted a self-criticism of the Aidit line for its collaboration with Sukarno and began a Maoist-style guerrilla campaign on Java and the outer islands, like Kalimantan. The PKI managed to hold on to some pockets of support, and its guerrilla strategy bore some minor fruits, but in the main it was effectively wiped out as a serious contender for state power.[34] In South America, Maoism came as Castroism, when leftists went into armed struggle against the state from Argentina to Venezuela. As the French political activist Régis Debray put it in 1965, only armed struggle by well-trained militants can destroy the bourgeois state apparatus—a precondition for a successful revolution that will not be destroyed by a military coup.[35] Not one South American country had a reprieve from Castroism, and even as these suffered disastrous failures and a generation of leftists perished before the police guns, the strategy remained alive. The military usurped control of the historical dynamic, destroyed a generation of militants, and took advantage of the situation to foment a decade of military rule. Powerlessness, already a social fact in large parts of the bruised nations, grows out of the barrel of a gun.[36]

As Sukarno fell, no significant word of protest came from New Delhi, Belgrade, Rangoon, Cairo, or Accra. Tepid disavowals of the violence came from their foreign ministries, but little else. Indonesia's Sukarno had played a crucial role in the creation of the political platform of the Third World, and Bandung had been its omphalos. Yet there was silence. The personal or political demise of the five major leaders of the progressive tendency in Bandung reveals much about the collapse of solidarity: Nehru died in 1964, both U Nu and Nkrumah had been recently deposed by military coups, Nasser's role had been weakened by the collapse of his United Arab Republic, and Tito had begun a genial rapprochement with the USSR. Nehru, U Nu, and Nasser had vexed relations with their domestic Communist parties. In 1959, Nehru used his maximum constitutional powers to eject a Communist state government in Kerala; U Nu had kept an arm's length from the Communist Party of Burma during his short-lived reign; and the Egyptian Communist Party had dissolved itself in 1965, and asked its members to cooperate with Nasser's regime.[37] The regimes of the Third World had little regard for their local Communist parties, and as long as this disdain made no impact on their relations with Moscow or Beijing, they had no obligation to speak for such atrocities as committed by the Indonesian army, the

Moroccan government (against the National Union of Popular Forces, and the assassination of its leader, Ben Baraka, on the streets of Paris in 1965), and the Congolese army (against the Mouvement National Congolais, and the assassination of its leader, Lumumba, in 1961, with Belgian collusion).

Both Sudan and Iraq remained a welcome part of the Third World and NAM. Sudan and Iraq, as well as Indonesia, formally continued to support the foreign policy objectives of the Third World. Indeed, Indonesia even formally adhered to the Bandung principles and this maintained the country in good stead at the political gatherings of the Third World.[38] During the genocide, the startlingly named Front Pancasila cheered on the army and helped conduct the mass murder.[39] Suharto's Pancasila only formally resembled the Panchsheela of Bandung—for the army general's five points included such conservative staples as "belief in the one supreme God," "the unity of Indonesia," and "democracy led by the wisdom of deliberation among representatives." The original Panchsheela did not refer to God, nor to the wisdom of the representatives, which could be another way of saying that the people should defer to their betters.[40] When Suharto's New Order spoke of unity, it might already have had in mind the invasion of East Timor (in 1975)—an annexation based on the army's notion of unity, not that of either the Indonesian people or the East Timorese.

At the 1977 NAM meeting in New Delhi, Sudan's representative held the delegates in thrall with a presentation on the need to restructure the United Nations so that it would be more democratic and thereby support the New International Economic Order. Iraq's delegate presented the second of two working papers after the Sudanese, this one on the need to have a more efficient NAM structure, with better coordination through a secretariat.[41] Neither Iraq, Sudan, nor Indonesia were laughed out of the room—their pogroms against the Communists in each case became the sacrosanct "internal affairs" of each country. The major Third World powers accepted Indonesia, Sudan, Iraq, and others simply because they signed on to the basic principles of non-alignment, and because they shared a similar international economic analysis.

The destruction of the Left had an enormous impact on the Third World. The most conservative, even reactionary social classes attained dominance over the political platform created in Bandung. As an adjunct to the military regimes, the political forces that emerged rejected the ecumenical anticolonial nationalism of the Left and the liberals for a cruel cultural nationalism that emphasized racialism, religion, and hierarchy. The latter took shelter in a manufactured vision of "tradi-tion"—they claimed to be the true spokespersons of the authentic cul-ture of their regions, as opposed to the "modern" or "Western" influence of the progressive Left. The myth of Bali as paradise and Arabs as puri-tanical, or Hindus as hierarchical and Africans as tribal—all these vi-sions of tradition emerged with a vengeance from the old social classes as a way to battle the Left, and once the latter had been shunned, claim that they were the authentic representatives of their civilization. "The Bali myth," the historian Robinson argues, for instance, "has helped to falsify history in a way that has served the people in power while silenc-ing those who have suffered injustice."[42]

Some U.S. government officials in the field bemoaned their cozy rela-tionship with oligarchies and militaries against the Communists. For ex-ample, the deputy chief of the U.S. embassy in Guatemala in the 1950s, Bill Krieg, noted that the reactionary forces were "bums of the first order" who "wanted money, were palace hangers-on," while the Com-munists "could work, had a sense of direction, ideas, knew where they wanted to go." They were "honest, very committed. This was the tragedy: the only people who were committed to hard work were those who were, by definition, our worst enemies."[43] The CIA and the old so-cial classes crushed the Left in many parts of the darker nations, en-livened the old social classes, and later—much later—found that they had created a monster they could not control.

TAWANG

At dawn on October 20, 1962, the hills of the Thag La ridge exploded in a series of blasts. The Chinese People's Liberation Army (PLA) began a long-awaited war with India that continued for a month with the PLA sweeping deep into Indian territory across its long border with China. Brigadier John S. Dalvi of the Indian armed forces was with his forward battalion near the ridge, where he had been posted several months before in anticipation of an Indian march against the Chinese forces. "As the first salvoes crashed overhead," Dalvi later wrote, "there were a few minutes of petrifying shock. The contrast with the tranquility that had obtained hitherto made it doubly impressive. The proximity of the two forces made it seem like an act of treachery."[1] Within two days, the Chinese assault not only pushed the Indian forces back but also cut off their retreat across the high-altitude passes that would have taken them back to reinforced Indian positions. The Chinese captured Dalvi and entered Brigade 7's main town, Tawang, where they met no opposition. Even as the war continued for a month, the PLA broke the back of the Indian defenses in days.[2]

In 1954, the two countries had signed the Five Principles of Peaceful Co-Existence, the Panchsheela, which called for mutual understanding and cooperation on all issues. At Bandung, Nehru and Zhou En Lai stood shoulder to shoulder to proclaim a new Asia. Nehru's closing speech proclaimed this new "spirit of Asia today." This is the Asia that is "dynamic; Asia is full of life. Asia might make mistakes, and has made mistakes in the past, but it does not matter so long as life is there in it. We can make advances if life is there, but if there is no life, all our right words, our right actions will not hold good, and whatever we have achieved will be lost."[3] Nehru's metaphysical poetry sat uneasily next to Zhou's practical forthrightness. When challenged about Chinese expansionism, Zhou noted, "We are ready to restrain our government and people from crossing even one step across our border. If such things should happen, we would like to admit our mistake."[4]

The People's Republic of China had common borders with many countries, but there were four that had border disputes with China: Burma, India, Pakistan, and the USSR. In 1920, the Karakhan Manifesto from the USSR repudiated the treaties between the Czarist regime and the Manchu Empire, with the statement that the Soviet Republic "renounces all the annexations of Chinese territory, all the concessions in China and returns to China free of charge and forever all that was ravenously taken from her by the Tsar's Government and by the Russian bourgeoisie."[5] In the late 1950s, the USSR would rescind this statement and insist on territory that it had abrogated. The breakdown came only from a question of territory. The border dispute provided an occasion to continue the Sino-Soviet doctrinal debate in a military fashion. Nevertheless, for at least two decades, when instability raged in China, the Soviet statement provided the window to an alternative mode of international relations—where the advantages of the imperial past would not determine the state of relations between contiguous states in the present.

The Soviet initiative in 1920 represents an unusual move in interstate relations, but it is not the only model for postcolonial boundary resolutions. China had an unclear border with Burma, where more than seventy thousand miles in the Wa region remained in dispute right up to 1956. The conflict got so bad in 1955 that the Burmese army fought a major encounter with the PLA in the Wa state, where the Burmese had been conducting operations against the Kuomintang army at the same time. The mess on the Sino-Burmese border could easily have led to war, as it did in the Sino-Indian sector. Yet the Burmese prime minister and a leading light at Bandung, U Nu, went to Beijing, forced the Chinese to the table, and negotiated their approach to the dispute and the actual border. Both the Burmese and the Chinese rejected the British borders at the same time as they assumed those older lines as guides for their new settlement. China absorbed some villages in the Kachin state, whereas Burma would have control over the Namwan Assigned Tract.[6] While the agreement began a process that ended in 1960 with a formal declaration of the border, within Burma the Kachin peoples rose in rebellion the following year because they had not been consulted in the arrangement, nor did they wish to be a part of China.[7] For all the talk of self-determination, neither U Nu nor Zhou had considered the views of those they had shuffled to one side or the other of the new international border. There was conflict, but it was not between states.[8]

The values on formal display in the Sino-Burmese negotiations had been enshrined at Bandung and Belgrade. The eighth principle in the Bandung communiqué pledged the countries to settle disputes "by peaceful means" within the framework of the United Nations.[9] While this principle was sacrosanct in rhetoric and sometimes in practice, it could not be sustained in many instances. India and Pakistan fought a border war over Kashmir before the British troops had even left the subcontinent, while the Israeli state and its Arab neighbors went to war as the former came into existence. The People's Republic of China threatened Formosa with an invasion, while Algeria and Morocco (1960) as well as Mauritania and Mali (1963) went to war over their various disputed boundaries. Wars over borders provided a major excuse for the growth of the military in each of these national liberation states, and even those that did not succumb to a military dictatorship created an immensely powerful military apparatus that suffocated the social justice side of national budgets. Border disputes that stem in many cases from both an inappropriate theory of the border and lines drawn for colonial reasons provided the postcolonial military with the pretext for its own ascendancy.

The PLA was battle hardened in war against the Japanese occupation, its civil war against the Kuomintang that ran from the 1930s right to the 1950s, and its assault on outlying regions like Tibet that continued to the late 1950s. As the PLA dug into its forward positions on the line that divided India and China, it had better equipment and far better battle readiness than the Indian army.[10] Following one of the precepts of Bandung, the Indian government tried to reduce the importance and size of, as well as the financial commitment to, the Indian army. In 1958, when the Indian army earned an increase in the budget to modernize its equipment and raise the salaries of soldiers, Congress leader Acharya Kripalani told the parliament, "We had believed that in a nonviolent India the last thing the Government would contemplate would be an increase in the military budget, but I am sorry to say, and I think that it would disturb the soul of the father of the nation [Gandhi], that in recent years there has been an increase."[11] Nehru's Congress Party did not expend foreign exchange on the import of foreign arms. The armed forces had to do with the British remainders and whatever could be produced domestically. From 1951 to

1962, the Indian treasury spent less on arms than either the British government before it or the Indian governments that would follow the Sino-Indian war. Despite the war with Pakistan in 1947–48, the Indian government reduced its military expenses to 2 percent of its total budget, and despite this relatively low amount, the armed forces reported savings from what it had been designated.[12] After the war, the Indian government would not stint on its military to become the world's largest importer of weapons by the 1990s.

Why did the PLA invade India in 1962? One answer is that India had threatened to invade China, and the Chinese did so preemptively. They had an intractable border dispute, and both sides began to encroach on each other's claimed territory.[13] Neither the Chinese nor the Indians decided to withdraw beyond sight of each other, call for arbitration, or create a demilitarized zone that might be several miles in depth as a way to cool tensions. Both governments padded their forces, brought them on to each other's heads, and set up a situation for war. Another way to look at the Sino-Indian border war is to see it as a commonplace occurrence in the new postcolonial states that had, as far as the borders went, begun to adopt a more "European" notion of nationalism than their own previous anticolonial form. The very idea of nationalism that had sustained the anticolonial movements would be challenged in the process of state formation. To remain on the level of the details of the Sino-Indian conflict from 1950–62 would inform us as to the reasons why the war took place, but it would not itself tell us about a broader problem for postcolonial states—the adoption of a mystical version of nationalism that had been alien to the anticolonial movements.

The Chinese built a road in the Aksai-Chin sector claimed by India, and they justified this not only as always having been part of Tibet (and therefore China) but as a crucial artery to join the Chinese provinces of Tibet and Sinjiang. Aksai-Chin is a barren region, where no one can survive year-round. By 1962, the Indian and Chinese armies stood at the many checkpoints that dotted the unmarked border. Border clashes from the mid-1950s resulted in the loss of some lives, but even those who did not perish spent months on end in the harsh high-altitude outposts where few would otherwise tread. When the snow got too heavy, the army abandoned the post, and each spring rushed back up to make sure that they were the ones to reclaim the spot and not the other side. This insane game went on for eight years.

Meanwhile, the Indian army moved to forward posts in the Tawang region, in northeastern India, into areas that were previously claimed by the Tibetans. Various ethnic communities for whom the border is an inconvenience people the Tawang region. Nations don't have natural borders, nor do most of them have well-defined historical borders. The tendency to see mountains or rivers as natural boundaries from the standpoint of security or ease of delineation is not universally accepted, nor does it everywhere have ancient roots.[14] Before mountains could be scaled or rivers could be forded, these geographic phenomena did provide a barrier for movement, but once humans learned to overcome these obstacles, they ceased to be effective barriers. Many premodern states did not put too much stake on the accurate delineation of the boundary, and the people who lived in its vicinity moved around for trade and pilgrimage with only minimal concern for the niceties of monarchal logic. Indeed, the Himalayas that run along the borders between today's states of Burma, Nepal, India, China, Pakistan, and Afghanistan are home to people at high altitudes whose lives rely on transit across the mountain passes to the plains for trade or religious pilgrimages. The boundary is not in the interest of these people, because in many cases it not only inconveniences trade or belief but also bifurcates a linguistic group or an ethnic community. People who see themselves as part of a community are rent by a logic that is antithetical to their own history.

In 1913, the British Indian government sent two surveyors to northeast India. Frederick Markham Bailey and Henry T. Morshead traveled along a well-trod trade route that would soon be known as the "Bailey Trail."[15] Bailey and Morshead found that traders and their yaks moved goods from the highlands of Tibet to the plains of Burma and India, without any care for passports or identification, without a sense that they lived in what had already become a disputed border region. When Christoph von Fürer-Haimendorf visited the Bailey Trail in 1944 as the special officer of the Indian External Affairs Department, he reported that the people in the region, the Monpa, had an oblique relationship with either Tibet, China, or India.[16] International borders meant little to them because their ancestors had hewed trails that created their own geography, their own mundane and spiritual maps. At the crossroads of this interconnected border region stood Tawang, a town dominated by a monastery (*gompa*) called Galden Namgyal Lhatse built between 1643 and 1647. The circumstances of the monastery illuminate the lack of importance borders had for the lives of the people. Lodre Gyaltso, known also as Merak Lama, allowed his horse to take him where it willed. The horse stopped, and Merak Lama named the place Tawang, "chosen by a horse."[17] The story mimics the Brahmanical *ashwamedha yagya*, the horse "sacrifice" of ancient Vedic India, where a monarch would allow a horse to run its paces, and all the ground the horse covered would be the monarch's terrain. The impulse of the horse determined the rough border of the Vedic kings, while the resting place of the horse along the fuzzy boundary between regions provided Merak Lama with the site for his monastery.

Bailey and Morshead were the advance team of a colonial state that had a classic approach to borders. Colonial powers based their borders on what they were able to conquer, and guarded these boundaries in terms of security rather than any other principle. The cartography of the Himalayas by the British had little to do with the needs and desires of the people who lived in the hills; it had everything to do with the creation of buffer states to protect their Indian empire from the threats by the Czarist Russians and the Manchu Chinese. In 1893, the British created the Durand line, which ran right through the homelands of the Pashtu speakers so as to maintain Afghanistan as a border territory between Russia and India, just as in 1914, the British fashioned the McMahon line to divide their Indian domains from those of the Chinese.[18] Security as the British understood it was the paramount reason for the way they understood the borders, and frequently they signed agreements with parties (such as King Abdul Rahman Khan in Afghanistan or Ivan Chen of the "Order of the Chia Ho" and the Dalai Lama for the Tibet-India border) whose own legitimacy would be questioned later. In the Durand and McMahon cases, the British simply drew up a line that met their security needs and got the line ratified by parties that had little option but to sign on.[19]

In the colony, the border provided security. In Europe, the border offered a divide between one nation and another. Indistinct zones between countries were redefined in the nineteenth century as nations came into their own.[20] Border technology (such as the quadrant and the theodolite as well as border cartography) supplied the means for the emergent European nations to produce finely wrought territorial markers and maps for their national imaginary. These new technologies met a social demand: to remove the nebulousness of the border and unify a nation. Border making was not neutral because it bore within it the values of European ethno-nationalism. From the mid-eighteenth century onward, European nation-states emerged out of the monarchies and baronies of earlier epochs. The idea that motivated many of these nation-states was that they must contain within them people of the same ethnicity or race—that the French and the Germans are divided not simply by language and custom but by the strains in their blood. While nationalism is indeed a modern phenomenon, nationalists enlivened their national demands with ancient stories of their nation, and therefore they saw their quest not as the production of a nation into a state but as the reclaiming of a nation under a state. The nation was always there, waiting for the nationalist to bring it into its own.[21] The creation of tradition and the accoutrement of nations strengthened the claim that a people, such as the English or the French, had a natural desire and need to be self-governed (where the "self" had racial connotations and did not simply designate a political unity).[22]

Anticolonial movements were conscious of these dual (security and racial) roots for border construction. Many of them had a great unease about the linkage between "national dignity" and territorial integrity. Multinational states had little need for chauvinist sensibilities about where the state started or stopped. Within the country, the division of the landmass was often conducted on lines that did not privilege the fault lines of race or religion; in India, for instance, the internal states were divided along the lines of language (which can be learned and therefore is not ontologically derived).[23] A strict border would inconvenience those who lived in the zone that straddled it, and in most cases, the harsh climate or terrain in the border region made its fortification unnecessary and impossible. When Soong Ch'ing-ling (Madame Sun Yat-sen) traveled to India in 1956 as China's vice president, she assured the national audience on All-India Radio that "friends may live far apart from each other, but friendship knows no barriers."[24] In late 1958, Nehru wrote to Zhou to set aside the "very minor border problem" and concentrate on larger matters. Zhou wrote back that the minor border matter "should not affect the development of Sino-Indian friendly relations. This small question can be settled."[25] Borders were a pragmatic issue, not a principled one.

Such high-minded ideas on internationalism and mutual respect for sovereignty (the basis of Panchsheela) could not withstand older ideological and cultural pressures. In China, the power of what some Communists called "Han chauvinism" or "Great Hanism" was strong. Liu Shao-chi's political report at the eighth National Congress of the Communist Party of China (September 1956) cautioned cadres not to fall prey to the idea that the Han people are the best, and that others are inferior, that only the Han can take charge of the minority communities (called "nationalities") and do their work for them.[26] In July 1957, Zhou went before the National People's Congress to caution the delegates against "big-nation chauvinism." "China is a big socialist country," he said, "so we must realize that the nationalist countries, whose social systems are different from ours, may have misgivings and fears toward China." Such statements offered an alternative to the virus of chauvinism and territorial fetishism that had become apparent in Tibet and in Formosa.[27]

If currents of ethno-nationalism emerged within and around the broader internationalism of Chinese Communism, similar leakages broke the barriers of Nehruvian secular internationalism. As the border dispute became more and more intractable, marginal political parties of the intransigent Right set the terms for the debate. The leader of the Swatantra Party told the Indian parliament that the Chinese were "soiling our motherland with their cancerous fingers."[28] When Zhou visited Delhi in 1960, Nehru stood beside him and said, "Not an inch of Indian soil would be yielded to China." Whereas Nehru was clear that the dispute was about "two miles of territory," his firmness came from the need to defend "national prestige and dignity."[29]

The reduction of dignity to territory had two important effects. First, it enabled previously subterranean chauvinism to parade in public. In India, the marginal Right took center stage as the defender of not only the border but also the ancient culture of India (which would be portrayed by these forces as Hindu). Tendencies against ethnic or religious minorities that would otherwise have no room in the broad expanse of secular national liberation squeezed into the public sphere, just as the state's own cultural institutions began to imagine the history of the state in ethno-cultural terms rather than anti-imperialist ones. From the rich resource of the past, state leaders drew elements to create the symbols and myths of the new nations; currency bore these emblems, as did national songs and history books. Anti-imperialism remained part of the agenda, but it now began to share the dais with an ideology that largely contradicted it: that the *nation* had always been there, that the freedom movements only returned it to its rightful place, and not that the nation had been produced by the national liberation movements. War encouraged chauvinism.

Second, the defense of the border and the talk of a military solution to a historical and political problem would have an adverse budgetary impact on state construction. An enhanced military establishment ate into the budgets and derailed the state's social development agenda. Monies spent on the military do not create a multiplier effect on the rest of the economy *in terms of social development*.[30] Indeed, military expenditure in the Third World distorts the national economic pledge to reverse the imperial drain and create a national economy whose incentive is social equity. Instead, the military expenditure drains capital toward the production of the means of destruction, begins to waste precious foreign exchange on the import of military technology, and destroys regional cooperation. One of the main levers to upturn the project of the Third World is militarization.[31]

After the 1962 war, the Indian government raised the percentage of the budget devoted to arms from an average of 2 percent (between 1951 and 1961) to an average of 4 percent of India's gross product (a full quarter of the central government outlay). The military's draw on the finances of the state raised the stature of the defense minister in the cabinet and state policy. Social development had to get in line behind security (which had been reduced to military defense) in the affairs of state. World Bank president Robert McNamara's study of military expenditure in the darker nations found that states had quintupled that one line item between 1960 and 1988; military expenditure increased at twice the rate of per capita income.[32] As precious capital went into the military, the rate of savings in these societies declined, just as these societies began to see a drastic reduction in social spending (education, health, and child welfare) as opposed to military expenditure.[33] In addition to its diversion of investment capital, the military drew on scarce human and material resources—people bore arms, they did scientific research for military purposes, and raw materials like chromium, cobalt, manganese, steel, uranium, and other such materials moved from civilian to military use.[34] By 1982, the United Nations offered the stark choice that either the world can "pursue the arms race," or else it can "move consciously and with deliberate speed toward a more stable and balanced social and economic development." But, the United Nations cautioned, "it cannot do both."[35]

As the Third World state diverted its foreign exchange toward the import of arms, it developed close relations with NATO and the Warsaw Pact. The main arms manufacturers and exporters came from either the Atlantic or the Soviet blocs, and the states of the Third World created special relationships to gain access to these producers. Often military arrangements were worked out to allow for the transfer of technology to the darker nations. For repairs and training, advisers from the Atlantic and Soviet blocs made frequent trips to the Third World—even to states that formally pledged their non-alignment. In 1973, the Soviet Union went to the UN General Assembly with a resolution to reduce global military expenditures by 10 percent and put that money into a fund for social development in the Third World. With all indications that the Atlantic powers would veto the measure, the General Assembly rewrote the resolution to ask the secretary general to study the matter.[36] The world's governments failed to cooperate effectively, and the measure died where it began. Every attempt to stem the arms trade or cut back on the vast increase in the global military budget was met with disdain or incomprehension—security and defense had come to be reality, whereas social development became idealistic.[37]

The 1962 Sino-Indian war tragically disrupted the dynamic of non-alignment, and therefore of the political platform of the Third World. Thereafter, India, which took a leadership role in the group at the United Nations on issues of disarmament and peace, was severely compromised by its own arms buildup. China's foreign policy wound its way from Bandung to a rapprochement with the United States and its impossible alliances with dictatorial regimes. As China began its new relationship with the United States, the Chinese government praised the Greek military junta (1972), took the side of Pakistan against the liberation of Bangladesh (1971), welcomed Nimeiri to Beijing after the dictatorship's massacre of its Communists (1971), sent emergency aid to the Sri Lankan government to defeat the left-wing Lanka Samaja Party's insurrection, and quickly recognized Pinochet's coup in Chile (it expelled the Chilean ambassador to China when he refused to support Pinochet).[38] The Sino-Indian war compromised the credibility of India and China.[39]

In 1966, the Indian writer Rahi Masoom Raza published his cheeky novel, *Aadha Gaon* (*Half a Village*). Set in Gangauli, a small town in Bihar on the banks of the Ganges, far from the border region, Raza's story takes the reader to the period when the partition of the subcontinent meant the mass migration of Hindus to India and Muslims to Pakistan—13 million people crossed the border and one million people died in the inevitable fracas when the two lines of enforced migrants met each other (or else when political forces of the Right began a vigilante massacre of each other). Deep inside what became India, the Muslim residents of Gangauli reject any idea that they must uproot themselves and go to Pakistan. "I am not going anywhere," said Mighdad, "Let those who feel ashamed of their buffaloes go. . . . I am here, with my soil and fields."[40] Some of Gangauli's residents thought that Pakistan would be the new name of a part of their village, the Muslim-majority areas would be renamed, and if they didn't already live there, they would have to move to this Pakistan. Tannu, Mighdad's brother, fights with a political worker who comes to convince

Muslims to move to Pakistan. He tells the politician that they will have to "harvest the crop of fear" because they have introduced firm differences where they were not so stark. "Allah is everywhere," he says courageously, "so how different is Gangauli from Mecca." The politician is outraged by this comparison, which brings from Tannu this rejoinder: "Gangauli is my town. Mecca is not my town. It is my home, just as Allah Mian's is the Kaaba. . . . Things built on a foundation of fear and hatred cannot be auspicious."[41] Raza wrote this novel in the aftermath of the Sino-Indian border war and while the Indo-Pakistan war of 1965 shook the subcontinent. The crop of fear had been harvested not just on the border and in the deaths that such wars occasion but also in the distortions bred into the social fabric of the nation and the economic agenda of the state.

CARACAS

On July 14, 1936, the magazine *Ahora* ran an editorial on its front page titled "Sembrar el petróleo" ("To Sow or to Plant Oil"). The year before, the longtime dictator of Venezuela, Juan Vincente Gómez, had died. The future seemed open for the country. Arturo Uslar-Pietri, well-known on the Caracas scene for his remarkable historical novel (*Las Lanzas Coloradas*, 1931), authored this farsighted piece. "Now all of Venezuela is oil. Not oil sown and transformed into harvests and factories, as it could and should have been; but oil flooding over and carrying away houses, plants and cattle in its path."[1] Oil, the most lucrative raw material found in the darker nations, carried great promise. As black gold, it had the ability to finance the social democratic dreams of populations that had slumbered too long in the shadow of empire. Yet the massive oil profits earned did not trickle down to the masses; the beneficiaries were the oil companies and the oligarchy.

As if testing Uslar-Pietri's thesis, in December 1936, the oil workers at the Maracaibo fields went on strike for better daily wages, better housing, and salary parity between Venezuelans and foreigners; the regime joined with the oil companies to refuse the demands, sent in the police, and decreed a mediocre rise in the daily wage as a sop.[2] The oil industry created an industrial proletariat, but their numbers remained low in this capital-intensive industry. When the oil workers made demands on their flushed proprietors, they earned no redress. The foreign (mainly U.S.) management recycled prejudices that did not answer the aspirations of the workers. The vice president of Venezuelan Gulf, W.T. Wallace, felt that there was no need to take care of these workers because "the native mind" cannot "conform to the accepted method of living," and if the workers do try to make their surroundings inhabitable, this comes "not on a real desire to conform to American practices, but from a desire to try to get something for nothing."[3]

In the 1950s, oil production doubled, and between 1948 and 1957 the oil industry produced revenues of $7 billion for the government. This amount was "greater than the whole previous total of public revenue since the colonization of the country by Spain."[4] This money, plus an enormous amount of foreign investment capital, flooded the country. It went toward a major construction boom in the city of Caracas. Freeways circled the valley, enclosing European-style apartment buildings and enormous shopping arcades (including the world's most profitable branch of Sears and Roebuck). The dictator Marcos Pérez Jiménez (1952–58) turned the oil revenues toward the reconstruction of urban Venezuela. The wealthy created a paradise in Caracas valley, while an enormous migration began to settle on the hillsides. These were not oil workers, who tended to live in company housing next to the oil fields toward the west of the country. The migrants came in response to the great social upheaval in Venezuela, caused in large part by the rapid economic growth spurred on by the oil profits. The gross national product increased by a dramatic 95 percent, and this buoyed the construction trade and the service industries for the rich. From 1950 to 1965, the years of oil expansion, the proportion of rural to urban dwellers grew from 48 to 66 percent. Pérez Jiménez's armies bulldozed the rough-and-ready urban villages and built vast public housing estates (*superbloques*). When this dictator was overthrown in 1958, his successors threw open the barrios to assuage the aspirations of the landless peasants who flooded the cities. As one scholar put it, "So concentrated was the trend that today more barrios trace their origin back to those first twenty-four months following the Revolution than to any other period."[5] The barrios remained a hotbed of political resentment and cultural ferment; from there would come the energy for revolution and disorder, for labor and reconstruction.

Oil promised salvation. The few countries that had enough oil for both domestic consumption and export earned significant amounts of foreign exchange. Oil had much more muscle than cocoa and coffee, than bauxite and iron ore. The lifeblood of postwar industrial capitalism, oil earned well for those who controlled it. The issue, from the first, was not so much the oil itself but control. Who controlled the oil? When inventors discovered what to do with the black gold in the 1850s, the main colonial states (including the United States and czarist Russia) quickly made it their mission to take control of this major energy resource. In 1850, fossil fuels supplied only 6 percent of the world's energy needs, while humans and animals provided the rest. A century later, human and animal power had declined to 6 percent, while fossil fuel use accounted for the remainder. By 1950, the main energy corporations organized themselves into seven conglomerates known as the Seven Sisters: Exxon (or Esso), Shell, BP, Gulf, Texaco, Mobil, and Socal (or Chevron).[6] Even though oil is a lucrative product, in its crude state it is nothing more than a raw material. To remove oil from the ground requires an immense capital outlay, both for exploration and extraction. This initial capital outlay is the carrot and stick used by the Seven Sisters. They came to the oil lands in the early years and staked out "concessions" for themselves. Their fates were interlinked. In one zone, Exxon would be the main partner, and in another BP—they operated as a cartel and dominated the supply of crude oil. Not only did the firms control the supply of oil but they also held the reins to the transportation, refinement, and sale of oil in its various forms. These seven firms, in 1950, controlled 85 percent of the crude oil production in the world outside Canada, China, the USSR, and the United States, and these firms acted together as a cartel of private companies to ensure that they not only got the best prices for crude oil but also controlled the entire oil market.

The regimes that ruled over the oil lands could have used the rent paid by the oil companies to increase the social wage—to expand public education, health, transport, and other such important avenues for the overall advancement of the people. Instead, the oil rent went toward the expansion of luxury consumption for the bureaucratic-managerial or monarchal elite—the oligarchy in Venezuela or the Ibn Saud clan in Saudi Arabia—and to oil the military machine (the oil war of Bolivia-Paraguay, 1932–35, was a preview of the 1967–70 Nigerian civil war).[7] In 1966, oil workers in Lagunillas, Venezuela, reflected that "oil has come and gone for us here. It would have been better for us if these machines had never come."[8] The profits for oil did not go toward social development—a failure that eroded the confidence of the local bourgeoisie in its own capacity. Uslar-Pietri's 1936 editorial reflected this anxiety and anger, this sense that despite the oil and its revenues, the Venezuelan government had been unable to open its hand to the afflicted.

In 1957 alone the Seven Sisters made $828 million in Venezuela, whose regime allowed them to remit all their profits without restrictions. As one U.S. banker noted, "You have the freedom here to do what you want to do with your money, and to me, that is worth all the political freedom in the world."[9] The United States supported the junta that came to power in the 1940s, whose goal was to maintain good relations with the oil cartel rather than pursue social development policies. In 1950, the U.S. State Department remarked that "all United States policies toward Venezuela are affected in greater or lesser degree by the objective of assuring an adequate supply of petroleum for the U.S., especially in time of war."[10] The oil wealth was not, therefore, reinvested for the overall development of the country. The junta reversed the land reforms of a decade previously, sold the land to private speculators, and moved Venezuela to become a net importer of food grains.[11] In the early 1950s, Creole Petroleum (a subsidiary of Exxon) did a poll that confirmed its worst fears: a majority of Venezuelans supported the nationalization of the oil industry.[12] Even the junta had to worry about the decline in oil prices, because this was the main source of its revenues. It sent a delegation to Saudi Arabia and Iran to see if the main oil lands could come to some agreement on prices, but they did not make a dent. The Saudis had a political beef with Venezuela: the latter had supported Israel's creation.

In 1958, the new relatively progressive government led by Acción Democrática (AD) expressed an interest in recouping a larger share of the oil profits, thus far absorbed by the Seven Sisters. Venezuela had been able to increase its share of the world oil market for serendipitous reasons. Mexico used to be a major provider of the world's oil (25 percent). After the Mexican Revolution (1911), the new regime attempted to get a better handle on its oil profits. The two major companies, U.S.-based Standard Oil and British-based Mexican Eagle, were chary about the nationalist noises from Mexico City. In 1934, after two decades of tussle, the general who had once guarded the oil region, Lázaro Cárdenas, became the president. A British official recognized his politics and yet admired his probity: "His Leftist inclinations make him the bugbear of capitalism, but all things considered it is to be regretted that there are not more men of his caliber in Mexican life."[13] The Depression, the overproduction of oil, and the stranglehold of the Seven Sisters led to a drop in the earnings for countries like Mexico. In 1937, its oil workers threatened to strike against their working and living conditions as well as the decline in their wages. Cárdenas appointed a commission to study the situation, and the commission reported that the wages and conditions of work needed to be improved, Mexican managers and technicians had to replace foreign ones, and the oil companies had taken Mexico for a ride. In 1938, Cárdenas nationalized the oil industry.

In retaliation, the Seven Sisters boycotted the purchase of Mexican oil, and the new national oil company, PEMEX, floundered. U.S. ambassador Josephus Daniels predicted that Mexicans would "drown in their own oil."[14] The Seven Sisters moved their focus from Mexico to Venezuela. Being a cartel, the Seven Sisters colluded in their political attack on Mexico, sent a message to the oil lands that they opposed the nationalization of the oil fields, and moved to another site where they were given beneficial treatment. Because of this shift to Venezuela, its oil production increased dramatically from 1943 onward, so that by 1957 the South American country produced a billion barrels of oil.

The AD regime reassessed Venezuela's position. The government could tax the oil profits. Before they moved in this direction, the Seven Sisters slashed the price of oil. The Seven Sisters faced competition from the USSR's sale of surplus oil on the open market as well as the entry of new oil companies outside the cartel (from Italy and Japan). The Seven Sisters also had to deal with the U.S. quotas on oil imports to stimulate domestic production. Even as the Seven Sisters began to lose their hold on the oil market, the decline still left them with over 72 percent of it by 1960.[15] To show their muscle, the Seven Sisters slashed the oil price twice between February 1959 and August 1960—they could spread their per barrel losses by capturing more of the volume of sales, whereas the taxes paid to the oil lands based on the per barrel posted price decreased immediately. The pain borne by the regimes of the oil lands pushed many of them toward a reconsideration of the shape of the international economy.

In the late 1940s, Raúl Prebisch complained about the low prices earned by the raw material producers because private cartels controlled international prices.[16] Whether the crop is cocoa, sugar, rubber, or oil, the structure of the commodity cartel did not differ much. The Economic Commission on Latin America and the Afro-Asian Organisation for Economic Cooperation both held deliberations on the creation of public commodity cartels as a power base against the private corporate cartels. They wanted the public cartels to achieve a stabilization of prices to benefit the raw materials' producers. The declining price of raw materials over time meant that the Third World would never be able to earn enough from the sale of raw materials to effect both meaningful social development and industrial growth. Many of the formerly colonial states had a problem: they had either been carved out as one-commodity producers or else they had developed into one-crop countries. With no economic diversification, these states additionally had less power than the private corporate cartel. They had only one crop, and unless other countries that produced the same crop banded together, they had to accept whatever terms the private corporate cartel offered. There could be no bargaining, and the prices remained abysmally low.

Because of the low level of capital available in the darker nations, the regimes tried to strengthen the one economic process that had already been perfected: the colonial crop. The regimes in the Third World relied on the singular colonial crop. They also had little capital to refine and process the crop to create some value before export. In other words, the raw material frequently left the old colonial rail lines and ports in its rawest form possible for transport, and brought a mediocre return to the former colony. The reliance on the singular crop or extractable raw material (or two crops and mined goods) meant that the national liberation state could not be too confrontational toward the only one who would buy the commodity and take it to the lucrative First World markets. As Egypt's Nasser put it, "Arabs know that their oil has to go to the customer before it has any value."[17] Finally, the low level of capital in the arsenal of the darker nations meant that they gave "reasonable" terms to the transnational conglomerates that worked in the private cartel, and had the funds to explore and excavate, cultivate and transport. The concessions given to these conglomerates meant that the regime frequently lost control over production, and would only be able to restrict the giants through licenses, increased taxation, and other minor irritations. The broad sovereignty over resources and labor had been long mortgaged for the capital infusion that was so necessary in the ruined landscape of the former colonies.

By 1980, of the 115 "developing countries," according to UNCTAD, at least half remained dependent on one commodity for over 50 percent of their export revenues. Most of these countries had come to rely on petroleum exports.[18]

The most common commodity on the following list is petroleum, although in the 1950s many of these nations had not yet produced petroleum at the rates they would in the 1980s. It made sense, then, that when the Seven Sisters played with the prices in the late 1950s, the regimes in the oil lands had to react. If they did not make any movement to challenge the Seven Sisters their livelihood would vanish.

Over 90 percent	Over 80 percent	Over 70 percent	Over 60 percent	Over 50 percent
Libya (petrol)	Trinidad and Tobago (petrol)	Niger (uranium)	Mauritius (sugar)	Ethiopia (coffee)
Iraq (petrol)	Gabon (petrol)	Burundi (coffee)	Mexico (petrol)	Cuba (sugar)
Nigeria (petrol)	Mauritania (petrol)	Chad (cotton)	Egypt (petrol)	El Salvador (coffee)
Saudi Arabia (petrol)	Iran (petrol)	Fiji (sugar)	Liberia (iron ore)	Cape Verde (fish)
Uganda (coffee)	Syria (petrol)	Vanuatu (oil seeds)	Seychelles (oil seeds)	Dominican Republic (sugar)
Venezuela (petrol)	Kuwait (petrol)	Angola (petrol)	Ecuador (petrol)	Tunisia (petrol)
Qatar (petrol)	Tuvalu (oil seeds)	Rwanda (coffee)	Indonesia (petrol)	Ghana (cocoa)
United Arab Emirates (petrol)	Zambia (copper)	Congo (petrol)	Suriname (alumina)	Mali (cocoa)
Algeria (petrol)	Maldives (fish)	Somalia (animals)	Jamaica (alumina)	Togo (crude fertilizer)
Bahrain (petrol)			Brunei (petrol)	
Yemen (petrol)				

Source: UNCTAD, *Handbook of International Trade and Development Statistics* (Geneva: United Nations, 1984), table 4.3D.

In April 1959, Nasser's Egypt and the Arab League hosted the First Arab Petroleum Congress, a gathering attended by representatives from the Arab nations (except Iraq, whose leader Qasim had a disagreement with Nasser) along with Venezuela and Iran. The congress gathered just as the Seven Sisters reduced the posted price for Middle East oil. Venezuela's representative, Juan Pablo Pérez Alfonzo, was an experienced

AD politician. Pérez Alfonzo made his political mark in 1943 during a debate in Venezuela over the oil concessions enjoyed by the Seven Sisters. Whereas the government won the right to tax oil profits, it did put off the rule of the Seven Sisters for another forty years. Pérez Alfonzo and his AD colleagues considered the Hydrocarbons Law a sellout. In 1958, Pérez Alfonzo joined the AD government as the minister of mines and hydrocarbons. He led the charge against the Seven Sisters, earned the government 60 percent of the oil revenues, and established the notion that Venezuela had sovereignty over its subsoil so that the entire oil industry was a public utility.[19] On his departure for Cairo from Caracas, Pérez Alfonzo noted, "We producers must try to find means to collaborate to avoid arbitrary fixing of prices."[20] Pérez Alfonzo, who refused to travel by car or use lights at night, had a mystical notion of Venezuela's petroleum reserves: petroleum, which had an intrinsic value, had been given to the people for posterity, and it was the duty of the guardians of the state to ensure its longevity.[21] His personal attitudes and practices with regard to petroleum did not come only from ecological motive but mainly from a nationalistic one. The reserves had to be saved for the future, not for themselves. Because of this idiosyncratic argument and because he was a close follower of Prebisch's theory of public commodity cartels, Pérez Alfonzo tried to maximize on the momentary advantage given to Venezuela by the Seven Sisters.

At Cairo, the powers did not make any great headway toward price control because all they settled on was a word-of-mouth agreement to defend the price of oil.[22] Franck Hendryk, legal counselor to the Saudi government, presented a paper at the congress in which he argued that "an oil-producing nation, by the law of civilized nations, may clearly in a proper case, modify or eliminate provisions of an existing petroleum concession which have become substantially contrary to the best interests of its citizens."[23] This inflammatory statement stunned the delegates, mainly because it came with the blessings of the Saudi petroleum minister 'Abdullah al-Tariqi. A devotee of Nasser, Tariqi was a commoner who had studied engineering in the United States before he returned to Saudi Arabia. Given a break by radical elements in the Saudi royal family (who were known as the "Free Princes"), Tariqi articulated a progressive agenda for Saudi oil profits. He annoyed the Arab-American Oil Company (Aramco) with his criticism of its economic and political hold on Saudi Arabia, and pressured the monarchy with his statements on the need for more democracy on the peninsula ("We will soon have a Constitution," he said in April 1958, "this country will shortly become a constitutional monarchy"). Not for nothing was he known as the "Red Sheikh."[24]

The Red Sheikh met secretly with Pérez Alfonzo to draft an agreement on the side of the conference that would be later known as the Maadi Pact.[25] Although the pact did not have any binding resolutions, it did set up the Oil Consultative Commission, which pledged to meet annually and push a five-point plan: to stabilize prices, integrate the operations of the industry so that the oil companies did not run rings around the oil lands, begin the refinement of oil products in the darker nations themselves, establish national oil companies "that would operate side by side with existing private companies," and coordinate "the conservation, production and exploitation of petroleum."[26] The two men made no formal agreement, but they created the basis for what became the oil producers' cartel.

Exxon egged on the nationalists with another price reduction (this time, by 7 percent of the posted price). When the oil producers met in Baghdad in September 1960, a month after the decrease, they came with a purpose: to form a public cartel of oil producers. After a week of deliberation, the group created OPEC. The five charter members nominally controlled or at least produced 82 percent of the world's crude oil exports: Venezuela (30 percent), Kuwait (18 percent), Saudi Arabia (14 percent), Iraq (10 percent), and Iran (10 percent). Pérez Alfonzo's opening statement reminded the delegates that oil is "an exhaustible, nonrenewable resource," that "world reserves of crude oil would not continue to expand forever," and so "our peoples cannot let flow, at an accelerated rate, their only possibility to pass without delay from poverty to well-being, from ignorance to culture, from instability and fear to security and confidence."[27] Export of the only lucrative raw material in these lands had to provide the basis for development, and if the leadership of these nations squandered that opportunity, it would be lost forever. From Pérez Alfonzo, the delegates got an awesome charge. The Nasserite delegates in the room would have already read something eerily similar in the Egyptian president's *The Philosophy of the Revolution* (1954), where he had placed oil as one of the three pillars of Arab socialism—its wealth would help the Arab nation come into its own. Oil, Nasser wrote, was the "vital nerve of civilization, without which all its means cannot possibly exist."[28] If the oil producers could put their hands on the spigot, Exxon would not be able to drive the prices down and waste the down payment for the liberation of the darker nations.

The lofty rhetoric around the Baghdad meeting produced a meager agenda for the public commodity cartel. The first resolution of the organization excoriated the Seven Sisters for their domination of the industry, and charged OPEC members to "demand that oil companies maintain their prices steady, and free from all unnecessary fluctuation."[29] If OPEC did nothing else, it was at least able to prevent a reduction in the price of oil. The oil exporters rationalized their taxation laws and cleared up all kinds of inconsistencies over whether royalties (rent) should be included with profits for taxation, or whether rent should be an outright payment. The Seven Sisters refused to allow the rent to be an additional burden, because they wanted the rent to be taken as a cost and not a credit, that it be an advance to be deducted from the overall tax. OPEC conceded to the Seven Sisters on this crucial point, although this would be an issue raised repeatedly at OPEC forums (often by the more radical elements within OPEC). Whatever the immediate limitations of OPEC, henceforth the Seven Sisters and the oil importing countries had to acknowledge its place in discussions over price (and therefore over production totals). Pérez Alfonzo left Baghdad in an upbeat mood, declaring, "The spirit which has animated our discussions is more important than the results achieved."[30] The major financial papers of the world ignored the foundation of OPEC, treating it as another one of those interminable Third World conferences that would have no value in the long run.

The bravura of OPEC, the idea that the darker nations could produce a cartel for their precious commodities to ensure a decent price, impacted the Third World. Various Third World political forums now tried to move a similar agenda as OPEC, to create various public cartels for the otherwise-cheap raw materials bought in a market created by the private transnational cartels mostly located in the First World (or else by prices set by the members of the Council for Mutual Economic Assistance). At the NAM meeting in Belgrade (1961), the issue came up for discussion, and in the halls of UNCTAD (from 1964) economists and politicians drafted and redrafted statements and agreements on Integrated Commodity Programs. The question was, how to create a cartel for a commodity not as obviously precious as petroleum? Prebisch at UNCTAD had his heart set on cocoa, while other parties created such platforms as the Inter-Governmental Council of Copper Exporting Countries and the International Bauxite Association. None of these had the impact of OPEC, and they all faltered on the mechanism to ensure stable prices and supply. When it came to the creation of a buffer stock of the commodity in question, UNCTAD lacked the funds to buy sufficient quantities to regulate the price and ensure stability.[31] A major disappointment in this was the failure of the OPEC nations to use their massive oil profits for the creation of such a fund to help stabilize other commodities.[32] Not only did the OPEC powers refuse to contribute to a global fund to stabilize raw material prices but they also had a poor record in their aid contributions to their neighbors and the Third World in general (only 6 percent of their flush profits).[33] Despite its political origins, OPEC became an economic cartel as it fought to defend oil prices and do little else. Certainly OPEC played an enormous part in the rise of the per barrel price of oil from $3 in 1973 to $36 in 1981, but by the 1999 Vienna meeting the major decisions were taken long before the powers met for a perfunctory three hours to ratify these prior resolutions. OPEC is now a hollow institution, in name a lion.

Despite OPEC's feint against the international world order, the petroleum exporting countries remained relatively powerless mainly because they did not dethrone the Seven Sisters. In fact, the collaboration between the Seven Sisters and OPEC squelched the growth of independent oil firms on the world market (such as the Italian State Oil Company, headed by the combative Enrico Mattei, and the Russian state oil ministry, Minnefteprom, as well as the U.S.-based family firms such as Getty and Hunt). These firms might have helped break down the Seven Sisters' suffocation of the market. The public oil cartel worked with the private cartel to close the market. The Seven Sisters benefited from OPEC, just as they did everything in their power to undermine it. For example, they began to explore other sources of oil in places like North Africa and off the shoreline of the Atlantic to enhance supply and reduce OPEC's bargaining power. When the opportunity presented itself, the Seven Sisters bargained with individual countries and gave them deals to bypass the OPEC price ceilings. U.S. president Eisenhower clearly understood this: "The Middle East countries in the new organization were concerned anyone could break up the organization by offering five cents more per barrel for the oil of one of the countries."[34] This happened numerous times in the early history of OPEC.[35]

One approach that nations of the Third World took toward concessionary cartels like the Seven Sisters was to nationalize the ownership of the oil fields, the plantations, or even the refineries—all the physical plant of the industry that had been rented from the state or else that worked within the authority of the state. To nationalize these assets disrupted the power of the Seven Sisters and other private cartels, but it did not overturn their overwhelming planetary power. Indeed, the immense political pressure on the oil lands to nationalize the assets had made such a move inevitable, so that in at least two cases (Saudi Arabia and Kuwait), the Seven Sisters "voluntarily" withdrew themselves from ownership of the fields. Nationalization of the oil fields moved the local power from the cartel to the domestic bourgeoisie that controlled or had substantial power over the managerial state. For instance, when Venezuela took action against the Seven Sisters in the 1960s, one commentator described the transfer of power in this way: "A planning apparatus and state-owned heavy industry complexes (a steel mill and aluminium industry in the Guayana province; petrochemical complexes in the northwest) were established. These further expanded and strengthened the position of the bureaucracy as an independent social force. But this did not give them control of the economic development process as a whole."[36] The Venezuelan state and the domestic bourgeoisie took charge of the extraction of the oil, but they did not control the process. They still had to cooperate with the Seven Sisters, which continued to exert enormous pressure on the oil industry. In sum, the nationalization of economic assets from transnational firms replicated the problems of political independence from colonialism; it was an advance, but it created an illusion of freedom. The Seven Sisters transferred the burdens of extraction on to the state, while it continued to enjoy the fruits of the industry. Furthermore, the state's newfound power over the fields and its ability to negotiate with the Seven Sisters over the prices and taxes moved it to bargain on two sides of the commodity cycle: with the oil workers for lower wages, and the Seven Sisters for higher prices. To raise the export receipt and increase the coffers of the state did not itself presage a strategy for the generation of equity.

If the public cartels and the strategy of asset nationalization did not always benefit the tropical working class, it should be said that the strategy also did not benefit those countries that did not have access to the higher-priced primary products. When OPEC maintained its price for oil, the darker nations without oil had a much higher import bill for the one energy source that had become indispensable for contemporary capitalism. While the radical members of OPEC, such as Libya in the early 1970s, did call for differential prices for the various nations of the world, OPEC's strictly economic vision precluded any such political arrangement. The only time OPEC openly indulged in a political battle was over the defense of Palestine, but even here Arab unity could not be counted on.[37] In general, commodity cartels did not always help the Third World and hurt the advanced industrial states: the latter often dominate the production of certain primary goods, such as agricultural commodities grown on factory farms by megacorporations, whereas the former often produce manufactured goods. High oil prices hurt the Third World states that have no domestic oil reserves, just as any cartel would only help those that have the commodity protected by it and not the others. Whereas the cartel approach certainly emboldened states, it did not have a general political strategy to build power in the totality of the Third World.

OPEC's boldest display of unity was during the embargo of 1973. A defeat to the Arab armies by Israel in 1967 strengthened a withered sort of Arab unity, while the Iranian Shah had a domestic compulsion to increase and modernize his military and police forces with oil revenues. The Venezuelan government, now under the conservatives, had long wanted an increase in revenues to maintain its tenuous hold on an increasingly impoverished society. The example for the oil hike came in 1970 from Libya. The new Revolutionary Command Council under Gaddafi raised the price of Libyan oil (whose advantages were its abundance, proximity to Europe, superior quality, and control by the Libyan state). Gaddafi declared, "The people who have lived 5,000 years without petroleum can live without it for many more decades in order to achieve their legitimate rights."[38] Neither the Atlantic powers nor the Seven Sisters could confront Gaddafi's defiance, and they caved with a "voluntary" price increase.

When OPEC raised the price of oil in October 1973, purportedly as a political weapon over the Yom Kippur war, it did not do so as a challenge to imperialism. Indeed, despite the confrontationist rhetoric of Gaddafi and others, OPEC's Saudi anchor derived advantages for the U.S. government in an intraimperialist show of force. In 1971, when President Nixon delinked the dollar from the gold standard, the administration puzzled over strategies to exert power over the global economy. One of these was a rise in the oil price, which would, the Nixon administration surmised, do at least two things for the United States: put an immense squeeze on the two main economic competitors, Western Europe and Japan; and earn profits for the oil lands, which would, in all probability, be recycled into U.S. financial institutions because the Gulf states, at least, did not have adequate productive capacity to absorb the petro-profits. The elimination of capital controls in the U.S. economy by 1974 further facilitated the recycling of these petro-profits (then held almost exclusively in dollars), and therefore the global enhancement of the status of the dollar as the instrument of "hard currency."[39] Since the oil states held their main currency reserves in dollars, it behooved them to help stabilize the U.S. economy (and work against the depreciation of the dollar, which contributed to the deindustrialization of the United States).[40] The 1973 price rise certainly improved the position of the oil lands momentarily, but in the long run it benefited the U.S. government and the major transnational firms that did business in dollars. Despite the best intentions of the public cartel, then, it did not necessarily inconvenience or challenge the structure of imperialism.

In 1974, in the afterglow of the OPEC oil embargo, the UN General Assembly adopted a curious document, the New International Economic Order (NIEO). The NIEO document had been in the works within the Third World (notably UNCTAD) for at least a decade, and at its 1973 Algiers summit, NAM espoused it.[41] Drawing from the best of dependency theory, NAM argued that despite the UN Decade on Development, the current international order not only failed to develop the darker nations but contributed to their underdevelopment.[42]

The NIEO came from the presence of OPEC and the stranglehold experienced by UNCTAD. Fortuitously, Algeria's President Boumédienne, who headed NAM in 1973, was also the head of an OPEC member nation. He brought the experience of the one to bear on the creation of an economic policy for the other. The NIEO had a number of concrete points for discussion, but the Third World could not get any movement from the advanced industrial states. In 1974, the UN General Assembly approved the "Charter of Economic Rights and Duties of States," which drew from the NIEO on such points as the nationalization of foreign assets (Article 2), the creation of raw material cartels (Articles 3 and 5), the creation of "multilateral commodity agreements" (Article 6), and the creation of a system to "promote just and equitable terms of trade" (Article 28). The bulk of the articles emphasized that there should be no penalty for the type of economic system chosen by a state, that each state is juridically equal, and that no state should use economic power against the interests of another people. The best of the motivation for OPEC lies in this living charter.[43]

The advanced industrial states fundamentally rejected the approach of the NIEO and fought it with all means necessary, including contempt. At the 1976 Nairobi conference of UNCTAD, Secretary of State Kissinger was blunt: "The United States better than almost any nation could survive a period of economic warfare. We can resist confrontation and rhetorical attacks if other nations choose that path. And we can ignore unrealistic demands and peremptory demands."[44]

As Kissinger offered these words, this gauntlet from the advanced industrial states and the United States in particular, an old man who had helped form OPEC wrote a sad letter to his family. After he regretted that death was on him at his Caracas home, Pérez Alfonzo penned this elegy for OPEC and the idea of commodity cartels in general. For him, oil was the devil's excrement. "I am an ecologist first of all. I have always been an ecologist first of all. Now I am not interested in oil any more. I live for my flowers. OPEC, as an ecological group, has really disappeared. Still I feel OPEC is a good instrument of the Third World. It just has not been used properly."[45] He died two years later.

ARUSHA

In 1967, the Tanzanian president Julius Nyerere dropped a bombshell in a nondescript town that functioned as the gateway to eastern Africa's most spectacular natural phenomenon. Founded in 1900 as a garrison town, Arusha is nestled at the base of Mount Meru and within sight of Mount Kilimanjaro and the Serengeti Plain. Here, at the executive committee of his Tanganyika African National Union (TANU), Nyerere unveiled what would become known as the Arusha Declaration. The opening line of the declaration, "The policy of TANU is to build a socialist state," discomforted the British and Tanzanian owners and managers of most of the country's resources (including the mines and the land). The announcement of socialism came alongside the recognition that its construction would not be easy in a formerly colonized state. Not only had the German and British colonial regimes stripped bare the economy of eastern Africa but they also left behind a state apparatus designed to exploit and not to liberate. The institutions of the state and the civil bureaucracy grew from a culture of imperial hierarchy, a value quite removed from the egalitarianism of national liberation (as illustrated by TANU's Arusha Declaration and its 1971 *Mwongozo* or Leadership Code). Hemmed in by pressures from the advanced industrial states, the aristocratic rural classes, and the emergent mercantile classes, the new state had little time. Things had to change in a hurry. But socialism requires imagination and time. It cannot be made in a hurry. To create socialism in a hurry without mass support, and institutions that can channel this support, led many Third World states to disaster.

The Arusha Declaration validated the twin principles of liberty and equality, individual rights and collective well-being.[1] The state had to eliminate poverty, ignorance, and disease. That was unimpeachable. But how should the state go about the process of elimination? What is the organizational form for the transformation of society? Should it be a centralized state alone, or does it need to cultivate democratic (perhaps local) institutions that could harness the energy, ingenuity, and enthusiasm of a population only recently freed? Tanzania's population was mainly resident in rural areas and dependent on agriculture. Any institutional change needed to address agriculture and its role in the society as well as the world. After many fits and starts, the Nyerere regime adopted the idea of the socialist village (*ujamaa vijini*) as the main organizational form for rural change. But the regime recognized that agrarian reform was insufficient. The national liberation regime had to solve some of the main demands of the population before its political capital ran out. In Tanzania, output in the subsistence sector was only 2 percent (while population growth was 3 percent). Even though Tanzania had a high rate of increase in food production, TANU inherited a crisis situation. Agriculture, in an industrial world, could not alone deal with the people's aspirations and needs. The international terms of trade had a bias against agricultural commodities. Since rural Tanzania (like the rural areas of the world) required industrial products, its dwellers had a disadvantage. Tanzania needed to grow an industrial sector to produce capital goods (machinery, for example), and to refine and process agricultural (and mined) raw materials. The agricultural reforms therefore needed to come in the context of a wide economic reform.

This was a tall order for any society, and more so for one battered by colonial rule. Such changes required both political will and investment capital. Most national liberation regimes recognized the perils of foreign aid and commercial loans from banks in the advanced industrial states. These monies had the tendency to trap the postcolonial economy into a dependent relationship with the institutions of the First World (Soviet aid was limited as compared to what was available from Europe and the United States). "To burden the people with big loans," noted the Arusha Declaration, "the repayment of which will be beyond their means, is not to help them but to make them suffer. It is even worse when the loans they are asked to repay have not benefited the majority of the people but have only benefited a small minority."[2] Instead of foreign aid or commercial loans, the national liberation states developed a three-pronged approach to development: the nationalization of the commanding heights of the economy (finance, infrastructure, energy, crucial raw material extraction, and capital goods production), the development of the agricultural sector, and the encouragement of industrialization. The plan expected the capital for industrialization to come from the nationalization of finance and an increase in the agricultural surplus. Nationalization put financial decisions in the hands of the state rather than transnational corporations, and it arrested the hemorrhage of capital. Whatever funds could be assembled helped toward the main challenge before Tanzania: to kick-start the rural economy and create equality in rural areas. Given the limited time frame to engineer agricultural reform and industrial growth, the national liberation state acted fast. In the Arusha Declaration, Nyerere bemoaned the logic that one had to first build capitalism and then socialism, because the act of doing the former would produce social wealth, but it would also squelch the political dynamic of national liberation that afforded an opportunity for such social transformation. "The mistake we are making," he wrote, "is to think that development begins with industries. It is a mistake because we do not have the means to establish many modern industries in our country."[3] First agricultural change, and then industrial growth.

The Third World agenda, for states such as India and Egypt, was not socialist as much as welfarist. The state centralized and nationalized the commanding heights of the economy to ensure that its dominant classes gained some purchase on a complex international economy (which was at any rate weighted against them). These states were concerned for their citizens' welfare, as we shall see below, but they did not pledge themselves to the creation of an egalitarian society. Tanzania under Nyerere's TANU attempted something more than the welfarism of India and Egypt. The Arusha Declaration drew from the socialist experiments: there was an insistence that the state must create equity among the population, and that this equity needed to be crafted at the level of production and not simply consumption.

The main problem with the Arusha-TANU project, however, came not in its goals but in its implementation. Like most Third World nationalisms, Arusha-TANU failed to differentiate the population. Since the bulk of Tanzania's population lived in rural areas, the declaration called for the state to "pay heed to the peasant." The policies it created targeted the landless peasantry, and among them the special role of women in agricultural production and reproduction.[4] What the Arusha-TANU strategy failed to delineate was how the mechanism for the delivery of its policies would utilize landless peasants, especially women. Instead, the state talked of the people, and yet it stood apart from them. TANU did not isolate special class allies among the peasantry and build institutions for them that would be the vehicle for social change. Rural trade unions for landless peasants were not formed in the service of either the 1967 ujamaa or the 1973–75 villagization programs. The state concentrated on the peasants and ignored the crucial role of organized labor in the "modern" sector (the dockworkers, postal workers, diamond miners, railway workers, sisal plantation workers, and others who led a series of strikes between 1958 and 1961 to win independence from Britain).[5] The TANU regime came to power, abolished the trade unions, and collected the unions' personnel into one government-authorized union, the National Union of Tanganyika Workers (1964). The natural allies of a socialist experiment were marginalized. There was no well-developed strategy for how the state planned to build power for its ideas.[6] Instead, the state stood above the people, directing them, preaching "socialism from above."[7]

In 1961, Tanzania barely exported any industrial goods. Agriculture dominated the domestic economy, and agrarian commodities were the main export items. As world agricultural prices remained low and often fluctuate quite wildly, Tanzania's economy malingered. To move to grow industries without capital, and with little accumulated capital from the centuries, would be a fool's errand. Not only did the socialist government of Nyerere recognize this, but so too did the World Bank in an influential report.[8] The World Bank, along with Nyerere's government, found that Tanzania's social ecology did not have villages as much as dispersed homesteads.[9] A challenge to any administration would be to amalgamate the efforts of these individual units into something more economically productive. The German colonizers had formed villages to facilitate missionary work, but their failure had drawn the British to valorize the independence of the African yeoman.[10] The relatively low density of population allowed the countryside to remain outside the orbit of world trade. Now, with the plans for the new nations and the expectations of progress, the Nyerere government acted.

In the early 1960s, the national liberation state did not bother smallholders who grew crops for the subsistence economy. Their only intervention in this sector was to provide the smallholders with minor improvements in their farming techniques.[11] The dispersed peasantry that suffered in years of poor rainfall could be served with better irrigation systems. The state also provided smallholders with mechanized implements and seeds for cash crops to replace subsistence farming. The introduction of cash crops did not go down well with the farmers. The export (cash) crops required expensive fertilizers and seeds, all of which cost money up front. In case the export market failed them, the farmers were stuck without access to food. Cotton, coffee, and tobacco had volatile international prices, and the farmers resisted their cultivation in all kinds of ways.

When the government's "improvement" scheme faltered, it tried a more radical approach called "transformation." The regime encouraged peasants to move to experimental farms called "village settlements" where they worked cooperatively to increase, theoretically, the value of their efforts. On these farms, mechanical implements and fertilizers replaced manual labor (mainly the hand hoe). The people, in Nyerere's terms, had to learn to live in "proper villages."[12] Of the millions who lived in rural Tanzania, only 3,500 families moved to set up these village settlements, which had cost the government upward of two million pounds. The famous French agronomist and sometime UN Food and Agriculture Organization adviser René Dumont wrote a report in 1969 that came close to the government's own view of the creation of villages: the scheme had produced appalling results, but it did "appear desirable, on condition that it did not cost too much."[13] The Arusha Declaration took stock of the several failures in the agricultural policy and offered an aggressive defense of the regime's strategy to grow the fields rather than build the factories. In the wake of the declaration, the regime announced not a withdrawal from village settlement but an expansion, now to be called the ujamaa program, with the total transformation of rural areas into socialist villages.

A few months after the Arusha Declaration, Nyerere's regime decided that it had simply worked to promote small-scale capitalist agriculture rather than socialism.[14] The improvement of farm life without any attempt to transform the feudal relations between the farmers and their markets was insufficient. The communal ideas that Nyerere felt were inherent in peasant life and that predated capitalism were getting swept away with capitalist agriculture. Ujamaa was to craft a modern shell for this communal husk.[15] Nyerere's regime called all peasants to move to ujamaa villages within the decade. The state resettled three million people, about 20 percent of Tanzania's population. The resettled farmers lived together in a village and worked cooperatively on the outlying fields. They pooled their resources to buy any inputs, and they pooled their produce for the market. The ujamaa policy had two major flaws. First, while the collectivization radically transformed the social relations of the farmers with their market, Nyerere did not construct ujamaa as a means to refashion the gendered aspects of social power. For Nyerere, the community of the farmers "would be the traditional family group," with all the implications of gendered power that this implied.[16]

Second, the policy left the regime no time to persuade a peasantry that had to be coerced into villages under the government's control. The government set in motion various "operations" to galvanize peasants to move to the villages (1971 Operation Dodoma, 1972 Operation Kogoma, and 1973 Operation Pwani). R.R. Matango described the chaos in his home district of Inchungu (Mara). "Many peasants in Inchungu were taken by surprise to see armed militiamen, climbing on top of their houses, taking away the thatch, in some cases the iron-sheets were torn off, doors and windows removed or smashed into pieces; houses pulled down in many cases." The state militia destroyed the old villages and moved the villagers to new sites. "People rushed in panic to build temporary accommodations in unplanned village sites. The entire division was in motion. Moving, moving in panic to the unplanned villages. Thus creating new villages in areas which are not even surveyed, on water, on school or dispensary— virtually no facility to maintain the population there or any plans to bring any, but only to serve the purpose of moving into the Development Villages. This haphazard, skimble-skamble movement has created problems which need urgent government attention and resources."[17] Without surveys, homes were built on fertile cotton soil or around areas where the land was without adequate irrigation. Socialism in a hurry in the Third World, in this manner, became undemocratic and authoritarian.

Tanzanian ujamaa is quite of a piece with a vast number of examples of Third World development or Third World socialism in a hurry. Most of the Third World states hurriedly built industrial factories and dams, cleared forests, and moved populations. This labor came for many reasons, of which the most important was to rapidly increase the productive capacity of the new nation, to make a Great Leap Forward into a moment of prosperity before the political capital of the liberation movements had been spent. Developed productive forces would generate the economic well-being that could only be created out of sacrifices demanded by political movements which had won political freedom from colonial rule or the rule of oligarchs. The intentions of the leadership, by all accounts, were not malevolent. Yet its modernist dream—to administer nature and society, and build vast industrial monuments without either a democratic governance structure or a mobilized population—led to the worst excesses of commandism and bureaucratism.[18] In India, in the period from the late 1940s to the late 1980s, the state displaced some 25 million people, while in the same period, the Chinese shifted 40 million people. These are the dramatic figures, because these states have substantial populations, but in small countries the percentage of the population that the state shifted by its bureaucratic commandism is staggering (in Tanzania, a fifth of the population was resettled).[19] The disregard for people's desires and the cannibalization of the ecological lifeworld both turned masses of people away from the Third World project as well as destroyed the habitat for the creation of justice. The state acted above the people, without care to build allies among the peasantry and allow them to force change through their organizations.

The ujamaa program began with the assumption that the national liberation regime should create a democratic economy that worked in the interests of the vast mass of the people. Since most of the people in the formerly colonized world in general and in Tanzania in particular lived rural lives, Nyerere's 1961 slogan resonated with them: "While other countries aim to reach the moon we must aim for the time being, at any rate, to reach the village."[20] Whatever Nyerere's intentions and those of the many Third World governments that had similar agricultural schemes (from Algeria to Burma, and on), the move to consolidate agriculture had the net effect of trying to *control* the peasantry, to agglomerate peasant production under the domination of the national liberation state.[21] Once collected, peasant production in the Third World would now be made subservient to the dynamics of world trade (and imperialism) rather than the subsistence needs of the localities that could have governed their development.[22] To render the relatively autonomous petty commodity sector subservient to the state, the regime abolished the marketing cooperative movement in 1975. Formed to gain better prices for agricultural produce (notably cotton), the movement brought some benefits to the peasantry. But the state decided to buy directly from the growers, often at prices set by the central government. Additionally, in 1972, the regime adopted the counsel of the U.S. consulting agency, McKinsey and Co., which advised it to replace the local government agencies with "development teams" that reported directly to central government ministries. These teams, wrote a scholar at the University of Dar es Salaam, "effectively replaced the local government system with an elaborate system of vertical information and planning flows centralized to the higher echelons of the government and party."[23]

The worst aspect of the Tanzanian and many Third World agricultural schemes is that because they worked in a hurry, and because they often had the view that the peasantry *should* simply follow rather than be guided by them, policies that might have been valuable corroded by the use of force. The Third World leadership in power seemed to follow Fyodor Dostoyevsky to the letter: "Well, then, eliminate the people, curtail them, force them to be silent. Because the European enlightenment is more important than people." If the modern state used violence as principally an immanent condition to discourage popular uprisings and keep the people in line, in the context of Third World modernism and bureaucratism violence became a means to realize the agenda of the state. In a review of ujamaa that understood the value of its ideals, the agricultural economist Philip Raikes wrote, "The implementation of the policy evoked some of the more frightening recesses of the bureaucratic mind."[24] Nyerere, in October 1967, understood that the ujamaa project as his regime constructed it would be implemented by force, and so he tried to see if his moral authority could turn the tide for persuasion. "We are not simply trying to organize increased production; we are trying to introduce a whole new way of life for the majority of our people. This can only be done once the people understand its purposes and voluntarily decide to participate."[25] In these words, Nyerere suggested that the regime should allow the people to hear from the government and then "voluntarily" follow its opinions. But the words of one person are hardly able to ameliorate or even transform the policies of a regime, even in one that gave so much power to an individual. Nyerere's policy had greater traction than his best intentions.[26] If the multitude that worked the land did not have a stake in it, then they would neither be motivated to increase its capacity nor would they benefit from it. Only compulsion motivated them to work hard.

People, because that is our wont, dissented in brave and innovative ways even when the state could neither provide avenues for nor tolerate dissent. The peasants of the Morogoro and Arusha regions ate the maize seeds rather than plant them, sold their subsidized fertilizers in the underground market, pretended not to understand instructions, tried to involve witchcraft against the local party officials, and organized demonstrations against villagization.[27] Elsewhere, people flocked to dam submergence sites and corralled them, or else struck against faster work rules in dangerous factories or mines. The level of dissent was matched by the rising tide of antilabor legislation and the violent reaction of the state. Police firings, mass arrests, assassinations of labor and people's leaders—all this became commonplace in the public sphere of the Third World.

Despite these major flaws, the Arusha experiment at the very least attempted to dethrone the powerful role played by the established social classes. Most of the darker nations tailored the Third World agenda to protect and even nourish the dominant classes. These regimes did not abjure land reforms or industrialization but carried them out in the service of the dominant classes. There was a great concern for the life and liberty of the working people, but mainly in the manner of noblesse oblige. In 1961, after two five-year plans, India's Nehru rued the failure of his regime to tend to the sufferings of the population. Rather than create even the semblance of equality, social development had grown the divide between the affluent and the afflicted. "Large numbers of people have not shared in [the increase in the nation's wealth] and live without the primary necessities of life. On the other side you see a smaller group of really affluent people. They have established an affluent society for themselves, anyhow, although India as a whole may be far from it. I think the new wealth is flowing in a particular direction and not spreading out properly."[28] Instead of doing much to turn the divide around, the state simply tried to siphon more welfare toward the poor. Short of socialism, the national liberation state in places like India wanted to produce higher growth rates. As output increased, regardless of the means to do so, the state would have a larger aggregate pool of capital and resources to distribute to the population. Market socialism or the mixed economy was a socialism of consumption not production. In the attempt to industrialize and create agricultural change, there was only a muted effort to change the relations and methods of production. The process of industrial as well as agricultural production remained similar to that found in any advanced capitalist country: workers had no say in the process of production, which was run by a detached management class. Deliberation was kept to a minimum. Socialism made its appearance in the marketplace and on the threshing floor—to more equitably divide the spoils rather than to more equitably produce them in the first place.

Even those Third World states most prone toward the creation of a domestic bourgeoisie and the protections of the dominant (rural and urban) classes clamored for land reform in the 1950s. At the UN General Assembly, their bloc put forward a resolution for land reform several times (1950, 1952, 1954, 1957, and 1960). The resolutions, while somewhat different, all pushed the view that land reform was "one of the main prerequisites for the general improvement of agricultural productivity."[29] Until the early 1960s, the general consensus was that if the Third World did not improve its agricultural output, it would not be able to break out of its low level of economic productivity. Industrial growth required some measure of agrarian dynamism, because taxes on and export earnings from the latter would help pay for the creation of a domestic industry.

While the postcolonial regimes wanted to see agricultural growth increase, not all of them were eager to see the rural landed lose their means and political clout. In 1932, the El Salvadorian rural elites engineered the massacre of twenty thousand peasants who occupied private land and opposed export-led agriculture.[30] Latin American history is filled with many such rebellions and mass reprisals. In 1944, when the leading Indian capitalists enjoined the state to protect their businesses with tariffs, they asked the Congress not to indulge itself with the reconstruction of agrarian relations in the new India. Any change might raise the expectations of the peasantry.[31] When India won its freedom, the Congress relied on rural power brokers to deliver the vote. It did not want to alienate the landowners who financed these agents of the party.[32] To avoid substantive land reform and yet adopt its slogan, the regime rested easy in the work of "saints" like Vinoba Bhava, who "created an illusion among the peasants that some landlords were indeed generous and magnanimous."[33] In the Philippines, the Land Reform Act of 1955 froze land relations in plantation-like conditions, with only a few modest allowances given to the landless workers.[34] These states valorized the undifferentiated peasant or farmer: the Indian *kisan* and the Egyptian fellahin (or even the Latin American campesino). The farmers, even if they were the rural dominant class, were treated as the backbone of the nation, the salt of the earth.

In some instances, land reforms came about when the regimes felt that anything short would result in a red revolution. Samuel Huntington's formula worked in states such as South Korea, Japan, and Taiwan (where land reform was conducted at the barrel of Japanese and later U.S. guns): "The willingness of landowners to lose their property through land reforms short of revolution varies directly with the extent to which the only alternative appears to be to lose it through revolution."[35]

The consensus over land reform changed in the 1960s as a new kind of agrarian solution entered the Third World. In 1945, the Rockefeller Foundation had piloted a program in Mexico to increase the agricultural yield using high-yield seeds and new agricultural methods (such as petrochemical fertilizers, pesticides, and mechanized farm implements). Mexico's wheat crop grew geometrically, and by 1964 this net grain importer began to export wheat.[36] The World Bank joined hands and broadcast this "Green Revolution" around the world. On almost half the land area of the Third World agricultural growth rates skyrocketed. In India, for instance, the technological solutions increased aggregate food availability. But there were problems. The growth had enormous regional imbalances, and the environmental impact of the highly noxious fertilizers created long-term problems. Further, the technological additives to the process raised the costs for the farmers. The Green Revolution also favored larger farms, and so it decreased both the call for land reform and its importance. At the 1967 Punta Del Este Conference of Latin American states, the delegates called for a reassessment of "unjust structures of land tenure and use," but this was window-dressing. The U.S.-born and Latin American UN Food and Agriculture Organization agronomist Solon Barraclough, who wrote the final declaration at Punta Del Este, was clear about the hollowness of these calls for land reform: "These post-1961 land reforms were for the most part, however, merely cosmetic. Often they were programs primarily designed to colonize state lands (often at unacceptable human and ecological costs) and to bail out large estate owners in economic difficulties by buying their lands for resettlement."[37] By 1972, when these same Third World powers gathered in Stockholm to found the UN Environmental Program, their main grouse was not the need for land reform but the prices of the technological inputs for Green Revolution–style agriculture. Transnational chemical firms charged high prices for the fertilizers, while agribusinesses enjoyed the rents on the high-yield seeds.[38] The Green Revolution had replaced the red one.

The lack of will toward the reconstruction of rural social relations in most of the darker nations did not mean that the state abandoned the landless and the small farmers to their own misery. It had a plan for them, but not one that dealt with their principle disadvantage: their lack of power in their localities and lack of control over the main instruments of production (land, water, and credit). Most Third World regimes provided rural credit to small farmers, although this capital was often insufficient for their needs (in line with the Green Revolution dynamic, the All-India Rural Credit Committee of 1969 argued that commercial banks should provide rural credit, when these banks favored trade and industry).[39] In lieu of land reform, the Third World turned toward the question of food security. The idea of food security can be traced back to the creation of the UN Food and Agriculture Organization in 1945. Then, food security was only one part of a package that included comprehensive land reform and the creation of commodity cartels.[40] By the late 1960s and early 1970s, the work of the organization was reduced to the provision of food security. This goal was enshrined in the 1974 Universal Declaration on the Eradication of Hunger and Malnutrition ("Every man, woman and child has an inalienable right to be free from hunger and malnutrition"). Socialist reorganization (socialized production) was squandered for welfarist handouts (socialized distribution and consumption). To manage the problem between farm prices and shop prices, the state in most cases created an institution to buy food grain (at fair prices to the farmer) and then sell these grains in fair price shops across the country, all done through government programs like India's Public Distribution System or Indonesia's Badan Urusan Logistic Nasional. Most of the regimes in the Third World created these programs to keep prices stable in urban areas, cut down on private trade (which it deemed to be exploitative), and ensure that farmers could make a living growing essential food products (through what in India was called the Minimum Support Price scheme). These schemes of socialized distribution and consumption enabled small farmers to enter into cooperatives to pool their produce and attain fair prices. Milk, food grain, and (coffee and cocoa) bean cooperatives thrived in the Third World into the late 1980s.

In the 1980s, the World Bank rued the failure of land reform. World hunger remained, and yet rural welfare was to end. In the language of neoliberalism, the World Bank concluded that global hunger could only be alleviated "by redistributing purchasing power and resources toward those who are undernourished."[41] In other words, by comprehensive land reform and the reconstruction of rural social relations.

Tanzania tried to move a socialist agenda, but like much of the Third World, it did so without a genuine attempt to organize the population into the ideas. It tried to act from above. When villagization failed, the state resorted to an embarrassing policy. A country with the highest rate of food grain production in Africa in the early 1960s now imported $180 million of food grains in late 1974. This exhausted Tanzania's foreign exchange reserves and set it up to beg for foreign aid.[42] Then the state welcomed U.S.-based agribusinesses to build large (fifty-thousand-acre), capital-intensive farms. The Green Revolution bailed out ujamaa.[43] Nyerere was left with his frustrations. In October 1975, Nyerere traveled to Mwanza where he berated the local Department of Agriculture for its poor advice to the peasants and demanded that those peasants who had been pushed into an ecological quagmire be resettled according to their wishes.[44] When Nyerere voluntarily left office in 1985, he retired to an experimental farm. He wanted to practice in his own small way the agricultural transformation that had eluded the Third World.

The pitfalls of the Third World bore heavily on it. Created by a wave of struggle, the new nations neither reorganized social relations effectively nor disrupted the colonial-type state structure bequeathed to it. By making alliances with the old social classes and adopting the colonial bureaucratic structure, the new nations essentially vitiated the Third World agenda. Military rule or military force became the order of the day, as the Third World regimes drove their demobilized populations to do what they had envisioned. The people who had driven the anticolonial struggles and had welcomed the Third World could only be seen by the new nations as compliant followers, or else as inert, or as foes. But despite all this, the political capital of the Third World remained and the project might have outlived its own pitfalls but for the frontal assault it faced in the 1970s. A debt crisis and a policy of planetary reorganization fostered by the First World assassinated the Third World.

Part 3
ASSASSINATIONS

NEW DELHI

By 1983, New Delhi was a city transformed. In the 1910s, the British crafted it as the modern twin of what became Old Delhi. Designed by Edwin Lutyens, the city was built to be the capital of the British Indian empire. Monumental buildings, wide avenues, and grassy expanses defined the city, although sharp racial tensions rent the old part from the new. When the British departed in 1947, the city suffered the trauma of Partition. As India and Pakistan emerged, battles between Hindus and Muslims escalated. Muslim refugees crowded into a sixteenth-century fort, while Hindu and Sikh migrants from Pakistan settled Delhi's western expanse. Like many postcolonial cities, Delhi and New Delhi bore all the rotten marks of empire, and a desire among its inheritors to get along with the job of accumulation. Being the capital of a state with a great tendency to be centralized, New Delhi housed a massive bureaucracy as well as those who had come in to build a metropolis that never stops growing. In 1941, a little more than 90,000 people lived in the city. The Partition influx increased the total to 1.7 million by 1951. By 1983, more than 6.5 million people lived there.

Monuments are commonplace in Delhi. From the Qutab Minar near the airport to the Red Fort at the other end of the city, Delhi's sights constantly rattle visitors. In the early 1980s, the city added more grandeur. In 1982, New Delhi hosted the Asian Games. New stadiums and residential buildings as well as conference centers grew across the city. An additional advantage was the entry of color television to the country. Stadiums grew in a city that had only recently ejected its poor to its outskirts. If Prime Minister Indira Gandhi's election slogan had

New Delhi, 1983: Indian prime minister Indira Gandhi receives Cuban president Fidel Castro at New Delhi Airport for the Non-Aligned Movement conference. © BETTMANN/CORBIS

once been *garibi hatao* (remove poverty), most people had come to understand it as *garib dilli se hatao* (remove the poor from Delhi). The conference venues regularly hosted all manner of international commercial and political gatherings. In 1983, these buildings welcomed the seventh NAM Summit Conference.

NAM came to New Delhi at a crucial time for Indira Gandhi. The daughter of Nehru, Gandhi spent her entire life in Indian politics. When Nehru died in 1964, Indira Gandhi took on a major role in the Congress Party. In 1966, she won elections and was prime minister until 1977. She returned to power in 1980 with a weakened mandate because of the excesses of the martial law (Emergency) regime she ran from 1975 to 1977. When NAM came to Delhi, the city was under siege. A fractious election in 1983 resulted in the defeat of Gandhi's party in the southern states of India. A film star, N.T. Ramarao, broke the Congress Party's hold in Andhra Pradesh, while an important foe during the Emergency (the Janata Party) won in neighboring Karnataka. In Assam, the opposition (except the Communists) called for a boycott of the elections. The Congress Party won a pyrrhic victory (only 2 percent of the population voted), as violence between Assamese, Bengalis, and Bobos rent the state. In Nellie, Assam, five thousand refugees were killed (Tariq Ali called this the "My Lai massacre multiplied by ten").[1] Gandhi traveled to Assam, offered a conciliatory statement ("I cannot find words to describe the horrors"), stood by the newly elected Congress Party state government, and returned to Delhi to host NAM.

New Delhi allows us to write the obituary of the Third World.

When the NAM delegates arrived in Delhi, they saw pictures of the Nellie massacre in every major newspaper and magazine. It haunted the proceedings, and reminded most of the leadership of their own Nellies.

The NAM that gathered in Delhi was in transition. A major line struggle broke out in the 1970s and remained unresolved through the Delhi meeting. Neither of the two sides left NAM. Instead, both remained, although one of them gained the upper hand in Delhi and has since come to define NAM. The victory of that camp, those that welcomed IMF-driven globalization, is as responsible for the assassination of the Third World as the social forces (imperialism and finance capital) that were its major adversaries from the 1950s onward. Most of the 101 members of NAM in 1983 did not hold fast to one or the other of the two lines at the conference. Nevertheless, the line struggle infected the proceedings and ended up determining the outcome of the final resolution.

The first line held the view that the principal problem for the planet was uneven capitalism. Endemic poverty and the theft of social wealth continued as a result of the policies set in place to benefit those who claimed title to the planet's resources. No single nation represented the gains of uneven capitalism, although the U.S. government began to speak as if it were the leader of the gainers. Between the 1966 Tricontinental and the 1979 sixth NAM meeting in Havana, a number of important events transpired. A Marxist revolution in Ethiopia (1974) inaugurated a set of defeats for the imperialist bloc. In 1975, the National Liberation Front defeated the United States in South Vietnam and the Pathet Lao took Vientiane. That same year, five Portuguese colonies in Africa seized their independence after the Salazar dictatorship ended in Lisbon. In 1978–79, the Marxists seized control of Afghanistan, the New Jewel Movement took power in Grenada, and the Sandinista revolution prevailed in Nicaragua. Additionally, a number of African regimes (such as in Benin, Madagascar, Liberia, and Libya) adopted Marxism-Leninism as their official ideology.[2] The mood in Havana was exuberant. After at least two decades of quiet, the USSR began to quite openly back many of these national liberation movements, which were also greatly helped by the Cuban medical and military teams (particularly in Angola). It was these victories and the close fealty offered by the Soviets that drew from Jamaica's Michael Manley this assessment at the 1979

NAM: "We may call ourselves communists, socialists, or humanists or simply progressive. But all anti-imperialists know that the balance of forces in the world shifted irrevocably in 1917," which burnished the recent victories in the glory of the still highly regarded October Revolution. The conflict was between the capitalist and Communist worlds, and non-alignment, did not mean neutrality in that struggle.[3] The Havana meeting raised the question of a formal anti-imperialist alliance between NAM and the USSR—a move pushed by Castro and the Cuban delegation. Interventions from Yugoslavia, India, and Burma held Castro back, although the final declaration was still tilted entirely against U.S.-led imperialism.

Between Havana and New Delhi, a great deal occurred to dampen this enthusiasm. Cuba slumped into a major debt crisis (by 1982, the government owed $3 billion, three and a half times the value of its exports to the First World). The Soviet Union could not assist Cuba because it was internally weak and weakened internationally. Inadequate economic growth in the late 1970s (demonstrated by a failure to make most of the generous targets of the 1976–80 five-year plan) was compounded by a lack of global support for the 1979 Soviet invasion of Afghanistan. The United States and its major Atlantic allies seized on the opening afforded by a weakened Soviet Union. Ronald Reagan's forward policy extended the increase in military expenditure initiated by Jimmy Carter. A few failed military interventions (particularly in Lebanon) resulted in the creation of the Reagan Doctrine, which encouraged the use of proxy armies in the field against left-wing regimes. The Nicaraguan contras, the Afghan mujahideen, the União Nacional para a Independência Total de Angola, and the Cambodian Khmer Rouge are the apposite examples. This heightened disparity on the global stage constrained the line pursued by the left-wing forces, whose leader at NAM was Castro.

In New Delhi, it was left to Castro to carry the standard for the Third World. His speech to the NAM delegates rehearsed the NAM agenda from 1961 onward and demonstrated how the unfolding debt crisis portended the end of the Third World. The Cuban government distributed a longer version of the speech, *The World Economic and Social Crisis*, at the conference, and within the year it appeared in different countries, in different languages.[4] While the Cubans worked the conference rooms, the Soviets worked the halls. The Soviets sent a large delegation to Delhi; they distributed a number of booklets about the crucial role of NAM in the quest for world peace. By New Delhi, however, the Soviet influence was lessened; yet that of Castro and the Cubans remained substantial. Partly this has to be attributed to Castro's personality, to his charisma (he was the only one to get a standing ovation after his speech). But it is also because the Cuban regime articulated an independent line that appealed to the emotions of the NAM delegates, even as many of them walked away from the NAM heritage. As the outgoing chair of NAM, Castro turned over the chair of the NAM conference to Indira Gandhi, his "sister," who was the new leader of the movement.

Castro's main antagonist in New Delhi was the Singaporean deputy prime minister Sinnathamby Rajaratnam. A founder of the People's Action Party with Singapore's strongman Lee Kuan Yew, Rajaratnam brought the island nation into NAM in 1970 and helped create the Association of Southeast Asian Nations (ASEAN) in 1977. In Delhi, Rajaratnam circulated a speech that offered a resolutely anti-Soviet, pro-U.S. position. "We are witnesses to our own slow-motion hi-jacking," wrote this former columnist of the *Straits Times*, "and if we do not wake up to this fact and do something to abort it then the ship of non-alignment and all those who sail in it may wake up one day to find that they have docked in a Soviet port." In a series of speeches made at the United Nations, ASEAN, and NAM, Rajaratnam argued that the world entered a "systematic crisis" in the 1970s.[5] Economic stagnation and superpower détente led to a dangerous situation for the darker nations. No longer were they able to insinuate themselves into one or the other bloc and reap some rewards. The Atlantic and Warsaw powers drew the various regional rivalries to engineer proxy wars. Countries, he contended, should not be motivated by allegiance to either capitalism or Communism; they needed to be motivated by national interest. For instance, Singapore needed to trade with both the United States and China, regardless of the political-economic systems adopted by both. This did not mean that Singapore should tolerate its domestic Communists, however, because "the people have made it abundantly clear that Communism is not for them."[6] The national interest invoked by Rajaratnam was actually the class interest of a section created by import-substitution industrialization.

Rajaratnam urged NAM states to disregard the bipolar conflict, but he also proposed that they revoke state-centered development for neo-liberal growth. "The policies that work best," he told the UN General Assembly in 1979, "are those based on free market competition, with government's role limited to protecting the people against the heinousness and injustices unrestrained competition could inflict and redistributing the fruits of competition without deadening the competitive spirit."[7] Rajaratnam spoke for a rising new class across the NAM states. Industrial, agricultural, and financial elites who gained through several decades of import-substitution policies now outgrew their training wheels and restraints. Reasonable growth and considerable accumulation by this class gave them the confidence to exert their own class interests over the needs of their population. Many of the most aggressive leaders of this class had been born toward the end of the era of full-blown imperialism. They had experienced neither colonialism nor anticolonialism. The structures that enabled them to flourish now seemed to be shackles. The intellectual leaders of this class spent time in international institutions (such as the IMF and the World Bank). Here, these intellectuals experienced the change from a Keynesian development model (that the state should intervene to create demand by social welfare and social wage policies) to a monetarist accumulation one (that the state should withdraw to the simple function of managing the money supply and ensuring low levels of inflation). People such as India's Montek Ahluwalia and Manmohan Singh as well as Venezuela's Moisés Naim and Miguel Rodriquez are good examples of this tendency. In addition, migrants to the advanced industrial states who made good turned their capital and expertise to the homeland during the era of stagflation in their host countries; people such as India's Sam Pitroda and Taiwan's Miin Wu brought their skills and worldview to bear on the development of the new information technology sector in their homelands. This infusion of skills and business philosophies enthused the emergent bourgeoisie in the darker nations, which saw the future through their eyes rather than the lens of the Third World agenda. This class was not motivated to become an economic proxy for the Atlantic powers. It believed in its capacity and wanted the opportunity to flourish. As Rajaratnam said, "I do not think we are going to get any free ride however much we shout. The hitchhikers will most certainly be left behind."[8] Rajaratnam's gauntlet was thrown down in New Delhi to check the "shouting."

It was left to Indira Gandhi, the chair of NAM, to mediate the Castro and Rajaratnam lines. Some aspects united the two. Both agreed that the 1970s portended disaster for the darker nations. The debt crisis among them combined with the stagflation in the Atlantic powers and the chaos in the Soviet economy were all dangerous. Proxy wars increased, and the international community betrayed a lack of will to deal with the complex, solvable human problems (dramatically, the famines of Ethiopia and Sudan in the late 1970s and early 1980s). Whereas one called for more state intervention on the side of people's needs (Castro), the other wanted less state intervention in favor of managed private initiative (Rajaratnam).

Gandhi did not tackle the disagreement openly. Her stewardship of NAM was deft. She minimized the Havana tilt to the Left and yet protected the institution from too close an association with the United States. What occurred under her watch and beyond was not so much a political association with one or the other camps in the world but a general ideological move toward the new consensus being pushed by the Atlantic powers and the international financial organizations. Her speech was a nostalgic appreciation of her father's role in the creation of NAM. In the midst of her speech she offered a definition of non-alignment, which sounded radical only because it bore no relation to the shifts in the planet's political economy: "Non-alignment is national independence and freedom."[9] The weakened USSR slowly capitulated to the aggressive military demands of the United States. While the voluntary disembowelment of the USSR came eight years later, its effective deterioration was apparent. International relations abhors a vacuum: as the USSR withdrew from its forward posture, the Atlantic powers, led by the United States, rushed in. The United States came to a leadership position not simply militarily but also economically. It broke the back of the postwar financial architecture that allowed currencies to float against each other and be stabilized by gold. In exchange, and through a complicated mechanism, the dollar emerged as the bellwether of the world economic system. This gave the United States an unmatched power in the world, as most of the financial elites pledged themselves objectively to protect the superpower and its dollar (in which they held their wealth). The uneven bipolarity of the Cold War era was already in transition, as the U.S.-led camp took control over world events. To be non-aligned now did not have the meaning that it had thirty years before.

The Third World agenda understood that the economic suffocation of the darker nations came not only from abstract economic principles but crucially because these principles had been set up through the political intervention of powerful actors. The rules of international trade, for instance, were not simply those of an a priori economic theory but were devised by the powerful to suit their interests. Because of this analysis, any reform had to be both about the politics of the economy (who writes the rules) and the economics of politics (who holds the economic muscle to allow themselves to write the rules). The interrelationship between economics and politics defined the work of the Third World agenda.

This fundamental linkage was opened in New Delhi. The delegates deliberated on economic issues, but they did not do so in the framework of the 1973 NAM's NIEO. The NIEO, adopted by the United Nations in 1974, was about the need to create new international rules to promote economic sovereignty and cooperation. Cooperation without sovereignty would mean that the powers with the greater economic muscle would simply continue to dominate the world economy, and regardless of their best efforts, their historical advantages would endow them with unequal power. To remedy this, the NIEO idea came with a set of proposals to rearrange the power relations in the world, including commodity cartels, a more just monetary policy, increased industrialization, control of transnational corporations, and a strong UN commitment to economic and human rights.[10]

In New Delhi, the more powerful (and therefore vocal) NAM delegates suggested that economic issues should be seen as technical problems, which could be sorted out by technocrats.[11] The political framework that suffocated the choices for the technocrats left the discussion table. The reaction to the debt crisis is illustrative. When some states proposed that the darker nations should simply refuse to pay their external debt, the more influential in NAM squelched this option. They felt that this would only provoke the G-7 to reprisals and would not improve their bargaining power. Rather than even an outright debt payment strike as a tactic to help restructure the debt, the "moderate" members argued that the restructuring of debt should happen individually and in negotiation. In other words, individual contracts between the indebted state and its debtors should be the approach rather than the totality of the Third World against their creditors (the G-7 governments or commercial houses located within the G-7).

The Third World leadership accepted that there was no other alternative to the economic logic of the G-7, although within that logic its leaders might fight to better the deal that they are able to get. Indeed, at the 1987 NAM meeting, the Indian prime minister and outgoing chair of NAM Rajiv Gandhi put it bluntly: "The stronger we are economically the more respect we shall get from the economically strong."[12] By this argument, economic growth was a sufficient criterion for political power, and indeed it might lead to political power. Such an approach detached the national liberation insistence that political and economic power could only be gained in tandem and not in sequence. In addition, the new NAM failed to acknowledge the manner in which the G-7 used the global rules for its own interest. For example, the G-7 objected strongly when the NAM states created tariff barriers to protect their economies, but by UNCTAD's count, the G-7 states themselves had over seven hundred nontariff barriers (such as government subsidies, quantitative restrictions, and other technical standards to block the import of certain goods into their protected markets).[13] A refusal to combat the rules meant an occlusion of these benefits to the G-7's advantage.

The adoption of what became globalization (or the hegemony of neoliberal economics) came not only from imperialist pressure but also from those forces within the countries that fundamentally disagreed with the strategic direction of social development *chosen* by the political parties of national liberation. Other routes could have been taken in the early 1980s, but only a few isolated places such as Cuba attempted to go in this direction. The countries that led NAM into this new dispensation were in a slightly better position than the rest of the darker nations. By 1983, the NAM states produced less than a tenth of the world's industrial output, although transnational corporations controlled three-quarters of the industrial output in these states. Among the NAM states, five produced more than 80 percent of this total industrial output: Brazil, South Korea, India, Mexico, and Argentina.[14] These states (notably India, the East Asian "Tigers," and Brazil) played a crucial role in the derailment of the Third World agenda.

The changes in the general character of NAM were reflected in the changes within India. By the mid-1970s, India's economic agenda floundered. The long-standing failure to reconstruct agrarian relations, an excessive reliance on industrial development over any other sector, a burgeoning military sector (particularly after the 1962 war with China and the 1965 war with Pakistan), and the oil crises of the late 1960s produced distress and anger across the country. A dissatisfied population rose in a host of rebellions, whether the Communist-led food movement of late 1965, the Maoist Naxalite movement of 1967, the United Women's Anti-Price Rise Front of 1973, the Nav Nirman movement of 1974, the Railway Strike of 1974, or the Jayaprakash Narayan movement in Bihar of 1974.[15] This broad, nationwide set of movements mainly led by the Left, but also joined in some places (such as the Jayaprakash Narayan movement) by a combination of the Left and the Right, assaulted the nationalist credentials of the Congress Party. The party of the freedom movement claimed to rule with the anticolonial nationalist agenda, but it adopted economic policies inimical to the vast mass of the population. To circumvent this criticism, the Indira Gandhi government nationalized the banks in 1969, signed an Indo-Soviet Defense Treaty in 1971, and ran on the garibi hatao (remove poverty) platform for the general election of 1971. The bank nationalization seemed to be along the grain of national liberation, but it actually accomplished two things: it centralized finance capital in the interests of the industrialists, and it offered moderate doses of credit to political allies, "small and middle entrepreneurs," and the agrarian elite who had been unable to generate capital since the economic stagnation of the mid-1960s. The rhetoric of socialism came alongside a set of policies designed to maintain the unequal political economy.

In reaction to the growing unrest, Indira Gandhi's regime declared the Emergency, withdrew the Constitution, and began to rule by decree.[16] Although the formal Emergency rule only lasted two years, from 1975 to 1977, it disrupted the Congress Party's ability to pose as the living heir to the national liberation heritage. In the first few days of the Emergency, in October 1975, Gandhi announced a twenty-point program that followed to the letter a series of demands made by the World Bank to the government of India. The program directed the animus of the state against what it considered the two enemies of progress: petty smugglers, and hoarders of goods and money. Sops for students and landless peasants as well as the urban middle class and the industrial elite attempted to stitch together support for the goals of the regime. Scrupulous attention to the landless peasantry in the program came alongside a novel development: the "liberalization of investment procedures" (point 14) for industrial development. In other words, the state proposed to allow foreign capital to enter the areas hitherto held in the state's trust (what had been called the commanding heights of the economy), and proposed to scale back on its regulation of industry and business. The scraps to the landless peasants would come to mean nothing in time as the state essentially handed over the keys to the kingdom to the industrial elite and foreign capital. When the Emergency ended in 1977 and much of its program withered, the drive to liberalize the economy, draw in foreign capital, and welcome a relationship with the IMF remained.

Unwilling to generate substantial growth or effective equity, in times of crisis the darker nations borrowed heavily from commercial lenders and international finance agencies. Once in debt, states such as India compromised their economic sovereignty to the IMF, which acted as the insurance for the loans provided by the advanced industrial states. To bolster its credentials with the international lenders, the Congress Party regime went after labor unions and economic controls (including subsidies). In 1982,

the Congress Party government passed the Essential Services Maintenance Act and the National Security Act in tandem, to secure labor and
accumulation by force as "labor" became "antinational." The government
cracked down on the Bombay mill workers' strike of 1982–83.[17] The experience of Mexico cast a long shadow on India's growing debt. Mexico,
an oil-rich country, defaulted on $80 billion in public-sector debt in 1982.
Forty countries joined Mexico in arrears, and a year later another twenty-
seven had to restructure their massive debt. The total debt in the bruised
nations was $500 billion, which at the time threatened the financial stabil-
ity of the world market (given that much of this debt was owed to commercial banks).

The Third World agenda crafted so skillfully, and with its major limitations, withered. The idea of nationalism began to change. Anticolonial nationalism disavowed a strict cultural or racial definition of the
nation. Forged in opposition to imperialism, this nationalism created a
program and agenda that united people on a platform of sovereignty in
all domains of life. With political freedom came the possibility of economic and cultural freedom. If there is divergence on what kind of economic model to follow, few disagreed with the view that they needed to
create secular and democratic republics. The two pillars of Third World
nationalism are economic autarky and secular democracy. The latter
challenged the new states to abjure the divisive techniques of colonial
administrators as well as transform cultural differences from a liability
to an asset. The former went by the name of socialism. It allowed the
new states to be patriotic without being chauvinistic. Patriotism in the
Third World states was not to be a "zealous love of country" in an abstract, mystical way. National patriotism came in the defense of the principles of the republic.

The abandonment of economic sovereignty lost the national liberation
regimes one of their two principal pillars of legitimacy. When IMF-led
globalization became the modus operandi, the elites of the postcolonial
world adopted a hidebound and ruthless xenophobia that masqueraded as
patriotism. Low economic tariffs and high cultural boundaries formed the
contours of the new legitimating strategy for the former Third World.
"Foreign," in the new dispensation, ceased to refer to finance capital and
transnational firms; increasingly, this term would refer to domestic minorities and anyone whose cultural presence provided a valuable means to
distort the nationalist sentiments of the population. Dominant classes in
these states adopted two postures, and sometimes both: an eagerness to be

untethered from their societies and/or linked to their population through ascribed identities of faith and race. The domestic elites were always a weak link for the national liberation agenda. When the benefits of import substitution produced a more aggressive and self-confident bourgeoisie, this class wanted to break the cross-class alliance. This class looked forward to a rearrangement of alliances, with a closer relationship with the "West" for economic gain and consumer pleasure. The erosion of the Third World state allowed this class to carry the standard of the First World. In India, by the early 1980s, this class was the size of the French population. In the early 1980s, Indira Gandhi's son, Rajiv, represented this class within the Congress Party; his technocratic vision of development clashed loudly with the national liberation one.

With the demise of import substitution and no other plans for economic sovereignty on the table that appealed to the masses, the Congress Party lost its claim to anticolonial Third World nationalism. Its leaders knew this implicitly, because Indira Gandhi's clique immediately fanned the flames of ethnic and religious difference to reclaim their electoral majority. The appeal to the "Hindu" majority against the secessionism in the Punjab and Assam as well as against Muslims and oppressed castes opened the door for the corruption of the idea of anticolonial nationalism. The massacre at Nellie, for instance, was a result of this venal appeal. By the late 1970s and early 1980s, the Congress Party was met toe to toe on this line, and it was found wanting by a *genuinely* cruel cultural nationalist political force, the Bharatiya Janata Party (BJP).

The BJP grew out of a violent and macho tradition of national patriotism that drew more from Nazi notions of nationalism (blood and soil) than from that of anticolonial nationalism. Its enemies were not foreign capital and domination but the Muslims and the Communists. The BJP staked its claim to patriotism as the Congress Party spent the late 1970s and the 1980s offering India for sale to the highest bidder and the aggressive dominant class. But when the BJP had a chance to govern in the 1990s and until 2004, it cloaked itself in the patriotism of cultural nationalism at the same time as it too opened the door to national wealth, especially in the sale of formerly nationalized assets at low prices. The BJP, for all its *swadeshi* (indigenism), followed the liberalization track to the letter, with one of its main leaders, L.K. Advani, promoting "globalization with our feet solidly rooted in swadeshi." The BJP created the Ministry of Disinvestment. Cultural nationalism opened the door for IMF-driven globalization.

During his assessment of the "systemic crisis" of world affairs, Singapore's Rajaratnam reflected on the degradation of the idea of nationalism. "Nationalism, initially a positive and constructive force in Third World countries," he said, "has now entered a destructive and reactionary phase. It is now reproducing in the Third World the errors and distortions that European nationalism did in its immature phase of history." The new nationalism "has entered its phase of racial, religious and cultural persecutions. The solidarity which transcended racial, religious and cultural differences has weakened or totally collapsed in many Third World countries."[18] Rajaratnam's clear-sighted 1979 assessment suffered from one major limitation. The great hope of the bourgeois social imagination was that the international order be based on free markets and individual identities, and that the deracinated latter be able to benefit from the unhampered former. Rather than realize Rajaratnam's dream, what manifested itself was the simultaneous growth of IMF-driven globalization and parochially cruel nationalism. Sectarian nationalism in the formerly colonized world is not only an adequate form of globalization, especially as the socialist bloc collapsed later in the 1990s, but it seems to be the form that IMF-driven globalization has taken since the late 1970s.

The Atlantic powers played a crucial role in giving cover to the emergent elites of the postcolonial states. They put pressure on the Third World institutions and freed up the impatient upwardly mobile elites. The first indication of this exuberant pressure was on display at the Multilateral Trade Negotiations of the Tokyo Round (1973–79) of GATT and at the 1982 UN Convention on the Law of the Sea. In both these instances, the G-7 offered concessions on small reforms and obduracy on the significant questions.[19] The G-7 promised not to "dump" cheap raw materials on vulnerable economies and to share the minerals on the deep seabed. While all this came on the surface, the rules betrayed the real motivations: the new rules for international regulations were not binding, and they allowed the G-7 to conduct side agreements with individual states. Between Algiers (1973) and the UN resolution on the NIEO (1974), the G-7 had made all kinds of bilateral and regional relationships with the states of the new nations. These relationships provided individual states with some marginal advantages, as they weakened the solidarity of the Third World and secured the permanence of the unequal structure. When the leaders talked about the NIEO in New Delhi in 1983, they evoked the language of Algiers, but not its meaning.

What they meant instead of the total reconfiguration of the world political economy was globalization with a human face. The economic and political dominance of the G-7 would continue, as long as their individual states got some bargains, and as long as everyone made the correct noises about "development" and "democracy."

The saddest gesture of the hollowed out language of NAM came in the narrowed vision for the Integrated Programme for Commodities. At the 1976 Nairobi UNCTAD IV meeting, NAM's members, without dissent, agreed to the creation of a Common Fund of $6 billion to ensure the stability of commodity prices. The G-7, led by the United States, squelched this demand, and eventually agreed to the creation of a fund with only $400 million to finance buffer stocks, and $350 million to do commodity research and development. As two analysts found, these pledges showed that "even if some commodity agreements are successfully concluded, thereby adding to the capital available, a genuinely integrated programme is unlikely to be implemented. Thus what is likely to be achieved will not make a radical difference to problems faced in the commodity sphere and to the situation and prospects of most developing countries."[20]

Economic issues were delinked from the politics of economics. At the same time, the political issues were removed from any consideration of the inequities of the power and privilege in the world. No longer did NAM produce a long, almost unwieldy laundry list of declarations and resolutions on each and every revolutionary struggle. Neither did NAM conduct an analysis of imperialism or the role of the bipolar Cold War in the sharpening of conflicts around the planet. At a 1976 NAM meeting in Colombo, Sri Lanka, Mozambique's Samora Machel tried to raise the question of proxy wars and how the Atlantic powers had begun to select "acceptable options" in conflict situations. The G-7 (and the international media) characterized these "puppet movements" as moderate and reasonable, while their adversaries were considered to be terrorists. Machel's intervention on this theme went nowhere.[21] Nor did any political discussion about the arms industry. In 1972, the Third World expended $33 billion on arms, already a vulgar amount. A decade later, the figure totaled $81 billion. In 1977, the Cuban government proposed that $650 billion wasted on the world arms trade be transferred into a capital infusion into the Third World. The G-7 did not consider the proposal, the corporate media mocked it, and NAM did not give it serious attention. The politics of NAM moved to symbolism. The creation of a powerful unity to change the political manipulation of the planet in the bipolar Cold War was destroyed.

The 1983 NAM concentrated on three political matters: the rights of the Palestinians, freedom for the South Africans, and the zone of peace in the Indian Ocean. By 1983, it was de rigueur, almost depressingly predictable, to demand rights for the Palestinians and the South Africans. The genuflection toward the Palestinians and the South Africans came, however, without any word on the support given by the Atlantic powers (particularly the United States) for both the Likud regime in Israel and the Afrikaner apartheid state in South Africa.[22] At the 1964, third NAM Summit in Cairo, the Third World called for the establishment of denuclearized zones around the world (such as a Zone of Peace in the Indian Ocean). The 1959 Antarctic Treaty and the 1963 Treaty of Tlatelelco laid the groundwork for this demand. India conducted a nuclear test in 1974, and the United States maintained an enormous base in the Chagos Archipelago (Diego Garcia) that housed nuclear weapons.[23] This did not enter into the framework of the political resolution.

There was no longer any frontal assault on the institutions of imperialism that sustained and extended global inequality—not just economic inequality but also political and cultural inequality. In terms of political equality, none of the G-77 powers challenged the veto power of the five nuclear states that sat as permanent members of the UN Security Council. If cultural equality was important, at least the NAM countries might have challenged the unrepentant show of superiority by the G-7 in its self-definition as the "greatest countries in the world," but also as the global, private monopoly media shuffled off the lives of the majority of the planet as opportunities to concentrate on hunger, famine, and refugees.

A great deal had changed between the rise of the Third World and the New Delhi meeting. In the decades that led to the creation of NAM in 1961 and for at least a decade after that, hope reigned over the populations of the world. National liberation movements of minimal military strength vanquished vast empires, and attempted to create just societies and a just world. The farsighted imagination created by the Third World is well represented in the speeches of its leaders at international gatherings, but also in the enthusiasm and sacrifice of the citizenry to create these new nations. The internal shortcomings and contradictions of the Third World states were significant, and intellectuals, politicians, and popular movements had little illusion about these. Castro handed over the baton to Indira Gandhi, and yet he remained the moral embodiment of what the Third World was. He was received like a rock star. The refrain he used here was "to struggle." The Third World, born in struggle, had to struggle to put its agenda on the table, and now had to struggle to realize it. That was Castro's view. But who would struggle for this agenda in a world where the effective power of the Third World was dramatically curtailed? If those in the room had no intention of following through with these suggestions, then why did Castro earn this extended applause? Did this mean that even as those who began to represent the bruised parts of the world created class alliances with their fellows in the First World, and even as they abandoned the agenda of the Third World for fellowship with the doctrine of U.S. primacy and IMF-driven globalization, they retained an emotional bond to the Third World's days of rage? None of the leaders and few of their regimes had the will or the capacity to genuinely represent the masses that offered their allegiance to them in one form or another. The lack of struggle for an expansive social justice agenda meant that the forms of social solidarity engendered by the dominant classes shifted from secular anticolonial nationalism to cultural nationalism. "Struggle" would cease to mean the determined struggle to create socially just collectivities.

For us, the first task is to untangle the policies of the IMF in the aftermath of the debt crisis. In the 1970s, the IMF shifted its three-decades-old mission from the provision of short-term credit to countries with current account deficits (lender of the last resort) to the use of its crucial finances as a weapon to demand structural economic changes mainly in the bruised nations. In other words, the new IMF eroded the institutions of state sovereignty fought for by the global institutions of the Third World (UNCTAD and NAM). The assault by the IMF is not easy to understand, and it demands a facility with economic discourse that I have tried to make as accessible as possible (in the next chapter, "Kingston"). When the IMF and the World Bank worked over the already-battered Third World, many of their salacious elites looked across to the Pacific Rim of Eurasia and found small states with high growth rates. These dominant classes longed to be part of the U.S. consumer dream and abandon what appeared to be the intractable poverty of the Third World landscape. Their dreams had a flimsy foundation, mainly because they did not have a proper analysis of the cause of this rise of the "East Asian Miracle." Nevertheless, the dream of the East Asian road provided an alternative path for the "development" of the dominant classes in the darker nations that liberated themselves from the Third World (as I will show in the chapter "Singapore"). But this is not sufficient, because I cannot in this history ignore the millions of people who continue to live in the former Third World, and whose ruling cliques have abjured the creation of an agenda for liberation. Secular anticolonial nationalism ceased to provide the foundation for their sense of social solidarity, and it was replaced by a cruel, cultural nationalism that either drew on forms of social solidarity provided by religion, reconstructed racism, or undiluted class power (the final chapter, "Mecca," will illuminate this). The Third World came to be assassinated by this confluence of factors and processes.

KINGSTON

A hundred years after Christopher Columbus arrived on the island of Jamaica in 1494, the Arawak population of a hundred thousand dwindled to a handful. In time, the entire population was cleansed, and the island was peopled by English colonial officials and plantation owners as well as enslaved Africans and indentured Indians. Captive labor grew the sugarcane that provided the main economic resource of the island. Rebellions came over time, and these generated a strong consciousness of distaste for the brutality and paternalism of colonial rule. It took centuries for independence to come, and when it did come in 1962, it was overdue.

Just as the abolition of slavery advanced the cause of human freedom and yet left the formerly enslaved people in decrepit socioeconomic conditions, so too did national independence move history forward and yet do little for the everyday dilemmas of Jamaicans.[1] When the British took down the Union Jack from the island, they could very well have sung the youthful lyrics from Bob Marley's second album, except that the British didn't leave much money behind:

> I brought the money like your lawyer said to do
> Ain't nothing funny, babe, I am still in love with you
> Said I'm leaving you tomorrow
> I'll cause you no more sorrow
> One more cup of coffee then I'll go.

The new regime of Nelson Manley's People's National Party crafted a social development agenda to counter the chainless bondage of postcolonial life. Drawing from the work of W. Arthur Lewis, a comrade and friend of Prebisch, the Jamaican government pursued the policy of "industrialization by invitation." A system of leases permitted the government to channel industrial investment into those areas of the economy that allowed for social development.[2] Economic policy generally drew from the import-substitution theory, and the government relied on targeted direct foreign investment, notably in the bauxite sector. The latter provided Jamaica with most of its foreign exchange earnings. Discovered in the 1940s, the bauxite reserves fell prey to Canadian and U.S. firms starting in 1952. These firms have since dominated the extraction of the mineral, with Jamaica becoming the largest exporter to North America in the 1960s.[3] But as with sugar and tourism, the Jamaican people did not benefit from their natural resources. The only return to Jamaica came in the way of modest taxes to the government, meager wages to the working class, and a small tribute to the Jamaican managers at the mines and plantations—for this reason, what Jamaica exported despite its fabulous resources was cheap labor, and what it gained for that was a pittance toward its grandiose development aims.[4]

The Manley-Lewis approach to development resembled in all its essentials the policy followed by most of the formerly colonized states. Unable to draw on foreign capital (the Puerto Rican model) and unwilling to cut off ties with the capitalist world system (the Cuban model), the Manley-Lewis policy hoped to harness whatever domestic funds it could find as well as accumulate state revenues from the sale of bauxite. The capital raised would go toward some measure of social development.

Indeed, for a formerly colonized state, the Jamaican economy in the two decades after the end of colonial rule grew at a respectable annual rate of 7 percent on average, and per capita income rose by almost 4.5 percent. But because Jamaica's government had effectively leased its economic sovereignty to the wiles of foreign capital, the growth that the economy experienced was not able to sustain itself. The fundamentals of the economy, like that of much of the Third World, did not befit the rhetoric of freedom.

Despite the decent rate of growth, Jamaica could not raise the funds to cover its import bill; over 60 percent of the goods used in the country came from abroad (including energy and consumer goods, but also about half its food). Unable to cover its import bill as a result of a failure to diversify its economy, the Jamaican government relied on foreign investment and tourism to balance its books. The erratic, but almost always low prices of its minerals (bauxite) as well as its plantation crops (bananas and sugar) meant that the balance of payments suffered from a chronic deficit. Loans from commercial banks, sympathetic governments, and international agencies became not an emergency stopgap but a regular budgetary feature. Like many other formerly colonized states, Jamaica came to rely on foreign direct investment not as capital for development or even emergency means but as a routine part of its annual financial policy. Aid became just that: relief to a structurally unbalanced budget. The lack of economic diversification and the use of foreign investment for the repayment of loans instead of social development led to an increase in unemployment from just above 10 percent in 1960 to just under 25 percent by 1972.[5]

By the early 1970s, the government reactivated its efforts to break Jamaica out of its impoverished chrysalis at the nether end of global capitalism. Manley's son Michael ran a ferocious and successful political campaign against the global economic system that stacked the decks against countries like Jamaica. Once in power, Michael Manley promoted the construction of democratic socialism for Jamaica, but his regime did not try to disassociate itself from the world capitalist system, or even the overwhelming dominance of financiers of the commercial or IMF variety. Keeping Jamaica hooked up to the infusion of foreign aid or investment meant that the government had to respond to the demands of the foreign money managers rather than the long-term developmental needs of the people of Jamaica. Short-term returns to the investors dominated the planning even of the democratic socialist state.

The decline in the terms of trade shifted the priorities of the national liberation state; indeed it created a new project for the state—what political scientist Susanne Soederberg calls the "competition state."[6] Each state competed with other states to provide the best conditions for private portfolio capital. Because of the general crisis of the domestic economy, its population could not deliver sufficient taxes on its income and profits. This capital infusion, then, was more important to the competition state than its own domestic population. The needs of the investors drove state policy.

This is not to say that Michael Manley's regime did nothing to try to promote Jamaican interests.[7] The administration's democratic socialist regime initiated a series of measures that challenged the hegemony of the G-7 states, even as it did not demand the structural adjustment of the capitalist order. The first and most impressive move came in the 1974 formation of the International Bauxite Association (IBA). At the founding conference in Conakry, Guinea, seven of the major bauxite producers (Australia, Guinea, Guyana, Jamaica, Sierra Leone, Surinam, and

Yugoslavia) descried the overwhelming domination of "multinational corporations in the exploitation and processing of bauxite and the marketing of its produce."[8] Transnational corporations sucked the benefits from the extraction of mineral resources like bauxite. The combined power of the companies worked against the mutual competition between states. Guinea and Jamaica, for instance, competed against each other to the benefit of transnational firms. The IBA wanted the states to shift this power imbalance. If these states operated together, the transnational firms might have to kowtow to them.

The Manley government sought control over the domestic bauxite industry from a handful of transnational corporations. A substantial levy on the price of the aluminum ingot content in the bauxite drew several hundred million dollars for the treasury in the matter of a few months, and after substantial deliberation the government took over majority (51 percent) control of the bauxite mines.[9] But control over the domestic production and revenue of bauxite was not sufficient, as the crucial cooperation of the Third World failed to materialize. Brazil did not join the IBA. Australia joined Brazil in selling bauxite for less than the IBA's agreed price. This destroyed the IBA, which soon became simply an office in Kingston.[10]

Bauxite was not the only unprocessed commodity to experience a sharp decline in its price into the early 1980s. If the 1970s saw a marginal rise in the price of certain nonpetroleum commodities, by the 1980s there was an across-the-board drop in these prices.[11] Single commodity export-dependent countries lost earnings of as much as $290 billion between 1980 and 1991 as a result of the decline in their terms of trade. For sub-Saharan Africa, the impact was gruesome. For much of the region, nonfuel primary commodity goods amount for about one-third of the state's export earnings. The decline in the term of trade meant that these countries lost on average about 5 percent of their gross domestic product, and thereby dampened their state's budgetary flexibility.[12] The decline in the terms of trade in the 1980s is not mystical.[13] It occurred for a variety of reasons. Agriculture in the G-7 states posed a significant problem, as these states both subsidized production and used costly fertilizers and irrigation systems to enhance productivity.

The bauxite trade was hit hard by shifts in the use of aluminum. Many industries used plastic in its stead, so that in the 1970s Jamaican bauxite exports declined by a third. In this same period, Jamaica's cane sugar exports declined by 22 percent as the First World market moved toward beet sugar and artificial sweeteners.

By the end of the 1980s, some commodity cartels remained in business, such as the London-based International Cocoa Organization, but others closed up shop, such as the Association of Coffee Producing Countries, which ended its run in 2002. From the late 1990s onward, the lack of viability of the World Trade Organization to act on behalf of the farmers of the former Third World showed decisively that their prices would remain low as subsidies to the producers in the G-7 remained legal. From bauxite to cotton, farmers and miners in the darker nations faced perilous times.

Burned by the failure of its cartel maneuver and unwilling to challenge the authority of global capitalism in general, the Manley government also pursued regional cooperation options. Jamaica took a leadership role in moving the Caribbean Community and Common Market (Caricom) from a free trade area into a customs union—that is, from an area without tariffs between the various countries in Caricom to an area with a common external tariff policy against those outside it. The Manley regime initiated a dialogue about the transformation of Caricom into a common market, but it did not go anywhere, Even Caricom failed its self-image as states demanded concessions for their own tariff policies or else cut side deals with the Caribbean Development Bank.[14] These were difficult times, and the leadership of these nations had no easy choices. They stumbled around in search of a way out of the debt trap, and even those such as Cuba only managed with considerable assistance from the already-faltering Soviet economy.[15]

In the early years of Michael Manley's democratic socialism experiment, Jamaica's main reggae artist became the voice of the Third World. In 1973, Marley and the Wailers released *Burnin'*, their second major international hit after the previous year's *Catch a Fire*. On this album, the Wailers produced a series of songs that reflected the rage of those who began to feel increasingly marginalized by their own state and the international order: "Get Up, Stand Up," "I Shot the Sheriff," "Burnin' and Lootin'," and "Oppressed Song."[16] One of them, the title track, set the tone with regard to the difficulty of finding the "boss" who controlled the system of everyday economic curfews:

This morning I woke up in a curfew.
Oh God, I was a prisoner too.
Could not recognize the faces standing over me.
They were all dressed in uniforms of brutality.
How many rivers do we have to cross,

Before we can talk to the boss?
All that we got, it seems we have lost,
We must have really paid the cost.

And then, because of the structural failure of the Third World agenda,

That's why we gonna be
Burnin' and lootin' tonight . . .
Burnin' all illusions tonight.

By 1976, the Jamaican balance of payments registered a deficit (in Jamaican dollars) of $231.3 million, and the net foreign exchange reserves fell precipitously from a positive balance of $136.7 million in June 1975 to a negative one of $181.4 million in December 1976. World inflation, high oil prices, and a drop in commodity prices effected the reserves, as it did those of most of the darker nations. In 1960, the total debt of the 133 states that the World Bank counted as part of the "developing countries" held a total public and private debt just short of US$18 billion. In ten years, the debt had escalated to $75 billion, and when Jamaica went into fiscal crisis, it was $113 billion. By 1982, the debt had reached the astronomical figure of $612 billion. While many scholars and commentators blame the oil crisis of 1973–74 for the ballooning debt, this is a superficial argument. The rise in oil prices due to the action of the OPEC cartel only exacerbated tendencies that had already stymied the social development of the formerly colonized states. The distorted development agenda followed by most of the Third World, whether those that adopted or shunned socialism, and the imperialist pressure faced by these states produced a structurally impoverished international political economy. When the oil crisis hit, it provided the conjuncture for the Third World's structural rot.

Many of the states mired in debt struggled to raise funds. As the NIEO strategy faltered, the Third World states turned to commercial banks to cover their debt. Borrowing without any ability to pay back the loans and the interest was the precipitating cause of the debt crisis for the Third World. In 1974–75, the nonpetroleum exporting states of the Third World had to come up with $80 billion to finance their external deficits. Of this, about $36 billion came from private sources.[17] Commercial banks in the G-7 that found that the rate of return within the advanced industrial states declined as productivity rates grew flat, turned eagerly to fund the Third World states. They divided the "emerging markets" into at least two categories: the "fast-growing exporters of manufactures" such as Brazil, the Philippines, and South Korea, and the "new rich commodity exporters" such as copper exporters Peru and Zambia, and even Zaire (copper, cobalt, and manganese). But the banks would not dole out their capital without cover from the IMF.[18] If the IMF sanctified the state with a short-term standby agreement, it provided a "seal of approval" for more funds. The IMF loans often fell far short of the amount needed, so the IMF acted as insurance for the private commercial banks. U.S. banks took the lead. For example, as the economist Emma Rothschild notes, twenty-one of the largest U.S. banks lent in excess of $5 billion to Brazil and Mexico each. The money swept into the Third World, but not without a prospect of return. In 1975, Rothschild reports, "each of the five largest U.S. banks made more than 40 percent of its profits from foreign operations. Chase was an extreme case. It earned 64 percent of its profits abroad, as compared to only 22 percent in 1970."[19]

These commercial banks made a prudent decision. Their investment in the structural poverty of the Third World's balance-of-payments debt crisis paid handsome returns. But the situation seemed illogical. How could the impoverished pay back these enormous loans? Even the capitalist press worried for the profligate banks. "It doesn't show on any maps," *Wall Street Journal* editors quipped, "but there's a new mountain on the planet—a towering $500 billion of debt run up by the developing countries." Because the situation "looks starkly ominous" to some, the paper continued, it might create a chain reaction of defaults and bank failures that resembles the major depression of the 1930s. It takes a lot for the booster of free market capital to drum up such a pessimistic outlook.

The defaults did not come because the IMF, backed by the U.S. government and the newly confident elites of the darker nations, strong-armed governments into the cannibalization of their resources to maintain the payment schedules. After the Mexican collapse of 1982, the U.S. government proposed the Brady Plan (1989), which had two elements. First, the banks lent money to cover the debt if the country provided assurances to pay back the loan and the debt, and second, the IMF and the U.S. Department of the Treasury sanctified the loan if the country entered a process of significant economic reform. These reforms were planned to construct competition states and cut down the elements of the responsive state created by the national liberation regimes.

The indebted states could not fully or finally pay back the loaned amounts because they did not have the structural capacity to raise their exports above their imports, nor could they claw back from the devaluations of their local currencies that resulted as part of the IMF package.[20] Nevertheless, they serviced their debts with an annual interest payment either raised through more credit or else through the diversion of the surplus that might have gone toward social welfare (health, education, and other such areas of the social wage).

By 1983, capital flows reversed, as more money came from the indebted states to the G-7 than went out as loans and aid. In other words, the indebted countries subsidized and funded the wealthy nations. In the late 1980s, the indebted states sent an average of $40 billion more to the G-7 than the G-7 sent out as loans and aid; this became the annual tribute from the darker nations. By 1997, the total debt owed by the formerly colonized world amounted to about $2.17 trillion, with a daily debt-service payment of $717 million. The nations of sub-Saharan Africa spent four times more on debt service, on interest payments, than on health care. For most of the indebted states, between one-third and one-fifth of their gross national product was squandered in this debt-service tribute. The debt crisis had winners: the financial interests in the G-7.

If the G-7 commercial banks gained from the loans they continued to extend to the new indebted world, they did not win alone. To blame the oil crisis of 1973–74 for the implosion disguises another beneficiary of the rise in oil prices. During the first six months of 1974, when the fiscal effects of the oil crisis became clear, the G-7 enjoyed a $6 billion surplus with the nonpetroleum exporting Third World states, but it suffered a $41 billion deficit with the oil exporting states. A year later, the nonpetroleum states owed $21 billion, whereas the G-7 owed the oil group $21 billion.[21] The scale had been balanced. The rise in oil revenue for the G-7 had been offset by the surplus owed by the oil-less Third World. Furthermore, the oil states, as we saw earlier, held their profits largely in U.S. dollars, which meant that as the U.S. dollar abandoned the gold standard in 1971, its own standing in the global economy remained high because petrodollars kept it in demand.[22] The rise in petrodollars allowed the United States to abandon the very macroeconomic restrictions it demanded of the Third World, and therefore run a deficit to strengthen its domestic economy and expand its already-considerable military.

The debt crisis and the general disunity in the Third World over its response to this predicament offered an opening to the G-7 and its international agencies, notably the IMF, to demand immense concessions from the indebted states. The debt crisis was the Trojan horse for an assault against the abbreviated project for the construction of Third World sovereignty.

The IMF did not provide short-term assistance without prejudice. At its founding meeting in 1944, the Indian delegation proposed that the IMF should "assist in the fuller utilization of the resources of economically underdeveloped countries." The principle powers (led by the United States) rejected this formulation. For them, the IMF should simply be an instrument to ensure that countries in debt be encouraged with loans to cover their deficit rather than erect trade barriers to shore up their economy. The IMF, for the United States particularly, would be one more instrument to maintain a tariff-free capitalist system. As Article 1, no. 5 put it, the IMF would "give confidence to members by making the general resources of the Fund temporarily available to them under adequate safeguards, thus providing them with opportunity to correct maladjustments in their balance of payments without resorting to measures destructive of national or international prosperity." India's proposal aimed to extend the IMF's ambit from monetary policy and macroeconomic stabilization to the development needs of the emergent Third World. This could not be allowed for an institution intended to teach the world the fundamentals of neoclassic, free market economics.[23] IMF policy not only encouraged the export of capital but also drove the export of the capitalist relations of production to the darker nations.

In 1954, the government of Peru came to the IMF for a short-term loan. The IMF did not provide the loan with the hope that Peru's government would make good use of it. Instead, the IMF demanded one condition: that Peru's economy must maintain a stable exchange rate. Gradually the IMF created procedures for accountability and punishment, generally as a poor report against the country that might lead to a dearth of commercial finance. States outside the G-7 that took IMF money had to submit to a total makeover of their political and economic relations. In March 1980, the World Bank would give these sorts of policies a name, "Structural Adjustment loan," which would soon be called the Structural Adjustment Policy (SAP). Jamaica and other countries in the 1970s had to submit to SAP loans avant la lettre.

In December 1976, as Marley took the stage at Kingston's National Heroes Park for his Smile Jamaica concert, Manley's government acceded to the IMF.[24]

We're gonna help our people, help them right.
O Lord, help us tonight.
Cast away that evil spell, throw some water in the well, and smile
In Jamaica, c'mon and smile

The IMF plan was rigorous. First, it called on the government to devalue its currency to discourage imports and increase its ability to export its products. The policy intended to shift the import-substitution thrust to an export-oriented economy. Second, the government had to discourage an increase in wages to keep down the need to import goods. Third, the IMF called for the reduction of state expenditure and a contraction of the role of the state in the economy (no more price controls and subsidies). Fourth, the state needed to sell off its public-sector assets and enhance the private enterprises. Finally, the state had to hamper the money supply and raise interest rates to induce "fiscal discipline." If Marley asked Jamaica to smile in late 1976, a few months earlier his wife, Rita, wrote a different song. "Them crazy," she wrote in a song that Bob sang in the summer. "Them crazy. We gonna chase those crazy baldheads out of town. . . . Here comes the con man, coming with his con plan. . . . We gonna chase those crazy . . . baldheads out of town."

The IMF arrived with one prescription to fit all ailments, whether in Jamaica in 1976 or Sudan and Zaire in 1979, and elsewhere.[25] The elements of IMF policy included such items as a tighter money supply, a devalued currency, high interest rates, reduced governmental expenditure, lower wages, and an assault on tariffs and subsidies. The logic of the social wage gave way to that of austerity. The IMF urged the indebted nations to submit themselves to complete integration in the world capitalist system, and not try to create either autarkic modes of economic protection or even reforms to privilege domestic development. Rather than deal with the short-term balance-of-payments crisis for what it was, the IMF in the 1970s used the financial crisis as the means to demand deep shifts in the political and economic arrangements devised by the Third World. In other words, the IMF went after every policy initiated by its fellow international agency, UNCTAD. Rather than consider that the problem of debt stemmed from the dilemma of mono-export economies, capital-starved former colonies, or unfinished class struggles within the Third World, the IMF put the problem on the nature of the state. The IMF rebuked the fact that the Third World state attempted to engineer development, indeed that it took on the role of surplus management.

In Jamaica, the immediate effects of IMF policy fell on the rural and urban working class. Inflation soared as the Jamaican dollar faced significant devaluation and prices of basic goods began to skyrocket (chicken up 74 percent, salt-fish 285 percent, milk 83 percent, flour 214 percent, and cooking oil 71 percent).[26] The IMF austerity regime dropped real wages by as much as 35 percent in 1978 alone. By 1980, the unemployment rate in Jamaica soared to 30 percent or perhaps more. About 60 percent of Jamaican households began to rely primarily, if not exclusively, on the income of women, many of whom worked in unrewarding sweatshops in Kingston's free trade zone. In that zone, 80 percent of the employees were single mothers whose desperation to keep their families alive meant that three-quarters of them worked overtime.[27] One of these women, Debbie, told a 1988 surveyor that she earned $30 every two weeks, and "when it comes time for my draw down, I put it into the Credit Union and try to keep it for utility bills. But I'm always behind. Sometimes I have to do without light or water or gas and beg my neighbours until I can catch up." When Debbie was not able to work overtime, she had to join the higglers (the female street vendors): "I go to the market with a few dollars to buy essentials like seasonings, callaloo (greens) and the cheapest fruits. I go later in the day when the prices are lower; I check prices and haggle. It takes a lot of energy." Journalist Joan Ross Frankson, who reported this survey, offers her summary: "By imposing structural adjustment policies on Jamaica the World Bank and its IMF partner have reversed the old rule about women and children being saved first. In this harsh new ocean there are no lifeboats—and women and children must simply sink or swim."[28]

Jamaica's problems with IMF policies mimicked what had occurred elsewhere. The UN Development Program as well as other agencies recorded their own doubts almost as soon as the IMF began to structurally adjust the national liberation state.[29] There were even doubters within the IMF. In 1990, a senior IMF economist studied the IMF-enforced stabilization measures from 1973 to 1988, the period when the structural adjustment bombed the Third World. His measured study found that "the growth rate is significantly reduced in program countries relative to the change in non-program countries."[30] The IMF medication produced a patient with contracted economic activity, the destruction of the capacity for long-term economic growth, the cannibalization of resources (what is known as "asset stripping"), and a consequent return to being an exporter of raw materials. Much of this resulted in rising inequality in terms of class and gender, in addition to widespread environmental devastation.

In the 1960s, the Third World states organized into UNCTAD had pledged not to attack the already-strained consumption ability of their citizens. Funds for development could not be garnered from additional taxation, these states promised, because they would not be able to draw more from a relatively impoverished population. After two decades, when the IMF era eroded the sovereignty of the national liberation states, it became routine to demand that these hollow states now pound more and more surplus from their exhausted populations to pay back already-fattened commercial banks and international agencies. Macro-economic stability became a more important actor on the world stage than the citizens of the national liberation states. In 1977, Michael Manley complained, "We cannot continue to be told that the price of balance of payments support through the IMF may involve measures that cause mass starvation."[31] If Manley worried about the ability of the working class to survive, the IMF took a harsh approach to sacrifice. In 1981, IMF director Jacques de Lavosiere called for "sacrifices on the part of all: international financing will serve no purpose if spent on consumption as if there were no tomorrow."[32]

Sacrifices could not be demanded without the expectation that they would result in protest. Early victims of IMF policies vigorously battled their governments for their accession to the IMF conditions. From Egypt to Peru, Sudan to Ecuador, Bolivia to Liberia—the streets of the Third World rang with the cries of "The Poor Can't Take No More" (as street graffiti in Kingston put it).

> Come we go burn down Babylon one more time
> Come we go chant down Babylon one more time . . .
> Men see their dreams and aspirations crumble in front of their face
> And all their wicked intentions to destroy the human race . . .
> Come we go chant down Babylon one more time.

Babylon knew that its demands would not come without a response. In early 1980, the Independent Commission for International Developmental Issues, chaired by the former socialist chancellor of West Germany Willy Brandt, published "North-South: A Program for Survival," which became known as the Brandt Report. The report had been commissioned by the World Bank's Robert McNamara to find out why the process known as "development" had failed to produce justice. Toward the end of the report the commission noted, "The Fund's insistence on drastic measures has tended to impose unnecessary and unacceptable political burdens on the poorest, on occasion leading to 'IMF riots' and even downfall of governments."[33] Jamaica had both these riots and the downfall of its government. The Manley government could have disavowed the IMF demands, refused to cover its deficit, and turned to Cuba and others for assistance. But this was a dangerous strategy given the overwhelmingly military response that would have come from the United States (as the Nicaraguans found after the successful Sandinista revolution of 1979, and as the Cubans continued to experience). Instead, Michael Manley accepted the IMF funds and tried to ameliorate its demands, to produce structural adjustment with a human face. Manley objected to the IMF's demand that the state cut its social programs, as this was "the price of survival for the democratic system."[34] Of course the IMF did not budge and the Manley government's budget had to give, and give again. As Manley hesitated, the commercial banks refused to proffer loans. When these came, the conditions were onerous. By the end of 1980, the per capita income in Jamaica fell by 40 percent.

This pressure and the unemployment not only damaged the credibility of the Manley government but also called into question the viability of democratic socialism, or indeed any alternative to capitalism. As economist Richard Bernal noted, "The [IMF's] actions and programs gave credibility to the charge that the government was guilty of economic mismanagement and that democratic socialism was impractical and unworkable."[35] IMF-led globalization promotes the view that the national liberation state is an overbearing and inefficient institution. Rather than allow the state to determine and regulate the process of the economy, IMF policies uphold "market forces" or the "market" as the most efficient agent for economic activity. When the IMF officials told the Jamaicans that politics should be taken out of the market, what they meant, Bernal underscored, was that the state should abdicate its formal accountable role in the management of the social surplus. The market will take care of everything.

Manley called for an election. He wanted to make it a mandate against the IMF and its prescriptions. This was always a tough sell, because it is hard to make abstract domination a coherent, emotive election issue. The opposition led by Edward Seaga's pro–United States Jamaican Labour Party was able to make the election turn on the current state of the economy, rather than the external pressures from IMF-driven globalization. Things looked bad for Manley. On the streets of Kingston, the wall painters wrote, "IMF = Is Manley's Fault."[36] Eight hundred people died in this most contentious and violent election. Seaga rode to victory.

Seaga inherited a broken economy. His party crafted the *National Programme for Reconstruction*, including the rebuilding of parts of the public sector.[37] When Manley spoke of the public sector, the U.S. government rebuked him; when Seaga did, they championed his leadership in the rebuilding of necessary infrastructure. The difference was political. A pro-Atlantic Jamaica could be a counterpoint to insurgent Nicaragua and Grenada as well as Cuba. In the same way, on the Pacific Rim, the U.S. government funded dictatorships in Indonesia and the Philippines despite the "nationalist" noises by Suharto and Marcos. Suharto declared 1966 to be the "Year of Self-Reliance," and threatened to nationalize the oil industry. Suharto's economic program included a cocktail of import substitution, industrialization by invitation, and an open door to the extraction sector (U.S.-based Caltex held a commanding position in oil, while U.S.-based Freeport-McMoran dominated copper). As long as Suharto facilitated the work of the transnational corporations and joined the United States in a geopolitical alliance, all else was forgiven.[38] Marcos, in 1973, ordained a constitution that reneged on the open-door policy for U.S. firms, yet he allowed these same firms through the back door with "service contracts." Additionally, Marcos signed Presidential Decree no. 66 to create the Bataan Export Processing Zone (EPZ); foreign-owned firms in this EPZ received enormous tax exemptions and repatriated their profits.[39] This was a harbinger of Marcos's export-oriented industrialization strategy, one welcomed by the U.S. treasury and the G-7. Seaga, too, spoke publicly about the need for an efficient public sector at the same time as he encouraged the two major bauxite transnational firms (Kaiser and Reynolds) to expand their operations on the island. Marcos, Suharto, and Seaga mastered the art of political illusion: by a sleight of hand, they posed as efficient nationalists as they opened their countries to unregulated corporations. The national bourgeoisie, represented in Jamaica by Seaga, camouflaged their enthusiasm for "reform" by making the claim that there is no alternative and the IMF made us do it as well as by touting the amount of U.S. and IMF money that flowed into the country as a result of the reforms.

Proximity to the Pentagon and the U.S. White House enabled such states to gain financial benefits. The U.S. government poured money into Jamaica: US$100 million per year in cash, and the purchase of millions of tons of bauxite for its "strategic stockpile."[40] In addition, the U.S. treasury vouched for these states with the international agencies, such as the IMF and other commercial and development banks. Short-term capital flooded in on very favorable terms. That the U.S. government dominated the IMF by dint of its contribution to the total fund and that it, along with the four other advanced industrial states (the United Kingdom, France, Germany, and Japan), controlled the World Bank, allowed it to have an inordinate control over the decisions of these crucial bodies.[41] The IMF provided Seaga's Jamaica with $600 million between 1981 and 1983 to underwrite the reform process. This inflow of capital did not prevent the free flow of the Jamaican economy. In 1981, the island's gross domestic product was $3 billion, but three years later it fell to $2 billion (the per capita annual income also dropped from $1,340 to $923). IMF-driven globalization exacerbated the collapse of the Jamaican economy, overseen by its great ally, Seaga. In 1984, an IMF riot broke out in Kingston. Eleven people died.

The institutional impact of IMF-driven globalization was heavy. The new reforms pushed by Seaga's government resulted in a weakened responsive state. Between the mid-1980s and 1989, Jamaica's government fired about a third of its public employees "both through privatization of public companies and through central government layoffs."[42] The state hired fewer people, had fewer regulators of the market, and therefore had little capacity to discharge its constitutional responsibilities. Not only did the IMF-driven reforms call for privatization and disinvestment in the economy, it also insisted on the withdrawal of the state from any interference in the management of social wealth (through a redistribution of food or via welfare) and the regulation of economic activities. The national liberation state was disemboweled in this process.[43]

The withdrawal of the neoliberal, competition state from the provision of social welfare and the protection of sovereignty did not mean that all the state institutions were weakened.[44] The neoliberal state now stakes itself more on repression than on responsiveness. Its role is as a crime fighter and a warrior against subversion. The assaults on the "rude bwoys" and Rastafarians predated Seaga's rule, but intensified within it. In 1980, the Private Sector Organization of Jamaica hosted Seaga's attorney general and minister of national security, Winston Spaulding, as well as the chief of staff of the Jamaican Defense Force brigadier Robert Neish and the police commissioner Wilbert Bowes. Spaulding reported that crime was intolerable, and to take care of it the police must "be free to go out there and get the gunmen." Seaga's cabinet backed the security forces entirely.[45] From 1979 to 1986, the Jamaican police killed more than two hundred people per year. An Americas Watch report summarized the police strategy as "a practice of summary executions by the police; a practice of unlawful detentions by the police at times accompanied by police assaults on detainees; and a practice of confining detainees in police station lock-ups under squalid and degrading conditions."[46] In the conditions of total social and economic collapse, gang violence or community protection against gang violence became the order of the day. Social anomie intensified alongside IMF-driven reforms, and the neoliberal state responded with the bullet.[47]

The armed forces not only went after the discarded parts of the Jamaican population but also used the right of eminent domain to expel people from their land. In the 1970s, the major bauxite firms took charge of almost two hundred thousand acres of farmland and displaced hundreds of thousands of farmers. These farmers "watched helplessly as the transnational firms bulldozed their homes and small provision grounds to take out the red dirt from the ground, sending this dirt to the sea on conveyor belts, where ships could carry them to provide jobs in the aluminum industry in Europe and North America."[48] The ejected farmers either went overseas and remitted money to distraught relatives, or they turned to the increasingly lucrative marijuana trade.

The state's withdrawal of regulation left the transnational corporation without any check. The mysteries of fiscal policy devalued the role of the citizen (with rights in the state) and elevated the power of the foreign corporations. In 1960, a U.S. scholar defined transnational corporations as entities "which have their home in one country but which operate and live under the laws of other countries as well."[49] This definition, however, missed one of the most crucial dynamics of the transnational corporation: to abjure jurisdictions and laws—in sum, to operate outside regulation and oversight. Carl Gerstacker of Dow Chemicals wistfully told the White House Conference on the Industrial World on February 7, 1972, "I have long dreamed of buying an island owned by no nation and of putting the world headquarters of the Dow Company on the truly neutral ground of such an island, beholden to no nation or society."[50] What Gerstacker hoped for did not come in the form that he desired (an island) but in the power that the transnational corporations wielded as a result of the demotion of the national liberation states. As such states withdrew from the task of economic regulation and the management of the surplus, transnational corporations filled the vacuum.[51] Of course the national bourgeoisie of these states, themselves children of two or more decades of import substitution or else the state bureaucracy, not only welcomed the transnational firms but also went into joint ventures with them or else went to work for them. The transnational corporation did not threaten the sovereignty of the national liberation state; that had already occurred through the impact of IMF-led globalization.[52]

The transnational corporations that blossomed from the 1970s onward emerged only because of a tremendous transformation of technology.

The fragmentation of the production process allowed firms to disarticulate the factory and shift parts of what was once a centralized assembly line across continents. This could only take place alongside the development of a communications network (via satellites), a transportation network (computerized shipping, containerization, and lower air freight costs), an international accounting and credit system (cash management through computers), and weaker international taxes on the transit of partially finished goods. All these developments allowed for the integration of production on a world scale. When national liberation states shifted their priorities from import-substitution, people-oriented development toward export-led, growth-driven development, they created EPZs that cut taxes and defended corporations against all regulation. Jamaica's Kingston EPZ used to be a warehousing and transshipment facility. In 1982, the state converted it into a production site, and soon thereafter added the Montego Bay EPZ (1985) and the Garmex EPZ (1987). Technological changes and the encouragement of the formerly colonized states through a withdrawal of laws enabled the transnational corporation to flourish.[53] In 1980, a study of the world's hundred-largest economic units found that thirty-nine of them were not states but transnational corporations.[54]

The more astute movements recognized the power of transnational corporations. After Chile's socialist president Allende nationalized the country's copper mines, he asked the UN Economic and Social Council to investigate the activities of global corporations. In 1973, after Allende's ouster and murder, the United Nations created the Centre on Transnational Corporations (UNCTC). Following a long period of deliberation and study, the UNCTC drafted a provisional transnational corporation code of conduct in 1976, but after dozens of consultations and meetings, the code died when the United Nations closed down UNCTC in 1993.[55] The UNCTC created an archive on corporate malfeasance and the fiscal irregularities due to a lack of international standards for accounting. All the principles and procedures being produced by the UNCTC would have posed a great challenge to the kind of fallacious operations maintained by Enron.[56] Over the course of the 1980s and into the 1990s, the UNCTC played a quixotic role, as the G-7 powers took advantage of the Third World's collapse to exert the power of the transnational corporation into the bureaucratic world of the United Nations. By February 9, 1998, when UN secretary general Annan signed a joint statement with the International Chamber of Commerce (represented by leaders from Coca-Cola, Goldman Sachs, McDonald's,

Rio Tinto Zinc, and Unilever) that read, "Broad political and economic changes have opened up new opportunities for dialogue and cooperation between the United Nations and the private sector," the advantage went decisively to IMF-led globalization over the Third World. Furthermore, the statement hoped that the United Nations and the International Chamber of Commerce would "forge a close global partnership to secure greater business input into the world's economic decision-making and boost the private sector in the least developed countries." What they wanted was the establishment of "an effective regulatory framework for globalization," or in other words, as little influence as possible in the capitalist relations of production.[57] This convergence effected the UNCTAD, the new home of the UNCTC.

When the UNCTC went to the UNCTAD, it became a part of the Division of Investment, Technology, and Enterprise Development—in other words, it became a cheerleader for transnational corporations. The UNCTAD, born by the efforts of the Third World, now produces investment guides for global conglomerates so that they can have "comparative information on investment opportunities" in the "least developed countries" (this is a project with the International Chamber of Commerce).[58] The UNCTAD is now a booster of trade within the current unfair structure of the international political economy, not the heart of the international struggle led by the Third World to challenge and change the structure itself. Where Prebisch called for a revision of the terms of trade and outright grants instead of loans, the current head of the UNCTAD, Rubens Ricupero, asks for an increase in the volume of trade alone. "Many poor countries run big balance of payments deficits, usually filled by aid flows and remittances from overseas," he told the 2004 UNCTAD conference. "A major aim of all least developed countries should be to reduce their aid dependence and external indebtedness." All this is along the grain of the old UNCTAD, but how does change happen? "Capital accumulation and trade are the engine of growth, and international trade is the fuel for the engine. If the fuel dries up, the engine will not run."[59] What the darker nations must do is to increase their exports within a structure that pays too little for them (terms of trade) or does not value their inputs (labor).

The demise of democratic socialism in the late 1970s had immense sociopolitical ramifications. During the 1970s, the Jamaican women's movement, mainly exercised through the democratic socialist political party, grew in strength.[60] After Manley's regime took power, the Women's Auxiliary of his party pushed a strong transformative agenda. The government felt the pressure, created the Women's Bureau in the Prime Minister's Office, and championed legislation to benefit women especially. When confronted with high female unemployment, Manley's government passed the Special Employment (or Crash) Programme to hire women to conduct public works. A backyard day care initiative and free educational services (including school meals and uniforms) freed up household budgets. Better minimum wage laws, equal pay rules, and a campaign against the concept of the illegitimacy of children rounded out the array of laws and rules. When the political and economic situation worsened in 1977, the Women's Auxiliary joined with the Marxist Committee of Women for Progress to create the Joint Committee for Women's Rights. This new forum pushed a maternity leave law, fought against price increases, and exposed cases of hoarding by markets. In this period, the campaign for women's liberation had an agenda and an organization. But with the IMF-led reforms, this dynamic collapsed. The state no longer provided an avenue for building the power of working-class women. The political organizations withered, or turned elsewhere for funds and support.

This elsewhere is significant. Private foundations in the Atlantic states came forward to provide small amounts of funds to those organizations that weathered the demise of the state's responsiveness. Some of these groups took over the state's function to provide the basic amenities of survival (health care, literacy, and sustenance). The World Bank lauded them for doing what the national liberation state did routinely.[61] The groups that pushed for systematic change or had strong political views had their funding cut. Sistren, a political and cultural outfit in Jamaica, started out in the 1970s as a beneficiary of the democratic socialist regime. When that fell apart, it was able to continue only because of North American foundation money. One of its leaders, Honor Ford-Smith, recalls how the Inter-American Foundation ceased funding Sistren when it insisted on joining an "unacceptable political" activity, an antiapartheid rally.[62] The Jamaican women's movement and the Women's Bureau of the democratically socialist state pushed a slew of laws to transform the social condition of women. These new groups could not exercise this sort of leverage. They were only able to offer support or express their discontent. The institutional apparatus within the state to carry forward the women's liberation agenda no longer existed.[63]

In 1979, scholars and politicians from around the Third World met in Kingston for an international conference on the trauma of the planet's political economy. The gathering produced "The Terra Nova Statement on the International Monetary System and the Third World." If the IMF put itself forward as an unblemished institution of global reform, those in Kingston saw it as an instrument for the perpetuation of inequality. The G-7 dominated the IMF procedures and policies, and regarded its rules as being for the darker nations and not for the advanced industrial states. For this reason, the G-7 did not adhere to the IMF structural adjustment demands against budget deficits and subsidies. The G-7 broke the rules when it wanted to and treated "the Fund with impunity when they wished."[64] The IMF served the G-7, and not the G-77. That was the lesson of "The Terra Nova Statement."

The statement showed that whereas almost a hundred Third World states accounted for less than 37 percent of the IMF's voting power, the five leading industrial powers controlled more than 40 percent, while the United States alone held 20 percent of the votes in the IMF. The fund was controlled by the United States and other advanced industrial states. Indeed, the U.S. government was fully aware of this, pointing out to itself that it would only promote the policies of these international bodies if "we are capable and willing to pursue important policy objectives in the banks by exercising the leverage at our disposal."[65] "The Terra Nova Statement" said that "the IMF, acting on behalf of the major industrialized capitalist countries, has assumed a growing role as a financial and economic policeman in Third World countries."[66]

The Third World, in crisis, offered a variety of reforms for the world political economy, but few listened. At Terra Nova itself, the delegates recognized that major "internal structural reforms" were needed, such as tight capital controls, control over foreign trade, and better management of local production. None of this came in line with IMF-led globalization, and most of this would be outlined at the South-North Conference on the International Monetary System and the New International Order in Arusha, Tanzania (June–July 1980). "The Arusha Initiative," like "The Terra Nova Statement," understood that the IMF had compromised its integrity by a too-close relationship with the G-7. The G-77 needed to reform the IMF to make it "supportive of a process of global development, especially for the countries of the Third World, which contain the majority of the world's poor." A new international monetary policy that could do this would need to achieve monetary stability, restore reasonable levels of employment and sustainable growth, and check inflation in the world economy.[67] To do this, the IMF would have to curtail the immense power of the G-7 to dominate production and prices, exchange rates, and world trade.

From such principled objections and objectives, "The Arusha Initiative" laid out four "main attributes of a new monetary system":

(1) Democratic management and control, or in fact the rearrangement of the policy that allows the largest donor to have the greatest say (as in the IMF);

(2) Universality, or a demand that all states participate in international agreements;

(3) The establishment of an international currency unit as the means of exchange and as the primary reserve asset, this to circumvent the global power of the dollar;

(4) Immediate "resource transfer" to undo the vast imbalance in the world system.

By the early 1980s, such proposals read like undecipherable hieroglyphics.

At Terra Nova, the participants acknowledged that any democratic reform against the IMF-led globalization agenda would face major political problems. If a government did not have the support of its population when it took on the G-7 and the abstract forces of economic domination, it would be ejected. For that reason, "the government should adopt forms of popular mobilization, organization and education which enable it to secure the active cooperation of the supporting social alliance, and the moral authority to ask for sacrifices. Experience shows that people make sacrifices willingly when they know that this is for a better future, and tolerate errors in management which are a natural part of the learning process."[68] These sacrifices would be far from the austerity of the post–Third World epoch.

SINGAPORE

As Jamaica's hopes clotted, dreams of other islands, these on the Pacific Rim, soared. The emergence of Japan as an economic giant surprised many, particularly since World War II devastated the country. Close on the heels of Japan came the states that the press dubbed the Four Tigers or Dragons (Hong Kong, Singapore, South Korea, and Taiwan), and then just behind them came the Four Cubs (Indonesia, Malaysia, Thailand, and the coastline of mainland China). Between 1960 and 1990, as the Third World's numbers plummeted, Japan and the Tigers turned in spectacular economic results. Not only did these five countries experience a higher growth rate than most other countries or regions on the planet but they also made significant inroads into global trade. In the thirty years after 1960, the Tigers' share of total world exports increased from 1.5 to 6.7 percent. Their share of total exports from the Third World rose from 6 to 34 percent, as their share of Third World manufacturing exports rose from 13.2 to an unbelievable 61.5 percent.[1] Unlike most great leaps forward of this kind, the Tigers did not grow at the cost of extreme domestic inequality. By 1990, all the Tigers showed a substantial improvement in income distribution, with Hong Kong and Singapore at the front, and South Korea and Taiwan not far behind.[2] In 1993, the World Bank released *The East Asian Miracle*, the first in a promised series of policy research documents written for the general public on development policy issues.[3] The title itself provides an indication of the breathlessness with which the World Bank saw the remarkable growth rates and relative economic equity produced in these Asian rim states.

New York, September 1976: Singaporean foreign minister S. Rajaratnam gives the UN General Assembly a piece of his mind. © BETTMANN/CORBIS

The Tigers' success dampened the enthusiasm for the Third World's exertions to transform the world order. If these small Asian countries could break through the constraints of the international political economy, why can't others do so? Singapore, about the size of Jamaica and also independent in the early 1960s, had the privilege of being the second most competitive economy in the world (after the United States). The gross domestic product of this small island grew from 1965 to 1990 by an average of 6.5 percent per year (double that of comparable places). The remarkable growth rates in these few decades eclipsed those of Singapore's former colonial ruler, England.[4] The engine for this explosion was Singapore's exports of manufactures. In 1960, only 7.2 percent of Singapore's gross domestic product came from manufactured exports, whereas by 1990 manufactured exports accounted for a little more than three-quarters of the gross domestic product. The massive economic growth lifted the standing of the entire population. The principle beneficiary of this expansion was the top 3 percent of Singaporean society, the elite who controlled the fields of finance (Lien Lin Chow, Khoo Teck Puat, the Lee family, and Wee Chor Yeow), real estate (Ong Beng Seng, Kwek Leng Beng, and Ng Teng Fong), and the media (the Shaw family). Singapore's elite is not flashy, but by three decades after the country's independence, it has been able to exert itself in global markets, as global players.[5]

Singapore is not unique. First millionaires and then billionaires appeared up and down the Pacific Rim as well as in the more established capitalist economies of the Third World. Taiwan produced Tsai Wan-Lin (banking and insurance) and Y.C. Wang (chemicals). Hong Kong delivered Li Ka-Shing (real estate and telecommunications), Kwok Tak-Seng (real estate), and Lee Shau Kee (real estate). South Korea conjured Huang Jen-Chung (finance) and Wong Ta-Ming (industrialist), and so many others. These men (and most are men) operated as sirens for the newly confident bourgeoisie across the Third World: people such as India's Birlas and Tatas, Brazil's Antonio Ermíro de Moraes and Julio Bozano, and the Philippines's Tan Yu and Jamie Zobel de Ayala, among others. One of the common cultural traits of the haute bourgeoisie is the assumption that their wealth is well gained, that it has come by the ingenuity of a founder and is maintained by the exertions of the family. No magnate or titan believes that they have got what they have by dint of state intervention or by chance. The success of East Asia's islands and their well-known entrepreneurs attracted the bourgeoisie in the rest of the Third World, and disenchanted them from the road taken by their own societies. By the 1980s, when the debt crisis wracked the rest of the Third World, its elites looked to the Pacific Rim for inspiration and a model. For the bourgeoisie of the darker nations, Singapore was Mecca.

By the 1980s, Singapore and the other Tigers possessed not only impressive growth rates but also the spectacle of advanced capitalist success. In 1965, as Singapore won its independence, its foreign minister, Rajaratnam, identified his country as a "global city." A chain of cities (Singapore–Hong Kong–Seoul–Taipei–Tokyo) would "share and direct, in varying degrees of importance, a world-wide system of economics."[6] The East Asian miracle, for Rajaratnam, was located in the city. This was not the industrial town of the nineteenth century. These cities represented the new mobile epoch of IMF-driven globalization. The idea of the global city ignored production, emphasized consumption, and made money through distribution. In these cities, the cathedrals of capitalism at their heart eclipse much else: the skyscrapers dominate the skyline, obscuring their own history and contemporary struggles. Singapore and Hong Kong, with immensely complex populations, both celebrated their diversity and enjoined their citizenry to revel in the present. "So what if Singapore has no landscape, in any full sense of the word?" writer Peter Schoppert asks. "Perhaps it is better to be lost than found. Who needs all the bloody ballast of land and destiny. Singapore is about routes, not roots: an intersection point of the trajectories of a thousand journeys. Singapore is the sum of a hundred diaspora: at night, it seems everyone is dreaming about somewhere else."[7] The city is the home for the confident bourgeoisie and an aspiring middle class, who eagerly want to break their bonds with the countryside and their domestic working class. Seoul and Taipei stand in for the hinterland of South Korea and Taiwan, while Hong Kong and Singapore are freed from the rest of the planet—little oases of capital and goods that have none of the problems of countries with an economically diverse landmass.

Singapore–Hong Kong, Dubai–Kuwait, and elsewhere symbolize the mobility of capital and goods, but not the production of anything. The global city hides its production sites in the shadows. Hidden, too, are the low wages in the EPZs (in South Korea, 11 percent of U.S. wages) and the gender disparities in the workplace (women in South Korea make about half what men do for the same job).[8] These annoying facts of continued distress for large numbers of people who lived in the Tigers or the hinterland of the Tigers (and therefore provided it with mobile and often disenfranchised labor) did not imperil the enthusiasm of the World Bank. The darker nations finally produced a miracle.

And it needed to be made universal. The World Bank's prescription for those Third World regimes in debt had the air of old, neoliberal wine in new miraculous Asian bottles. "These market-oriented aspects of East Asia's experience," it wrote, "can be recommended with few exceptions."[9] The World Bank report grudgingly acknowledged the role of governmental intervention of the Third World variety, but then hastily cast it aside: "More institutionally demanding strategies have often failed in other settings and they clearly are not compatible with economic environments where the fundamentals are not securely in place. . . . In parts of Sub-Saharan Africa and Latin America, and elsewhere in Asia . . . activist government involvement in the economy has usually gone awry. So the fact that interventions were an element of some East Asian economies' success does not mean that they should be attempted everywhere, nor should it be taken as an excuse to postpone needed market-oriented reforms."[10] The World Bank spoke for a bourgeoisie eager to deny the governmental intervention that birthed it as well as to shirk off any lingering governmental regulations laid out for nationalistic aims. It also, significantly, spoke for the treasury departments of the G-7 and the financial elites who lived in the global cities of London, New York, and Tokyo. Moreover, the construction of the "miracle" enabled the Tigers to exert themselves in the NAM forums against the line proposed by Castro and the Left. Galloping growth had a more solid foundation for its arguments than galloping inflation. Because the miracle (as early as 1973) was talked about with the barest of concern for the facts, it carried greater weight than the reality of the East Asian road.

The World Bank report and the self-image of the Tigers minimized the main historical facts.[11] The sensation of Singapore and the other Tigers came in large part from a set of advantages exceptional to them. For one, the colonial experience of the Tigers was objectively beneficial. Seized by the British as commercial bases for their China trade, Singapore (1819) and Hong Kong (1841) inherited few of history's problems. There was little agriculture, and what there was soon vanished before the hunger for buildings (Hong Kong not only urbanized its landscape but also reclaimed land from the sea for its airport and residential areas). Both Singapore and Hong Kong thrived as duty-free ports for opium and other commodities. These were paradises of capital, where the problem of production (and hence workers) was shipped elsewhere. These were almost purely entrepôts.[12] Occupied by the Japanese, Taiwan and Korea experienced an assault on their landlord class and forced land reform. Feudalism disappeared at the butt of an Arisaka rifle. In addition, the Japanese colonial machine exported its *zaibatsu*-state complex for capitalist development. The zaibatsu (called *chaebol* in Korean) is an industrial conglomerate that controls finance, production, and distribution as well as cultivates a proximate relationship with the state. The zaibatsu-state alliance created a filial ideology that crushed dissent and infantilized workers, so that the factory became a curious amalgam of barracks and home. This was to be exported to Korea and Taiwan. In the 1930s, the Japanese economist Katane Akamatsu's theory of the "flying geese" appealed to the zaibatsu and the Japanese imperial state—the lead goose (Japan) developed technologies and products; as it developed newer lines, it turned over the older ones to its colonies (Taiwan and Korea), and so it developed them as it went ahead.[13] Both the Japanese and the British established strong state structures and made the dominant classes subservient to these state institutions.[14] The potentialities of capitalist development along the Pacific Rim were well laid by colonial rule.[15]

World War II devastated the Pacific Rim. It left Singapore in shambles. The growth of the Communist movement in Malaysia and Singapore threatened the British hold on the region. A brutal war between the British and the Communist Party ran from 1948 until Malaysia's independence in 1957. In Singapore, the Communist movement developed mass support among the Chinese working class. Aware of the growing strength of the Left, an England-educated group led by Lee Kuan Yew created the People's Action Party (PAP). PAP made an alliance with the Communist trade unions to throw out the British. For the first elections of 1959, PAP developed a manifesto that reflected its eclectic ideology— a mix of socialism, pragmatism, multiculturalism, and nationalism.[16] In 1961, as PAP gained confidence, it ejected its left wing (which re-formed as the Barisan Sosialis, the Socialist Front). In 1963, the PAP state engineered Operation Cold Store to "obliterate the BS's [Barisan Sosialis's] top level leadership."[17] PAP's lead economist and first finance minister of Singapore, Goh Keng Swee, warned the cabinet not to be swayed by either the lures of the free market or socialism. What Singapore needed, he argued, was the guided development of its free enterprise.[18]

Lee Kuan Yew, the leader of PAP, came from an established, moneyed Chinese Singaporean family. He attended the best of the English-medium schools (Raffles Institution and Raffles College) and took his degree at Fitzwilliam College (Cambridge). Lee was devastated when the brief merger with Malaysia (1963–65) ended with anti-Chinese riots organized by chauvinist Malaysian political organizations. Lee cried before the television cameras, telling his new island nation that this was a "moment of anguish" for him.[19] The Hobbesian nature of modern politics distressed Lee, whose aristocratic background required a more hierarchical form of administration. Singapore, he told some journalists a few days after independence, "should be a Republic. We do not have a Sultan, nor a Raja." The Singaporean republic was not, to Lee's taste, "excessively democratic."[20] Democracy not only had the tendency to devolve into mob rule (as in Malaysia, 1965) but it also wasted the talents of the educated classes. At a lecture at Harvard University in 1968, Lee explained that a highly politicized state absorbed the talents of people who would otherwise be involved in the productive economy. The educated, in that setting, "were not put to the best use," and those who entered the combative arena of politics were "gifted more in arousing their people than in mundane matters of administration and economics."[21] Politics interfered with the necessary work of development; the ideological framework developed by Lee for PAP secluded the world of politics from Singaporean society, and tried to turn the attention of the people toward an increase in the growth rates. Political differences were suppressed toward the creation of a "strong" economy. The sinister named Operation Cold Store was an early indication of the ejection of politics from Singaporean society. The Tigers emulated each other on this score: two consecutive dictatorships (led by Park Chung-Hee and Chun Doo-Hwan) controlled South Korea from 1960 to 1988; in Taiwan, the Kuomintang ruled a one-party state from 1949 to 1996; and Hong Kong remained a British colony until 1997. None of these states had even the pretense of political democracy.

Even as the Third World's bourgeoisie lavished praise on the East Asian miracle in the 1980s, during the 1950s and 1960s, the Tigers traveled a familiar route, albeit with better basic conditions (land reforms and institutions such as the chaebols for industrial organizations). Singapore's PAP, led by the charismatic Lee, followed Goh Keng Swee's advice on state intervention. The Development Plan (1960–64) adopted the import-substitution industrialization strategy. Whatever funds could be harnessed went into state-owned enterprises and the expansion of the state functions itself. As part of its commitment to the creation of a strong state, PAP, like many of the Pacific Rim political parties, created policies to hamper the political growth of the middle class. In 1966, Lee told a branch meeting of PAP that the economically powerful needed to help create a strong state, because "you know, you can be the world's biggest millionaire. But if the country collapses you are in trouble."[22] That same year, Lee's confidant Rajaratnam announced to the nation that "the average citizen" must not equate "his immediate self-interest as the national interest. He must try and hitch his self-interest to the national interest because in the long run if the country disintegrates into political anarchy and economic chaos the pursuit of self-interest becomes impossible."[23] The interventionist state took charge of development, while the people, especially the middle class, were required to put their innovations and enthusiasm into economic development and private initiative.[24] The superficial side of this strong state was the ban on spitting and the compulsory haircuts at Singapore's Changi Airport. The state not only sent the middle class home or to their businesses, it also went into the homes to engineer family size.[25] The object of statecraft, Lee Kuan Yew told journalist Fareed Zakaria, "is to have a well-ordered society."[26]

In addition to its congruence on some NAM economic issues, Singapore joined the Third World at its many forums. At the first press conference after independence, when a reporter asked Lee if Singapore would seek admission into the Afro-Asian Conference, he answered, "What else? Are we to be outcasts? Surely we are not. And I would imagine that all the heads of Governments and heads of State and Governments that I have met in Africa, in Asia, will know that I am not a stooge. . . . There is no hope of survival if I do not have people who are friends, who are prepared whatever their reason—they may be selfish reasons, that is irrelevant to me so long as I am not playing stooge to them—but they ensure my survival."[27] At this time, Singapore's friends were in the Third World, but its first priority was in its region. In 1967, it engineered the creation of ASEAN, which adopted the NIEO principles at its inaugural meeting. As late as 1979, ASEAN reiterated its commitment to a special fund to help control commodity prices.[28] In 1970, Singapore entered NAM. In this period, Singapore was not, in Lee's words, a stooge for anyone.

When Singapore broke from Malaysia in 1965, it had to reassess the import-substitution strategy because now the small island alone did not have a sufficient domestic market to carry through the program. This specific event, the caesura from Malaysia, caused the cabinet to move the island state toward an export-oriented manufacturing path. It is in this context that Rajaratnam spoke of the island nation as a global city. To transform Singapore into a major transshipment entrepôt and manufacturing site required an enormous infusion of capital. Like Taiwan and South Korea (as well as Japan), the scale of capital was beyond the capacity of the domestic population. It had to come from elsewhere. The secret to the Tigers' sensation lies in this original infusion of capital, because only with it could their various institutional advantages shine.

A large amount of the investment capital came from PAP's ability to capture domestic savings. The government maintained the Central Provident Fund, the cache of social security payments for all workers. Investment for the state-owned enterprises and other ventures came from this capital fund. But this was insufficient. Additional money came from U.S. government aid, although this played less of a role in Singapore than in Taiwan ($13 billion) and Korea ($5.6 billion). The investment-as-aid that went into Taiwan and Korea dwarfs the aid that went to the rest of the Third World from both the United States and the USSR. Because most of these East Asian and Southeast Asian countries enjoyed the security umbrella created by the United States, they spent much less than they might have on their militaries.

More than domestic savings and foreign aid, the Tigers in the 1960s relied on investment from transnational corporations. Lee Kuan Yew recognized early that his goal was "to make Singapore into an oasis in Southeast Asia, for if we had First World standards then business people and tourists would make us a base for their business and tours of the region."[29] To draw in tourists and finance capital required lenient rules and clean streets. Lee provided the latter through his authoritarian state; his government created the conditions for the former in haste. It worked: between 1960 and 1990, Singapore enjoyed the world's highest investment ratio. In 1967, Singapore's Economic Expansion Incentives Act provided these firms with enormous tax benefits; when it increased these temptations in 1970, the IMF warned against being "overgenerous."[30] By 1973, Singapore abolished quotas and tariffs to create a free-trade port. It created EPZs, which blossomed because the state removed all income taxes and allowed them to function without regulation.[31] PAP also squelched trade unions and absorbed any syndicalism into its own domesticated National Trades Union Congress (between 1978 and 1997, Singapore only had two strikes). As a result of this suppression, Singaporean labor by the 1970s was cheapened. All this came as the New International Division of Labor emerged: the breakdown of the production process, the improvement in the transport of goods and communication across continents, and the relative lack of skills needed in production allowed the East Asian rim to become a major manufacturing hub for transnational corporations. Rajaratnam's vision for the global city included the construction of a container complex. When this was built in 1972, it made Singapore the major transshipment station in Southeast Asia (within a few years, Singapore was the third-busiest port in the world after Rotterdam and New York). Even as transnational firms outsourced production to the EPZ factories, much of the ownership of these subcontracted factories remained in East Asian (indeed Japanese) hands.[32] Harsh work regimes, using mainly female workers without any union protection or state regulation, allowed the new platforms for world production to engineer high rates of growth.[33] While the bulk of the planet suffered from a downturn in economic fortunes, East Asia benefited.[34]

Singapore's direction worried its leadership. The high rates of investment did not change the nature of the Singaporean economy; it produced low-end goods for the world market. Singapore needed to go after the high-end, high-value goods to hasten its development and break out of its dependency on foreign capital. Starting in 1979, PAP inaugurated a new targeted investment strategy. It gave immense incentives for foreign capital to invest in industrial manufacturing, tourism, trade, transport, and communication as well as "brain services" (medical and financial).[35] This "Second Industrial Revolution" required an infusion of skill and a new kind of investment. The import of skill was not new to the Tigers. Because of Communist insurrection and insurgency, the well-educated and upwardly mobile professionals fled to Taiwan and Hong Kong (from China), South Korea (from the North), and Singapore (from China and Malaysia). These professionals brought with them mercantile and technical skills that came gratis to their host societies. In the early years, all the Tigers invested heavily in their human capital: state-funded and managed educational systems that stressed technical skills, and an enhanced social wage that drew and maintained populations (in Singapore, the state provided housing to all but a few of its citizens). Additionally, the Tigers borrowed heavily from technological inventions developed elsewhere.[36] In 1980, Singapore inaugurated an international "search for talent" through its Professional Information and Placement Service and Committee for Attracting Talent to Singapore. Skills were needed, and the state went out to import them. The result was a type of "fragmentary industrialization," where certain sectors dependent on foreign capital zoomed ahead while others lagged behind.[37]

Singapore developed its high-technology firms, but structurally its economy remained dependent on foreign investment (mainly from transnational corporations and private portfolio investment). As Japanese investment dried up in the late 1980s, Chinese investment kicked in. China, boosted by the human capital growth of its socialist era and the EPZ performance on its coastal rim, generated investment for the East Asian manufacturers. It also operated as a major importer of raw materials and finished industrial goods from the region.[38]

PAP's broad antipolitics message combined with this structural dependence on foreign investment constrained Singapore's political role in the world. In 1966, Rajaratnam's National Day message walked the country through the argument. Singapore is "an overcrowded island with no natural resources of our own," said the foreign minister. "Our prosperity and well-being depends primarily on our being able to trade with and render services to other countries. . . . Essentially our policy is not to go out of our way to make enemies but if others persist in treating us as enemies then we will take such measures as we think fit to protect ourselves against them."[39] Singapore could not afford to make those who invested in it anxious or angry. At the 1973 NAM meeting, the Tigers attempted to uncouple the linkage between economic and political reform of the world order; the Third World challenged the political framework that guided economic decisions, and argued for the political reconstruction of the economic order. Rajaratnam, who led the delegation, insisted that economic issues be taken up in isolation from the political divides. Singapore's insistence on this question came from the ideological predilections of its ruling party, but more so from its own constrained political position vis-à-vis those who invested in its economy. Politically independent Singapore was actually deeply economically dependent.

Singapore's leadership on this question within NAM is perhaps the most potent long-term consequence of the Tigers' miracle. By the 1980s, NAM was infected with the belief that economic development is a technical problem that should not be bothered with the question of power. The Tigers' example and leadership drove the Third World abandonment of the political critique of the economic order. The debt crisis shook the Third World agenda at about the same time as the Tigers experienced their economic takeoff. Whereas the Tigers continued to attend the Third World forums, they now did so to promote their path as well as combat the ideas of import substitution and anti-imperialist cooperation. As the NIEO lapsed, the Tigers championed the New International Division of Labor. The Tigers became their own boosters.

Hubris struck the East Asian miracle just as it seemed poised for a thousand-year period of co-prosperity. In 1997, the Thai *bhat* failed, setting off a chain reaction across the rim until the Tigers had to go to the IMF with their hats in hand for a bailout. What had struck the rest of the Third World from the late 1970s onward, hit East Asia two decades later. While the Tigers' collapse appeared structural, as the dust settled it became clear that they had been the victims of financial speculators whose fickle entry and exit from the currency markets caught the East Asian states not so much in an insolvent position as in an illiquid one.[40]

East Asia, buffered by authoritarian states and protected by U.S. primacy, had engineered a miracle, but in the end the East Asian Tigers suffered a drop in prices for their goods and the liberalization that they willing underwent in the 1980s devastated them. A substantial part of the industrial growth from the Tigers' EPZs came from their role as the assembler and component supplier of the world's electronics, notably computer, industry. When the price of computers dropped, the cost of the silicon chip began to resemble the potato chip. A commodity is a commodity after all, and when global factors begin to devalue the labor that goes into its manufacture, the computer chip market can approximate the market for any raw material.[41] China's sheer economic size allowed it to weather the storm, and its stability provided a lifeline for parts of the East Asian world.[42] The commodity price drop explains not only the downturn but also the structural closeness of the Tigers to the rest of the darker nations.

There is another important element that shows the similarity: that the East Asian crisis of 1997 happened partly because of the liberalization of the currency markets conducted by the managers of these states in collaboration with the IMF. In the early 1990s, under pressure from the IMF, the G-7, and other major financial interests, the governments of the East Asian rim undertook "radical financial deregulation," which is to say, they "removed or loosened controls on companies' foreign borrowings, abandoned coordination of borrowings and investments, and failed to strengthen bank supervision."[43] The South Korean government, for instance, abolished its Economic Planning Board, let the Treasury Department take charge, and watched from the sidelines as private firms borrowed heavily from overseas banks in contravention of the broad principles that produced the South Korean miracle. These policies allowed speculators to trash the currencies of East Asia. At the 1996 Asia-Pacific Economic Cooperation meeting in Manila, those invested in trade liberalization dominated the meeting, and demanded that the East Asian countries immediately succumb to liberalization at least in the electronics and computer sector.[44] The demand for liberalization, heard loudly in the Third World, also resounded in East Asia. If liberalization entered the Third World agenda as its poison pill after the debt crisis, in East Asia liberalized currency and capital policies engendered the economic collapse. The laden cart of debt, in this case, followed the horse of impatient capital.

The 1997 crisis did not impact Singapore directly. The strong state's control over monetary policy sheltered the island nation. Yet after the crisis, it too moved toward the liberalization of its financial markets. Part of the management over the crucial Central Provident Fund went into private hands. The state allowed private citizens to use their retirement savings in the stock market, even to buy shares of foreign firms in foreign currencies. In addition, the government issued government debt bonds, which created an interest rate market for the Singaporean dollar.[45] The foundations of Singapore's safe house are now in question.

Two remarkable reactions came from within the East Asian countries. First, the new bourgeoisie of East Asia (and the former Third World as well) found liberalization to be exhilarating. They wanted the good times to continue despite the currency collapse and the growing inequality within their own societies. As far as they were concerned, whether they lived in New Delhi or New York, Tokyo or Toronto, they lived in *America*. Fast fortunes and fast times became the hallmarks of their existence, and since many had studied in the United States or worked for U.S.-based transnational corporations, they wanted to create an endless and insulated world of consumerism and profits that resembled nothing so much as a Hollywood movie. The actual inequality and structural adjustment of the United States itself did not register on their radar: they only saw certain blocks of Manhattan as "America."

Taiwan's Club 51 provides a cartoonish example of this sensibility. In 1996, members of Taiwan's elite created an organization (Club 51), whose manifesto called on the island to join the United States as its fifty-first state. The club urged the Taiwanese elite not to conduct "individual immigration," which it deemed "selfish and short-sighted." Rather than migrate as individuals, the club proposed that the elite gather together and fight for all of Taiwan to become part of the United States. This was the "Taiwan State-Building Movement." If the elite did not go in this direction, the club warned, then Taiwan would suffer the fate of Hong Kong and be merged into Communist China.[46] While China's role in East Asia instigated Club 51, certainly the organization of the haute bourgeoisie toward an alliance with the United States is not restricted to the case of Taiwan or Hong Kong.[47]

Others too wanted to forge an alliance with the United States, either through free-trade agreements or else through military pacts that would lead to advantageous economic arrangements for the bourgeoisie.

In 2005, Lee's son, Singapore's current prime minister, Lee Hsien Loong, delivered an address on the "Singapore Elite." He pointed out that the first generation of the elite fought against colonialism and struggled to craft a state. The second generation was not schooled in social struggle or national construction. It is prone to self-interest or class over national interest. For this reason, Lee offered the typical bromides about the elite's "moral obligation to give back to society" and the "spirit of patriotism," although he recognized that "a sense of obligation and patriotism are not things that we can dictate or implement." Instead, the elite could only be enjoined to act in a manner less venal than is apparent.[48]

What such developments show is that among sections of the bourgeoisie, there is a slow erosion of national loyalty and the growth of cosmopolitan extranational sentiments that are more in tune with a global bourgeois calculation of economic interest. We might be on the threshold of the creation of a genuine global bourgeoisie—at least in style, if not in structure—and therefore a political realignment among certain states whose bourgeoisie is eager for a pro–United States engagement, even as this might be counterproductive for the vast mass of its population. This genuine global bourgeoisie is motivated less by national agendas and more by the patriotism of the bottom line as well as the need for the validation of their cultural heritage.[49]

It is the globalization of these turbo elites that provoked much of the planetary euphoria in the 1990s—with the collapse of the Second World and Third World, nothing would stand before the broad unity of the sophisticated classes across the globe. The vapid desire for a quick fix to the contradictions of the bruised nations came from a generation that had been raised within the Third World project rather than within formal colonialism. What the elites who were produced by this project saw as constraints, their parents' generation would have seen as the necessary architecture for the production of freedom. The new generation of structural adjustment wanted the accoutrement of advanced industrial capitalism without a sense of the historical process that makes this possible. The fire sale of the public assets of the Third World should be seen in the context of this impatience for private wealth rather than the development of the nation. The capricious growth of private bank accounts, of course, does nothing for the society in which one lives. The limits of this class after the 1970s are hardly its fault; rather, the caprice is a result of the structural adjustment of the Third World.[50]

The second development out of the East Asian crisis is the return to primordial culturalism. Faced with the charge that the East Asian collapse took place because of corruption, Singapore's Lee Kuan Yew reverted to his strong belief that only Confucian values create stability and growth, even if these values had some flaws. "There are certain weaknesses in Confucianism," he admitted. "You owe a duty to your family and loyalty to your friends, to help and support them. That's Confucianism. But this value is degraded when you use public resources through your official position to do your duty to your family and be loyal to your friends."[51] Singapore's leader did not ask for an abandonment of Confucianism but for a more intense return to it, a return to "Asian values."[52] As IMF-led globalization tore into the heart of the Third World, we see an increased attention to these cultural values as nationalism itself is perverted from its national liberation meaning to cultural nationalism. The only explanation that makes the East Asian miracle impossible as an exportable model allows Lee Kuan Yew to save face. Singapore and East Asia are not alone: the rest of the world in structurally adjusted times also takes refuge in culture as a salve from the cruelties of turbo capitalism.

MECCA

In May 1962, Crown Prince Faysal of Saudi Arabia welcomed 111 ulema, learned Muslim men, to the city of Mecca. They came to conduct the hajj, the annual pilgrimage of Muslims to their holiest city. These ulema also came to reform a moribund organization, the World Muslim Congress. Under Faysal's eye, they discussed the problems faced by Muslims in the Arab lands and elsewhere, and created the Rabitat al-alam al-Islami, the World Muslim League (WML). The final declaration of the conference was blunt: "Those who disavow Islam and distort its call under the guise of nationalism are actually the most bitter enemies of the Arabs, whose glories are entwined with the glories of Islam."[1] The WML, therefore, organized to disrupt the growth of Third World nationalism and its secular sense of community, and to recall in its place the sublime bonds of religion. With Saudi largesse, the WML set up offices across the Muslim world, from Indonesia to Morocco, and went to work against the growth of secularism and socialism.

Seven years later, in Jeddah, Saudi Arabia, King Faysal, after the initiative of King Hussein of Jordan, called for the creation of a governmental-level body to do much the same work as the nongovernmental WML. The meeting in 1969 created the General Secretariat of the Muslim League along with the Organization of the Islamic Conference (OIC). The OIC formed an international Islamic news agency, set up Islamic cultural centers, and held regular conferences to consolidate its broad line struggle against Third World nationalism and Communism. The twenty-three foreign ministers of Muslim countries who attended the gathering agreed "to promote co-operation among the Islamic states and establish institutional bases for pan-Islamism."[2]

The WML and the OIC were the international face of what the Saudi regime conducted domestically. Faysal unleashed all domestic social forces against the growth of Third World nationalist ideas within Saudi Arabia. Nasser and the Free Officers were popular in Egypt certainly, but also in the broader Arab world (including on the Arabian Peninsula). Strikes and attempted palace coups were crushed. Repression did not stop the ideological power of Nasserism and Third World nationalism in general. A more potent brew was needed. Faysal's maternal family had instructed him in the worldview of Wahhabism, a school of Islam that called for a return to the social forms of the seventh century. The Saudi dynasty was born in the eighteenth century thanks to a pact made between its founder and the progenitor of Wahhabism, Muhammed ibn 'Abd al-Wahhab.[3] Nevertheless, over the years, most of the Saudi royal family had enjoyed a pragmatic relationship with Wahhabism: they accorded it respect in public, but lived wilder lives in private (including during long sojourns to Europe).

Faysal was different. He was a true believer.[4] He accepted the tenets of Wahhabism—to wit, that Islam needed to be restored to its pristine state and that the believers must scrub out all the innovations of the centuries. Rationalism and folklore were equally to be disdained. The rules for society came from a puritanical common sense married to the holy texts (as well as the work of al-Wahhab and that of an earlier scholar, ibn Taymiyya). Nothing more was needed. Faysal drew from the institutional advantages of his belief to counter the growth of Third World nationalism. By 1970, he reorganized the Ministry of Justice so that the ulema ran it, and siphoned oil funds toward the creation of an Islamic rather than secular public sphere in Saudi Arabia that spent its time fulminating against godless Communism and Nasserism. An emergent civil society died an early death.

Faysal is an emblem of many other such leaders and the social forces they represented. Such people, such Faysals, rejected Third World nationalism, its secularism and its socialism as well as its type of modernity. If not always in practice, Third World nationalism was ideologically predisposed to the dismissal of hierarchy, and the domination of certain classes and clans. This was anathema to people like Faysal. They rejected the rationalism of Third World nationalism in favor of vestigial structures such as religious Puritanism, racialism, and tribalism. While Nasserism and

Communism promised equality, the Saudis proffered a celestial equality as long as the populace accepted the hierarchy of the world. Against the Third World agenda, across the planet, the old social classes set loose various kinds of unreconstructed cultural ideas to discipline their populations. From Mecca, the WML worked on behalf of a rigorous masculine Islam. But it was not alone. The danger of Communism and liberation theology in South America drew a terrific response from regional elites as well as the mainline Christian churches: they promoted pre–Vatican II Catholicism, encouraged the close relationship between the church and the juntas, and unleashed Pentecostalism on a population tired out by the failures of their various mundane political hopes. This Christian counter-reformation is the mirror image of what came out of the WML and its kin organizations.[5]

Religion is not the only social form that is mobilized by the elevated levels of the old social classes. The reinvention of tribalism and other atavistic ideas is equally central. Joseph Désiré Mobutu, raised in the Belgian Congo by European friars, led the coup against the left-wing prime minister Patrice Lumumba in 1960.[6] Lumumba's Congolese National Movement Party took the newly freed Congo leftward and disadvantaged European capital (particularly those interested in the vast extractable resources of the new state). Mobutu, backed by the Belgians and the United States, overthrew and killed Lumumba, and then took charge of the country. Within a few years, to consolidate his position, Mobutu conducted the Zaireanization of the Congo: he changed his name (Mobutu Sese Seko) and that of his country (Zaire), and insisted on a series of cultural returns to an idea of the pure cultural heritage of Zaire. Meanwhile, Mobutu pillaged the treasury of Zaire, and gave lucrative contracts to European and U.S. transnational corporations. The tribalism promoted by Mobutu and backed by many of the First World states enhanced his power. Mobutu stole an estimated $5.5 billion from his country at the same time as he tried to portray himself as a Zairean like any other. Respect for Zairean culture was more important than respect for the Zairean people. Such atavisms provided cover for an all-out assault against the social forces of secularism and socialism, the best traditions of Third World nationalism.

In the early years of the Third World era, these reactionary social forces (tribalism and religionism) had no direct involvement in the anti-colonial fight. In that epoch, they sat out or else supported the imperial battalions, and commanded little loyalty. The succession of coups against monarchs in the Arab lands (Egypt, Iraq, and Libya) is one indication of the ideological frailty of the Saudi regime by the early 1960s. What the Saudis and others did, however, was to prepare the terrain of culturalism in direct and self-conscious opposition to Third World nationalism. Nevertheless, their own ability to move an agenda was hampered by the bulwark of nationalism as well as the state-centered development strategy mapped out and followed by the new regimes. The Saudis sent Crown Prince Faysal to Bandung for the 1955 conference, where an avuncular Nasser shepherded around a cagey Faysal. When they returned from Indonesia, Egypt came to the aid of the Saudis as British forces from Oman seized an oasis within Saudi borders. The Saudis and Egypt signed a mutual border pact. Saudi Arabia lent Egypt money in August 1956 when European commercial lenders froze its funds during the Suez crisis.[7] The rapprochement with Egypt was not singular. At this same time, under the rule of Faysal's brother Saud, the kingdom made overtures to the Soviet bloc (two princes went to Prague on a mission for Soviet arms, and the Saudi monarch met the Soviet ambassador to Iran).[8] There was little expectation for the Saudis to become a full-fledged member (and bank) of the Third World. What most parties understood was that the kingdom was being compelled by circumstances and the power of Third World nationalism into its orbit. This was, after all, the age when influential clerics from Egypt to Iran wrote books that justified Islam as the "dialectical synthesis" of capitalism and Communism. They promoted Islam as a modern solution to modern problems and an addition to the main ideologies of the bipolar world because Islam "combines the virtues of both, it goes further than either by giving man ineffable bliss—spiritual satisfaction."[9] Islam of the Wahhabi variety and other such atavistic ideologies withered in the plain light of Third World nationalism.[10]

Saudi Arabia was no ordinary society. It was the center of the oil lands. Oil came into the picture for Saudi society in the early years of ibn Saud's rule (1933). Hastily, ibn Saud signed concessions to U.S.-British oil firms. The corporations flourished. The Saudis acted as rentiers of a reservoir that holds a quarter or more of the world's oil, while the U.S. and British governments offered security for the longevity of the antidemocratic regime. Checks from the oil concession enabled the ibn Saud family to go on a massive construction spree: they built palaces in Jeddah and Riyadh (their clan city and state capital), and provided bursaries to their vast extended family. In Mecca, the heart of their kingdom, the Saudis used the oil wealth to bolster the city's historic attraction: the annual hajj pilgrimage. As global transportation improved, more and more thousands of people made their hajj (half a million people came from outside the kingdom during Faysal's reign). In 1956, the Saudi Ministry of Health took over the operation of the hajj, using some of its extensive oil wealth.[11] To facilitate this increase in traffic, the Saudi state extended and rebuilt the Masjid al-Haram, the main mosque in Mecca and site of the important *kabah* (the contract for this work went to a Yemeni migrant, Mohammed Awad bin Laden). Saudi largesse went toward the profligate consumption of the royal family and religious charity. By 1958, the oil-rich land was in debt by $480 million.[12]

Crown Prince Faysal, who exerted his own authority against his brother King Saud, went to the IMF in 1957, and earned some credits in lieu of a tighter fiscal policy and a devalued rial. The oil merchants thrived, but the Saudi people suffered. The monarchy continued to draw $300 million per year as its oil royalty. The stalled state expenditure exacerbated the population's already-diminished set of expectations. They were tinder for Nasserism, Third World nationalism, and Communism. Clans that lost out to ibn Saud's were smothered by resentment, while the Shia of the eastern provinces were marginalized by the increased role of Sunni Wahhabism in Saudi statecraft. The eastern region, home to the massive oil fields and Aramco, was also a hive of worker unrest. In 1953, the workers at Aramco conducted an unsuccessful two-week strike to form a union. Then, in July 1956, when King Saud came to Dhahran mass demonstrations greeted him. The workers wanted basic rights, while the population wanted the removal of the growing U.S. military base that comforted the four thousand U.S. employees of Aramco and guaranteed Aramco's hegemony over the area.[13] In the Saudi section of the Dhahran Air Base, officers mutinied in support of the workers. They were caught and killed. The year before, at the Taif Air Base in the western mountains of the kingdom, Saudi troops mutinied in Nasser's name. They were executed. In this context, Nasser arrived in Saudi Arabia in 1956. To cheering crowds in Dhahran and Riyadh, this Arab titan announced, "Arab Oil for Arab People." These Nasserite currents came to the fore in the early months of 1958. In January, Egypt, Syria, and Yemen formed the United Arab Republic, and in July, the Free Officers in Iraq overthrew the Hashemite monarchy. By March, Saudi frustration with Nasser had reached a high pitch. The crown tried to assassinate him as his aircraft approached Damascus International Airport.

The Nasserite threat was always greater than that of the Communists, who in Saudi Arabia numbered few. The Organization of Saudi Communists operated under the aegis of the National Renewal (later,

Liberation) Front from 1954 onward. Only in the 1960s did peninsular Marxism make its mark—in Yemen and Oman. The 1962 nationalist revolution in Yemen provided a haven for the export of Third World nationalist and revolutionary ideas across the region. Yemen supported the Popular Front for the Liberation of Oman that was the main instrument in the widespread rebellion in Oman's Dhofar Province. When the Marxists seized power in South Yemen in 1967, the Popular Front was renamed the Popular Front for the Liberation of Oman and the Arabian Gulf. The Saudis, now much more militarily confident than they were in the 1950s, financed the resistance against South Yemen and that of the Omani government against the Popular Front. They were scrupulous in the extrication of the Left from the peninsula. What remained were rump groups, such as the Arabian Peninsula People's Union, the Voice of the Vanguard, the Revolutionary Nadji Party, and (in 1975) the Communist Party of Saudi Arabia.

Nasserism, like a virus, entered the palace walls. Within the large family of ibn Saud, dissatisfaction and grievances festered. As brothers fought brothers over matters grave and petty, a group of young princes gathered in Beirut. Their leader was Prince Talal bin Abdulaziz, the "Red Prince," who not only preferred the vibrant life of Beirut and Cairo to the staid palace life in Riyadh but also married Mouna as-Solh, the daughter of the nationalist prime minister of Lebanon (and one of the founders of the Arab League), Riad as-Solh. In the late 1950s, Talal and the Free Princes (al-umara'al-ahrar) formulated their plans, and in 1960, they acted. Talal broached the idea of a National Council in 1958, and now the Free Princes moved to gain public support. They had no mass base, and since they did not have the support of their clans, they failed to penetrate Saudi society. All they could rely on were the shenanigans of the palace. As Faysal and Saud fought, the Free Princes gained and then lost. To undercut Faysal, Saud elevated Talal from minister of transport to minister of finance. Tariqi, the "Red Sheikh," was already in charge of the oil lands. Another ally was Prince Nawwaf ibn Abd al-Aziz, who told the Cairo press in May 1960, "There is a trend towards convening a national assembly for the first time in Saudi Arabia, drafting the first constitution of the state and setting up a supreme court and a supreme planning commission. The problem is how to accomplish the mission."[14] Faysal rejected Talal's formal proposal in June, and Saud too dismissed the draft constitution in September. Talal used the bulk of 1961 to create secular social institutions in Saudi society and ameliorate unemployment through public works. The Free Princes appeared to be on the road to accomplish a left-wing palace coup, to do what the Free Officers did without the use of the military.

Then Faysal moved against Talal. The ulema, led by the Grand Mufti Muhammed ibn Ibrahim Al al-Shaikh and the head of the League of Public Morality Amr ibn Hasan, challenged Talal's labor law. They claimed its generosity was un-Islamic. Pressure on Saud and the Free Princes from these social quarters galvanized Faysal to action. In March 1962, he took over from his ailing brother. Aramco had long wanted Tariqi to be fired from his post as head of petroleum. This was Faysal's first action. Talal tried to gain some purchase on the situation. Since Faysal's clique worked solely within the discourse of Islam, Talal argued for the interpretation of Sharia or Islamic law on the basis of *ijtihad* (the individual interpretation of the Koran and the Sharia). The feint failed. Talal and his group withdrew to Beirut. The Free Princes were squashed. Most recanted and returned to their bursaries. Talal went between Cairo and Beirut, a permanent dissident, an individual without a party and a mass base.

Not long after Faysal's coup de grâce against the Nasserites and the Communists, he hosted the WML. Faysal had a senior partner in Aramco, and behind them was the U.S. government. The U.S. government gave "wholehearted support" to the WML as an instrument to roll back Third World nationalism and dent the USSR by appeal to its large Muslim population (perhaps 45 million).[15] In July 1960, the U.S. treasury secretary and Texas oilman Robert Anderson told the National Security Council that "Middle East oil was as essential to mutual security as atomic warheads." Five years later, at a U.S. State Department conclave, Aramco head Thomas Barger revealed that the United States had played a long-standing role in the destabilization of Nasserism and Third World nationalism: "There was an appropriate government role aimed at preventing unthinking use of oil as a political weapon by radical Arabs." The best way to prevent this use of oil was to prevent "Arab unity."[16] To isolate the Russians and the British as well as block the aspirations of Third World nationalism, U.S. president Eisenhower held a summit in 1957 with the Saudis and enunciated his doctrine. The Eisenhower Doctrine was framed to contain Communism in general, but in the specific instance of the Middle East to promote the Saudis and other monarchical forces (such as the Shah of Iran and the kings of Jordan and Iraq) as an alternative to Nasserism.[17] By 1957, the U.S. government had coordinated an anti-Nasser policy with the Saudis. In eastern Saudi Arabia, the CIA agent James Russell Barracks confirmed the existence of "an extensive program" to fund small religious cells (these are the direct ancestors of Osama Bin Laden's Advice and Reformation Committee or Hayat Annaseyha Wa'ahisla).[18] In 1958, the United States provided Saudi Arabia with $25 million through the Foreign Assistance Act. Some of the money went toward the reinforcement and modernization of the Saudi army with U.S. arms in lieu of the Saudis renewing the U.S. lease for the Dhahran Air Base.

When Faysal welcomed the ulema to Mecca and they formed the WML, the United States welcomed its ally's new ideological gambit.[19] The ulema decided that the WML should meet each year during the hajj, and thanks to Saudi pressure it earned nongovernmental accreditation at the United Nations. The WML did not establish an entirely new network. It revived and connected older Muslim organizations around the world. These had lapsed under the weight of anticolonialism, and many of them failed the ideological and institutional transition into modernity. The WML among other social agents provided the energy, money, and program for their recovery. The French ambassador to Saudi Arabia, Georges de Bouteiller, described the WML's operations as "tentacular." The WML's tentacles reached deep into those parts of the world inhabited by Muslims.[20] Rather than play the neutral institutional coordinator, the WML pushed the agenda conjured up by the Saudi regime to diminish Nasserism and Communism.[21] The creation of a Muslim public sphere (periodicals, libraries, and schools), disaster relief, or social welfare charity, and the promotion of organizations that championed the Sharia—all this took place around two simple propositions articulated in the WML manifesto: that the WML must "combat the serious plots by which the enemies of Islam are trying to draw Muslims away from their religion and to destroy their unity and brotherhood," and that the WML must vanquish Nasserite nationalism and Communism from the Arab lands.[22] The dismissal of all ideologies other than Islam for both Muslims and Arabs can be traced to the stern views of the Muslim Brotherhood, which declared that nationalism and Communism should be considered as *shu'ubi* (anti-Arab).

The WML became the conduit for the export of Saudi religious doctrine—missionaries traveled to the Muslim lands, and apart from the annual gathering during the hajj, the WML organized continental conferences and the establishment of offices on each of the continents. The WML produced and circulated tracts on the condition of Muslims in the Communist lands, whereas it said little about anti-Muslim sentiment in the capitalist lands. But most clearly, the WML went after the ideologies of nationalism and Communism—and turned them into enemies of Islam. The WML rejected the idea of *qaum* (a nation of equals) and promoted the idea of *ummah* (a community of believers). The historian Benedict Anderson argues that for the development of nationalism, three "fundamental cultural conceptions" had to lose their "axiomatic grip" on human consciousness: the endowment of sacredness to a language (Sanskrit, Arabic, or Latin), the acceptance of the divine monarch, and an idea of time that did not distinguish between history and cosmology.[23] What we have in the strategy of the WML is a reversal of history, to turn back the development of nationalism and promote a transnational community based on a sacred language, divine monarchies (if not an actual king, then certainly the concept of the caliph), and time as eternal return. History travels in a crooked line, as the WML fought to establish a reactionary idea of community at the center of popular consciousness in large parts of the Third World, from Morocco to Indonesia. The "Islamic nation," as Faysal put it, is more important than the concrete nations that organize the world, whose own status in this model is nothing more than provisional compared to the divinely imagined community.

Between 1965 and 1966, Faysal traveled to the major conservative Muslim states in Asia and Africa, starting in Tehran, then going to Sudan, Turkey, Morocco, Guinea, Mali, Tunisia, and Pakistan. In the latter, Faysal offered a vision of Islam as a glue for the peoples of the Third World and demanded unity against radicalism: "It is in these moments, when Islam is facing many undercurrents that are pulling Muslims left and right, east and west, that we need time for more cooperation and closer ties to enable us to face all the problems and difficulties that obstruct our way as an Islamic nation, believing in God, His Prophet and His Laws."[24] In 1969, the Saudis organized the OIC, and in 1972 they led the way for the creation of the World Assembly of Muslim Youth. The Saudi monarchy, led by Faysal, promoted a virulent form of Islam over the heterodox forms that grew across Africa and Asia, and over the democratic urges of the Arab and other peoples. The Saudis pushed a reactionary form of Islam to quell the resentment among their own population that increasingly suffered the indignity of life in a theocracy ruled by a dissipated family. In the 1960s and into the 1970s, the WML played a marginal role, with its organizations providing succor to scholars and activists who felt beleaguered in their societies for their anachronistic ideas about modernity and statecraft. Developments in the world soon provided them with the opportunity to lead rather than be left behind as the arc of history bent backward.

In 1979, a group of devout Muslim activists organized into the Movement of the Muslim Revolutionaries of the Arabian Peninsula laid siege to the Masjid al-Haram. They defended their actions as the only way to take back the holy shrines from the "drunkards" who "led a dissolute life in luxurious palaces."[25] The princes "seized land," "squandered the state's money," and left the people in a state of oppression and corruption.[26] Simultaneously, but independently, the Shia of eastern Saudi Arabia came out in mass demonstrations (many of them were oil workers in ARAMCO's fields). The National Guard crushed both the siege and the rebellion. The egalitarian noises from the Iranian Revolution (but not so much the Islamic republic that followed it) petrified the Saudi royals and indeed the entrenched elites across the Third World. A monarchy pressed into service by the United States could not be protected from a mass upsurge; despite the Iranian Revolution's capture by the clerics, the energy that overthrew the Shah's state came from a cross section of society. In Iran, the traditional elites (the clerics) expunged the modern elites (the royalty and the parasitic bourgeoisie it cultivated). Such "traditional" forms moved on the Saudi monarchy as well. Faysalism, however, was able to harness the traditional leadership to its project. During the 1979 siege, the monarchy forced the ulema to issue a fatwa against the Movement of the Muslim Revolutionaries. Shaykh 'Abd al-'Aziz ibn Baz of the Institution of Ifta' and Scholarly Research did as he was told, and even authorized military intervention into the Masjid. The ulema in Saudi Arabia were quick to line up with the monarchy.

The oil price rise after 1973 provided Saudi Arabia with the singular ability among the darker nations to buy off its citizenry. A few years of liquidity in the 1970s allowed the state to increase the social wage, although the monarchy did not fundamentally change the dependent basis of the Saudi economy. Saudi industry produced less than 2 percent of the gross national product, and dates remained the second-largest export item after crude and refined oil. What passed for a bourgeoisie in Saudi Arabia basically earned money as brokers and real estate dealers, rather than as industrialists. The royal state commanded the economy, and its princes functioned as a sort of quasi-bourgeoisie. A small part of the massive oil profits went toward infrastructure, but since the 1960s an increasing amount was channeled by the Saudi Arabian Monetary

Agency to the main centers of capital (New York, Zurich, and London). In the fundamentals, Saudi society reflected the same problems as much of the Third World: a one-commodity economy, with a poorly developed industrial sector, a large state apparatus, a growing military (costing about 14 percent of the gross national product), and a languished population. At the whim of fickle oil prices, the Saudi economy went into a nosedive beginning in the late 1970s, when the political unrest was most visible. The World Bank recommended that the Saudi state shore up its fundamentals, and the royal family conducted a self-directed structural adjustment during the 1980s. It sliced the social wage and most infrastructural development, devolved control of the oil fields to transnational corporations, increased military expenditure, and privatized sections of the state. This period of austerity was not extended to the transnational corporations or the holders of private capital (including the wealthiest princes). King Fahd told a conference of Saudi businesspeople in 1985, "I hope that your main purpose will be capital investment in Saudi Arabia or any friendly country, but this does not mean any restriction on free investment."[27] The Saudis privatized parts of the state, and yet saw little respite as Saudi oil profits bled to commercial banks in the G-7 and to heal the widening deficits in the United States.

For a society with a young population and growing structural unemployment, the social and cultural consequences of austerity were great. As dissent and protest grew, the Saudis met this both through outright repression and an ideological campaign. In 1976, the Saudi royals welcomed the head of the religious police (*mutawwa'a*) into the cabinet.[28] The control of antisocial behavior operated as a useful device to constrain the growth of dissent. Chauvinisms of various kinds were encouraged. The royals called for the "Saudiization" of the workforce as a means to turn the blame for unemployment on the five million foreign contract workers (almost a third of the total Saudi population). The promotion of domestic organizations with links to the WML worldview (such as Ahl al-Dawa and Jamaa al-Tabit) enabled the canalization of youthful discontent into a misogynist and antimodernist sensibility— better to curtail modern aspirations rather than try to meet them at the expense of the entrenched global hierarchy. Finally, the Saudi state promoted the export of its dissatisfied and devout sections to fight against the vestiges of Nasserism and Communism in the Muslim lands. At the fourth Islamic conference of foreign ministers in Benghazi, Libya (1973), the leaders established a Jihad Fund "to utilize the Fund for the assistance of Islamic liberation movements, for extending help to Islamic centres and societies abroad as well as in cases of natural disasters, and for building schools and hospitals."[29] An "ad hoc committee" took charge of the fund in Jeddah. The export of extremism enabled the undemocratic regimes to undo any domestic criticism, and turn the minds of their populations toward Israel or Communism. To concentrate on *dar ul-harb* (the house of war, where Muslims are not in power) provided an alibi to forget the nonexistence of a humanitarian program in *dar ul-Islam* (the house of Islam) itself. When these extremists tried to raise the issue of the un-Islamic lifestyles and policies of the monarchies, the state cracked down on them. It was far easier to worry about Muslims in the USSR and Palestine than to organize against these authoritarian monarchs and the class that surrounded them.

The WML went to work overseas in two different venues. In states with a majority Muslim population, or which considered themselves Islamic states, the WML and its affiliated, tentacular organizations filled the gap as the state withdrew from the provision of public services. As IMF-driven globalization desiccated the state, the Islamist organizations moved in to offer those services. The IMF institutions prodded the postcolonial states in the 1970s to give up on the delivery of public goods such as education, health care, and relief services, and allow private or charitable entities to do the work. In Pakistan and Egypt, for instance, as the state slowly eroded its public educational system, the exponential growth of cheap Islamic schools provided opportunities for lower-middle-class and working-class youth. In Marxist states with Muslim populations, the WML and its allied organizations went on the offensive. Here, they armed groups of young men often trained in religious seminaries and sent them to destabilize these left-wing regimes. The exporting of these men took place in earnest after the 1979 mosque siege revealed the discontent within Saudi society. The examples here are the attempts by WML subsidiaries to overthrow the Marxist governments of South Yemen and Afghanistan as well as to promote the rise of Islamists from Sudan to Indonesia.

The WML impacted the planet, but most spectacularly in southern Asia. Between 1977 and 1978, Afghanistan's Marxists took power in Kabul, and Pakistan's Islamist military dictator, Zia ul-Haq, dismantled the state-centered social welfare schemes and replaced them with privatized Islamization. On one side of the Hindu Kush mountains a Marxist regime implemented the social reform agenda of the constitution drawn up in 1964 (land reform and women's rights), while on the other side an

Islamist dictatorship dismantled the state on behalf of certain vestigial structures. The People's Democratic Republic of Afghanistan promulgated the Land Reform Proclamation 6 (July 1978) that canceled debts and dismantled the usurious credit schemes run by feudal moneylenders. Alongside this, the People's Democratic Republic of Afghanistan promoted a wide women's rights agenda, as enunciated by politburo member Anahita Ratebzad: "Privileges which women, by right, must have are equal education, job security, health services, and free time to rear a healthy generation for building the future of the country. Educating and enlightening women is now the subject of close government attention."[30] The mainly urban Marxists made several elementary errors with their land reforms; they came to power before they were able to build up a sufficient base in the countryside. The Marxists' program failed for a host of reasons: internecine struggle within the Marxist coalition, interference from the KGB, uprisings by tribal warlords, and armed hostility from the Islamist political parties. That the Marxists invited the Soviets into the country in 1979 showed their weakness and proved to their detractors that they were epigones of the USSR. As such, the CIA-WML-backed conservatives within Afghanistan and Pakistan had threatened the government, which was the reason they turned to the Soviet Union. All this was irrelevant as the Soviets entered an unwinnable situation, further alienated the people from their government, and gave legitimacy to the jihadists who now repackaged themselves as freedom fighters. It did not help the Marxist cause that the Soviet army engaged in a rash of brutal campaigns in the countryside that sent millions of people toward Iran and Pakistan as refugees.

The government of General Muhammad Zia-ul-Haq, chief martial law administrator in Pakistan; the WML; and the CIA gave moral and material support to both the warlords and the Islamist political parties.[31] The U.S. government made an alliance with forces committed to landlordism, authoritarianism, and misogyny. When the USSR sent in troops to protect its allies in the Kabul government from the CIA-supported insurgency of warlords and Islamists, the U.S. government smelled an opportunity. U.S. national security adviser Zbigniew Brzezinski recalled that he counseled President Carter in 1978 to provide aid to the conservative warlords and Islamists because "this aid would induce a Soviet military intervention." Such a move, Brzezinski noted, would give "the USSR its Vietnam War."[32] The USSR already suffered from serious structural economic problems. The massive planned industrialization that dashed this backwater into the front ranks of the world had now become a millstone. In the 1920s, only a fifth of the Soviet economy comprised the industrial, technological, and construction sectors, whereas by the 1980s the percentage had risen to more than two-thirds. The huge factories were not technologically modernized, and they relied on an enormous sacrifice from their workers to keep the obsolete rust belt afloat.[33] An oil boom in the 1970s gave the USSR a new lease on life, which the leadership squandered.[34] The United States felt that it could bleed the USSR in Afghanistan, but that behemoth already ran into a grave crisis that was probably unaffected by the Afghan war (except inasmuch as the Soviet casualties created a moral problem).

The Afghan and Pakistani people are the real victims of the wars from 1978 on, and they bled more than anyone else. If the Afghan tragedy is by now well-known, the effect on Pakistan is less clear. In 1977, Zia's dictatorship made an alliance with the Jamaat-i-Islami, a generally unpopular outfit that represented far-right views on social issues (notably on women's and minority rights). As part of the Pakistan National Alliance, the Jamaat reaped the benefit of Zia's cutback in educational funding—money now came in from the WML, the International Islamic Relief Organization, the Saudi and Kuwaiti Red Crescent, the Saudi General Intelligence Department, the Saudi royals, and other such private avenues. This money created a web of religious schools (madrassas): from nine hundred madrassas in 1971, the number swelled to eight thousand by 1988.[35] This faith-based education came as a result of the CIA-Saudi initiative to ideologically and militarily train Afghans and Pakistanis for the jihad against the Soviets. In addition, the WML through the Office of Services (Maktab al Khidmat, which was started by Osama Bin Laden's mentor, Abdullah Azam), recruited men to both fight and do relief work in the region (as the Egyptian Muslim Brotherhood attracted large numbers of professionals, the bulk of those who came to do relief work also contributed to the ideological narrowness promoted in Pakistan). The military, which once held fast to secular, professional values, also fell into the web of the WML-type groups. It recruited from these madrassas, and worked closely with jihadist groups in Kashmir and Afghanistan. A former Pakistani soldier and now leader of the right-wing Tanzeemul Ikhwan, Mohammed Akram Awan, boasted, "We can extend Jihad beyond our boundaries only after we have achieved our objective at home."[36] The secular institutions of Pakistan took a beating from Zia's alliance with the CIA-Saudis, with Afghanistan as pretext.

The IMF-driven globalization of the 1970s ravaged the main pillars of state sovereignty. As it undermined the idea of nationalism, conservative social forces and various powerful social classes gathered together to offer an alternative vision of what it meant to be patriotic, indeed what it meant to be nationalistic. The secular-socialist nationalism of the Third World agenda withered before the rise of a cultural nationalism now deeply invested in racial, religious, and such atavistic differences. The return of divisive religiosity into the center of statecraft, the new conversations about culture as a code for race, and other such objectionable entrances into public life became commonplace. The conservative social forces rejected equality and cultural diversity for hierarchy and cultural superiority. It is routine in many of these social programs to utterly disregard the equal rights of women and valorize women in social roles that tie them to the family. If these new forces did not write openly against equality, their texts of superiority showed that one people (race or religion) are better than another, and hence people are not equal. National liberation regimes had not been able or did not try to dethrone the old social classes and the older forms of social solidarity but they did create mechanisms to create national solidarity. Public schools, military service, voluntary labor, and other such institutions attempted to make equality a real social value and part of the experience of the citizenry. If the social classes do not mingle, there can be no real national solidarity. That said, once the state ceased to make this token effort, the significance of the older, generally unmolested class bonds now attained a great deal of purpose.

Saudi Arabia's government, along with its royalist allies and the U.S. regime, put together the elements for a full frontal assault on socialist governments and Communist movements, so that Sudan and Afghanistan, with a substantial Communist presence, became central players in Saudi Arabia's forward policy.[37] They unfurled the green flag of the prophet to galvanize the corpse of the Saudi monarchy. But this is not the story of Saudi Arabia alone. It is the story of how the dominant forces among the old social classes exerted themselves during the epoch of IMF-driven globalization. The pursuit of structural adjustment and the abandonment of the social transformation agenda for the new states encouraged these dominant classes to expunge Third World nationalism for a type of cultural nationalism. It was far easier to construct legitimacy for their new globalized states that disavowed the rights and needs of their own citizenry by making horizontal cultural connections across vertical class lines. As many governments in the darker nations devolve the economic and democratic agenda of the Third World, the dominant classes in each of these states promote their legitimacy and discipline their populations through cultural conservative ideas rooted in religion and racialism. Globalization and cultural nationalism are not opposites or irreconcilable doubles; they exist together, they feed off each other. Indeed, cultural nationalism is the Trojan horse of IMF-driven globalization. The mecca of IMF-driven globalization is therefore in the ability to open one's economy to stateless, soulless corporations while blaming the failure of well-being on religious, ethnic, sexual, and other minorities. That is the mecca of the post–Third World era.

CONCLUSION

Debt hangs heavy for the bulk of the planet. In 1970, when the Third World project was intact, the sixty states classified as "low-income" by the World Bank owed commercial lenders and international agencies $25 billion. Three decades later, the debt of these states ballooned to $523 billion. An impoverished conversation on debt yields no agenda to combat this fundamental ailment for the former Third World. These are not "poor" countries. Over the course of these three decades, the sixty states paid $550 billion in principle and interest on loans worth $540 billion. Yet they still owe $523 billion. The alchemy of international usury binds the darker nations.

At the 1986 NAM Summit in Harare, Zimbabwe, a group of leaders under the initiative of Malaysia's Prime Minister Mahathir Mohamed created the South Commission. They wanted a serious study of the political and economic problems of the NAM states, and some pointers for action. To chair the commission, NAM chose Tanzania's former president Julius Nyerere. Nyerere summarized the Third World project in five words: "growth and hope—then disillusionment." The hope of the anticolonial era was translated into an agenda, a project that the new states struggled to enact. It was unique in world history for the majority of the world to agree on the broad outlines of a project for the creation of justice on earth. But it did not last. External and internal pressures crippled the project. "That [Third World] hope has now vanished. For there was a gradual realization that such progress as was made in the first three decades after 1945 did not imply any fundamental change in the status or real development prospects of

The Brijuni Islands, Yugoslavia, July 1956: The Titans at Brijuni, enfolded by the sounds of Suez. COURTESY OF THE NEHRU MEMORIAL MUSEUM AND LIBRARY, NEW DELHI

Third World countries. Dependency was increasing rather than decreasing, poverty was persisting and the income gap between the Rich North and the Poor South was getting wider."[1] According to the World Bank, "In 1960 per capita GDP in the richest 20 countries was 18 times than in the poorest 20 countries. By 1995 this gap had widened to 37 times."[2] The divergence between the North and the South grew as the Third World fragmented. But even this spatial metaphor of the North and the South is insufficient; it ignores the mature class hierarchies that had grown within each of the countries in the South and the North.

The South Commission's report, released in 1990, argued that the adjustment strategies of the IMF-led globalization weakened the Third World as a political force. The UNCTAD, the G-77, NAM, and others faded into insignificance. One consequence of this demise was that no credible political force existed to champion a debt abolition or relief strategy for the planet. On the debt question, the report noted that "the vulnerability of individual developing countries vis-à-vis the North made it impossible for them to make an effective collective stand on the debt issue and to go beyond broad statements of policy."[3] The South had no control over the North or even the ability to initiate matters of collective concern. The Third World, in other words, had been dissolved.

As the South Commission met and wrote its report, a series of crucial events transpired. In 1985, the Communist Party of the Soviet Union began a long transition toward economic liberalization (perestroika) and political openness (glasnost). Six years later, the party was overwhelmed and the USSR collapsed. Consequently the bipolar Cold War ended. While this major development occurred, the United States as the leader of the Atlantic powers began to exercise its long-held project of primacy over the planet. The invasion of Panama (1989) was a dress rehearsal for the new epoch. It was followed by the war on Iraq, the dismemberment of Yugoslavia, and other displays of aerial bombardment. The unchecked Atlantic alliance now used military power to reshape polities. An older doctrine of primacy remained the mantra in Washington, and its elites maneuvered the U.S. population into a well-laid trap. During the course of the Cold War, the U.S. government operated as the hub of a well-projected set of allied spokes that put pressure equally on the USSR and the Third World. With the effective demise of both, and with the maintenance of U.S. military power intact, the U.S. policymakers were drawn into a fallacy: that they should no longer pull back, but that they should drive a forward policy to reshape the world using U.S. military power in the interests of a transnational turbo elite. The U.S. government eagerly accepted the leadership of a global coalition of dominant classes (it used a combination of free markets or "soft power" and military force or "hard power" in different doses since 1989 onward). The U.S. defense and treasury departments went to work to ensure that resources continue to flow toward transnational corporations, and that the dollar remain the main hard currency.

The ruling classes in the darker nations no longer had any institutional incentive to respond to the grievances and aspirations of their populations. Sections among these elites are often more predisposed to the tics of the various stock indexes then they are to the demands of their populations. Mumbai's Dalal Street and the Dar es Salaam Stock Exchange thrive when their own citizens feel pain. And the higher the stock indexes, the better the bond rating for a country. In other words, the neoliberal strategy allows a state to better its competitive position if its population suffers more. Demands on the neoliberal state from social movements or political parties are met with repression, dismissal, or ideological hostility. Police firings against protesters are routine, but so is the statement that the opposition has no alternative to the neoliberal one. But most important, the ruling classes also turned to more subtle ideological stratagems. The cultivation of cultural nationalism as the social cement in an otherwise-political wasteland is a cause and consequence of the collapse of the Third World. Racial and religious political organization is not prepared to confront capital along with its central role in the creation of planetary distress. Rather, religious and racial organization is now the social balm for hopelessness and helplessness. IMF-driven globalization undermines the possibility of egalitarianism. Racialism and religiosity ridicule equity on behalf of a traditional, mostly hierarchical order. Neither this globalization nor traditionalism is capable of being true to the dreams of freedom and the demands for equality that govern the souls of modern humans.

Distress produces its own contradictions. Grievances and anger manifest themselves in different ways, dependent on the kinds of traditions available in different countries. Where the Left has been obliterated, the festering anger at the growing inequality produced fiery hatred and violence as well as a kind of authoritarian populist nationalism. Attacks against minorities or else fantasies of an armed war against the United States and its allies grow in those regions (such as Sudan and Indonesia) that were once home to growing progressive movements. In other areas, such as Latin America, acronyms presumed dead resurfaced (MAS in Bolivia came back to win elections in 2006) and revolutionaries reappeared to articulate popular grievances in a different vocabulary (guerrillas in Venezuela are now in government). Social movements arose in the darker nations to challenge the neoliberal states with national liberation values: land movements, water movements, indigenous rights movements, and others have culminated in electoral victories or else in the imagination of alternatives to IMF-driven globalization. Many of these struggles draw on resilient ideological resources (such as Marxism, anarchism, and populism). Confident Communist parties, indigenous unions, and broader movement platforms are some of the organizations that have assembled the popular anxieties about global asymmetries. The unchecked growth of U.S. power has renewed the emotional attachment to national sovereignty, if not among elites, then certainly among those who have been disadvantaged by the collapse of the Second and Third World projects. The transformation in Latin America, the clogged feint in the Middle East, and the reorganization of alliances among China, Russia, and others has paused the juggernaut of U.S. power.

But in this renewal of energy, there is as yet little evidence of an alternative institutional agenda to replace the assassinated Third World project. The current weight of Atlantic power, joined by Australia and Japan, limits the scope for maneuver by elected officials in the poorer nations. A handful of them continue to band together to gain some benefit, or push one kind of policy or another. In 1989, a few NAM states created the Group of Fifteen (G-15).[4] Their first communiqué described the way that all these countries "are undertaking far-reaching economic reforms and structural adjustment measures . . . to enhance the competitiveness, upgrade the technological level and improve efficiency." To do this, the states seek to "mobilize domestic savings and attract foreign financial resources."[5] The G-15 wanted a more urgent response to the debt crisis, although there was no mention of debt forgiveness. The main themes were to increase world trade, open up northern markets to southern goods, and increase growth rates. The NAM agenda was narrowed in these neoliberal times. The second meeting of the G-15, in Caracas (1991), showed the frayed tempers of the managers of the poorer nations. "Our national economies are being restructured and liberalized at considerable social cost and human hardship, while the industrialized countries continue to run large fiscal deficits, to pay billions of dollars in subsidies to inefficient industries and to agricultural production, and to maintain and even intensify tariff and nontariff trade barriers that block exports of developing countries. These asymmetries endanger the viability of the South's own efforts and could lead to social and political instability."[6] Many of the discrete elements of the NAM agenda (UN reform, the need for the UNCTAD and a Common Fund for Commodities, and technology transfer) returned to the G-15. There was, however, no lucid vision for the new dispensation. Neither is there a strong institutional formation to tackle U.S.-driven primacy.

A lack of coherence and dynamism allows the regimes to operate within the rules set by IMF-driven globalization, within the broad ideology of neoliberalism. The reform agenda remains, but it now more often is used by a group of powers to make gains in their national or regional interest. The call for UN reform, for instance, devolved into a call by the Group of Four (Brazil, Germany, India, and Japan) for them to win permanent seats on the Security Council. South Africa, which emerged from apartheid in this new world era, pushed the New Partnership for Africa's Development (NEPAD) in 2001. NEPAD's core elements included the privatization of basic infrastructure and the incorporation of the African economy into the world economy (regardless of the decline in terms of trade and the continuation of subsidy regimes in the Atlantic economies to the detriment of African commodities). The word partnership in

NEPAD, as with many such documents in the post–Third World, post–Second World era, has come to mean privatization (as in public-private partnerships). The narrow space for maneuver confronted the South Commission in the mid-1980s. It studied the devastation of the darker nations, and yet recommended "the establishment of market relations" as the solution.[7] The patchy and as yet contradictory global vision of the G-15 is neither of the caliber nor the scope of the Bandung agenda.

The limitations of IMF-driven globalization and revanchist traditionalism provoke mass movements across the planet. The battles for land rights and water rights, for cultural dignity and economic parity, for women's rights and indigenous rights, for the construction of democratic institutions and responsive states—these are legion in every country, on every continent. It is from these many creative initiatives that a genuine agenda for the future will arise. When it does, the Third World will have found its successor.

NOTES

Introduction

1. Frantz Fanon, *The Wretched of the Earth* (New York: Grove Press, 1963), 314. I have substituted "project" in place of "aim." The original is "Le Tiers-Monde est aujourd'hui en face de l'Europe comme une masse colassale dont le project doit être d'essayer de résoundre les problèmes auxquels cette Europe n'a pas su apporter de solutions." Frantz Fanon, *Les Dammés de la Terre* (Paris: François Maspero, 1961), 241.
2. George McTurnan Kahin, ed., *The Asian-African Conference: Bandung, Indonesia, April 1955* (Ithaca, NY: Cornell University Press, 1956), 43–44.

Paris

1. For two excellent histories, see Laurent Dubois, *Avengers of the New World: The Story of the Haitian Revolution* (Cambridge, MA: Harvard University Press, 2004), and *A Colony of Citizens: Revolution and Slave Emancipation in the French Caribbean, 1787–1804* (Chapel Hill: University of North Carolina Press, 2004).
2. Ousmane Sembene's *Le Camp de Thiaroye* (1987) portrays a West African force that returns from Europe after World War II, demands recompense for its time on the battlefield and in the concentration camps, and gets brutally murdered by the French at the movie's end.
3. That same year, Presence Africaine released Chiekh Anta Diop's *Nations Negres et Culture*, a book that sought to show the African roots of Egyptian civilization.
4. Aimé Césaire, *Discourse on Colonialism* (New York: Monthly Review Press, 2000), 32.
5. Ibid., 38–39.
6. John Locke, *Two Treatises of Government* (Cambridge: Cambridge University Press, 1988), 291.
7. Nguyen Ai Quoc, "An Open Letter to M. Albert Sarraut, Minister of Colonies," in *Ho Chi Minh on Revolution: Selected Writings, 1920–66*, ed. Bernard B. Fall (New York: Signet, 1968), 30.

8. Césaire, *Discourse on Colonialism*, 47–48.

9. Claude Bourdet, "J'accuse," *France-Observateur*, December 6, 1951.

10. From 1949 to 1951, a group of social and natural scientists met there to draft a statement against racism, although they had been motivated not so much by the racism in the tropics as by Nazi racism against Jews. Nevertheless, UNESCO drew on the expertise of many scholars, several of them from the French intelligentsia, to transform the insistence on biological difference to an appreciation for cultural diversity. In the early 1950s, UNESCO published a host of books against the ideology of colonialism. *The Race Concept: Results of an Inquiry* (Paris: UNESCO, 1951), 31.

11. Alfred Sauvy, "Trois Mondes, Une Planété," *L'Observateur*, no. 118, August 14, 1952. See also the essays, including one by Sauvy, in *Le "Tiers-Monde" sous développement et développement*, ed. Georges Balandier (Paris: Presses Universitaires de France, 1961). In 1960, Parisian intellectuals founded *Tiers-Monde*, a journal dedicated to the Third World (later renamed *Revue Tiers-Monde*), and in English, the term became common after Peter Worsley's *The Third World: Culture and World Development* (London: Weidenfeld and Nicholson, 1964).

12. *Winston S. Churchill: His Complete Speeches, 1897–1963*, ed. Robert Rhodes James (New York: Chelsea House, 1974), 7:7285–93.

13. Bernard Baruch made the comment in the South Carolina legislature on April 16, 1947 (*New York Times*, April 17, 1947), while Lippmann used the term in his *New York Herald Tribune* columns from July 1947 onward and collected them in his *The Cold War* (New York: Harper, 1947).

14. Göran Therborn, "From Petrograd to Saigon," *New Left Review* 48 (March–April 1968): 4.

15. John Ellis, *World War II: A Statistical Survey. The Essential Facts and Figures for All the Combatants* (New York: Facts on File, 1993).

16. Therborn, "From Petrograd to Saigon," 5.

17. Eugene Black, *The Diplomacy of Economic Development* (Cambridge, MA: Harvard University Press, 1960), 45.

18. Vijay Prashad, "Mother Teresa as the Mirror of Bourgeois Guilt," in *White Women in Racialized Spaces*, ed. Samina Najmi and Rajini Srikanth (Albany: State University of New York Press, 2002).

19. Caroline Elkins, *Imperial Reckoning: The Untold Story of Britain's Gulag in Kenya* (New York: Henry Holt, 2004), 49; David Anderson, *Histories of the Hanged: The Dirty War in Kenya and the End of Empire* (New York: W.W. Norton, 2004).

20. This was the thesis in Berthold F. Hoselitz, *The Progress of Underdeveloped Areas* (Chicago: University of Chicago Press, 1952).

21. Lilly Marcou, *Le Kominform* (Paris: Presses de la Fondation Nationale des Sciences Politiques, 1977), chapter 2.

22. Fernando Claudín, *The Communist Movement: From Comintern to Cominform* (New York: Monthly Review Press, 1975), part 2, 467.

23. Mary Ann Glendon, "The Forgotten Crucible: The Latin American Influence on the Universal Human Rights Idea," *Harvard Human Rights Journal* 16 (Spring 2003): 27–39. Cisneros's Cuba was then in a springtime of democracy—it had recently dispatched the autocrat Fulgencio Batista y Zaldívar in 1944, although he returned to power in 1952, to be removed again by Castro's legions in 1959.

24. *Conference for the Establishment of the United Nations Educational, Scientific and Cultural Organisation*, Institute of Civil Engineers, London, November 1–16, 1945 (Paris: UNESCO Archives, no. AG 41), 33.

25. Jawaharlal Nehru, *India's Foreign Policy: Selected Speeches, September 1946–April 1961* (Delhi: Publications Division, 1961), 77–78.

26. The idea of the "nation" in Europe was premised on shared blood or some sort of racial history—the French people being not just the people who speak French but those who *are* French in a cultural and racial way. For an excellent history of the process of nation formation along these lines, see Eugene Weber, *Peasants into Frenchmen: The Modernization of Rural France, 1870–1914* (Stanford, CA: Stanford University Press, 1976). For a strong statement against the grain of the European national project, see Benedict Anderson, *Imagined Communities: Reflections on the Origin and Spread of Nationalism* (London: Verso, 1991).

27. That Nehru and his like came from bourgeois backgrounds did play a role in their inability to understand the impatience of the working class and peasantry. Whereas the latter wanted justice in a hurry, Nehru and his ilk preached gradual change, and a transformation that would come without world war.

28. Peter T. Bauer, *Equality, the Third World, and Economic Delusion* (London: Weidenfeld and Nicholson, 1981), 83–84.

29. Hisham Sharabi, *Neopatriarchy: A Theory of Distorted Change in the Arab World* (New York: Oxford University Press, 1988), 7.

Brussels

1. My discussion of the atrocities relies on Sven Lindquist, *Utrota varenda jävel* (Stockholm: Albert Bonniers Förlag, 1992) (translated as *"Exterminate All the Brutes"* and published by The New Press in 1996); Jan Breman, ed., *Imperial Monkey Business: Racial Supremacy in Social Darwinist Theory and Colonial Practice* (Amsterdam: Centre for Asian Studies Amsterdam, 1990). There is also the Belgian foreign service officer Jules Marchal's four-volume history of the Congo for l'Harmattan (1996 onward), and finally, the Belgian anthropologist Daniel Vangroenweghe's extraordinary work, *Du sang sur les lianes. Léopold II et son Congo* (Brussels: Didier Hatier, 1986).

2. Quoted in Adam Hochschild, *King Leopold's Ghost: A Story of Greed, Terror, and Heroism in Colonial Africa* (New York: First Mariner Books, 1999), 166.

3. Quoted in ibid., 44.

4. Ibid., 282

5. In February 2002, the Belgian government accepted that it had participated in the assassination of Zaire's Patrice Lumumba in 1961. What it did not say, however, was that this was an act motivated by the Belgian mining interests and colonial officers who had much to gain from a region. Nonetheless, it did take responsibility for an act that damaged the anticolonial movement. That summer, the Belgian government commissioned a study by Professor Jules-Luc Vellut to report on Leopold's depravations by summer 2004, an event that coincided with a major exhibition at the Royal Museum for Central Africa in Brussels. Guido Gryseels, the museum's director, said of the events of the past, "It is a reality which touches the deepest part of the Belgian soul. We really haven't coped with it, and the revelations came as a real shock. We were brought up knowing that we brought civilization and good to Africa. [Allegations of brutality] weren't taught in schools." Andrew Osborn, "Historians Vow to Unearth Truth about Allegations of Genocide in Congo," *The Guardian*, July 13, 2002. See Samuel Nelson, *Colonialism in the Congo Basin, 1880–1940* (Athens: Ohio University Press, 1994); Georges Nzongola-Ntalaja, *The Congo from Leopold to Kabila: A People's History* (London: Zed, 2002). Belgium will discover that it brought barbarity to the Congo, or as one Dutch historian observed, the Congolese "became acquainted with white civilization in [this] manner." Breman, *Imperial Monkey Business*, 1.

6. I have used the papers of the League against Imperialism, available at the International Institute for Social History (IISG), Amsterdam. For background on Belgium's political situation in the interwar years, see Els Witte, Jan Craeybeckx and Alain Meynen, *Political History of Belgium* (Brussels: Vrije Universiteit Brussel University Press, 2000), 130–33.

7. "Belgische Resolution, 1927," no. 14, League against Imperialism Papers, IISG.

8. Several authors who mention the conference simply reduce it to a Communist "front organization," without any sense of the value that it held for those who traveled to it from Africa, the Americas, and Asia. For a recent example, see Sean McMeekin, *The Red Millionaire: A Political Biography of Willi Münzenberg, Moscow's Secret Propaganda Tsar in the West* (New Haven, CT: Yale University Press, 2003), 194–95.

9. Vladimir Ilyich Lenin, "Backward Europe and Advanced Asia," in *Collected Works* (Moscow: Progress Publishers, 1976), 19:99–100.

10. Vladimir Ilyich Lenin, "The Foreign Policy of the Russian Revolution," in *Collected Works* (Moscow: Progress Publishers, 1976), 25:85–87.

11. John Riddell, ed., *To See the Dawn: Baku, 1920. First Congress of the Peoples of the East* (New York: Pathfinder, 1993).

12. The Stalinist purges killed many of those who had been in Baku and played central roles in the creation of left political parties in their homelands: Jalaluddin Korkmasov of Dagestan, Nariman Kerbalai Najaf-oglu Narimanov of Azerbaijan, Pilipe Makharadze of Georgia, Tashpolad Narbutabekov of Turkestan, and Dadash Buniatzadeh and Ahmed Sultanzadeh of Iran.

13. This logic followed from the "Fourteen Points" enunciated by President Wilson, who in January 1918, announced in his point no. 5, "A free, open-minded, and absolutely impartial adjustment of all colonial claims, based upon a strict observance of the principle that in determining all such questions of sovereignty the interests of the populations concerned must have equal weight with the equitable claims of the government whose title is to be determined." From Wilson, it is not clear whose "government" is referred to in the last sentence. One can only assume he means the colonial government, which means that it gets to determine the entire process of rule and devolution.

14. George Wilson, *The First Year of the League of Nations* (Boston: Little, Brown, 1921), 75.

15. Jawaharlal Nehru, *Toward Freedom* (New York: John Day, 1941), 125.

16. "Manifest des Brüsseler Kongresses gegen den Imperialismus, 1927," no. 10, League against Imperialism Papers, IISG.

17. "Resolution. Südafrika von den Delegierten der Südafrikanischen Union. D. Colraine, J. A. la Guma, J. Gumeda," no. 19, League against Imperialism Papers, IISG.

18. Helmut Müller, "Antikolonialer Widerstand im subsaharischen Afrika und Antiimperialistische Lige," *Die Liga gegen Imperialismus und für nationale Unabhängigkeit, 1927–1937* (Leipzig: Karl-Marx-Universität, 1987), 116–17.

19. Nnamdi Azikiwe, *Renascent Africa* (Accra: n.p., 1937).

20. Owen Mathurin, *Henry Sylvester Williams and the Origins of the Pan-African Movement, 1869–1911* (Westport, CT: Greenwood, 1976), 60–65.

21. W.E.B. DuBois, "To the Nations of the World," in *Report of the Pan-African Conference at Westminister Town Hall* (London: Pan-African Association, 1900). His speech is also available in Herbert Aptheker, ed., *Writings in Non-Periodical Literature* (Millwood, NY: Kraus-Thomson, 1982).

22. Immanuel Wallerstein, *Africa: The Politics of Independence* (New York: Vintage, 1961), 104; Penny M. Von Eschen, *Race against Empire: Black Americans and Anticolonialism, 1937–1957* (Ithaca, NY: Cornell University Press, 1997), 45.

23. George Padmore, ed., *History of the Pan African Congress: Colonial and Coloured Unity* (London: Hammersmith Books, 1963), 5.

24. Kwame Nkrumah, *I Speak of Freedom: A Statement of African Ideology* (London: Heinemann, 1961), xi–xiv.

25. "Resolution vorgeschlagen von der syrischen delegation," no. 22, and "Resolution gegen den französischen imperialismus in Syrien," no. 23, League against Imperialism Papers, IISG.

26. Gerhard Höpp, "Die arabischen Nationalrevolutionäre in Berlin und die Liga," and Mario Kessler, "Antikoloniale Bündnisse im syrischen Volksbefreiungskrieg, 1925–1927," in *Die Liga gegen Imperialismus und für nationale Unabhängigkeit, 1927–1937* (Leipzig: Karl-Marx-Universität, 1987).

27. Muhammed Khalil, *The Arab States and the Arab League* (Beirut: Khayats, 1962), 2:57.

28. Yeshoshua Porath, *In Search of Arab Unity, 1930–1945* (London: Cass, 1986) and Majid Khadduri, "Towards an Arab Union," *American Political Science Review* 1,000, no. 1 (February 1946).

29. John Charles Chasteen, *Born in Blood and Fire* (New York: W.W. Norton, 2001), 203.

30. One of APRA's main theorists and organizers was José Carlos Mariátegui, the greatest Marxist thinker outside the pale.

31. Quoted in Arthur P. Whitaker, *Nationalism in Latin America: Past and Present* (Gainesville: University of Florida Press, 1962), 63. For Haya de la Torre in Brussels, see Max Zeuske, "Haya de la Torre, die APRA und der Brüsseler Weltkongreß der Antiimperialistischen Liga," in *Die Liga gegen Imperialismus und für nationale Unabhängigkeit, 1927–1937* (Leipzig: Karl-Marx-Universität, 1987).

32. Olga Cabrera, "Julio Antonio Mella und die Gründung der kubanischen Sektion der Antiimperialistischen Liga," and Anja Alert, "Antiimperialistishce Liga und revolutionäre Bewegung Venezuelas," in *Die Liga gegen Imperialismus und für nationale Unabhängigkeit, 1927–1937* (Leipzig: Karl-Marx-Universität, 1987).

33. Víctor Alba, *Nationalists without Nations* (New York: Praeger, 1968), 73.

34. Arthur Whitaker and David Jordan, *Nationalism in Contemporary Latin America* (New York: Free Press, 1966), 167.

35. *Final Act of the Inter-American Conference on Problems of War and Peace*, Mexico City, February–March 1945 (Washington, DC: Pan-American Union, 1945), Articles 1 and 2.

36. Quoted in K.P. Karunakaran, *India in World Affairs* (Oxford: Oxford University Press, 1958), 85.

37. Even a canonical work like Evan Luard's *A History of the United Nations* (New York: St. Martin's Press, 1989) offers evidence for this interpretation.

38. Víctor Alba, *Nationalists without Nations: The Oligarchy versus the People in Latin America* (New York: Praeger, 1968), 59.

39. In November 1921, delegates from the Mongolian People's Revolutionary Party met with Lenin and asked if they should change their party into a Communist Party. In anticipation of the Second Congress of the Communist International in 1920, Lenin had written that the delegates must "adjust both Soviet institutions and the Communist Party (its membership, special tasks) to the level of the peasant countries of the colonial East. This is the crux of the matter. This needs thinking about and seeking concrete answers." Vladimir Ilyich Lenin, "Material for the Second Congress of the Communist International," in *Collected Works* (Moscow: Progress Publishers, 1972), 42:202. A peasant society with little industrial development and almost no proletariat, with a weak bourgeoisie and strong landlords, with weak national sovereignty and strong imperial control, could not immediately forgo an alliance with the old social classes and fight on all fronts at once. Instead, Communist forces should create "independent contingents of

fighters and party organizations" to both build the power of the working people and anticipate the time when proletarian parties "can emerge in them" for a full frontal assault on the national bourgeoisie. For this reason, Lenin told the Mongolians that "a mere change of signboards is harmful and dangerous." Quoted in "The Second Congress of the Communist International," in *Collected Works*, 31:241–44. National liberation had to be given its due, as Lenin argued in his debate with the Indian revolutionary M.N. Roy, even as it should not be allowed to squelch the independent organization of workers and peasants for a future and inevitable confrontation.

40. Quoted in George McTurnan Kahin, ed., *The Asian-African Conference: Bandung, Indonesia, April 1955* (Ithaca, NY: Cornell University Press, 1956), 40.

Bandung

1. John R.W. Smail, *Bandung in the Early Revolution, 1945–1946* (Ithaca, NY: Cornell University Modern Indonesia Project Monograph Series, 1964), chapter 6.
2. My thanks to Muhammed Dasuki, Bandung Padjadjaran University, Indonesia, and Agus Hadi Nahrowi for this translation.
3. Cees van Dijk, *Rebellion under the Banner of Islam: The Darul Islam in Indonesia* (The Hague: Martinus Nijhoff, 1981).
4. Quoted in George McTuran Kahin, ed., *The Asian-African Conference: Bandung, Indonesia, April 1955* (Ithaca, NY: Cornell University Press, 1956), 42.
5. P. Sitaramayya, *The History of the Indian National Congress* (Bombay: Padma Publications, 1946), 1:363–64.
6. Quoted in Kahin, *The Asian-African Conference*, 43.
7. Quoted in ibid., 44, 45.
8. Keith Buchanan, "The Third World," *New Left Review* (January–February 1963): 5–23, collects the demographic details and makes the case for a Third Worldist position regarding world revolution.
9. Quoted in Kahin, *The Asian-African Conference*, 45–46.
10. Which is why it is the only full document available in Kahin's influential collection from 1956.
11. Sukarno, *Sukarno: An Autobiography as Told to Cindy Adams* (Hong Kong: Gunung Agung, 1966), 26.
12. On the *ilustrados*, see Renato Constantino, *Dissent and Counter-Consciousness* (Quezon City, Philippines Malaya Books, 1970).
13. Most of the main facts are in George McTuran Kahin, *Nationalism and Revolution in Indonesia* (Ithaca, NY: Cornell University Press, 1952), Bernhard Dahm, *Sukarno and the Struggle for Indonesian Independence* (Ithaca, NY: Cornell University Press, 1969).
14. Kahin, *Nationalism and Revolution*, 108.
15. Rex Mortimer, *Indonesian Communism under Sukarno: Ideology and Politics, 1959–1965* (Ithaca, NY: Cornell University Press, 1974).
16. Geoff Simons, *Indonesia: The Long Oppression* (London: Macmillan, 2000), 161.
17. Carlos Romulo of the Philippines described Zhou like this: "At Bandung, Premier Chou En-Lai comported himself as one who had taken a leaf from Dale Carnegie's tome on *How to Win Friends and Influence People*. . . . At the Asian-African Conference, he was affable of manner, moderate of speech." Carlos Romulo, *The Meaning of Bandung* (Chapel Hill: University of North Carolina Press, 1956), 11. Nehru hosted a dinner for Zhou where the Communist leader was "cordial and pleasant." Tillman Durdin, "Chou, Anti-Reds Dine with Nehru," *New York Times*, April 21, 1955.

18. *China and the Asian-African Conference: Documents* (Peking: Foreign Languages Press, 1955).

19. In 1943, in Yan'an, China, Mao had offered the slogan "From the Masses, to the Masses" as a way to capture the tone that Communists should follow in their relationship to the "masses," an ambivalent term that referred either to the revolutionary classes (workers and peasants) or all the Chinese people. "This means: take the ideas of the masses (scattered and unsystematic ideas) and concentrate them (through study turn them into concentrated and systematic ideas), then go to the masses and propagate and explain these ideas until the masses embrace them as their own, hold fast to them and translate them into action, and test the correctness of these ideas in such action. Then once again concentrate ideas from the masses and once again go to the masses so that the ideas are persevered in and carried through. And so on, over and over again in an endless spiral, with the ideas becoming more correct, more vital and richer each time. Such is the Marxist theory of knowledge." Mao Tse-tung, "Some Questions concerning Methods of Leadership (June 1, 1943)," in *Selected Works* (Beijing: Foreign Language Press, 1976), 3:119.

20. Romulo, *The Meaning of Bandung*, 91.

21. Quoted in ibid., 22.

22. "Appraising Bandung," *New York Times*, April 24, 1955, E10; "Sir J. Kotelawala on Value of Bandung," *Times* (London), April 27, 1955; "Impact of Bandung on the Asian Community," *Times* (London), April 26, 1955. The publisher of the *New York Times* offered this patronizing judgment: "Our friends at the world's first assembly of African and Asian statesmen proved more numerous and more stanch than predicted." C.L. Sulzberger, "Bandung Draws Attention to a Problem," *New York Times*, April 23, 1955, 18.

23. Benedict J. Kerkvliet, *The Huk Rebellion: A Study of Peasant Revolt in the Philippines* (Berkeley: University of California Press, 1977).

24. Richard Clutterbuck, *The Long, Long War: The Emergency in Malaya, 1948–1960* (London: Cassell, 1967).

25. I am guided by Peter Gowan, "Triumphing toward International Disaster: The Impasse in American Grand Strategy," *Critical Asian Studies* 36, no. 1 (2004): 3–36.

26. Quoted in Samuel P. Huntington, "Transnational Organizations in World Politics," *World Politics* 25 (April 1973): 333–68.

27. Carlos Romulo, "What the Asians Expect of the U.S.," *New York Times Magazine*, June 19, 1955, 8, 55, 60–61; and *The Meaning of Bandung*, 41–43.

28. Romulo, "What the Asians Expect of the U.S.," and *The Meaning of Bandung*, 51–52.

29. Jawaharlal Nehru, *India's Foreign Policy: Selected Speeches, September 1946–April 1961* (Delhi: Government of India, 1961), 89.

30. Quoted in Kahin, *The Asian-African Conference*, 68.

31. Sulzberger, "Bandung Draws Attention to a Problem," 18.

32. "Sir J. Kotelawala on Value of Bandung," *Times* (London), 10; John Kotelawala, *An Asian Prime Minister's Story* (London: G. G. Harrap, 1956), 177–94.

33. The denial of Israel did not stem entirely from any perceived relationship that it had with the colonial powers. In his memoirs, the director general of the Israeli Mission of Foreign Affairs, Walter Eytan, dismissed the arguments made for the isolation of Israel by the new states of Africa and Asia as not "logical." In his view, "There seems little doubt that Moslem hostility to Israel is still the stumbling block." In general, he points out, "Israel's relations with Asia were bedeviled by the Moslem factor." The reason for the denial of Israel did not come from the "Moslem factor," but because, despite the entireties of India and Burma, Pakistan felt that its presence would upset the many Arab

states whose representation was crucial. Many Arab leaders, particularly the Jordanian and Saudi Arabian monarchies, used Israel as a convenient means to distract the attention of their own people from the appalling injustice of their states. Walter Eytan, *The First Ten Years: A Diplomatic History of Israel* (New York: Simon & Schuster, 1958), 183. For Pakistan's sentiments about the Arab states, see Kahin, *The Asian-African Conference*, 3. U Nu, with the support of Nehru, led the way to include Israel, but they could not succeed. Mizra Khan, "Israel-Burma Ties," *The Guardian*, no. 4, December 1957; Richard Butwell, *U Nu of Burma* (Stanford, CA: Stanford University Press, 1963), 186.

34. Thomas Hovet, *Bloc Politics in the UN* (Cambridge, MA: Harvard University Press, 1960), 79.

35. Nehru, *India's Foreign Policy*, 279.

36. Quoted in Kahin, *The Asian-African Conference*, 82.

37. Quoted in Sven Lindqvist, *A History of Bombing* (New York: The New Press, 2001), 31.

38. Quoted in Kahin, *The Asian-African Conference*, 83.

39. UN General Assembly Resolution 502 (VI), January 11, 1952.

40. Kahin, *The Asian-African Conference*, 83; UN General Assembly Resolution 914 (X), December 16, 1955.

41. The conventional history of the IAEA states that its formation came as a result of U.S. president Dwight Eisenhower's "Atoms for Peace" speech to the United Nations in 1953. Indeed, it was in this speech that Eisenhower broached the subject of an atomic energy agency to "set up a completely acceptable system of world-wide inspection and control." The idea comes from the speech, but eighty-one nations might not have come to the United Nations in 1956 eager to create such an agency without the Bandung conference of the previous year. International Atomic Energy Agency, *IAEA: What It Is and What It Does* (Vienna: IAEA, 1961); Mohamed El Baradei, *The Peaceful Use of Nuclear Energy: The Contribution of the IAEA* (Abu Dhabi: Emirates Center for Strategic Studies and Research, 2003).

42. In 1982, this was established in the declassified Truman Papers. A memorandum from the State Department to President Truman, dated May 28, 1952, notes, "The Soviet Union has contended with some success on the propaganda front that the Western Democracies do not wish reduction in arms but merely wish a vast intelligence operation. It is believed that if this proposal [an arms control working paper] can be introduced in time to be included in the First Report of the Disarmament Commission, which will be submitted to the Security Council about June 1st., some of the effect of the Soviet propaganda will be offset." UN Disarmament Commission, Folder no. 1, PSF, Truman Papers, Truman Library, Independence, MO. On the question of disarmament, the USSR was more reliable after Stalin's death in 1953: in 1955, the USSR proposed an end to nuclear tests, and it took four years of pressure to bring the United States and Britain to partially accept this position.

43. Bhagat Singh, "Why I Am an Atheist," in *Selected Writings of Shaheed Bhagat Singh*, ed. Shiv Varma (Kanpur: Samajwadi Sahitya Sadan, 1996), 123. Che Guevara, decades later, came to the same conclusion: "Terrorism is a measure that is generally ineffective and indiscriminate in its effect, since it often makes victims of innocent people and destroys a large number of lives that would be valuable to the revolution. Besides it hinders all the more or less legal or semi-clandestine contact with the masses and makes impossible unification for actions that will be necessary at a critical moment." Che Guevara, *Guerrilla Warfare*, trans. J.P. Murray (New York: Vantage Books, 1961).

44. If nuclear bombs deter nuclear wars, then why have the bombs in the first place? Why, logically, should two sides need to keep arsenals of things to ensure that those very things are not to be used? Why hold each other's populations hostage? Nuclear bombs

certainly do not deter conventional wars, since the nuclear age continues to be littered with the detritus of conflict. The original sin of Hiroshima produced a theology called deterrence, which is an opiate not to wash away the worries of poverty but to promote an authoritarian and militaristic state. The Bandung powers had another vision, now gone from the realm of governments.

45. George Perkovich, *India's Nuclear Bomb: The Impact on Global Proliferation* (Berkeley: University of California Press, 1999), 65; John Wilson Lewis and Xue Litai, *China Builds the Bomb* (Palo Alto, CA: Stanford University Press, 1988).

46. Mary Ann Glendon, *A World Made New* (New York: Random House, 2001), 11.

47. Quoted in Kahin, *The Asian-African Conference*, 79.

48. Ibid., 79–80. As the 1945 founding constitution of UNESCO noted, "The wide diffusion of culture, and the education of humanity for justice and liberty and peace are indispensable to the dignity of man and constitute a sacred duty which all the nations must fulfill in a spirit of mutual assistance and concern."

49. The rapprochement began in 1954, as illustrated in the correspondence between Khrushchev and Tito as well as in the May 31, 1954, Communist Party of the Soviet Union's presidium's resolution for normalization of relations between the USSR and the Yugoslavian federation.

50. Quoted in "President Tito on Bandung Talks," *Times* (London), April 28, 1955.

51. David Kimche, *The Afro-Asian Movement: Ideology and Foreign Policy of the Third World* (Jerusalem: Israel Universities Press, 1973), 84. Even the most ideologically unreconstructed Communist regime, the Albanians, welcomed the Bandung Conference and its agenda of Third World solidarity. Here is Enver Hoxha: "The Albanian people hailed the historic Bandung Conference and are wholeheartedly at one with all the peoples of Asia and Africa still in bondage, who are fighting to wipe out the odious yoke of colonialism once and for all. The Albanian people and their government have declared their adherence to the well-known Five Principles of Peaceful Coexistence among states of different social systems, which have been proclaimed by the governments of the People's Republic of China and the Republic of India." Enver Hoxha, "A Report to the 3rd Congress of the PLA," in *Selected Works* (Tiranë, Albania: Naim Frasheri Publishing House, 1975), 2:498.

52. Aryeh Yodfat, *Arab Politics in the Soviet Mirror* (Jerusalem: Israel Universities Press, 1973), 6; James Richter, *Khrushchev's Double Bind: International Pressures and Domestic Coalition* (Baltimore, MD: Johns Hopkins University Press, 1994).

53. Chen Jian, *Mao's China and the Cold War* (Chapel Hill: University of North Carolina Press, 2001); Alexandr Fursenko and Timothy Naftali, *"One Hell of a Gamble": Khrushchev, Castro, and Kennedy, 1958–1964* (New York: W.W. Norton, 1997); Fernando Claudín, *The Communist Movement: From Comintern to Cominform* (New York: Monthly Review Press, 1975).

54. Arthur Conte, *Bandoung, tournant de l'histoire* (Paris: Laffont, 1965), 38; and Kimche, *The Afro-Asian Movement*, 64. Much the same attitude prevailed in the United States during the run-up to the ill-fated Bandung II meeting in 1965. McGeorge Bundy, from the White House, wrote to the secretary of state's office to say, "The President wishes to encourage sympathetic non-aligned nations willing to speak up against those who are blindly critical of the U.S. position in Vietnam. . . . [The Department of State should] mount a substantial effort to . . . encourage those attendees friendly to us to organize themselves to prevent ostensibly unanimous anti-U.S. resolutions from passing." National Security Action Memorandum 331: Bandung II Conference, April 9, 1965, National Security File, NSAM File, Johnson Library, Austin, Texas.

55. Christoper Thorne, *The Issue of War* (New York: Oxford University Press, 1985), 30.

56. John O'Donnell, "Capitol Stuff," *New York Daily News*, May 6, 1955; Robert Alden, "Powell Bids U.S. Bar Colonialism," *New York Times*, April 23, 1955; "Red China Exposed—Not Dominant in Asia. Interview with Adam Clayton Powell, Jr.," *U.S. News and World Report*, 42–44.

57. Noam Chomsky, *Year 501* (Boston: South End Press, 1993), 45.

58. U.S. Department of State, *Foreign Relations of the United States, 1955–1957, Volume XXIII, Japan* (Washington, DC: Government Printing Office, 1991), 325–30.

59. NSC 5809. April 2, 1958. U.S. Department of State, *Foreign Relations of the United States, 1958–1960. Volume XVI, East Asia-Pacific region; Cambodia, Laos* (Washington, DC: Government Printing Office, 1992), 31–33.

60. Quoted in Butwell, *U Nu*, 27.

61. Ibid., 176.

62. Boutros Boutros-Ghali, *Le Mouvement Afro-Asiatique* (Paris: Presses Universitaires de France, 1969). In 1958, Boutros-Ghali edited a book on the nationalization of the Suez Canal, where he wrote that Nasser's act conformed "with international law and [was] compatible with the goals and principles of the United Nations." Boutros Boutros-Ghali and Youssef Chlala, *Le Canal de Suez, 1854–1957* (Alexandria: al-Bassir, 1958), iii. In a 1997 interview with Daniel Pipes, Boutros-Ghali defended this statement, saying, "The symbolic value of the nationalization of the Suez Canal was more important than the economic value or the consequences that followed. The 1956 nationalization in a way was a follow-up from the Bandung Conference of 1955; it had great importance to Third World countries." "Boutros Boutros-Ghali, 'I Support the Algerian Government,'" *Middle East Quarterly* 4, no. 3 (September 1997).

63. Kimche, *The Afro-Asian Movement*, 82.

Cairo

1. Gamal Abdel Nasser, *Egypt's Liberation: The Philosophy of the Revolution* (Washington, DC: Public Affairs Press, 1955), 54.

2. Ibid., 56.

3. Saïd K. Aburish, *Nasser: The Last Arab. A Biography* (New York: St. Martin's Press, 2004), 57–85.

4. In 1956, exiled Algerian leaders Ferhat Abbas and Tawfiq al-Madani met with FLN commanders in Cairo, and set up the FLN headquarters in the city. They were not alone. Alongside them, Cairo boasted offices for rebels from Basutoland, Cameroons, Eritrea, Kenya, Nigeria, the two Rhodesians, Rwandi-Burundi, South Africa, South-West Africa, Uganda, and Zanzibar.

5. Soha Abdel Kader, *Egyptian Women in a Changing Society* (Boulder, CO: Lynne Reinner Publishers, 1987), 101.

6. Margot Badran, *Feminists, Islam, and Nation: Gender and the Making of Modern Egypt* (Princeton, NJ: Princeton University Press, 1995), 150–51.

7. Quoted in *Afro-Asian Peoples' Solidarity Conference, Cairo, December 26, 1957–January 1, 1958* (Moscow: Foreign Languages Publishing House, 1958), 204–5. Hereafter *AAPSC*.

8. Kumari Jayawardena, *Feminism and Nationalism in the Third World* (London: Zed, 1986).

9. Nawal El-Saadawi, *The Hidden Face of Eve: Women in the Arab World* (London: Zed, 1980), 176.

10. Suruchi Thapar, "Women as Activists, Women as Symbols: A Study of the Indian Nationalist Movement," *Feminist Review* 44 (1994): 81–96.

11. Janet Afary, *The Iranian Constitutional Revolution, 1906–1911: Grassroots Democracy and the Origins of Feminism* (New York: Columbia University Press, 1996).

12. See, for example, Bobby Siu, *Women of China: Imperialism and Women's Resistance, 1900–1949* (London: Zed, 1982).

13. One good example of the conversation across regions is the influence of the Indian feminist Pandita Ramabai on the Indonesian feminist Raden Adjeng Kartini, as noted in Pramoedya Ananta Toer, "Jang Harus Dibabat dan harus Dibangun," *Bintang Timur*, September 7, 1962.

14. Quoted in Margot Badran and Lucia Sorbera, "In No Need of Protection," *al-Ahram*, July 24–30, 2003; Badran, *Feminists, Islam, and Nation*, 91–92.

15. Quoted in Badran, *Feminists, Islam, and Nation*, 235. For more on this, see Antoinette Burton, *Burdens of History: British Feminists, Indian Women, and Imperial Culture, 1865–1915* (Chapel Hill: University of North Carolina Press, 1994); Billie Melman, *Women's Orients: English Women and the Middle East, 1718–1918* (Ann Arbor: University of Michigan Press, 1995).

16. Carmen Ramos Escandón, "Women and Power in Mexico: The Forgotten Heritage, 1880–1954," in *Women's Participation in Mexican Political Life*, ed. Victoria E. Rodríguez (Boulder, CO: Westview Press, 1998); Susan K. Besse, *Restructuring Patriarchy: The Modernization of Gender in Brazil, 1914–1940* (Chapel Hill: University of North Carolina Press, 1996).

17. Francesca Miller, *Latin American Women and the Search for Social Justice* (Hanover, NH: University Press of New England, 1991), 116.

18. Margaret E. Galey, "Promoting Nondiscrimination against Women: The UN Commission on the Status of Women," *International Studies Quarterly* 23, no. 2 (June 1979): 276.

19. Ibid., 276–79.

20. Arvonne S. Fraser, "The Convention on the Elimination of All Forms of Discrimination against Women (the Women's Convention)," in *Women, Politics, and the United Nations*, ed. Anne Winslow (Westport, CT: Greenwood Press, 1995), 77–94.

21. All these details are in Badran, *Feminists, Islam, and Nation*, chapter 11.

22. If the Wafd was programmatically incapable of being true to equality, the Nasserites showed a pragmatic tendency to betray their own ideals, particularly on the question of women's rights. This is shown in Beth Baron, "The Construction of National Honor in Egypt," *Gender and History* 5, no. 2 (1993): 244–55.

23. *AAPSC*, 205.

24. Ibid., 251. Much the same began to occur in the Americas with the First Congress of Latin American Women, hosted at much the same time in Santiago, Chile. In 1963, at the second congress, held in Havana, Cuba, women from the Communist parties were joined by women who worked in various grassroots organizations, such as the Bolivian Housewives' Committee of Siglo XX and the Sisterhood of Salvadoran Women. Miller, *Latin American Women*, 158–60. For more on these various movements, see Gloria Ardaya Salinas, "The Barzolas and the Housewives Committee," and Isabel Larguia and John Dumoulin, "Women's Equality and the Cuban Revolution," in *Women and Change in Latin America*, ed. June Nash and Helen Safa (South Hadley, MA: Bergin and Garvey, 1985).

25. An Afro-Asian Conference on Women had been held in Colombo, Sri Lanka, in 1958, but that had only been open to women of the twenty-nine original Bandung states, and it hewed too closely to the official line of each state rather than being representative of the movements in these very same states. Sri Lanka's own major women's organization, the Eksath Kantha Peramuna, was dissolved in 1949, when one of its major political allies, the Communist Party, split with its other major ally, the then-Trotskyist Lanka

Sama Samaja Party. Jayawardena, *Feminism and Nationalism in the Third World*, 135. The Afro-Asian Federation for Women, on the other hand, placed a veteran activist, Bahia Karam, in charge, and she traveled across Africa and Asia to invite as many fighting organizations as she could find to the conference. In 1938, Cairo had played host to a conference of women's organizations on the question of Palestine, and many of those activists formed the core of the invitees to the 1961 meeting in Cairo.

26. Quoted in *The First Afro-Asian Women's Conference, Cairo, 14–23 January 1961* (Cairo: Amalgamated Press of Egypt, 1961), 10. Hereafter *TFAAWC*.

27. Quoted in ibid., 42.

28. Two classic analyses of the role of women in a revolutionary situation are Frantz Fanon, "Algeria Unveiled," in *A Dying Colonialism* (1959; repr., New York: Grove Press, 1967); Che Guevara, *Guerrilla Warfare* (1961; repr., New York: Vintage, 1967). Surrounded by the experience of Vilma Espín, Celia Sanchez, and Haydée Santamaria in the hills of the Sierra Maestra, Guevara wrote, "The part that the woman can play in the development of a revolutionary process is of extraordinary importance. It is well to emphasize this, since in all our countries, with their colonial mentality, there is a certain underestimation of the woman which becomes a real discrimination against her." *Guerrilla Warfare*, 86. Following this enlightened statement, Guevara resorts to descriptions of women's work in the most stereotyped way, with the woman as auxiliary, comfort, cook, and nurse. The actual experiences of women in the Cuban, Algerian, and Guinea-Bissauan revolutions are far more complex, as women entered combat and took on leadership roles, even as these were challenged by men who, despite their left analysis, did not want to relieve themselves of patriarchal privileges. Vilma Espín, "The Early Years," in *Women and the Cuban Revolution*, ed. Elizabeth Stone (New York: Pathfinder Press, 1981); Stephanie Urdang, *Fighting Two Colonialisms: Women in Guinea-Bissau* (New York: Monthly Review Press, 1979); Danièle-Djamila Amrane-Minne, *Les Femmes dan la guerre d'Algerie: entretiens* (Paris: Karthala, 1994).

29. As the political document put it, "Acquisition of national independence is an essential prerequisite to women's rights. Democracy and justice can become mere words without meaning if women, who comprise more than half the population in any Asian and African state, remain isolated from political life. Nor can the Eastern world be established if the sexes do not cooperate on an equal footing. They must enjoy the rights of equality with men in their political domain in such a way that the laws arranging them may reflect the re-vindication of the rights of women, their children and the rights of their people." Quoted in *TFAACW*, 25.

30. Ibid., 25.

31. "Rights should not be only stipulated in law, they must be implemented. To turn laws into reality depends on the unity and organization of women. It involves patient and painstaking work. It requires aid and abetment of all people of goodwill. But it is the only way which can lead to the real equality of men and women, the fullest emancipation of womanhood and the greatest development of the nation." Quoted in *TFAACW*, 52. In 1928, Nehru offered a vision for the necessity of the autonomous organization of women and other oppressed groups within the nationalist framework, because justice is not a product of benevolence: "I should like to remind the women present here that no group, no community, no country, has ever got rid of its disabilities by the generosity of the oppressor. India will not be free until we are strong enough to force our will on England and the women of India will not attain their full rights by the mere generosity of the men of India. They will have to fight for them and force their will on the menfolk before they can succeed." Quoted in Jayawardena, *Feminism and Nationalism*, 73.

32. Quoted in *AAPSC*, 206–7.

33. Quoted in ibid., 249–50.

34. In 1920, Najiye Hanum of the Communist Party of Turkey laid out a similar agenda at the Baku Conference of the Toilers of the East. "I will briefly set forth the women's demands. If you want to bring about your own emancipation, listen to our demands and render us real help and cooperation. 1. Complete equality of rights. 2. Ensuring to women unconditional access to educational and vocational institutions established for men. 3. Equality of rights of both parties to marriage. Unconditional abolition of polygamy. 4. Unconditional admission of women to employment in legislative and administrative institutions. 5. Establishment of committees for the rights and protection of women everywhere, in cities, towns, and villages. There is no doubt that we are entitled to raise these demands. In recognizing that we have equal rights, the Communists have reached out their hand to us, and we women will prove their most loyal comrades. True, we may stumble in pathless darkness, we may stand on the brink of yawning chasms, but we are not afraid, because we know that in order to see the dawn one has to pass through the dark night." Najiye Hanum, *To See the Dawn: Baku, 1920—First Congress of the Peoples of the East*, ed. John Riddell (New York: Pathfinder, 1993), 206–7.

35. Quoted in *TFAACW*, 26–28. The final point is poorly phrased, because in many parts of the world tilling is monopolized by men, so by this standard, men would get land rights, not women. A better phrase, for universal applicability, would have been "land to those who work it" (the phrase that emerged in the Mexican Revolution of 1911, and has since become a slogan across the Spanish-speaking world of the Americas).

36. This is what Partha Chatterjee analyzes in "Nationalist Resolution of the Woman Question," in *Recasting Women: Essays in Colonial History* (New Delhi: Kali for Women, 1989), although from the essay one does not get the sense that nationalism itself remained a wide ideological arena, within which many continued to struggle despite these resolutions on a broader feminist agenda. For a critique of his views, see Himani Bannerji, "Resolution of the Women's Question," *Economic and Political Weekly*, March 11–17, 2000; Uma Chakravarti, "The Myth of 'Patriots' and 'Traitors': Pandita Ramabai, Brahmanical Patriarchy, and Militant Hindu Nationalism," in *Embodied Violence: Communalising Women's Sexuality in South Asia*, ed. Kumarai Jayawardena and Malathi De Alwis (London: Zed, 1996).

37. Quoted in *TFAACW*, 29.

38. Mervat Hatem, "Economic and Political Liberation in Egypt and the Demise of State Feminism," *International Journal of Middle East Studies* 24 (1992): 233.

39. Urdang, *Fighting Two Colonialisms*, 243.

40. Quoted in ibid., 258–59.

Buenos Aires

1. Raúl Prebisch, "The Economic Development of Latin America and Its Principle Problems," *Economic Bulletin for Latin America* 7, no. 1 (February 1962): 1–12. At the same time as Prebisch made his innovations, the German-born, U.S.-based economist H.W. Singer developed a similar approach. H.W. Singer, "US Foreign Investment in Underdeveloped Areas: The Distribution of Gains between Investing and Borrowing Countries," *American Economic Review* 40 (1950): 473–85. In the academic literature, their theory is known as the Singer-Prebisch thesis. Their work substantially followed the insights in Paul Rosenstein-Rodan, "Problems of Industrialization of Eastern and South-Eastern Europe," *Economic Journal* 53, nos. 210–11 (June–September 1943): 202–11.

2. Quoted in Víctor Alba, *Nationalists without Nations: The Oligarchy versus the People in Latin America* (New York: Praeger, 1968), 106. To accomplish this, Pelligrini set up Argentina's first national bank; decades later, Prebisch would run its descendant. On the flight of capital to Europe, see Alba, *Nationalism without Nations*, 58–59.

3. Arturo O'Connell, "Argentina into the Depression: Problems of an Open Economy," in *Latin America in the 1930s: The Role of the Periphery in the World Crisis* (New York: St. Martin's Press, 1984).

4. Quoted in Eduardo Galeano, *Open Veins of Latin America: Five Centuries of the Pillage of a Continent* (New York: Monthly Review Press, 1973), 229.

5. Joseph Page, *Perón: A Biography* (New York: Random House, 1983), 171. Perhaps Perón got the idea of his phrase from a remarkable story written by his fellow Argentine Jorge Luis Borges, "Tlön, Uqbar, and Orbis Tertius," in *El Jardín de senderos que se bifurcan* (Buenos Aires: Sur, 1941). Miranda quoted in Arthur P. Whitaker, *Nationalism in Latin America: Past and Present* (Gainesville: University of Florida Press, 1962), 50.

6. Whitaker, *Nationalism in Latin America*, 50.

7. On the Nazi connection, notably with Perón and Mercedes-Benz, see Gaby Weber, *La Conexion Alemana* (Buenos Aires: Edhasa, 2005).

8. The biographical details and Prebisch's relationship with Perón are well covered in Edger Dosman, "Markets and the State in the Evolution of the 'Prebisch Manifesto,'" and Adolfo Gurrieri, "The Ideas of the Young Prebisch," *CEPAL Review* 75 (December 2001): 67–80. The entire issue is dedicated to the work of Prebisch.

9. Prebisch studied the terms of trade for England between 1873 and 1938. His analysis of the decline in the terms of trade from the 1870s found validation in an unlikely recent source, Paul Cashin and C.J. McDermott, "The Long-Run Behavior of Commodity Prices: Small Trends and Big Variability," *IMF Staff Papers* 49, no. 2 (2002): 175–99.

10. H.W. Singer, "The Terms of Trade Controversy and the Evolution of Soft Financing: Early Years in the UN," in *Pioneers in Development*, ed. Gerald M. Meier and Dudley Seers (New York: Oxford University Press, 1984), 297.

11. UN Department of Economic Affairs, *Measures of the Economic Development of Under-Developed Countries* (New York: United Nations, 1951), 35.

12. Michal Kalecki, *Essays in the Theory of Economic Fluctuations* (London: Allen and Unwin, 1939), 149.

13. Michael Hogan, *The Marshall Plan: America, Britain, and the Reconstruction of Western Europe, 1947–1952* (New York: Cambridge University Press, 1987). Importantly, the monies lent had to be paid back, and the recipient countries had to buy goods produced by U.S. firms, a nice way for the U.S. government to subsidize its own industrial sector. Hogan shows how the Marshall Plan owes much to the New Deal.

14. W.W. Rostow, *The Stages of Economic Growth: A Non-Communist Manifesto* (Cambridge: Cambridge University Press, 1960).

15. Max Weber, *The Protestant Ethic and the Spirit of Capitalism* (New York: Scribner, 1956), 68. R.H. Tawney, based on similar material, draws the opposite conclusion in his Holland Lectures of 1922, in *Religion and the Rise of Capitalism* (New York: Mentor, 1947).

16. "In India, and to a less extent in Ireland," the economist Alfred Marshall wrote in 1890, "we find people who do indeed abstain from immediate enjoyment and save up considerable sums with great self-sacrifice, but spend all their savings in lavish festivals at funerals and marriages. They make intermittent provision for the near future, but scarcely any permanent provision for the distant future." In other words, the lack of long-term thrift, and not the theft of the surplus by English imperialism, accounts for poverty in India and Ireland. Marshall noted that "the great engineering works by which [Indian]

productive resources have been so much increased, have been made chiefly with the capital of the much more self-denying race of Englishmen." Capital, he argues, "depends much on social and religious sanctions," and the Indians and Irish just don't have the racial capacity to generate capital sums for development. Alfred Marshall, *Principles of Economics. An Introductory Volume* (London: Macmillan, 1910), 225.

17. Dadabhai Naoroji, *Poverty and Un-British Rule in India* (London: Sonnenschein, 1901), 216. On Naoroji and the drain, I am guided by Bipan Chandra, *The Rise and Growth of Economic Nationalism in India* (New Delhi: People's Publishing House, 1991).

18. Or to discover that certain cultures already had "Protestant" values within them, as in Milton Singer's monograph *When a Great Tradition Modernizes: An Anthropological Approach to Indian Civilization* (New York: Praeger, 1972).

19. Galeano, *Open Veins of Latin America*, 33.

20. The debate on the effect of the "price revolution" is contentious, particularly among economic historians. For a summary, see Peter Ramsey, ed., *The Price Revolution in Sixteenth Century England* (London: Methuen, 1971). Ramsey's collection includes Earl Hamilton's "American Treasures and Andalusian Prices, 1503–1660: A Study in the Spanish Price Revolution," *Journal of Economic and Business History* 1 (1928): 1–35, which set the terms of the ongoing debate. For a more recent work, see John TePaske, "New World Silver, Castile, and the Philippines, 1590–1800," in *Precious Metals in the Medieval and Early Modern Worlds* (Durham, NC: Duke University Press, 1983).

21. In 1903, Indian economist R.C. Dutt noted on this point, "For when taxes are raised and spent in a country, the money circulates among the people, fructifies trades, industries and agriculture, and in one shape or another reaches the mass of the people. But when the taxes raised in a country are remitted out of it, the money is lost to the country for ever, it does not stimulate her trades or industries, or reach the people in any form." R.C. Dutt, *Economic History of India*, quoted in Chandra, *The Rise and Growth*, 656.

22. Raúl Prebisch, *Toward a Dynamic Development Policy for Latin America* (New York: United Nations, 1963), 17–18.

23. Prebisch, "The Economic Development of Latin America," 1.

24. David Ricardo, *On the Principles of Political Economy and Taxation* (London: Penguin, 1971), 152. Ricardo's ideas have had an enormous impact on the science of economics—so much so that the justification for "free trade" in our own day is largely built around his analysis. The canonical text is Paul Krugman and Maurice Obstfeld, *International Economics: Theory and Policy* (New York: HarperCollins, 1994).

25. What enabled England to hold a comparative advantage over Portugal in Ricardo's time was not the "power bestowed by nature" but a series of bilateral commercial treaties (such as the 1703 Methuen Treaty) imposed by force on Portugal by England. When Ricardo put pen to paper, Portugal had become "a virtual commercial vassal of England." "The English," historian Leonard Gomes points out, "found that war as an instrument of policy could be both effective and profitable." The comparative advantage secured by England not only over Portugal but over much of the world would be won by its mercantilist policies: where the English state operated to harness England's resources and protect its economy, at the same time it promoted the subordination of the economic destiny of the rest of the world to England. Leonard Gomes, *The Economics and Ideology of Free Trade: A Historical Review* (Cheltenham, UK: Edward Elgar, 2003), 14–15. The two classic texts on the history of the Anglo-Portuguese trade are Sandro Sideri, *Trade and Power: Informal Colonialism in Anglo-Portuguese Relations* (Rotterdam: Rotterdam University Press, 1970); Harold Fisher, *The Portugal Trade: A Study of Anglo-Portuguese Commerce, 1700–1770* (London: Methuen, 1970).

26. "The flaw in [the assumptions of comparative advantage] is that of generalizing from the particular. If by 'the community' only the great industrial countries are meant, it is indeed true that the benefits of technical progress are gradually distributed among all social groups and classes. If, however, the concept of the community is extended to include the periphery of the world economy, a serious error is implicit in the generalization. The enormous benefits that derive from increased productivity have not reached the periphery in a measure comparable to that obtained by the peoples of the great industrial countries. Hence, the outstanding differences between the standards of living of the masses of the former and the latter and the manifest discrepancies between their respective abilities to accumulate capital, since the margin of savings depends primarily on increased productivity." Prebisch, "The Economic Development of Latin America," 1.

27. John Maynard Keynes to David Waley, May 30, 1944, in *The Collected Writings of John Maynard Keynes*, ed. Donald Moggridge (Cambridge: Cambridge University Press, 1980), 26:42.

28. Clair Wilcox, *A Charter for World Trade* (New York: Macmillan, 1949), 47.

29. George McTuran Kahin, ed., *The Asian-African Conference: Bandung, Indonesia, April 1955* (Ithaca, NY: Cornell University Press, 1956), 76–78.

30. Prebisch, "The Economic Development of Latin America," 1.

31. The only successful example was OPEC, created in 1960. A less successful attempt was the 1981 International Agreement on Cocoa.

32. "Joint Declaration on International Trade and Development," UN General Assembly, 18th Session, November 1963.

33. "Cooperation for the common good, from which each country will emerge better equipped for the modern economic struggle and which, in any case, will increase goods and services exchanged between Afro-Asian countries, will extend right to the heart of economic life by examining and cooperatively dealing with the problems of production in all aspects. The following are some of those aspects: (1) Capital formation and its allocation among production sectors; savings—form and agencies; (2) Expansion of consumer goods pari-passu with investment in heavy industry; diversification and specialization of production; (3) Technical education; socio-economic problems relating to workers." Quoted in *AFRASEC Conference Proceedings* (Cairo: Afro-Asian Organization for Economic Cooperation, 1961), 31.

34. Aldo Antonio Dadone and Luis Eugenio Di Marco, "The Impact of Prebisch's Ideas on Modern Economic Analysis," in *International Economics and Development*, ed. Luis Eugenio Di Marco (New York: Academic Press, 1972), 25–26. Prebisch dragged the Latin American countries to the table with the Afro-Asian delegates; he mended the frayed relationship between the nineteen Latin American states at the United Nations and the vast Afro-Asian bloc. For an indication of the splits, see Henry Raymont, "Latins at the UN Seek More Unity," *New York Times*, September 22, 1963, 23.

35. In 1949, Rao wrote a paper that showed how private capital would not move to the formerly colonized world for extra-economic reasons (racism and so on) as much as for economic ones (a low rate of return, unpredictable institutions, and so forth). If private capital is unpredictable, then the United Nations had to get involved in capital investments for the development of the formerly colonized world. Burma, Chile, Cuba, Egypt, India, Lebanon, and Yugoslavia pushed the proposal in the early years of the United Nations, to no avail. When Yugoslavia won a seat to the Economic and Social Commission in 1952, it pressed the SUNFED idea. Again it found resistance, mainly from the United States and England. The SUNFED proposal dithered at the United Nations from 1952 to 1957, when a tepid version of the original emerged as the Special

Fund, and then without any capital investment provision, as the UN Development Program (in 1965), and with a modicum of capital, as the UN Industrial Development Organization (in 1966). At UNCTAD's founding in 1964, the Yugoslavian economist Janez Stanovnik chaired the Committee on Financial Problems, which struggled hard to develop proposals for capital investment transfer. "The weight of the argument favoring an increase in the international financing of economic development," Stanovnik wrote, "lies neither in restitution nor in charity but in the sound economic logic of developing a new integrated world economy." In 1958, Stanovnik already guessed why the First World would resist the idea of a UN capital fund, because "financing economic development through the United Nations would shake the faith in private capital and private enterprise in the world." Since private enterprise was the religion of the First World, it would take a miracle for the United States and Europe to revise their free market theology. Janez Stanovnik, "1/1000 or 1/100?" *Review of International Affairs* 18, no. 423 (1967): 15, and "A Remarkable Achievement," *Review of International Affairs* 9, no. 187 (1958): 9. For more analysis, see Janez Stanovnik, *World Economic Blocs: The Non-aligned Countries and Economic Integration* (Belgrade: Edition Jugoslavija, 1962), and "Trade, Aid, and Economic Development," *Review of International Affairs* 15, no. 333 (1964).

36. Quoted in Kahin, *The Asian-African Conference*, 76. "The temporary help of foreign capital is necessary if this vicious circle is to be broken without unduly restricting the present consumption of the masses, which, generally speaking, is very low. If this capital is effectively used, the increase in productivity will, in time, allow savings to accumulate which could be substituted for foreign capital in the new investments necessitated by new technical processes and the growth of the population." Prebisch, "The Economic Development of Latin America," 13–14.

37. The Sultan of Oman Professor of International Relations at Harvard, Joseph S. Nye, refers to the UNCTAD as "Under No Circumstances Take Any Judgment." Such condescension from a man whose own post had been funded by a despot came without any acknowledgment that the UNCTAD had forced the World Bank to deal with the problem of equity. Joseph S. Nye, "UNCTAD: Poor Nations' Pressure Group," in *The Anatomy of Influence*, ed. Robert Cox, Joseph S. Nye, and Harold Jacobson (New Haven, CT: Yale University Press, 1973). In a note within the U.S. Agency for International Development in February 1965, the administrator told his staff, "Partly as a result of the UNCTAD conference in Geneva last summer, the World Bank and other international institutions have begun to reexamine their program." The United States did not want to change its own policy of less aid, more trade, but it did have to admit that the G-77 exerted power on the world stage. "Memorandum from the Administrator of the Agency for International Development (Bell) to the Executive Staff of the Agency for International Development," in *Foreign Relations of the United States, 1964–1968. Volume IX. International Development and Economic Defense Policy: Commodities*, ed. David Patterson, Evan Duncan, and Carolyn Yee (Washington, DC: Department of State, 1997), 304. In the summer of 1964, the U.S. representative to the Development Action Committee observed, "Virtually all delegates explicitly recognized the political importance of UNCTAD and the corollary necessity for coordination among DAC members in the face of the 75 [later 77]." "DAC High Level Meeting, July 23–24, 1964, Memorandum for the Files," in *Foreign Relations of the United States, 1964–1968, Volume IX*, 257.

38. This is the method laid out by John Perkins, *Confessions of an Economic Hit Man* (San Francisco: Berrett-Koehler, 2004).

39. R. Krishnamurti, "UNCTAD as a Negotiating Instrument on Trade Policy: the UNCTAD-GATT relationship," and Iqbal Haji, "Finance, Money, Developing Countries, and UNCTAD," in *UNCTAD and the South-North Dialogue: The First Twenty Years*, ed. Michael Z. Cutajar (New York: Pergamon Press, 1985).

40. Quoted in Graham Hancock, *Lords of Poverty: The Power, Prestige, and Corruption of the International Aid Business* (New York: Atlantic Monthly Press, 1989), 70. Little of this was private, because Black routinely made such comments in public, notably in 1962 at a speech to the UN Economic and Social Commission.

41. Quoted in Robert S. Walters, *American and Soviet Aid* (Pittsburgh, PA: University of Pittsburgh Press, 1970), 16–17. Eight years later, the U.S. government noted that it spent most of its foreign aid as military aid, since it needed to give "economic aid to help less developed countries receiving U.S. military aid to meet some of the economic and political burdens incurred by expanding the local defense establishment. The primary purpose therefore is military security, but some economic development may result as a by-product."

42. Although I am not going to go into it in any detail, from 1959, the People's Republic of China began to offer technical assistance and cooperative market arrangements with a number of African nations (as well as military training to those who still fought colonial powers). Guinea was the first country to create close economic ties with the People's Republic of China through interest-free loans and instruction in rice-growing techniques. Alan Hutchison, *China's African Revolution* (London: Hutchinson, 1975), 56; Udo Weiss, "China's Aid to and Trade with the Developing Countries of the Third World," *Asia Quarterly* 3 and 4 (1974): 203–314, 263–309. There was tremendous depth to these exchanges, for as Kathleen Baker shows, the Chinese low-cost, low-technology agricultural systems increased yields in Senegal. Kathleen Baker, "The Chinese Agricultural Model in West Africa: The Case of Market Gardening in the Region du Cap Vert, Senegal," *Pacific Viewpoint* 26, no. 2 (1985): 401–14.

43. During his report to the Central Committee of the Twentieth Communist Party Congress in 1956, Khrushchev stated that the Third World, "although they do not belong to the socialist world system, can draw on [the socialist world's] achievements in building an independent national economy and in raising their people's living standards. Today they need not go begging to their former oppressors for modern equipment. They can get it in the socialist countries, free from any political or military obligations." This, and the 1956 world tour by Khrushchev and Bulganin, inaugurated a major aid cycle from the USSR that lasted into the 1980s. Walters, *American and Soviet Aid*, 30.

44. Henry Trofimenko, "The Third World and U.S.-Soviet Competition," *Foreign Affairs* 59, no. 5 (Summer 1981): 1021–40.

45. Randall Stone, *Satellites and Commissars: Strategy and Conflict in the Politics of Soviet-Bloc Trade* (Princeton, NJ: Princeton University Press, 1996); Walters, *American and Soviet Aid*, 38–39.

46. Andrew Zimbalist and Manuel Pastor, "Cuba's Economic Conundrum," *NACLA Report on the Americas* 29, no. 2 (September 1995): 7–12. Cuba's reliance on a single commodity (sugar) was not simply because of its colonial-plantation past but also because of its role within the Soviet economic archipelago. Guevara, at the Second Economic Seminar of Afro-Asian Solidarity held in Algiers in 1965, pointed this out trenchantly: "The socialist countries must bear the cost of development of the countries which are now beginning to embark on the road to liberation. . . . The socialist countries are in a sense accomplices of imperial exploitation. The socialist countries have the moral duty of liquidating their complicity with the exploiting countries of the West." Quoted in Maurice Halperin, *The Taming of Fidel Castro* (Berkeley: University of California Press, 1981), 126.

47. Paul Baran, *The Political Economy of Growth* (New York: Monthly Review Press, 1962), 399. Baran's views found sympathy in Argentina, among groups such as the Movimiento de Izquierda Revolutionaria-PRAXIS. For more on this, see Carlos Strasser, ed., *Las izquierdas en el proceso político argentino* (Buenos Aires: Editorial Palestra, 1959). The work of the Movimiento de Izquierda Revolutionaria's Silvio Frondizi is central to this line of thought, which saw Perónism as the most advanced position of the national bourgeoisie, and that it was incapable of either social democracy or socialism. Horacio Tarcus, *El marxismo olvidado en la Argentina: Silvio Frondizi y Milcíades Peña* (Buenos Aires: El cielo por asalto, 1996).

48. I learned this from an old India FOIL hand who worked in both London and Calcutta. For an overview, see Rajesh Chandra, *Industrialization and Development in the Third World* (London: Routledge, 1992).

49. There was a fierce debate on the nature of class rule in postcolonial countries like India and Egypt. Some, such as economists Michal Kalecki and K.N. Raj, argued that the petty bourgeoisie dominated in these new nations, thereby creating "intermediate regimes" that could not be treated as full-blown capitalist ones. Kalecki's classic essay on the "intermediate regime" is collected in his *Essays on the Economic Growth of the Socialist and Mixed Economy* (London: Allen, Unwin, 1972). Raj's contribution is in "The Politics and Economics of Intermediate Regimes," *Economic and Political Weekly*, July 7, 1973. The strong rejoinder from the Communist intellectual and leader E.M.S. Namboodripad can be found in "On Intermediate Regimes," *Economic and Political Weekly*, December 1, 1973. The main charge made by Namboodripad was that Raj (and Kalecki) did not appreciate the role of the big bourgeoisie in societies like India, which had acceded to the import-substitution logic as a class bargain rather than for its own liquidation. Namboodripad's position is bolstered by the little-known Marxist analysis of India by Charles Bettelheim, *India Independent* (New York: Monthly Review Press, 1968), reviewed profitably by Prakash Karat in "A Political Economy of India," *Radical Review* 2, no. 1 (January 1971), which notes, "State capitalism is a policy approved by the big bourgeoisie" (37).

50. Raúl Prebisch, "North-South Dialogue," *Third World Quarterly* 2 (January 1980): 15–18.

51. In the 1940s, the United Nations had initiated a study that resulted in a report favoring land reform as a major policy for social transformation. This report became the touchstone of all UN efforts in the next two decades. *Land Reform: Defects in Agrarian Structure as Obstacles to Economic Development* (New York: UN Department of Economic Affairs, 1951).

Tehran

1. E.V. Abrahamian, "Social Bases of Iranian Politics: The Tudeh Party, 1941–53" (PhD diss., Columbia University, 1969), is a reasonable introduction to the party in its most fertile period.

2. Stephen Kinzer, *All the Shah's Men: An American Coup and the Roots of Middle East Terror* (New York: John Wiley, 2003); Mark Gasiorowski and Malcolm Byrne, eds., *Mohammed Mossaddeq and the 1953 Coup in Iran* (Syracuse, NY: Syracuse University Press, 2004).

3. At Bandung, the Iranian representative Djalal Abdoh informed the conference that Bulganin apologized to the Shah's regime for the USSR's support of the 1945–46 Democratic Party of Azerbaijan, for the oil concessions taken by the Soviets from their allies in the breakaway region and their use of the Red Army to check the Iranian army until

December 1946. Bulganin's apology meant that it put Tudeh on notice to tread carefully against the Peacock Throne. George McTuran Kahin, ed., *The Asian-African Conference: Bandung, Indonesia, April 1995* (Ithaca, NY: Cornell University Press, 1956), 20–21.

4. Malecki, for instance, indicated this with his paean toward the creation of a "mass civil order" that would neither sacrifice the individual nor society, that would favor neither the hierarchy of individuals nor the asphyxiation of society. Farzin Vahdat, *God and Juggernaut: Iran's Intellectual Encounter with Modernity* (Syracuse, NY: Syracuse University Press, 2002), 112.

5. Michael C. Hillmann, *A Lonely Woman: Forugh Farrokhʐad and Her Poetry* (Boulder, CO: Lynne Rienner, 1987), 83.

6. The collection *Nun va al-qalam*, while set in the past, is a nice allegory of Iranian society. It is translated as *By the Pen* (Austin: Center for Middle Eastern Studies, University of Texas, 1988).

7. This is the basic problem of his outstanding 1958 novel *Mudir-i madrasah*, translated as *The School Principal* (Minneapolis, MN: Bibliotheca Islamica, 1974).

8. Octavio Paz, *El Ogro Filantrópico: Historia y politica 1971–1978* (Barcelona: Editorial Seix Barral, 1983), 33–34, 45.

9. Uday Singh Mehta, *Liberalism and Empire* (Chicago: University of Chicago Press, 1999).

10. Jalal Al-e Ahmad, *Occidentosis: A Plague from the West* (Berkeley, CA: Mizan Press, 1984), 27–28. At Bandung, the delegates quietly noted the fact that "the existence of colonialism in many parts of Asia and Africa in whatever form it may be . . . suppresses the national cultures of the people." Kahin, *The Asian-African Conference*, 79.

11. L.P. Elwell-Sutton, *Persian Oil: A Study in Power Politics* (London: Lawrence and Wishart, 1955).

12. Al-e Ahmad, *Occidentosis*, 62–63.

13. See, for example, Jalal Al-e Ahmad, *Awraʐan* (Tehran: Kitabkhanah-i Danish, 1954), and *Jaʐirah-i Kharg* (Tehran: Kitabkhanah-i Danish, 1960).

14. When Amitav Ghosh traveled to Egypt in the late 1980s, he had a discussion with an imam with whom he debated the relative advance of Egypt and India. Frustrated into a corner, Ghosh bragged that India "even had a nuclear explosion," which Egypt "won't be able to match even in a hundred years." Representatives of two great civilizations vie with each other "to establish a prior claim to the technology of modern violence," with the "West," the gold standard, reduced to "science and tanks and guns and bombs." Amitav Ghosh, *In an Antique Land* (Delhi: Ravi Dayal, 1992), 234–36.

15. On Brazil, see the social scientist (and later ambassador) Mario Vieira de Mello's *Desenvolvimento e cultura: O problema do estetismo no Brasil* (São Paulo: Nacional, 1963).

16. Alioune Diop, "Opening Address," *Présence Africaine* (June–November 1956): 9. For an extended description of the conference, see James Baldwin, "Princes and Powers," *Nobody Knows My Name: More Notes of a Native Son* (New York: Dial Press, 1961).

17. The Senegalese economist Mamadou Dia turned the conference's attention from strictly cultural matters to the historical opportunity given to the leaders of the African liberation movements to deal with the economics of life, although he ignored the analytic centrality of the "economic" to the "cultural" analysis of Césaire. Bennetta Jules-Rosette, *Black Paris: The African Writers' Landscape* (Urbana: University of Illinois Press, 1998), 62–63.

18. "Négritude is a vague and ineffective ideology," said Stanislas Adoveti, the minister of culture and youth from Dahomey. "There is no place in Africa for a literature that lies outside of revolutionary combat. Négritude is dead." Quoted in Jules-Rosette, *Black Paris*, 71.

19. Aimé Césaire, "Culture and Colonisation," *Présence Africaine* (June–November 1956): 203–4.

20. Even those who sometimes promoted the idea, disavowed its conclusions: "As an Asian or an African," Al-e Ahmad wrote, "I am supposed to preserve my manners, culture, music, religion, and so forth untouched, like an unearthed relic, so that the gentlemen can find and excavate them, so they can display them in a museum and say, 'Yes, another example of primitive life.'" Al-e Ahmad, *Occidentosis*, 34. As Diop told his Paris audience, "Our heritage cannot perform the service which it should if it is codified and mummified in the interests of the museums and the curiosity seekers of Europe. The classics of a people must be given fresh reality, and therefore must be re-thought and re-interpreted by each generation. This should be so with ours." Diop, "Opening Address," 16.

21. Diop, "Opening Address," 12.

22. For the Brazil story, see Linda Rabben, *Unnatural Selection: The Yanomani, the Kayapó, and the Onslaught of Civilization* (Seattle: University of Washington Press, 1998). For the Indian story, see Archana Prasad, *Against Ecological Romanticism: Verrier Elwin and the Making of the Anti-Modern Tribal Identity* (New Delhi: Three Essays Press, 2003). On Central America, see Richard Adams and Santiago Bastos, *Las relaciones étnicas en Guatemala, 1944–2000* (Antigua Guatemala: Centro de Investigaciones Regionales de Mesoamérica, 2003). On the case of Namibia, see Robert Gordon, *The Bushman Myth: The Making of the Namibian Underclass* (Boulder, CO: Westview Press, 1992).

23. Césaire, "Culture and Colonisation," 207.

24. Ibid., 197.

25. "Nothing could be further from the truth than such a supposition. Nationalism is not what it seems, and above all it is not what it seems to itself." Ernest Gellner, *Nations and Nationalism* (Ithaca, NY: Cornell University Press, 1983), 56.

26. In 1963, the anthropologist Clifford Geertz noted, "Multiethnic, usually multilingustic, and sometimes multiracial, the populations of the new states tend to regard the immediate, concrete, and to them inherently meaningful sorting implicit in such 'natural' diversity as the substantial content of their individuality. To subordinate these specific and familiar identifications in favor of a generalized commitment to an overarching and somewhat alien civil order is to risk a loss of definition as an autonomous person, either through absorption into a culturally undifferentiated mass or, what is even worse, through a domination by some other rival ethnic, racial, or linguistic community that is able to imbue that order with the temper of its own personality. But at the same time, all but the most unenlightened members of such societies are at least dimly aware—and their leaders are acutely aware—that the possibilities of social reform and material progress they so intensely desire and are so determined to achieve rest with increasing weight on their being enclosed in a reasonably large, independent, powerful, well-ordered polity. The insistence on recognition as someone who is visible and matters and the will to be modern and dynamic thus tend to diverge, and much of the political process in the new states pivots around an heroic effort to keep them aligned." From the Third World intellectuals, we don't get the angst of Geertz, that multinationalism, regionalism, or Third Worldism will mean a loss of subjectivity. Clifford Geertz, "The Integrative Revolution: Primordial Sentiments and Civil Politics in the New States," in *The Interpretation of Cultures* (New York: Basic Books, 1973), 258–59.

27. Quoted in *Conference for the Establishment of the United Nations Educational, Scientific and Cultural Organisation*, Institute of Civil Engineers, London, November 1–16, 1945 (Paris: UNESCO Archives, no. AG 41), 49.

28. Nicholas B. Dirks, *Castes of Mind: Colonialism and the Making of Modern India* (Princeton, NJ: Princeton University Press, 2001); Edmund Leach, *Social and Economic Organisation of*

the Rowandu{ Kurds (London: P. Lund, 1940), 19; Talal Asad, "Two European Images of Non-European Rule," in *Anthropology and the Colonial Encounter*, ed. Talal Asad (New York: Humanities Press, 1973); Mahmood Mamdani, *Citizen and Subject: Contemporary Africa and the Legacy of Late Colonialism* (Princeton, NJ: Princeton University Press, 1996).

29. On composite culture, see Tara Chand, *Influence of Islam on Indian Culture* (Allahabad: Indian Press, 1963); Humayun Kabir, *The Indian Heritage* (Bombay: Asia Publishing House, 1946). Kabir became the minister of education in independent India.

30. Frantz Fanon, "Racism and Culture," *Présence Africaine* (June–November 1956):131.

31. As suggested in Diop, "Opening Address," 15.

32. Aimé Césaire, *Discourse on Colonialism* (New York: Monthly Review Press, 2000), 69–70.

33. Quoted in *Conference for the Establishment of the UNESCO*, 33. There was a recognized need, again at Bandung and elsewhere, to revive the long history of people-to-people contact that had been commonplace in the ancient world. Documented in Vijay Prashad, *Everybody Was Kung Fu Fighting: Afro-Asian Connections and the Myth of Cultural Purity* (Boston: Beacon Press, 2001), chapter 1.

34. *Afro-Asian Peoples' Solidarity Conference, Cairo, December 26, 1957–January 1, 1958* (Moscow: Foreign Languages Publishing House, 1958), 192.

35. Kahin, *The Asian-African Conference*, 79–80.

36. The best of the *Lotus* work was collected in the two-volume *Afro-Asian Short Stories: An Anthology* (Cairo: Permanent Bureau of Afro-Asian Writers, 1973). The collection included forty-one stories from such countries as Kenya (James Ngugi and Grace Ogot), South Africa (Alex La Guma), Malaysia (Tan Kong Peng), Japan (Dazai Osamu), India (Mulk Raj Anand), Iraq (Fouad Tokarly), and Palestine (Emil Habibi).

37. The Soviets played a crucial role here, because their Progress Publishers translated not only Russian books in a variety of non-European languages but also translated work from Urdu into Arabic and from Korean into Swahili. As a child, I ate up the cheaply distributed, but lavishly illustrated children's stories from Progress—they had Russian, African, Asian, and other folktales in good editions. In the 1970s, Progress also published a series called "Problems of the Third World," which included books by Russian and other authors on the dilemmas that had begun to face the new nations. For another view of this, see Pankaj Mishra, "The East Was Red," *The Guardian*, February 4, 2006.

38. On Portal, see Daniel Reedy, *Magda Portal, la pasionaria peruana: biografía intelectual* (Lima: Ediciones Flora Tristán, 2000).

39. Al-e Ahmad, *Occidentosis*, 63.

40. In some contexts, the attempt to indigenize democracy led to its suspension in its own name (the best example is of the logic elaborated by Julius Nyerere, who argued that a multiparty system would fragment a united Tanzania).

41. "Would the tree of liberty grow [in India], if planted? Would the declaration of rights translate into *Sanscrit*? Would *Bramin, Chetree, Bice, Sooder* and *Hallochore* [the first four being the textual *varnas* from the Vedas, the latter being a Persian term to refer to the sanitation workers] meet on equal ground? If not, you may find some difficulty in giving them to themselves." Jeremy Bentham, "Emancipate Your Colonies," in *The Works of Jeremy Bentham*, ed. J. Bowring (1830; repr., New York: Russell and Russell, 1962), 4:417.

42. Quoted in *Afro-Asian Peoples' Solidarity Conference*, 135.

43. UNESCO, *Fundamental Education: Common Ground for All Peoples* (Geneva: UNESCO, 1947). The Afro-Asian Women's Conference in Cairo recommended a series of approaches toward the eradication of illiteracy, and many of these entered the life of the Third World movements. The most important initiatives included the provision of grants for the creation of libraries, the production of popular educational books,

and adult education. These moves, however, would not work if the classroom treated the students as passive receptacles for a mainly urban-oriented curriculum. The materials for the class had to be "compatible to the conditions of life and work," and the struggle against illiteracy had to be part of a "larger popular movement aided by the popular organizations." *The First Afro-Asian Women's Conference, Cairo, 14–23 January 1961* (Cairo: Amalgamated Press of Egypt, 1961), 30.

44. Shabnam Virmani's 1996 documentary, *When Women Unite: The Story of an Uprising*, is about women in Andhra Pradesh who are organized in a literacy circle and then begin a statewide campaign against cheap liquor. It is an excellent document on the power of contemporary literacy campaigns linked to political-social reform movements. Equally impressive is the "total literacy campaign" in Kerala's Ernakulam district. See P.K. Michael Tharakan, *The Ernakulam District Total Literacy Programme: Report of the Evaluation* (Trivandrum, India: Centre for Development Studies, 1990); Kerala Sastra Sahitya Parishad, *Lead Kindly Light: Operation Illiteracy Eradication. A Report on the Intensive Campaign for Eradication of Illiteracy in Ernakulam* (Trivandrum, India: KSSP, 1991).

45. For a terrific account, see Jonathan I. Israel, *Radical Enlightenment: Philosophy and the Making of Modernity, 1650–1750* (Oxford: Oxford University Press, 2001).

46. The best empirical alarm against this trend is in Pervez Hoodbhoy, *Islam and Science* (London: Zed Books, 1991). The best philosophical rejection is in Meera Nanda, *Prophets Facing Backwards: Postmodern Critiques of Science and Hindu Nationalism in India* (New Brunswick, NJ: Rutgers University Press, 2003).

47. This is from his *Dar Khedmat va Khianat Rushanfekran*, a work that draws from the framework and concepts of Antonio Gramsci's work on organic intellectuals. See Vahdat, *God and Juggernaut*, 119–20. One contemporary Iranian continues Al-e Ahmad's quest, even if his direction is far more suffused with a reverence toward canonical Islam than Al-e Ahmad (who was more keen on esoteric Islam and its folkloric roots). See AbdolKarim Soroush, *Reason, Freedom, and Democracy in Islam: Essential Writings of AbdolKarim Soroush* (Oxford: Oxford University Press, 2000).

48. Al-e Ahmad, *Occidentosis*, 30.

49. Ibid., 79.

50. Quoted in Darius M. Rejali, *Torture and Modernity: Self, Society, and State in Modern Iran* (Boulder, CO: Westview Press, 1994), 140.

51. "A Change of Ideas," *Time*, September 27, 1963, 79.

52. He suffered the fate of being associated, after his death, with the Iranian Revolution, and then began to be seen by some as one of the intellectual progenitors of the Islamic regime. See Val Moghadam, The Revolution and the Regime: Populism, Islam, and the State in Iran," *Social Compass* 36, no. 4 (1989): 429; Mehrzad Boroujerdi, "*Gharbzadegi*: The Dominant Intellectual Discourse of Pre- and Post-Revolutionary Iran," in *Iran: Political Culture in the Islamic Republic*, ed. Samih Farsoun and Mehrdad Mashayekhi (London: Routledge, 1992).

53. Simin Daneshvar, *Savushun* (Washington, DC: Mage Publishers, 1990). An alternative translation is *A Persian Requiem* (London: Halban, 1991).

54. Forugh Farrokhzad, "Kasi Keh Mesi-e Hichkas Nist," *Arash* 10 (Summer 1966), in Hillmann, *A Lonely Woman*, 65–68.

Belgrade

1. Fernando Claudín, *The Communist Movement: From Comintern to Cominform, Part 2* (New York: Monthly Review Press, 1975), 390–91.

2. Quoted in François Fejtö, *Histoire des démocraties populaires* (Paris: Editions du Seuil, 1969), 85–86.

3. The Italian Communist Party's general secretary Palmiro Togliatti laid out his party's position in 1956 as "polycentrism," or the "national roads to socialism." *VII Congresso del PCI* (Rome: Editori Riuniti, 1956), 45. Moscow remained an important center of the movement, but as Togliatti affirmed, each national Communist Party would develop its strategy and tactics based on its analysis, and not on that of Moscow itself. This is a far cry from the Eurocommunist manifesto of 1976, where the Western European parties announced, "Once Moscow was our Rome, but no more. Now we acknowledge no guiding center, no international discipline." Fernando Claudín, *Eurocommunism and Socialism* (London: New Left Books, 1978), 54.

4. The Yugoslavs did accept investment capital and foreign aid from the Western European states and the United States. In July 1949, Tito justified this infusion: "When we sell our copper to buy machines, we are not selling our consciences, but only our copper." Quoted in Claudín, *The Communist Movement*, 509.

5. Because Bandung was a conference of Africa and Asia, Yugoslavia could not attend, but the Brijuni summit allowed Nasser and Nehru to join Tito in the creation of a framework that exceeded the continents and included those with a Third World vision. From the standpoint of Europe, additionally, the region that became Yugoslavia was treated as savage and lesser, somewhat in a similar manner to the rest of the Third World. Perhaps this legacy had something to do with the sympathetic welcome accorded to Yugoslavia into the ranks of the Third World. Larry Wolff, *Inventing Eastern Europe: The Map of Civilization on the Mind of the Enlightenment* (Stanford, CA: Stanford University Press, 1994).

6. Indeed, when Algeria's first president, Ahmed Ben Bella, traveled to Belgrade in 1964, he thanked Tito's government because "as a small country [it] nevertheless, contributes towards the settlement of world problems," and because its version of socialism is "the best of all, since it pays attention to democracy and harmonizes socialism and democracy." Alvin Z. Rubinstein, *Yugoslavia and the Nonaligned World* (Princeton, NJ: Princeton University Press, 1970), 88.

7. The USSR's hasty recognition of Israel in 1948 and its temerity over India's claims in Kashmir isolated it further from the ruling class in Egypt and India.

8. The details are in Robert J. McMohan, *The Cold War on the Periphery: The United States, India, and Pakistan, 1947–1965* (New York: Columbia University Press, 1994); Dennis Kux, *India and the United States: Estranged Democracies* (Washington, DC: National Defense University Press, 1992).

9. Douglas Little, *American Orientalism: The United States and the Middle East since 1945* (Chapel Hill: University of North Carolina Press, 2002), 166–67.

10. Gabriel Kolko, *Confronting the Third World: United States Foreign Policy, 1945–1980* (New York: Random House, 1988), 62. U.S. establishment literature consistently missed the point of non-alignment, always ready to impute the worst motivations to the states that assembled for peace. Arthur Holcombe, *Peaceful Coexistence: A New Challenge to the United Nations* (New York: Twelfth Report of the Commission to Study the Organization of Peace, Research Affiliate of the American Association for the United Nations, 1960); Richard V. Allen, *Peace or Peaceful Coexistence?* (Chicago: American Bar Association, 1966).

11. Sukarno's opening address to the 1961 NAM Conference took on this point directly, "Non-alignment is not neutrality. Let there be no confusion on that score. No, non-alignment is not neutrality. It is not the sanctimonious attitude of the man who holds himself aloof—'a plague on both your houses.' Non-aligned policy is not a policy of

seeking for a neutral position in case of war; non-aligned policy is not a policy of neutrality without its own colour; being non-aligned does not mean becoming a buffer state between the two giant blocs. Non-alignment is active devotion to the lofty cause of independence, abiding peace, social justice, and the freedom to be free. It is the determination to serve this cause; it runs congruent with the social conscience of man." Quoted in *The Conference of Heads of State or Government of Non-Aligned Countries* (Belgrade: Editions Jugoslavija, 1961), 27. The idea of non-aligned or noncommitted had been well laid out in the 1950 5th Session of the United Nations by Yugoslavia's Foreign Minister Edvard Kardelj: "The peoples of Yugoslavia cannot accept the assumption that mankind must today choose between the domination of one great power or another. We consider that there is another path, the difficult but necessary path of democratic struggle for a world of free and equal nations, for democratic relations among nations, against foreign interference in the domestic affairs of the people and for the all around peaceful cooperation of nations on a basis of equality." Rubinstein, *Yugoslavia*, 29. Non-alignment for the NAM group was not a legal concept but a political and moral space. Lars Nord, *Nonalignment and Socialism* (Stockholm: Raben and Sjögren, 1974), 58–59.

12. For the dam itself, Nasser toyed with the various powers for finances, but he settled for the earnest offers from the United States and the World Bank. British Foreign Secretary Harold MacMillan saw that Nasser wanted to "induce both the West and the Soviets to bid up each other's price." Harold MacMillan, *Tides of Fortune, 1945–1955* (New York: Harper and Row, 1969), 635.

13. Quoted in Little, *American Orientalism*, 171. For more on this, see Geoffrey Aronson, *From Sideshow to Center-Stage: U.S. Policy toward Egypt, 1946–1956* (Boulder, CO: Lynne Rienner, 1986), 256; Townsend Hoopes, *The Devil and John Foster Dulles* (Boston: Little, Brown, 1973).

14. Quoted in Melvyn Leffler, *A Preponderance of Power: National Security, the Truman Administration, and the Cold War* (Palo Alto, CA: Stanford University Press, 1992), 18–19.

15. Quoted in H.W. Brands, *The Specter of Neutralism: The United States and the Emergence of the Third World, 1947–1960* (New York: Columbia University Press, 1989), 273.

16. "The Brioni Document. Joint Communiqué by President Tito, President Nasser, and Premier Nehru," *Review of International Affairs* 7, nos. 152–53 (1956).

17. As prelude to the Belgrade meeting, Tito went on an extended tour of liberated Africa in 1961. Before Ghana's parliament, Tito honored the delegates as being the antithesis of the fascists and colonial rulers who had dominated the world. "Millions of ordinary people have entered the stage of history," he said, and "they will not allow a handful of irresponsible belligerent people to gamble with their destiny." Josef Broz Tito, "Speech in the Parliament of the Republic of Ghana," in *Selected Articles and Speeches, 1941–1961* (Zagreb: Naprijed, 1963), 345. There are two more useful documents on Tito's trip: *President Tito's Visit to Friendly African Countries* (Belgrade: Edition Jugoslavija, 1961); Obren Milicevic, *With Friends in Africa* (Belgrade: Edition Jugoslavija, 1961).

18. After Belgrade, the NAM Head of State Conferences have been held in the following cities: Cairo (1964), Lusaka (1970), Algiers (1973), Colombo (1976), Havana (1979), New Delhi (1983), Harare (1986), Belgrade (1989), Jakarta (1992), Cartagena de Indias (1995), Durban (1998), and Kuala Lumpur (2003). There have also been other conferences of foreign ministers and lesser representatives over the years.

19. There are a lot of warts in the life of the three giants, and much has been written of Tito's authoritarian tendency and distortion of internal democracy in the party. For an analytic account by Tito's sometime ally and then vehement critic, see Milovan Djilas, *Tito: The Story from Inside* (New York: Harcourt Brace Jovanovich, 1980). Much the

same has been said of Nehru and Nasser (see Saïd K. Aburish, *The Last Arab: A Biography* [New York: Thomas Dunne Books, 2004]).

20. This political diversity made it impossible for NAM to become a bloc in the conventional sense. In an assessment of the history of NAM in anticipation of the Second NAM Conference at Cairo, the former Yugoslavian representative to the United Nations Miso Pavicevic wrote, "It has been repeated many times that the Belgrade Conference was not held with the intention of forming a third bloc or still less an exclusive club. The object of the Belgrade Conference and of the policy of the non-aligned countries has always been to narrow the area of bloc conflict and build a world of peaceful and active co-existence. The fact that an increasing number of countries are adopting the policy formulated at the Belgrade Conference is both an outstanding result and a forceful proof of the vitality and rightness of this policy. Bloc arguing is alien to the very nature of the policy of the non-aligned countries, and so is any attempt to enclose it within narrow limits, which must be surpassed by life." Miso Pavicevic, "Why a New Conference of Non-Aligned Countries?" *Review of International Affairs* 15, no. 333 (1964): 5.

21. Quoted in *The Conference of Heads of State or Government*, 69.

22. It was not until this concerted pressure from the Third World and the tension of the 1962 Cuban Missile Crisis that the two countries began to seriously entertain inspections, a confidence builder that led in great part to the 1968 Treaty on the Non-Proliferation of Nuclear Weapons. The treaty provided the scaffolding for the bulk of the nuclear disarmament agreements that followed. To many in the Third World, the U.S. obduracy on the nuclear question did everything to sour their sense of the superpower. The 1946 Baruch Plan appeared to be a ruse to allow the United States to preserve its technological and military dominance. Further, when the USSR voted in the 15th Session of the United Nations (1960) against nuclear tests, and when it declared a unilateral moratorium on tests in 1985, the United States did not respond in kind. Indeed, on September 18, 1959, when the USSR submitted a memorandum to the 14th Session of the United Nations in favor of total disarmament, the rest of the nuclear elite read it silently.

23. *The Conference of Heads of State or Government*, 87 (Haile Selassie), 99 (Nkrumah), 254–55 (final resolution).

24. Ibid., 264.

25. The permanent seats and veto had nothing to do with nuclear weapons. In 1945, only the United States had nuclear capability, but soon thereafter the USSR, England, and France joined it. When the People's Republic of China replaced Taiwan in the United Nations (and on the Security Council) in 1971, it had a nuclear bomb (having tested it in 1964). As it turned out, then, the five Security Council members are nuclear powers, although when the Third World demanded the expansion of the council, this was not the case. After India tested nuclear weapons in 1974, it was not invited into the club. Historical advantage, not nuclear capability, gave the Security Council members veto power over the world's affairs.

26. In late 1954, Tito told the Indian Parliament, "Up to now the United Nations has failed to settle many questions of international significance mainly because of organizational faults, such as the right to veto in the Security Council, and so on, and then again because of the tendency to divide into blocs has been apparent in the Organisation from the very beginning, and this has hampered the proper functioning of this international institution." Josef Broz Tito, "Speech in the Indian Parliament," in *Selected Speeches and Articles, 1941–1961* (Zagreb: Naprijed, 1963), 162.

27. Quoted in *The Conference of Heads of State or Government*, 70.

28. Rubinstein, *Yugoslavia*, 10. In 1964, the Yugoslavian Foreign Ministry's Josip Djerdja offered a sympathetic and critical analysis of the role of the United Nations for NAM:

"[Regular meetings of NAM representatives at the United Nations] should be seen as the embryo of a necessary and constant consultative procedure which would make it possible for the non-aligned countries to cooperate more effectively in constantly expanding the field of activity toward peace and progress. The non-aligned countries have again identified their activity with the efforts of the United Nations which in a more peaceful and just world should act as a regulator of equitable cooperation and an instrument of general development in a world which is diverse but which should be freed from the danger of the existing differences and diversities serving as a motive or cause of friction and antagonism. Democratization of the United Nations and a course toward some necessary corrections in the mechanism of the world organization and in its Charter, which are given prominence in the Cairo program, are nothing but an indication that the non-aligned countries are looking forward with sober confidence to the days when the UNO will assume this important role." Josip Djerdja, "The Cairo Programme of Action," *Review of International Affairs* 15, no. 350 (1964): 2–3.

29. Cuba's President Osvaldo Dorticós, who had attended the 1961 and 1964 meetings of NAM, expressed his joy that with this plank, NAM "made clear that non-alignment is not the same as neutrality but that it only means not participating in some military bloc." Quoted in Jorge I. Domínguez, *To Make a World Safe for Revolution: Cuba's Foreign Policy* (Cambridge, MA: Harvard University Press, 1989), 222.

30. Amilcar Cabral, "National Liberation and Peace, Cornerstones of Non-Alignment," in *Revolution in Guinea: Selected Texts by Amilcar Cabral,* ed. Richard Handyside (New York: Monthly Review Press, 1969), 55.

31. Edvard Kardelj, *Socialism and War: A Survey of Chinese Criticism of the Policy of Peaceful Coexistence* (London: Methuen, 1960), 148. Kardelj's defense of the Soviet intervention in Hungary draws from this theory, but it does not follow his own presumptions to the end. While his book questions the intervention by a stronger power into a weaker one when other solutions offer themselves, in his address to the Federal People's Assembly, he defends the intervention on the grounds that any delay would have increased the suffering of the Hungarian working class. He did, however, call the intervention the "lesser evil," and not the greater good. Edvard Kardelj, *Review of International Affairs* 12, no. 161, special supplement (1956).

32. Cabral, "National Liberation and Peace," 53. Cabral was not alone. Here are some others on the same point: "Today, in the entire continent of Africa, from Algiers to Cape Town, from Lobito to Lusaka, Africa's Freedom Fighters are up in arms and will lay down their lives rather than their arms in the struggle for the total liquidation of colonialism. Protracted constitutional devices designed to defeat the attainment of freedom and independence will no longer be tolerated." Nkrumah, quoted in *The Conference of Heads of State or Government,* 103. "I am sure that, like the Cuban people, all other peoples represented here who have been the victims of imperialist and colonialist aggression, wish to live in peace with the aggressor countries. It is not a mere whim which prompts us to oppose them. We are being forced into taking up arms and giving battle, and no Government which wishes to maintain the dignity and sovereignty of its nation can refuse the challenge." Dorticós, quoted in *The Conference of Heads of State or Government,* 128. "The elimination of colonial relationships and of neo-colonialistic attempts at preserving the substance of colonialism in changed circumstances is today equally to the advantage of colonial peoples and the peoples of metropolitan countries. Full support to peoples and countries struggling against colonial domination for their fundamental rights is, at the same time, one of the basic prerequisites for an effective eradication of sources of war and of dangers threatening world peace." Tito, quoted in *The Conference of Heads of State or Government,* 161.

33. Quoted in Maurice Halperin, *The Taming of Fidel Castro* (Berkeley: University of California Press, 1981), 118–19.

34. Nehru, at the 1961 NAM, noted that "we should approach [the nuclear powers] in a friendly way, in a way to win them over and not merely to denounce them and irritate them and make it even more difficult for them to follow the path we indicate to them." Quoted in *The Conference of Heads of State or Government*, 115.

Havana

1. A mainstream history of these interventions is available in Stephen Kinzer, *Overthrow: America's Century of Regime Change from Hawaii to Iraq* (New York: Times Books, 2006).

2. Dwight D. Eisenhower, *Waging Peace, 1956–1961* (Garden City, NJ: Doubleday, 1965), 523.

3. Jorge I. Domínguez, *To Make a World Safe for Revolution: Cuba's Foreign Policy* (Cambridge, MA: Harvard University Press, 1989), 84.

4. Maurice Halperin, *The Taming of Fidel Castro* (Berkeley: University of California Press, 1981), 163.

5. Régis Debray, *Strategy for Revolution: Essays on Latin America* (New York: Monthly Review Press, 1971); Frantz Fanon, *Wretched of the Earth* (New York: Grove Press, 1965); Lin Biao, *Long Live the Victory of the People's War!* (Peking: Foreign Languages Press, 1965).

6. The Latin American delegates had been in Brussels in 1927. Cuba had been present at NAM 1961. Cuba was also a major supporter of the Algerian War. Piero Gleijeses, *Conflicting Missions: Havana, Washington, and Africa, 1959–1976* (Chapel Hill: University of North Carolina Press, 2002). In April 1961, the Fourth Session of the Council of Solidarity of the Afro-Asian peoples in Bandung welcomed the first Latin American delegation to an Afro-Asian gathering. The Cubans who came to Bandung joined in a resolution to condemn the U.S. aggression on the island at the Bay of Pigs. Then, in December, the Cubans traveled to Gaza (Palestine), where the Executive Committee of the Organization of the Solidarity of Afro-Asian Peoples decided to host a conference of the three continents—a move pushed by Cuba. The Cubans then went to Mexico City to attend the First Latin American Conference for National Sovereignty, Economic Emancipation, and Peace (1961), which passed a declaration on behalf of the Tricontinental. Finally, at Moshi (Tanzania), the Third Conference of the Solidarity of the Afro-Asian Peoples in 1963 chose Havana as the site for the Tricontinental at the request of the Cuban delegation.

7. There was agreement on all the usual issues: the analysis of imperialism, colonialism, underdevelopment, nationalization, racial discrimination, and cultural development. *First Solidarity Conference of the Peoples of Africa, Asia, and Latin America: Proceedings* (Havana: Solidarity Conference of the Peoples of Africa, Asia, and Latin America, 1966), 148–55.

8. Ibid., 166.

9. *The Tricontinental Conference of African, Asian, and Latin American Peoples: A Staff Study, Subcommittee to Investigate the Administration of the Internal Security Act and Other Internal Security Laws of the Committee of the Judiciary of the United States Senate* (Washington, DC: U.S. Government Printing Office, 1966), 21; *First Solidarity*, 129. Eisenhower well knew the value of Vietnam for the U.S. government's geostrategic plans: "What do you think caused the overthrow of President Sukarno in Indonesia? What do you suppose determined the new federation state of Malaysia to cling to its

independence despite all the pressure from outside and from within? Well, I could tell you one thing: the presence of 450,000 American troops in South Vietnam had a hell of a lot to do with it." Quoted in Jonathan Neale, *A People's History of the Vietnam War* (New York: The New Press, 2003), 72.

10. Che Guevara, "Message to the Tricontinental" (originally published by the Executive Secretariat of the Organization of the Solidarity of the Peoples of Africa, Asia, and Latin America, Havana, April 16, 1967), in *Guerrilla Warfare*, ed. Brian Loveman and Thomas Davies Jr. (Lincoln: University of Nebraska Press, 1985), 202. Che's statement followed a 1962 speech by Castro: "It is the duty of every revolutionary to make the revolution. In America and in the world, it is known that the revolution will be victorious, but it is improper revolutionary behavior to sit at one's doorstep waiting for the corpse of imperialism to pass by." Quoted in Domínguez, *To Make a World Safe for Revolution*, 116.

11. Guevara, "Message," 209, 213.

12. Daniel James, *Che Guevara: A Biography* (New York: Stein and Day, 1969), 188.

13. The Soviet position is explained in Herbert Aptheker, *The Truth about Hungary* (New York: Mainstream Publishers, 1957).

14. Mao Tse-tung, *People of the World, Unite and Defeat the U.S. Aggressors and All Their Lackeys* (Peking: Foreign Languages Press, 1967), 14.

15. David Kimche, *The Afro-Asian Movement: Ideology and Foreign Policy of the Third World* (New York: Halsted, 1973), 201–2.

16. A.W. Singham and Shirley Hume, *Non-Alignment in an Age of Alignments* (London: Zed Books, 1986), 92.

17. See Gérard Chaliand, *Armed Struggle in Africa* (New York: Monthly Review Press, 1969); Perry Anderson, *Le Portugal et la fin de l'ultracolonialisme* (Paris: François Maspero, 1963).

18. Kwame Nkrumah, *Neocolonialism: The Last Stage of Imperialism* (New York: International Publishers, 1966), x.

19. Ibid., 258.

20. Kwame Nkrumah, *Handbook of Revolutionary Warfare* (New York: International Publishers, 1968), 42.

21. Amilcar Cabral, "The Weapon of Theory," in *Revolution in Guinea*, trans. Richard Handyside (New York: Monthly Review Press, 1972), 91.

22. Ibid., 102.

23. Ibid., 107. Cabral and Fanon are quite separate from the revolutionary groups that take their inspiration from George Sorel: to strike fear in the heart of empire. Cabral and Fanon are less invested in the psyche of the imperial forces, and more in the colonized.

24. Much the same trajectory as the PAIGC marked the Palestine Liberation Organization, formed in 1964, but not on the armed path before the defeat of the Arab armies in the Six Day War (1967).

25. *First Solidarity*, 63.

26. The victory of FRELIMO in Mozambique gave a fillip to the struggle of ZANU and the Zimbabwe African People's Union across the border in Rhodesia to overthrow South Africa's puppet.

27. The cult of the gun produced little tangible freedom for the Third World, and indeed, as we shall see in the next chapter, it facilitated dictatorships by malign leaders who cloaked themselves in militancy to fend off challenges to their rule.

28. Singham and Hune, *Non-Alignment*, 219.

29. Amilcar Cabral, "Tell No Lies," in *Revolution in Guinea*, 89.

30. Cabral, "The Weapon of Theory," 91–92.

Algiers

1. Mohammed Harbi, *1954: La guerre commence en Algérie* (Paris: Complexe, 1984), 34; Alistair Horne, *A Savage War of Peace: Algeria, 1954–1962* (London: Macmillan, 1977), 101–2; Djamila Amrane, *Les Femmes algériennes dans la guerre* (Paris: Plon, 1991); Arslan Humbaraci, *Algeria: A Revolution That Failed* (New York: Praeger, 1966). These texts inform much of the history that I will lay out on the FLN and the Algerian War of Independence.

2. Quoted in Edward Behr, *The Algerian Problem* (London: Hodder and Stoughton, 1961), p. 86.

3. Hadj's organization resisted, faced the guns of the FLN, and dissolved. Hadj himself went into exile in France. Mohammed Harbi, *Le F.L.N.: Mirage et réalité* (Paris: Jeune Afrique, 1980). I have derived much of my narrative from the writings of Mohammed Harbi, who was once a leading figure in the FLN and a member of Ben Bella's first cabinet. When Ben Bella was overthrown in 1965, Harbi was imprisoned. He escaped in 1971, and then went into exile in France in 1973. One more useful history from Harbi is the co-written (with Benjamin Stora), *La Guerre d'Algérie, 1954–2004* (Paris: Robert Laffont, 2004). The point on the front not being a party is from David Macey, *Frantz Fanon: A Biography* (New York: Picador, 2000), 258; and the MTLD and later the FLN's Mabrouk Belhocine, William Quandt, *Revolution and Political Leadership: Algeria, 1954–1968* (Cambridge, MA: MIT Press, 1969), 213.

4. Frantz Fanon, *Toward the African Revolution* (New York: Monthly Review Press, 1967), 53.

5. Jean-Paul Sartre, preface to *The Wretched of the Earth*, by Frantz Fanon (New York: Grove Press, 1963), 10.

6. Fanon, *Toward the African Revolution*, 114, and *The Wretched of the Earth*, 191–92.

7. Maria Lazreg, *The Eloquence of Silence: Algerian Women in Question* (New York: Routledge, 1994), 123.

8. For a contemporary analysis of the masculine state, see Iris Marion Young, "The Logic of Masculinist Protection: Reflections on the Current Security State," *Signs* 29, no. 11 (2003): 1–25. See also Amina Mama, "Sheroes and Villians: Conceptualizing the Colonial and Contemporary Violence against Women in Africa," in *Feminist Genealogies, Colonial Legacies, Democratic Futures*, ed. M. Jacqui Alexander and Chandra Talpade Mohanty (New York: Routledge, 1997).

9. National liberation and national consciousness, Fanon writes, "instead of being the all-embracing crystallization of the innermost hopes of the whole people, instead of being the immediate and most obvious result of the mobilization of the people, will be in any case only an empty shell, a crude and fragile travesty of what it might have been." Fanon, *The Wretched of the Earth*, 148.

10. *La Charte d'Alger. Ensemble des Textes Adoptés par le Premier Congrès du parti du F.L.N.* (Alger: FLN Commission Centrale d'Orientation, 1964), 104–7. I borrow some of the translations from Robert Malley, *The Call from Algeria: Third Worldism, Revolution, and the Turn to Islam* (Berkeley: University of California Press, 1996). Kenya's Jomo Kenyatta also argued for a single-party state, but he offered a crucial caveat. Kenyatta noted that the number of parties that one has in a country does not determine the nature of rule; that is, two-party systems might produce tyrannical and undemocratic regimes, while one-party states could be democratic. The main innovation of the modern era is not the two-party democratic system but the "mass party," where political legitimacy is drawn not simply as an abstraction from the people but where the people act everyday to produce the state's work and its rules. Cherry Gertzel, Maure Goldschmidt, and Donald Rothchild, eds., *Government and Politics in Kenya* (Nairobi: East Africa Publishing

House, 1969), 113. "In a certain number of underdeveloped countries," wrote Fanon, "the parliamentary game is faked from the beginning. Powerless economically, unable to bring about the existence of coherent social relations, and standing on the principle of their domination as a class, the bourgeoisie chooses the solution that seems to it the easiest, that of the single party." Fanon, *The Wretched of the Earth*, 164.

11. Quoted in Henry F. Jackson, *The FLN in Algeria: Party Development in a Revolutionary Society* (Westwood, CT: Greenwood Press, 1977), 108.

12. Quoted in Quandt, *Revolution and Political Leadership*, 194. Fanon had anticipated this as well: the "fruitful give and take from the bottom to the top and from the top to the bottom which creates and guarantees democracy in a party" vanishes. The party becomes a "screen" for the leadership to hide behind, and while the party continues, "party life" is suspended. The people are sent "back to their caves." Fanon, *The Wretched of the Earth*, 170, 183.

13. François Borella, "La constitution algérienne: un regime constitutionnel de gouvernement par le parti," *Revue algérienne des sciences juridiques, politiques, et économiques* 1 (January 1964); Jackson, *The FLN in Algeria*, chapter 5.

14. One view has it that "Ben Bella moves as though he were alone. He is intent on his own vision and seems scarcely aware of what people about him are saying." Horne, *Savage War*, 540. Another says that he never had statues erected in his honor, and he did not name streets after himself. David Ottaway and Marina Ottaway, *Algeria: The Politics of a Socialist Revolution* (Berkeley: University of California Press, 1970), 81–82.

15. Ottaway and Ottaway, *Algeria*, 94–95. For an exuberant reaction to Ben Bella's regime, see Daniel Guérin, *Ci-git le colonialisme* (Paris: Mouton, 1973).

16. When the French government decided to withdraw from Algeria in 1962, the large French settler population decided to either take what it could carry or destroy the rest. The Organisation Armée Secrète bombed industrial and mercantile establishments in urban Algeria, while the army withdrew from the rural areas with a scorched-earth strategy.

17. Ottaway and Ottaway, *Algeria*, 57.

18. Ibid., 63–64; John Entelis, *Algeria: The Revolution Institutionalized* (Boulder, CO: Westview Press, 1986), 141; Thomas Blair, *"The Land to Those Who Work It": Algeria's Experiment in Workers' Management* (Garden City, NY: Anchor Books, 1970).

19. *La Charte*, 44–45, 63.

20. Ottaway and Ottaway, *Algeria*, 41.

21. Much the same tale could be told of the Mexican Revolution. The Mexican Revolution that broke out in 1910 settled into national construction in the six-year administration of General Lázaro Cárdenas del Rio (1934–40). Cárdenas's regime drew on massive peasant support for the revolution to force land reforms on the landed aristocracy. The hacienda gave way to the *ejidos*, the communal lands that earned capital support from the Banco Nacional de Credito Ejidal. While few debate that the Cárdenas policy dented the power of the large landholders, most contemporary historians question the efficacy of the democracy put in place by the regime. Marjorie Becker, *Setting the Virgin on Fire: Lázaro Cárdenas, Michoacan Peasants, and the Redemption of the Mexican Revolution* (Berkeley: University of California Press, 1996); Ben Fallaw, *Cárdenas Compromised: The Failure of Reform in Postrevolutionary Yucatán* (Durham, NC: Duke University Press, 2001). In 1938, Cárdenas's government annexed Mexico's oil resources and formed a national firm, PEMEX, to ensure that the resources of the nation benefit its people and not monopoly oil conglomerates. In 1938, Cárdenas's political allies formed the Partido de la Revolución Mexicana, but in 1946, the new governors of the state aptly renamed the party, Partido Revolucionario Institucional. Indeed, while Cárdenismo's social justice agenda continued to provide rhetoric for the regime, the "corporatist

structure given form during the Cárdenas *sexenio* became little more than bureaucratic channels of political control." Tom Barry, *Zapata's Revenge: Free Trade and the Farm Crisis in Mexico* (Boston: South End Press, 1995), 25. Large corporations dominated agriculture and eclipsed the ejidos, while PEMEX became an instrument of the industrial elite rather than for national liberation. The Cárdenas era in Mexico is not alone: it is strikingly similar to developments during the presidency of Getúlio Vargas in Brazil (1930–45) and Juan Perón in Argentina (1946–55), both of whom nationalized key sectors of the economy and attempted to conduct land reforms. Their mandarin approach to "reform" and their reticence toward devolution of power led to their downfall, either at the hands of a far more conservative military or else to their former allies who would not countenance even their mild social reform agenda.

22. The story is recounted in Ricardo Rene Laremont, *Islam and the Politics of Resistance in Algeria, 1782–1992* (Trenton, NJ: Africa World Press, 2000); Abder Rahmane Derradji, *A Concise History of Political Violence in Algeria, 1954–2000: Brothers in Faith, Enemies in Arms* (Lewiston, ME: Mellen Press, 2002).

23. Gerard Chaliand, *L'Algérie est-elle Socialiste?* (Paris: Maspero, 1964), 89; Ottaway and Ottaway, *Algeria*, 84.

24. Much the same sort of thing occurred in Egypt, where the number of bureaucrats increased by over 60 percent in the 1960s and their incomes rose by over 200 percent. Mahmoud Abdel-Fadil, *Development, Income Distribution, and Social Change in Rural Egypt, 1952–1970* (Cambridge: Cambridge University Press, 1975), 49; Robert Mabro and Samir Radwan, *The Industrialization of Egypt, 1939–1973* (Oxford: Clarendon Press, 1976), 239.

25. Ottaway and Ottaway, *Algeria*, 85.

26. Fanon is contradictory here. He later says, "The single-party is the modern form of the dictatorship of the bourgeoisie, unmasked, unpainted, unscrupulous and cynical," when he has earlier noted that the bourgeoisie's pressures are only one part of the reason for the national liberation party's move to the single-party solution. Fanon, *The Wretched of the Earth*, 165.

27. This "naturalness" was well recognized by an Algerian partisan, a woman who felt betrayed by her revolution: "We thought we would earn our rights. We thought they would naturally be recognized later." Lazreg, *The Eloquence of Silence*, 140.

28. *La Charte*, 105.

29. Julius Nyerere, *Freedom and Unity* (Dar es Salaam: Oxford University Press, 1967), 312.

30. Ho Chi Minh, "Political Report Read at the National Conference of the Vietnam Workers' Party Held in February 1961," in *Selected Works* (Hanoi: Foreign Languages Publishing House, 1961), 3:255. Third World Communists had also been schooled by a lengthy tradition within the Marxist tradition that began almost as soon as the Bolsheviks experienced the problems of bureaucratization within the Soviet Union. At the 1922 conference of the Communist Party, Lenin offered a searing commentary on the gradual disentanglement of the party-state from the population. "The task," he told this contentious conference, whose main topic for discussion was the New Economic Policy, "is to learn to organize the work properly, not to lag behind, to remove friction in time, not to separate administration from politics. For our administration and our politics rest on the ability of the entire vanguard to maintain contact with the entire mass of the proletariat and with the entire mass of the peasantry. If anybody forgets [the importance of mass contact] and becomes wholly absorbed in administration, the result will be a disastrous one." Vladimir Ilyich Lenin, "Political Report to the Central Committee of the RCP (B)," in *Collected Works* (Moscow: Progress Publishers), 33:263–309. Such questions were commonplace in the worker council type of Communism of the 1920s—and

provoked the works of Antonio Gramsci—and the German worker council movement (although here the highly skilled workers predominated over the rest). On the Italian case, see Paolo Spriano, *The Occupation of the Factories: Italy 1920* (London: Pluto Press, 1975). On the German example, see Sergio Bologna, "Class Composition and the Theory of the Party at the Origin of the Workers-Council Movement," *Telos 3* (Fall 1972): 4–27.

31. Paulo Freire, *Pedagogy in Process: The Letters to Guinea Bissau* (New York: Seabury Press, 1978), collects his insightful letters to the commissioner of state for education and culture, Mario Cabral.

32. Le Duan's essays and speeches on this theme are collected in *On the Right to Collective Mastery* (Hanoi: Foreign Languages Publishing House, 1980).

33. Fanon, *The Wretched of the Earth*, 169.

34. Ottaway and Ottaway, *Algeria*, 127.

35. The South African militant Ruth First described the absorption of the armed corps with a sense of what had been lost by the victory of this colonial remnant under the command of the revered Boumédienne: "At the very moment of Algeria's independence victory, after seven years of grueling war, the very forces which supplied the dynamics of Algeria's revolution were displaced. The forces of the interior, liberated by a guerrilla war which might have led to a genuine popular mobilization for a new political system, were overtaken, even suppressed, by a highly centralized, authoritarian and bureaucratic armed structure. From this time onwards, Algerian independence politics were not peasant-based, as the rural revolt which sustained the war had been; nor were they fired primarily by the worker, student and intellectual militants of the cities, who in great street demonstrations and in the Battle of Algiers had thrown their weight behind the FLN in the face of security force terrorism. They became the contests of elite groups, among them the professional officer corps of the career army, manipulating for political and economic vantage points." Ruth First, *The Barrel of a Gun: Political Power in Africa and the Coup d'Etat* (London: Penguin, 1970), 95.

36. Jean-Pierre Durand, "L'agriculture sacrifiée," in *L'Algérie*, ed. Patrick Eveno (Paris: Le Monde, 1994).

37. Quoted in Malley, *The Call from Algeria*, 152.

38. After the coup, the Communists merged with the left core of the FLN to create the Socialist Vanguard Party of Algeria. An old FLN veteran, El Hachemi Chérif, who hailed from the Kabyle region of Djurdjura, led it. The party worked illegally until 1989. In 1993, it was renamed Ettehadi, and then in 1999, split into the Democratic and Socialist Movement and the Algerian Party for Socialism and Democracy. They are largely ineffectual, although they maintain a lonely vigil against the rise of both neoliberalism and Islamic fundamentalism.

39. Fanon, *The Wretched of the Earth*, 169.

40. Ibid., 166, 168.

41. Ibid., 166.

La Paz

1. Robert O. Kirkland, *Observing Our Hermanos de Armas: U.S. Military Attachés in Guatemala, Cuba, and Bolivia, 1950–1964* (London: Routledge, 2003), 110.

2. Pierre Vilar, *A History of Gold and Money, 1450–1920* (London: Verso, 1991), and "The Age of Don Quixote," *New Left Review* 68 (July–August 1971): 59–71.

3. John Hillman, "The Mining Industry and the State: The Politics of Tin Restriction in Bolivia, 1936–1939," *Bulletin of Latin American Research* 21, no. 1 (January 2002): 40–72; and Manuel Contreras, *The Bolivian Tin Mining Industry in the First Half of the Twentieth Century* (London: Institute for Latin American Studies, 1993).

4. Eduardo Galeano, *Open Veins of Latin America: Five Centuries of the Pillage of a Continent* (New York: Monthly Review Press, 1978), 163. For an excellent study of the tin miners of Bolivia, see June Nash, *We Eat the Mines and the Mines Eat Us: Dependency and Exploitation in Bolivian Tin Mines* (New York: Columbia University Press, 1993). For a remarkably good study of the relations between the campesinos and the miners, see Silvia Rivera Cusicanqui, *Oppressed but Not Defeated: Peasant Struggles among the Ayamara and Quechua in Bolivia, 1900–1980* (Geneva: United Nations Research Institute for Social Development, 1987).

5. Gloria Ardaya, *Política sin rostro: mujeres en Bolivia* (Caracas: Nueva Sociedad, 1992); Laurence Whitehead, "The Bolivian National Revolution: A Twenty-First-Century Perspective," in *Proclaiming Revolution: Bolivia in Comparative Perspective*, ed. Merilee Grindle and Pilar Domingo (Cambridge, MA: Harvard University Press, 2003), 32.

6. Herbert S. Klein, "Social Change in Bolivia since 1952," in *Proclaiming Revolution*, 232; James Dunkerley, *Rebellion in the Veins: Political Struggle in Bolivia, 1952–1982* (London: Verso, 1984); James Kohl, "Peasant and Revolution in Bolivia, April 9, 1952—August 2, 1953," *Hispanic American Historical Review* 62, no. 4 (1982): 238–59.

7. On the prerevolutionary agricultural upsurge, see Laura Gotkowitz, "Revisiting the Rural Roots of the Rebellion," in *Proclaiming Revolution*, 164–82. On the disregard for rural radicals, see Kohl, "Peasant and Revolution in Bolivia."

8. The details are in William Brill, *Military Intervention in Bolivia: The Overthrow of Paz Estenssoro and the MNR* (Washington, DC: Institute for the Comparative Study of Political Systems, 1967); Kirkland, *Observing Our Hermanos de Armas*, 103–4.

9. Kirkland, *Observing Our Hermanos de Armas*, 104.

10. Piero Gleijeses, *Shattered Hope: The Guatemalan Revolution and the United States, 1944–1954* (Princeton, NJ: Princeton University Press, 1991).

11. Kenneth Lehman, *Bolivia and the United States: A Limited Partnership* (Athens: University of Georgia Press, 1999).

12. John F. Kennedy, *Alliance for Progress: Text of an Address Delivered at the White House, March 13, 1961* (Washington, DC: Pan American Union, 1961).

13. Kirkland, *Observing Our Hermanos de Armas*, 108.

14. Lehman, *Bolivia and the United States*; Dunkerley, *Rebellion in the Veins*.

15. Gavin Kennedy, *The Military in the Third World* (London: Duckworth, 1974), appendix A. Kennedy tends to include any and every incidence, including coup attempts that are, as he says, "doubtful" and others that are announced by regimes for their "propaganda needs" (337). Nonetheless, his figure is a useful indication of the incidence and claims of coups in the darker nations.

16. Frantz Fanon, *The Wretched of the Earth* (New York: Grove Press, 1963), 202.

17. Ibid.

18. Guillermo Centeno's fine 1984 short on women in the territorial army, *Mamá se va a la Guerra*, provides a nice, wry look at what "civilian defense" meant by the 1980s. For an overview of the Mariana Grajales platoon before the revolution, see Teté Puebla, *Marianas in Combat: Teté Puebla and the Mariana Grajales Women's Platoon in Cuba's Revolutionary War, 1956–58* (New York: Pathfinder Press, 2003).

19. Quoted in Peter Wyden, *Bay of Pigs: The Untold Story* (New York: Simon & Schuster, 1979), 295.

20. The great anomaly is India, where the military remained strong and did not move on the parliament. In 1975, the Indian prime minister, Indira Gandhi, suspended the Constitution to declare emergency rule, but widespread protests over two years led to the revocation of these measures. The military sat out of this conflict. Apurba Kundu's *Militarism in India: The Army and Civil Society in Consensus* (London: I.B. Tauris, 1998) develops the view that the Indian military top brass are averse to coups because they have internalized the idea of a professional officer corps. This is a useful argument, although limited by the example of Pakistan, which had the same kind of professional culture and opposite results.

21. The best summary is in William Blum, *Killing Hope: U.S. Military and CIA Interventions since World War II* (Monroe, ME: Common Courage Press, 1995).

22. Institute for Defense Analysis, *A Study of U.S. Military Assistance Programs in the Underdeveloped Areas*, April 8, 1959; Final report and papers of the Draper Committee, Accession #67–9, Dwight D. Eisenhower Library, Abilene, Kansas.

23. Gabriel Kolko, *Confronting the Third World: United States Foreign Policy, 1945–1980* (New York: Pantheon, 1988), 133. One of the most important theorists of this tendency was Morris Janowitz, who worked on the University of Chicago's Committee for the Comparative Study of New Nations. His classic work is *The Military in the Political Development of New Nations* (Chicago: University of Chicago Press, 1964), which he rewrote and expanded as *Military Institutions and Coercion in the Developing Nations* (Chicago: University of Chicago Press, 1977). Another significant work in this field is John Johnson, *The Role of the Military in Underdeveloped Countries* (Princeton, NJ: Princeton University Press, 1962).

24. On this, see Thomas Skidmore, *The Politics of Military Rule in Brazil, 1964–1985* (Oxford: Oxford University Press, 1988). Quote from Michael Crozier, Samuel P. Huntington, and Joji Watanuki, eds., *The Crisis of Democracy: Report on the Governability of Democracies to the Trilateral Commission* (New York: New York University Press, 1975), 166–68. On the Trilateral era, see Stephen Gill, *American Hegemony and the Trilateral Commission* (Cambridge: Cambridge University Press, 1991).

25. Samuel P. Huntington, *Political Order in Changing Societies* (New Haven, CT: Yale University Press, 1968), 136.

26. On this point Huntington remained consistent, because he made much the same argument for the role of the U.S. military in its own history. Samuel P. Huntington, *The Soldier and the State: The Theory and Politics of Civil-Military Relations* (Cambridge, MA: Harvard University Press, 1959).

27. National Security Council, "U.S. Overseas Internal Defense Policy," August 1, 1962; Kolko, *Confronting the Third World*, 133.

28. Transparency International, *Global Corruption Report 2004* (London: Transparency International, 2004), 13.

29. James Dunkerley, *Power in the Isthmus: A Political History of Modern Central America* (London: Verso, 1988), 439–43.

30. Steve Striffler, *In the Shadows of State and Capital: The United Fruit Company, Popular Struggle, and Agrarian Restructuring in Ecuador, 1900–1995* (Durham, NC: Duke University Press, 2002), could be read in such a way that the 1964 reforms *produced* a higher level of peasant consciousness and thereby undermined the very junta that created the reforms in the first place.

31. John Fitch, *The Military Coup d'Etat as a Political Process: Ecuador, 1948–1966* (Baltimore, MD: Johns Hopkins University Press, 1977); Martin Needler, *Anatomy of a Coup d'Etat: Ecuador 1963* (Washington, DC: Institute for the Comparative Study of Political Systems, 1964).

32. While there is an immense diversity of reasons and logics for each coup, I want to concentrate on two clusters of coups: those that are conducted by a military leadership annoyed by civilian incursions into its authority, and those that are conducted by the lower ranks within the military against the relationship of the domestic oligarchy or monarchy with imperialism. An additional important cluster that I will ignore here, but that bears mention, is the coup that takes place when one regional or clan group within the military conducts a coup in the name of the clan or region against the rest of the nation; the classic example here are the two coups of 1966 (in Burundi and Nigeria, where the Tutsi and the Ibo aristocracies dominated, respectively).

33. Huntington, *Political Order*, 194. For an overemphasis on the intramilitary reasons for the coup, see William Thompson, *The Grievances of Military Coup Makers* (London: Sage, 1973).

34. Huntington, *Political Order*, 221.

35. Ibid., 137.

36. Ibid., 220. Again, Huntington does not discriminate between liberal democratic states and national liberation states. In an important essay from the 1970s, he noted that the First World suffered from "an excess of democracy." He offers the army as an example of an institution that is better left outside democratic demands, and suggests that there is much to be learned from it for the larger polity. Samuel P. Huntington, "The United States," in *The Crisis of Democracy*, 113–14.

37. Robert McNamara, "Security in the Contemporary World," Defense Science Board, June 6, 1966, 880–81.

38. Ruth First, *117 Days: An Account of Confinement and Interrogation under the South African Ninety-Day Detention Law* (London: Bloomsbury, 1988).

39. Ruth First, *South West Africa* (London: Penguin Books, 1963).

40. A selection of her work is available in Don Pinnock, ed., *Voices of Liberation, Volume 2, Ruth First* (Pretoria: Human Sciences Research Council, 1997).

41. The debate on the caudillo is well represented in Hugh Hamill, ed. *Caudillos: Dictators in Spanish America* (Norman: University of Oklahoma Press, 1992). In this collection, Glen Dealy's "The Public Man" offers the cultural explanation, whereas Eric Wolf and Edward Hansen's "Caudillo Politics: A Structural Analysis" provides the view that I accept. A patient criticism of the notion of the "tribal leader" is in Talal Asad, "Two European Images of Non-European Rule," in *Anthropology and the Colonial Encounter*, ed. Talal Asad (London: Ithaca Press, 1975).

42. Ruth First, *The Barrel of a Gun: Political Power in Africa and the Coup d'Etat* (London: Penguin, 1970), ix.

43. Ibid., 5.

44. Ibid., 6.

45. Huntington, *Political Order*, 4.

46. Karl Marx, *Capital, Volume One* (London: Penguin, 1976), 479.

47. First, *Barrel*, 217–18.

48. The U.S. footprint is well documented in Peter Kornbluh, *The Pinochet File: A Declassified Dossier on Atrocity and Accountability* (New York: The New Press, 2003), and the subject of a debate between Kenneth Maxwell (Council on Foreign Relations) and William D. Rogers (vice chair of Kissinger Associates). The debate was conducted over 2003–4. Maxwell, director of Latin American Affairs at the council, resigned when *Foreign Affairs*, the council's journal, refused to allow him to answer Henry Kissinger's longtime associate Rogers's denials of U.S. involvement and Kissinger's heavy hand in Chilean relations. Scott Sherman, "The Maxwell Affairs," *The Nation*, June 21, 2004.

49. Pablo Neruda, *Canto General*, trans. Jack Schmitt (Berkeley: University of California Press, 1991), 161.

50. U.S. Senate Select Intelligence Committee, *Alleged Assassination Plots Involving Foreign Leaders*, 94th Congress, First Session, Report No. 94-465, November 20, 1975 (Washington, DC: Government Printing Office, 1975), 277.

51. Certainly, Egypt had a strong social reform tradition that dated back to the early nineteenth-century rule of the Albanian migrant, Mohammad Ali. All the efforts of his regime came to little before the stranglehold placed on Egypt by the English led by Lord Palmerston. The English promoted the weak Ottoman control over the region rather than a strong Egyptian state, as the former would allow them not only to dominate the region but thereby control the waterway to India, China, and East Africa. Afaf Lutfi al-Sayyid Marsot, *A Short History of Modern Egypt* (Cambridge: Cambridge University Press, 1985), 54–75.

52. Fatemah Farag, "Labour on the Fence," *Al-Ahram*, May 11–17, 2000.

53. Quoted in Ruth First, *Libya: The Elusive Revolution* (London: Penguin, 1974), 102.

54. For a useful assessment of Chávezism, see Richard Gott, *In the Shadow of the Liberator: Hugo Chávez and the Transformation of Venezuela* (London: Verso, 2000). For less exuberant analyses, see Margarita López-Maya and Luis Lander, "Refounding the Republic: The Political Economy of Chavismo," *NACLA Report on the Americas* 33, no. 6 (May–June 2000): 21–23; Steve Ellner and Daniel Hellinger, eds., *Venezuelan Politics in the Chávez Era: Class, Polarization, and Conflict* (Boulder, CO: Lynn Rienner, 2003).

55. Quoted in Walter Laqueur, *The Soviet Union and the Middle East* (New York: Routledge, 1959), 219. Nasser himself had penned a deeply anticommunist tract whose views remained with him until his end in 1970, *Nahnu wa'al'Iraq wa'al-shuy u'iyah* (Beirut: Dar al-Nashr al-Arabiyah, 1959); Saïd K. Aburish, *Nasser: The Last Arab* (New York: Thomas Dunne Books, 2004), 98.

56. First, *Barrel*, 462.

57. Neruda, *Canto General*, 206–7 (translation slightly modified).

Bali

1. Pablo Neruda, *Canto General*, trans. Jack Schmitt (Berkeley: University of California Press, 1991), 139–40.

2. Soekarno, *Nationalism, Islam, and Marxism* (Ithaca, NY: Cornell University Press, 1970).

3. Rex Mortimer, *Indonesian Communism under Sukarno: Ideology and Politics, 1959–1965* (Ithaca, NY: Cornell University Press, 1974), 49.

4. Ibid., 366–67.

5. Ibid., 372.

6. In 1958, a U.S. Joint Chiefs of Staff memorandum defended this payment to the military based on its analysis that it was "the only non-Communist force . . . with the capability of obstructing the . . . PKI." Peter Dale Scott, "The United States and the Overthrow of Sukarno, 1965–1967," *Pacific Affairs* 58 (Summer 1985): 239–64.

7. Indeed, Sukarno welcomed a large delegation from the armed forces into his 1959 cabinet, while he virtually shut out the PKI. Mortimer, *Indonesian Communism*, 110. For useful military modernization analyses of the Indonesian army, see Guy Pauker, "The Role of the Military in Indonesia," in *The Role of the Military in Underdeveloped Countries*, ed. J.J. Johnson (Princeton, NJ: Princeton University Press, 1964); Daniel Lev,

"The Political Role of the Army in Indonesia," *Pacific Review* 36, no. 4 (Winter 1963–64): 349–64.

8. Quoted in Mortimer, *Indonesian Communism*, 79.

9. The numbers will, perhaps, never be established. An extensive survey is in Robert Cribb, ed., *The Indonesian Killings of 1965–1966: Studies from Java and Bali* (Clayton, Victoria: Monash University, Centre of Southeast Asian Studies, 1990); Hermawan Sulistyo, "The Forgotten Years: The Missing History of Indonesia's Mass Slaughter (Jombang-Kediri 1965–1966)" (PhD diss., Arizona State University, 1997), 52–54.

10. We are fortunate to have an excellent monograph on the events in Bali that offers a long-term history of the various conflicts on the island, but gives due credence to the extraordinary forces that led to the massacre. Geoffrey Robinson, *The Dark Side of Paradise: Political Violence in Bali* (Ithaca, NY: Cornell University Press, 1995). For a useful summary from Kesiman, a village on Bali, see Leslie Dwyer and Degung Santikarma, " 'When the World Turned to Chaos': 1965 and Its Aftermath in Bali, Indonesia," in *The Specter of Genocide: Mass Murder in Historical Perspective*, ed. Robert Gellately and Ben Kiernan (Cambridge: Cambridge University Press, 2003).

11. For an excellent account of the construction of the idea of Bali, see Adrian Vickers, *A Paradise Created* (Berkeley, CA: Periplus Editions, 1989).

12. Robinson, *Dark Side of Paradise*, 297–303. For an eyewitness account, see John Hughes, *The End of Sukarno* (Sydney: Angus and Robertson, 1968).

13. Vickers, *A Paradise Created*, 170.

14. Dwyer and Santikarma, "When the World Turned to Chaos," 295.

15. See, for example, Seth S. King, "Indonesians Deny Peking's Accusation That Troops Sacked Building in Drive Against Reds After Plot," *New York Times*, October 20, 1965, 4. For many of the details, see Robinson, *Dark Side of Paradise*, chapter 11. Iwan Gardono Sudjatmiko's dissertation suggests that the PKI's strategy led to the massacre—a conclusion that is along the grain of that fed to the media by the U.S. embassy in Jakarta, but not borne out by the wider context of the genocide. Iwan Gardono Sudjatmiko, "The Destruction of the Indonesian Communist Party: A Comparative Analysis of East Java and Bali" (PhD diss., Harvard University, 1992), 232ff.

16. *Indonesia: Malaysia-Singapore; Philippines*, vol. 26, *Foreign Relations of the United States, 1964–1968* (Washington, DC: Department of State, 2001), 338–39.

17. Ibid., 386–87.

18. Robinson, *Dark Side of Paradise*, 282. In 1959, the military modernization scholar Guy Pauker offered the Indonesian military as an example of a strong force that the United States should encourage as an antidote to Communism. Pauker's analysis provided the blueprint for Suharto's coup. Guy Pauker, "Southeast Asia as a Problem Area in the Next Decade," *World Politics* 11 (April 1959): 325–45.

19. David Easter, *Britain and the Confrontation with Indonesia, 1960–1966* (London: Tauris, 2004), and " 'Keep the Indonesian Pot Boiling': Western Covert Intervention in Indonesia, October 1965–March 1966," *Cold War History* 5, no. 1 (February 2005): 55–73.

20. UN General Assembly, no. 2027 (20), "Measures to Accelerate the Promotion of Respect for Human Rights," November 18, 1965. On April 1, 2004, the Asian Legal Resource Center (Hong Kong) petitioned the United Nations to act on the 1965–66 massacres. Its petition begins with the following paragraph: "Incredibly, to date the international community has failed to address the massacre of at least half a million persons in Indonesia orchestrated by General Soeharto during his rise to power in

1965–66. Whereas the victims of the Bali bombings of 2002, mostly non-Indonesians, found some measure of justice within months, nearly four decades later the survivors of this massive crime against humanity as yet pass unrecognised." Nothing has come of the petition to date.

21. On the tenth anniversary, Malcolm Caldwell edited *Ten Years' Military Terror in Indonesia* for the Bertrand Russell Peace Foundation (Nottingham, UK: Spokesman Books, 1975)—just as the Indonesian army received the green light from Washington to invade the island of East Timor.

22. The general tendency of the Comintern is covered in the two-volume work by Fernando Claudín, *The Communist Movement: From Comintern to Cominform* (New York: Monthly Review Press, 1976). Regional studies include Manuel Caballero, *Latin America and the Comintern, 1919–1943* (Cambridge: Cambridge University Press, 1986); Hakim Adi, "The Communist Movement in West Africa," *Science and Society* 61, no. 1 (1997); Apollon Davidson, Irina Filatova, Valentin Gorodnov, and Sheridan Johns, eds., *South Africa and the Communist International: A Documentary History*, 2 vols. (London: Frank Cass, 2003); Irina Yurieva Morozova, *The Comintern and Revolution in Mongolia* (Cambridge, UK: White Horse Press, 2002); Cheah Boon Kheng, *From PKI to the Comintern, 1924–1941: The Apprenticeship of the Malayan Communist Party* (Ithaca, NY: Cornell University South East Asia Program Publications, 1992).

23. William Shinn, "The 'National Democratic State': A Communist Program for Less-Developed Areas," *World Politics* 15, no. 3 (April 1963): 177–89.

24. Livio Maitan, *Party, Army, and Masses in China: A Marxist Interpretation of the Cultural Revolution and Its Aftermath* (London: New Left Books, 1976), 312–17.

25. Roger Kanet, *The Soviet Union and the Developing World* (Baltimore, MD: Johns Hopkins University Press, 1974), assesses the theories of the 1960s. There is a view that the Soviets proposed the class collaborationist approach, whereas the Chinese pushed the more radical approach. James Richter, *Khrushchev's Double Bind: International Pressures and Domestic Coalition* (Ithaca, NY: Cornell University Press, 2002). On the Chinese role, see Chen Jian, *Mao's China and the Cold War* (Chapel Hill: University of North Carolina Press, 2001). This is not borne out by the facts, which show that both Moscow and Beijing worked in the maw of a real strategic contradiction.

26. Charles Tripp, *A History of Iraq* (Cambridge: Cambridge University Press, 2000), 156–57. The ICP had already disbanded its military wing, the Union of Soldiers and Officers, prior to the coup, at the suggestion of the Free Officers. This would later be a fatal mistake, although it was a useful confidence-building step for the new republic. Hanna Batatu, *The Old Social Classes and the Revolutionary Movement of Iraq* (Princeton, NJ: Princeton University Press, 1978), 792–94.

27. Quoted in Samir al-Khalil, *Republic of Fear: The Politics of Modern Iraq* (Berkeley: University of California Press, 1989), 191, 226. Nasser's confidant Muhammed Heikal also wrote that Communism did not suit the Arab world. Some Communists themselves promoted this view, as for example the Syrian Communist leader Khaled Bakdash, who noted in the 1950s that not only was he "above all an Arab nationalist" but that Syria would remain "Arab nationalist and nothing else in addition." Quoted in Walter Laqueur, *The Soviet Union and the Middle East* (New York: Praeger, 1959), 300.

28. Batatu, *The Old Social Classes*, 903.

29. The Baath leadership was quite open about how the Party came to power "on an American train." Batatu, *The Old Social Classes*, 985–86.

30. I have offered examples of Soviet intransigence, but I could just as well have detailed the story of Beijing and the Pakistanis. For a pointed account, see Tariq Ali, "Revolutionary Perspectives for Pakistan," *New Left Review* 63 (September–October 1970): 43–55.

31. Alain Gresh, "The Free Officers and the Comrades: The Sudanese Communist Party and Nimeiri Face-to-Face, 1969–1971," *International Journal of Middle East Studies* 21 (1989): 393–409; Gabriel Warburg, *Islam, Nationalism, and Communism in a Traditional Society: The Case of Sudan* (London: Frank Cass, 1978).

32. Tariq Ali, *Bush in Babylon: The Recolonization of Iraq* (London: Verso, 2003), 89–101.

33. Ludo Martens, *Pierre Mulele and the Kwilu Peasant Uprising in Zaire* (London: Zed, 1993). Mulele's wife, Abo Leonie, recounts how poorly the guerrillas treated women. Socialism's ideals had only a faint footprint in the uprising. Ludo Martens, *Abo: Une Femme du Congo* (Brussels: EPO and l'Harmattan, 1995).

34. Ernst Utrecht, "The Communist Party of Indonesia (PKI) since 1966," in *Ten Years' Military Terror in Indonesia*, ed. Malcolm Caldwell (Nottingham, UK: Spokesman Books, 1975)

35. Régis Debray, *Strategy for Revolution: Essays on Latin America* (New York: Monthly Review Press, 1971), 72.

36. The Maoist strategy paid off dividends in Colombia. The Communist Party there had been devastated in the 1940s and 1950s, and its rump became the target of the Colombian elite and the U.S. government. When they went after the Communists in 1964, less than fifty Communists under the command of Manuel Marulanda Vélez went into the forests near Marquetalia and began a guerrilla war under the name of the Revolutionary Armed Forces of Colombia. Four decades later their war continues. Elsewhere, the Communists who moved to the gun had less success (although the Revolutionary Armed Forces of Columbia's current imbroglio is hardly a model of success). In next-door Venezuela, the left forces regrouped in the countryside as the Party of the Venezuelan Revolution under the leadership of Douglas Bravo and Ali Rodriquez (today the head of the Petroleos de Venezuela, the nation's oil company), and continued to fight an armed struggle as well as infiltrate the armed forces (Hugo Chávez's brother Adan was an important activist in the party).

37. George Lenczowski, *Soviet Advances in the Middle East* (Washington, DC: American Enterprise Institute, 1971), 88. These entries into government functioned as showcases for the Communist parties rather than opportunities to exercise genuine power. Carol Saivetz and Sylvia Woody, *Soviet-Third World Relations* (Boulder, CO: Westview Press, 1985), 50.

38. The Congress of the People in Indonesia's first decree in 1966 contained the following principles: "Indonesia should renounce its membership of any bloc or military pact; Asian problems should be solved by the Asians themselves, including the question of Vietnam; the UN resolution on decolonization has not been fully applied. Indonesia must always support every struggle for independence, whichever it may be; the strengthening of Afro-Asian solidarity should be the *principal part* of the independent and active foreign policy of Indonesia, a policy which is anti-imperialist and anti-colonialist; Afro-Asian organizations such as the Afro-Asian Islamic Organization should be strengthened. This is in conformity with the firm policy of Indonesia in respecting and applying the ten principles of *Bandung*." David Kimche, *The Afro-Asian Movement: Ideology and Foreign Policy of the Third World* (New York: Halsted, 1973), 230.

39. Robinson, *Dark Side of Paradise*, 298.

40. The attempt by Suharto's Golkar Party to dominate the political imagination of the Indonesian people is documented in Hans Antlöv, *Exemplary Centre, Administrative*

Periphery: Rural Leadership and New Order in Java (Richmond, UK: Curzon Press, 1995). The list of Pancasila is on 37.

41. A.W. Singham and Shirley Hune, *Non-Alignment in an Age of Alignments* (London: Zed, 1986), 173.

42. Robinson, *Dark Side of Paradise*, 306–7.

43. Quoted in Piero Gleijes, *Shattered Hope: The Guatemalan Revolution and the United States, 1944–1954* (Princeton, NJ: Princeton University Press, 1991), 193.

Tawang

1. John S. Dalvi, *Himalayan Blunder: The Curtain-Raiser to the Sino-Indian War of 1962* (Bombay: Thacker and Co., 1969), 264.

2. Neville Maxwell's *India's China War* (London: Jonathan Cape, 1970) has been indispensable for my short commentary on the war. Maxwell is more disposed to the Chinese view on the border dispute and the war (more so in his short monograph, *China's "Aggression" of 1962* [Oxford: Court Place Books, 1999]). I am less interested in the reasons for the war than in the fact of the war itself.

3. Quoted in George McTurnan Kahin, ed., *The Asian-African Conference: Bandung, Indonesia, April 1955* (Ithaca, NY: Cornell University Press, 1956), 73.

4. Ibid., 59.

5. Quoted in Maxwell, *India's China War*, 282.

6. Daphne Whittam, "The Sino-Burmese Boundary Treaty," *Pacific Affairs* 34, no. 2 (1961): 174–83; Richard Sola, *Chine-Birmaine: Histoire d'une Guerre Secrete 1949–1954* (Paris: Sudestaise, 1990).

7. Anthropologist Edmund Leach's 1954 monograph gives a vivid picture of the fluid identity of the Kachin peoples: *Political Systems of Highland Burma: A Study of Kachin Social Structures* (London: G. Bell and Son, 1954).

8. From the late 1960s, the Communist Party of Burma convened in the northeast, enjoyed Chinese support, and continued to harass the central government. By the mid-1980s aid declined. In 1989, sections of the Communist army took control over the party and signed a cease-fire with the Burmese junta, State Law and Order Restoration Council. Bertil Lintner, *The Rise and Fall of the Communist Party of Burma* (Ithaca, NY: Cornell University Southeast Asia Program Publications, 1990).

9. Kahin, *The Asian-African Conference*, 85.

10. William W. Whitson and Chen-hsia Huang, *The Chinese High Command: A History of Communist Military Politics, 1927–1971* (New York: Praeger, 1973); Harlan W. Jencks, *From Muskets to Missiles: Politics and Professionalism in the Chinese Army, 1945–1981* (Boulder, CO: Westview Press, 1982).

11. Quoted in Maxwell, *India's China War*, 183. In 1953, the historian B.S.N. Murti pointed out that India needed an army to foster a "psychology of peace, keeping her armed strength to the minimum level consistent with her basic defense requirements." B.S.N. Murti, *Nehru's Foreign Policy* (New Delhi: Beacon Information and Publications, 1953), 35.

12. The details are in Raju G.C. Thomas, *Indian Security Policy* (Princeton, NJ: Princeton University Press, 1986).

13. The absurdity of it all is that neither knew very much about the area they held in dispute. The Chinese wanted control over an area they knew as Wu Je, which the Indians called Barahoti. On July 18, 1955, the Indians sent a note to the Chinese, saying, "We are not aware of the exact location of Wu Je." *Notes, Memoranda, and Letters Exchanged, and*

Agreements Signed between the Government of India and China, 1959–1962 (White Paper) (New Delhi: Ministry of External Affairs, 1962), 1:13. In November 1958, the Chinese admitted that they had "not yet undertaken a survey of China's boundary." Ibid., 3:47.

14. Mingke Wang, "The Ch'iang of Ancient China through the Han Dynasty: Ecological Frontiers and Ethnic Boundaries" (PhD diss., Harvard University, 1992); Ainslie Embree, "Frontiers into Boundaries: The Evolution of the Modern State," in *Imagining India: Essays on Indian History* (New Delhi: Oxford University Press, 1989).

15. F.M. Bailey and H.T. Morshead, *Report on an Exploration of the North-East Frontier* (Simla, India: Government Press, 1914); F.M. Bailey, *No Passport to Tibet* (London: Travel Book Club, 1957).

16. Christoph von Fürer-Haimendorf, *Himalayan Barbary* (London: John Murray, 1955).

17. N. Sarkar, "A Historical Account of Tawang Monastery," in *Encyclopedia of India and Her States, Vol. IX: North-East India*, ed. Verinder Grover and Ranjana Arora (New Delhi: Deep and Deep, 1996).

18. Matthew Edney, *Mapping an Empire: The Geographical Construction of British India, 1765–1843* (Chicago: University of Chicago Press, 1997).

19. West Africa is an excellent example of how the wiles of colonialism carved up peoples who speak kindred African languages, but who now are divided by their European heritages. In the fourteenth century, Sundiata Keita established the Mali kingdom from the Atlantic coast to today's Nigeria. Because of the low population density of the African continent, the states had a greater interest in the control of population movement rather than control over land; land remained limitless, while people were few. Jeffrey Herbst, *States and Power in Africa: Comparative Lessons in Authority and Control* (Princeton, NJ: Princeton University Press, 2000). When the Portuguese came to the shores of the empire a few hundred years later, they established forts along the coast to facilitate their trade in goods and later people (such as in today's Guinea-Bissau and Cabo Verde). In the late 1600s, the British settled at the mouth of the Gambia River (some scholars suggest that the name comes from *Cambio*, the Portuguese word for trade/money). In their scuffles with the French over West Africa, the British seized the river and its environs, while the French held the area around the river. The river becomes today's Gambia, a sliver of a nation carved out of the former French colony of Senegal. At the Berlin Conference of 1885, the European powers and the United States agreed on their respective "spheres of influence" on the continent, with each of them to take possession of generous tracts of the continent based not so much on the historical development of regions and markets but the expectation of resources and their proximity to the coasts (for transshipment). The logic of African history would be secondary to the rationale of capitalist development in the paler nations. Almost half of the borders drawn by colonial rulers in the late nineteenth century came in straight lines—an indication that colonial efficiency and security had a greater role in the creation of the boundary than any other logic. Kenneth Barbour, "A Geographical Analysis of Boundaries in Late-Tropical Africa," in *Essays in African Population*, ed. K.M. Barbour and R.M. Prothero (London: Routledge, 1961). The British action over Gambia denied Senegal access to the river, which had been a British colonial possession and is now the lifeline of the groundnut economy that sustains it. When the groundnut prices fell in the 1970s and 1980s, the Senegalese and the Gambians began to talk about a confederation, but "national pride" and entrenched power bases held them back. Details on the linguistic and cultural divisions are available in several essays in A.I. Asiwaju, ed., *Partitioned Africans: Ethnic Relations across Africa's International Boundaries, 1884–1984* (New York: St. Martin's Press, 1985), such as Ade Adefuye, "The Kakwa of Uganda and Sudan," Bawuro Barkindo, "The Mandara Astride the Nigeria-Cameroon Boundary," and

from where I got most of the information on Senegambia, F.A. Renner, "Ethnic Affinity: Partition and Political Integration in Senegambia."

20. For centuries, the region between England and Scotland was known as "no-man's-land," the "Debatable Land," and the "liberties." Moss-troopers and freebooters, clans such as the Armstrongs and Maxwells, fought over the area outside the ambit of an established state. Alastair J. MacDonald, *Border Bloodshed: Scotland and England at War, 1369–1403* (East Linton, UK: Tuckwell Press, 2000). A similar story might be told of the border between France and Spain. Peter Sahlins, *Boundaries: The Making of France and Spain in the Pyrenees* (Berkeley: University of California Press, 1989).

21. Anthony Smith's analysis takes the European nationalists' claims of ethnic unity as their ground for political action at face value. Anthony Smith, *The Ethnic Origins of Nations* (Oxford: Blackwell Publishers, 1998).

22. Eric Hobsbawm is right to distinguish between the "revolutionary-democratic" nationalism of the French Revolution and like movements of the early nineteenth century and the much later ethno-linguistic nationalism. Eric Hobsbawm, *Nations and Nationalism since 1780* (Cambridge: Cambridge University Press, 1990). I believe, however, that despite the professions of the revolutionary democrats and the liberals, the states they created as the century wore on had a distinctly ethno-linguistic cast. Nation building, which followed the revolutions of the agitators, had an ethno-nationalist dynamic. For the later period, see Eugen Weber, *Peasants into Frenchmen: The Modernization of Rural France, 1870–1914* (Palo Alto, CA: Stanford University Press, 1976). The European nation-state did not take as its goal the creation of an ethno-linguistic state but assumed an a priori unity between an ethnic community and its ethnic state (the *Staatsvolk*). I have inverted Walker Connor's erroneous formulation, "A Nation is a Nation, is a State, is an Ethnic Group is a . . . ," *Ethnic and Racial Studies* 1, no. 4 (1978): 382. The problem of the ethnic minority that became dramatic in Nazi Germany already had its seeds in the idea of ethno-nationalism; most European nation-states had their own version of the "Jewish Question," among other such dilemmas about minorities. Furthermore, border regions between the so-called homogeneous nations became sites of dispute not on security or resource terms but on the basis of ethnicity: the Franco-German dispute over Alsace-Lorraine, the Czech-German dispute over the Sudetenland, and the Italian-Austro-Hungarian dispute over the Trieste-Trentino-Dalmatia region are examples of major border dilemmas. The Italian border dilemma provides an important category for analysis: irredentism. In 1878, the Irredentist political party emerged in the borderlands beside the Austro-Hungarian Empire to demand that Italy claim its "unredeemed land" (*terra irredenta*), to redeem the "natural" boundaries of the Italian nation (the movement it spawned, Italia Irredenta, pushed Italy into World War I. Naomi Chazan, ed., *Irredentism and International Politics* [Boulder, CO: Lynne Rienner, 1991]).

23. Prakash Karat, *Language and Nationality Politics in India* (Bombay: Orient Longman, 1973).

24. Soong Ch'ing-ling, *Good Neighbours Meet: Speeches in India, Burma, and Pakistan* (Peking: Foreign Languages Press, 1956), 21.

25. *Notes, Memoranda, and Letters*, 1:49.

26. This critique continues the broad argument developed in Lui Shao-Chi, *Internationalism and Nationalism* (Peking: Foreign Languages Press, 1952).

27. In Tibet, the debate raged in the 1950s, with Fan Ming, the deputy secretary of the Chinese Communist Party Tibet Work Committee, leading the fight against Han chauvinism. Tsering Shakya, *The Dragon in the Land of Snows: A History of Modern Tibet since 1947* (London: Pimlico, 1999), 167.

28. Maxwell, *India's China War*, 169. The Swatantra leader's views had a respectable lineage in Indian nationalist practice. In 1936, Gandhi inaugurated the Bharat Mata (Mother India) temple on the outskirts of Varanasi. Rather than worship a Puranic god in this temple, people were urged to worship a large map of India and its regional environment. The temple is not itself significant. It is a curious instantiation of what is far more common: the frequent invocation by the new nation's government of the idea of national integrity and the sanctity of the border.

29. Quoted in Maxwell, *India's China War*, 152, 117.

30. Emile Benoit points out that military expenditure creates an environment in formerly colonized countries for foreign aid—but this is not the same as military expenditure producing either economic growth or social development. Emile Benoit, *Defense and Economic Growth in Developing Countries* (Lexington, MA: Lexington Books, 1973). An updated version of this thesis is in Michael J. Mueller and H. Sonmez Atesoglu, "Defense Spending, Technological Change, and Economic Growth in the United States," *Defense Economics* 2, no. 1 (1990): 19–27. Since this article uses the United States as its empirical base, the thesis is altered; it is more in the grain of military Keynesianism than military development. For useful arguments on the negative effect of military expenditure in the formerly colonized world, see Jürgen Brauer and J. Paul Dunne, eds., *Arming the South: The Economies of Military Expenditure, Arms Production, and Arms Trade in Developing Countries* (New York: Palgrave, 2002). See also J. Paul Dunne, "Economic Effects of Military Expenditure in Developing Countries: A Survey," in *The Peace Dividend*, ed. Nils Gleditsch et al. (Amsterdam: Elsevier, 1996); J. Paul Dunne and Nadir Mohammed, "Military Spending in Sub-Saharan Africa: Some Evidence for 1967–1985," *Journal of Peace Research* 32, no. 3 (1995): 331–43; Malcolm Knight, Norman Loayza, and Delano Villaneuva, "The Peace Dividend: Military Spending Cuts and Economic Growth," in *Policy Research Working Paper no. 1577* (Washington, DC: World Bank Policy Research Department, Macroeconomics and Growth Division and International Monetary Fund, 1996).

31. Robin Luckham, "Militarism and International Development: A Framework for Analysis," in *Transnational Capitalism and National Development: New Perspectives on Dependence*, ed. José J. Villamil (Atlantic Highlands, NJ: Humanities Press, 1979).

32. Robert S. McNamara, "The Post–Cold War World: Implications for Military Expenditure in the Developing Countries," in *Proceedings of the World Bank Annual Conference on Development Economics* (Washington, DC: World Bank, 1992).

33. Saadet Deger and Ron Smith, "Military Expenditure and Growth in Less Developed Countries," *Journal of Conflict Resolution* 27 (1983): 335–53. The new nations that spend the most on war, according to the 2000 *Human Development Report*, remain at the bottom of the table for human development indicators. The link between social and military spending is made ad nauseam in Ruth Sivard, Arlette Brauer, Lora Lumpe, and Paul Walker, *World Military and Social Expenditures 1996*, 16th ed. (Washington, DC: World Priorities, 1996).

34. On raw materials, see Helge Hveem, "Minerals as a Factor in Strategic Policy and Action," in *Global Resources and International Conflict: Environmental Factors in Strategic Policy and Action*, ed. Arthur Westing (Oxford: Oxford University Press, 1986).

35. United Nations, *The Relationship between Disarmament and Development* (New York: United Nations, 1982), 154. According to the UN Development Program, it would take only a fraction of the world's military expenditure of over $800 billion to solve the problems of education (about 0.7 percent of the military expenditure), water and sanitation (1.1 percent), and basic health as well as nutrition (1.9 percent).

36. UN General Assembly, Resolution XXVIII, December 7, 1973.

37. When the literature on the Cold War writes of the Third World as a *passive* proxy in the superpower conflict, what is missed is that just as frequently it is the darker world that invites the major powers into its own regional and geopolitical dilemmas, which are often motivated by the *active* failure of the national liberation regional agenda. While it is generally true that regional solutions often brokered by the tropical countries fail, there are also many examples of well-conceived efforts that are undermined by imperialism. An apposite instance is the lack of regard for the Shanghai Cooperation Organization, formed in 2001 by Russia, China, Kazakhstan, Tajikistan, Kyrgyzstan, and Uzbekistan to solve the "instability of Afghanistan." U.S. allies and the U.S. State Department tried to undermine the process that created the Shanghai group, mainly because this would have meant that the United States would have to surrender power in the region to Russia and China—an unthinkable result for the strategy of U.S. primacy.

38. Livio Maitan, *Party, Army, and Masses in China* (London: New Left Books, 1976), chap. 13.

39. If the 1962 Sino-Indian war bespeaks a tragedy, the 1966–67 Nigerian civil war is a calamity for the Third World. The military expansion did not only take place for reasons of transborder instability. When the idea of the nation had begun to move away from its national liberation origins and into one that would be more familiar in the European context, the dominant ethnic community (often also the dominant class or military caste) exerted its power over minorities. When Nigeria won its independence in 1960, it found itself united against Britain, but divided by the legacy of division that had been fostered by the British. Despite the multiethnic character of the country, regional differences split the national liberation movement. The north of the country, dominated by the Hausa peoples, but also home to many Ibo, supported the Nigeria Peoples' Congress, whereas the mainly Yoruba south joined the Action Group, and the National Council for Nigeria and the Cameroons represented the primarily Ibo west. With no program to address the tensions between the communities, the government fell to a group of Ibo colonels in 1966 whose partisan brief on behalf of the suppressed Ibo threatened the republic. A coup led by mainly Hausa military officers quickly led to a countercoup, as a massacre of the Ibos in the north of the country began. As thousands died and many hundreds of thousands began to move to the predominantly Ibo region of southeastern Nigeria, the leadership there seceded and proclaimed the independent republic of Biafra. But since Biafra had valuable oil fields and any secession would undermine the republic of Nigeria, a civil war broke out. During the civil war, the army expanded from a mere 10,000 to 250,000 troops. The oil revenues from the rest of the country financed this expansion, and the military became the custodian of the oil wealth. Oil would be used not for social development but for the ferocious war machine assembled by the generals to hold together a country made by colonial logic. The French military industry supplied the army, as the French government hoped to gain a foothold in the oil concession. A million people died, and many hundreds of thousands suffered from a war-driven famine. Nigeria quickly absorbed Biafra, and even with the civil war over, the army, then the largest in Africa, could not be dismantled. It became a fact of life, and as much as the Indian army, a creature of fear. Elechi Amadi, *Sunset in Biafra: A Civil War Diary* (London: Heinemann, 1973); James Oluleye, *Military Leadership in Nigeria, 1966–1979* (Ibadan, Nigeria: University Press, 1985); Ken Saro-Wiwa, *On a Darkling Plain: An Account of the Nigerian Civil War* (London: Saros, 1989).

40. Rahi Masoom Raza, *Aadha Gaon* (Delhi: Rajmakal Prakashan, 1966), 219. For a detailed analysis, see Ravi Singh, "Life during the Partition: A Literary Geographic Narrative of Rahi Masoom Raza's *Adha Gaon* and Bhishma Sahni's *Tamas*" (paper, European Association of South Asian Studies Conference, 2004).

41. Raza, *Aadha Gaon*, 254–57.

Caracas

1. Quoted in Guillermo Morón, *A History of Venezuela* (New York: Roy, 1963), 199.

2. Stephen G. Rabe, *The Road to OPEC: United States Relations with Venezuela, 1919–1976* (Austin: University of Texas Press, 1982), 49; Rómulo Betancourt, *Venezuela: Oil and Politics* (Boston: Houghton Mifflin, 1979), 56–58.

3. Quoted in Judith Ewell, *Venezuela: A Century of Change* (Palo Alto, CA: Stanford University Press, 1984), 64.

4. UN Commission for Latin America, "Economic Development in Venezuela in the 1950s," *Economic Bulletin for Latin America* 1, no. 1 (1960): 23.

5. Talton F. Ray, *The Politics of the Barrios of Venezuela* (Berkeley: University of California Press, 1969), 6.

6. For an excellent introduction, see Anthony Sampson, *The Seven Sisters: The Great Oil Companies and the World They Made* (New York: Viking, 1975).

7. In the Gulf states, such as Saudi Arabia and the various other emirates, the regimes did not hire their own into the oil industry but imported temporary workers with no political rights. Nasra Shah, "Structural Change in the Receiving Country and Future Labor Migration: The Case of Kuwait," *International Migration Review* 29, no. 4 (1995): 1000–1022; Anh Nga Longva, *Walls Built on Sand: Migration, Exclusion, and Society in Kuwait* (Boulder, CO: Westview Press, 1997).

8. Eduardo Galeano, *Open Veins of Latin America: Five Centuries of the Pillage of a Continent* (New York: Monthly Review Press, 1973), 184.

9. Quoted in Rabe, *The Road to OPEC*, 129.

10. Ibid., 120.

11. John Powell, *Political Mobilization of the Venezuelan Peasant* (Cambridge, MA: Harvard University Press, 1971), 87–94.

12. Rabe, *The Road to OPEC*, 123.

13. Daniel Yergin, *The Prize: The Epic Quest for Oil, Money, and Power* (New York: Simon & Schuster, 1991), 274–75.

14. Quoted in Sampson, *The Seven Sisters*, 85.

15. Edith Penrose, *The Large International Firm in Developing Countries: The International Petroleum Industry* (London: Allen and Unwin, 1968).

16. Prebisch was not alone. In a 1942 note on "The International Control of Raw Materials," John Maynard Keynes deplored the "frightful price fluctuations which we have learnt to accept as normal." Rather than allow this to continue, Keynes proposed an International Commodity Control Programme to create buffer stocks and defend reasonable prices. These prices must be such that they would "yield to producers a standard of living which is in reasonable relation to the general standard of the countries in which the majority of them live. It is in the interest of all producers alike that the price of a commodity should not be depressed below this level, and consumers are not entitled to expect that it should. The desire to maintain more adequate standards of living for primary producers has been the mainspring of the movement towards commodity regulation schemes in recent years, and they may still remain necessary for this purpose." John Maynard Keynes, "The International Control of Raw Materials," in *The Collected Writings of John Maynard Keynes*, ed. Donald Moggridge (Cambridge: Cambridge University Press, 1980), 27:113.

17. Quoted in Nathan Citino, *From Arab Nationalism to OPEC: Eisenhower, King Sa'ud, and the Making of US-Saudi Relations* (Bloomington: Indiana University Press, 2002), 153.

18. UNCTAD, *Handbook of International Trade and Development Statistics* (Geneva: United Nations, 1984), table 4.3D.

19. Movimento Político Ruptura (Comisión Ideológica), *El imperialism petrolero y revolución venezolana* (Caracas: Fondo Editorial Salvador de la Plaza, 1977), 2:303.

20. Quoted in Pierre Terzian, *OPEC: The Inside Story* (London: Zed, 1985), 24.

21. This is the thesis in Juan Pablo Pérez Alfonzo, *Petróleo y Dependencia* (Caracas: Síntesis Dos Mil, 1971). For details on his life, see Eduardo Mayobre, *Pérez Alfonzo* (Caracas: El Nacional, 2005).

22. For basic information on the congresses, see the three annual numbers of Arab Petroleum Congress, *Information, Observations, and Documentation* (Beirut: Lebanese and Arab Documentations Office, 1959–1961).

23. Quoted in Citino, *From Arab Nationalism*, 152–53; Terzian, *OPEC*, 25.

24. Quoted in Terzian, *OPEC*, 88–89; Stephen Duguid, "A Biographical Approach to the Study of Social Change in the Middle East: Abdullah Tariki as a New Man," *International Journal of Middle East Studies* 1, no. 1 (1970): 195–220.

25. The special relationship between the two is nicely elaborated in Abdullah Taraki, "Arab-Latin American Cooperation in the Energy Field," in *Arab-Latin American Relations: Energy, Trade, and Investment*, ed. Fehmy Saddy (New Brunswick, NJ: Transaction Books, 1983); *Vigencia del pensamiento de Juan Pablo Pérez Alfonzo* (Caracas: Academia Nacional de Ciencias Economicas, 1990). The two men were introduced by *Petroleum Week*'s dynamic correspondent Wanda Jablonski at this little-used yacht club in the suburbs of Cairo.

26. Terzian, *OPEC*, 27–28. See also Abbas Alnasrawi, *Arab Nationalism, Oil, and the Political Economy of Dependency* (Westport, CT: Greenwood Press, 1991).

27. Quoted in Terzian, *OPEC*, 54.

28. Gamal Abd al-Nasser, *Philosophy of the Revolution* (Cairo: National Publishing House Press, 1960), 61.

29. For all the important public documents, see *OPEC Official Resolutions and Press Releases, 1960–1990* (Vienna: OPEC Secretariat, 1990).

30. Quoted in Terzian, *OPEC*, 54.

31. Jere Behrman, "The UNCTAD Integrated Commodity Program: An Evalution," in *Stabilizing World Commodity Markets: Analysis, Practice, and Policy*, ed. F.G. Adams and S. Klein (Lexington, MA: Lexington-Heath, 1978).

32. Raúl Prebisch, "Two Decades After," in *UNCTAD and the South-North Dialogue*, ed. Michael Z. Cutajar (Oxford: Pergamon Press, 1985).

33. Mohammed Imady, "Patterns of Arab Economic Aid to Third World Countries," *Arab Studies Quarterly* 6 (Winter–Spring 1984); Ibrahim F.I. Shihata, *The Other Face of OPEC: Financial Assistance to the Third World* (London: Longman, 1982).

34. Quoted in Citino, *From Arab Nationalism*, 155.

35. For example, when the Seven Sisters gave the Iranians and the Saudis a price break in 1964, or when the United States reduced its import quota to benefit Venezuela in 1967. In 1960, right after the creation of OPEC, Tariqi hoped that OPEC would prevent "dumping or price wars which could result in disaster for the exporting countries." This is indeed what happened. Rabe, *The Road to OPEC*, 160.

36. Wolfgang Hein, "Oil and the Venezuelan State," in *Oil and Class Struggle*, ed. Petter Nore and Terisa Turner (London: Zed, 1980), 241–42.

37. In 1972, the Egyptian government's main spokesperson, Mohammed Heikal, said that in light of the cozy relationship between Israel and the United States, the Arab nations should use oil as a weapon. The Saudis, however, refused to allow this. During the 1973 Israeli-Arab war, when the Palestine Liberation Organization called for the suspension of crude oil exports, OPEC dithered and then offered a moderate price increase at the request of Kuwait.

38. Quoted in Rabe, *The Road to OPEC*, 180.

39. Atif A. Kubursi and Salim Mansur, "The Political Economy of Middle-Eastern Oil," in *Political Economy and the Changing Global Order*, ed. Geoffrey Underhill and Richard Stubbs (London: Macmillan, 1994); David E. Spiro, *The Hidden Hand of American Hegemony: Petrodollar Recycling and International Markets* (Ithaca, NY: Cornell University Press, 1999); Peter Gowan, *The Global Gamble: Washington's Faustian Bid for World Dominance* (London: Verso, 1999), 21–22.

40. I have worked on some of this in *Keeping Up with the Dow Joneses: Debt, Prison, Workfare* (Boston: South End Press, 2003).

41. Robert Rothstein, *Global Bargaining: UNCTAD and the Quest for a New International Economic Order* (Princeton, NJ: Princeton University Press, 1979).

42. The eighteen-clause final document had at least the creation of public cartels or producer associations, like OPEC, to transfer power to raw material producers; the creation of commodity agreements for just prices; a link or "indexation" of export prices for raw materials to prices of imported manufactured goods; sovereignty over natural resources and economic activities, including the nationalization of assets within the territory of the state; the transfer of more aid (up to 0.7 percent of the gross national product of the advanced industrial states) and technology; the reduction of tariffs in the advanced industrial states that prevent the relatively free entry of manufactures from the darker nations; and the creation of a regime for world food.

43. "Charter of Economic Rights and Duties of States," General Assembly Resolution 3281 (29), UN GAOR, 29th Session, Supplement no. 31 (1975), 50.

44. Quoted in L.S. Stavrianos, *Global Rift: The Third World Comes of Age* (New York: Morrow, 1981), 798; Christopher Gilbert, "International Commodity Agreements: An Obituary Notice," *World Development* 24, no. 1 (1996): 1–19.

45. Mayobre, *Pérez Alfonzo*, 129; Terzian, *OPEC*, 85. Juan Pablo Pérez Alfonzo, *Hundiéndonos en el exremento del Diablo* (Caracas: Editorial Lisbona, 1976).

Arusha

1. The principles are "(a) To consolidate and maintain the independence of this country and the freedom of its people; (b) To safeguard the inherent dignity of the individual in accordance with the Universal Declaration of Human Rights; (c) To ensure that this country shall be governed by a democratic socialist government of the people; (d) To co-operate with all political parties in Africa engaged in the liberation of all Africa; (e) To see that the Government mobilizes all the resources of this country towards the elimination of poverty, ignorance and disease; (f) To see that wherever possible the Government itself directly participates in the economic development of the country; (g) To see that the Government gives equal opportunity to all men and women irrespective of race, religion, or status; (h) To see that the Government eradicates all types of exploitation, intimidation, discrimination, bribery and corruption; (i) To see that the Government exercises effective control over the principal means of production and pursues policies which facilitate the way to collective ownership of the resources of this country; (j) To see that the Government co-operates with other states in Africa in bringing about African unity; (k) To see that the Government works tirelessly towards world peace and security through the United Nations Organization." Julius Nyerere, "The Arusha Declaration: Socialism and Self-Reliance," in *Freedom and Socialism: Uhuru na Ujamaa* (Dar es Salaam: Oxford University Press, 1968), 232–33.

2. Nyerere, "The Arusha Declaration," 240. In the 1950s, the bulk of the aid went to

countries that bordered the USSR and China—as a security multiplier rather than the means for the economic liberation of those parts of the world. On Soviet aid, see Elizabeth Valkenier, *The Soviet Union and the Third World: An Economic Bind* (New York: Praeger, 1983). The literature on the problems of aid is vast: David Wall, *The Charity of Nations: The Political Economy of Foreign Aid* (New York: Basic Books, 1973); William Brown and Redvers Opie, *American Foreign Assistance* (Washington, DC: Brookings Institution, 1953); Sergei Shenin, *The United States and the Third World: The Origins of the Postwar Relations and the Point Four Program (1949–1953)* (Commack, NY: Nova Science, 2000); Teresa Hayter, *The Creation of World Poverty* (London: Pluto Books, 1981).

3. Nyerere, "The Arusha Declaration," 241–42.

4. The Pearson Report notes the emphasis on the landless peasantry: Lester B. Pearson (chair, Commission on International Development), *Partners in Development: Report* (New York: Praeger, 1969), 270. The Arusha Declaration mentions the need to recognize the labor of women, who "work harder than anybody else in Tanzania." Nyerere, "The Arusha Declaration," 245.

5. I am relying on William H. Friedland, *Vuta Kamba: The Development of Trade Unions in Tangayika* (Palo Alto, CA: Hoover Institution Press, 1969); Dudley Jackson, "The Disappearance of Strikes in Tanzania: Incomes Policy and Industrial Democracy," *Journal of Modern African Studies*, no. 2 (1979): 219–51.

6. This is a classic problem of populism. For a comprehensive look at African populism, see P.L.E. Idahosa, *The Populist Dimension to African Political Thought: Critical Essays in Reconstruction and Retrieval* (London: Turnaround, 2004).

7. Jannik Boesen, Birgit Storgård Madsen, and Tony Moody, *Ujamaa: Socialism from Above* (Uppsala: Scandinavian Institute for African Studies, 1977).

8. International Bank for Reconstruction and Development, *The Economic Development of Tanganyika: Report of a Mission Organized by the International Bank for Reconstruction and Development at the Request of the Governments of Tanganyika and the United Kingdom* (Baltimore, MD: Johns Hopkins University Press, 1961).

9. J.E. Moore, "Traditional Rural Settlement," in *Tanzania in Maps*, ed. Leonard Berry (London: University of London Press, 1971).

10. On the missions, see Klaus Fiedler, *Christianity and African Culture: Conservative German Protestant Missionaries in Tanzania, 1900–1940* (Leiden, Netherlands: Brill, 1996).

11. For evidence of the potential of the smallholders, see Hans Ruthenberg, ed., *Smallholder Farming and Smallholder Development in Tanzania: Ten Case Studies* (Munich: Weltforum Verlag, 1968).

12. Helge Kjekshus, "The Tanzanian Villagization Policy: Implementational Lessons and Ecological Dimensions," *Canadian Journal of African Studies* 11, no. 2 (1977): 274.

13. René Dumont, *Tanzania Agriculture after the Arusha Declaration: A Report* (Dar es Salaam: Ministry of Economic Affairs and Development Planning, 1969), 11; and Kjekshus, "The Tanzanian Villagization Policy," 275.

14. Nyerere recognized that improvement might simply create capitalist agriculture. "The small-scale capitalist agriculture we now have is not really a danger, but our feet are on the wrong path, and if we continue to encourage or even help the development of capitalist agriculture, we shall never become a socialist state." Julius Nyerere, "Socialism and Rural Development," in *Freedom and Socialism*, 344.

15. Ibid.

16. Ibid., 351.

17. R.R. Matango, "Operation Mara: The Paradox of Democracy," *Maji Maji* 20 (1975): 17–29; Kjekshus, "The Tanzanian Villagization Policy," 280.

18. I am in broad agreement with James Scott's argument that planning must listen carefully to local knowledge and know-how, because this not only creates the social basis for mass-scale consent for the plan but also teaches the often-arrogant bureaucratic elites a thing or two about areas of human life that they know little about (such as agriculture). James Scott, *Seeing Like a State: How Certain Schemes to Improve the Human Condition Have Failed* (New Haven, CT: Yale University Press, 1998). Scott's chapter on Tanzania is useful, but does not interrogate the special Third World developmentalist reasons for high modernism.

19. World Bank Environment Department, *Resettlement and Development: The Bankwide Review of Projects Involving Involuntary Resettlement, 1986–1993* (Washington, DC: World Bank, 1994). On political displacement, see Roberta Cohen and Francis Deng, *Masses in Flight: The Global Crisis of Internal Displacement* (Washington, DC: Brookings, 1998).

20. Quoted in Stanley Dryden, *Local Administration in Tanzania* (Nairobi: East African Publishing House, 1968), 42.

21. On Algeria, see François Burgat and Michel Nancy, *Les villages socialistes de la revolution agraire algérienne, 1972–1982* (Paris: Editions du Centre national de la recherché scientifique, 1984). On Burma, see Ardeth Maung Thawnghmung, *Behind the Teak Curtain: Authoritarianism, Agricultural Policies, and Political Legitimacy in Rural Burma* (London: Kegan Paul, 2003).

22. I am led by the classic work of Issa Shivji, notably *Class Struggles in Tanzania* (New York: Monthly Review Press, 1976), whose book inspired the useful Andrew Coulson, ed., *Socialism in Practice: The Tanzanian Experience* (Nottingham, UK: Spokesman, 1979). Tanzania is not alone in Africa on this. At a 1966 seminar, Senegal's Diop noted, "The peasants are mostly illiterate, unorganized and dispersed among 12,000 villages and rural townships. Primitive forms of production and organization and the superstructure corresponding to these forms lag far behind the requirements of the modern world, owing to which the winning of the peasantry in active struggle as the natural ally of the working class will obviously be a difficult task for some time to come." To make the peasants less dispersed would mean to gather them in controlled villages, such as the ujamaa scheme. Majhemout Diop, "Structure and Position of the Working Class in Senegal," in *Africa: National and Social Revolution* (Cairo: al-Talia, 1966), 102.

23. Deborah Fahy Bryceson, "Peasant Commodity Production in Postcolonial Tanzania," *African Affairs* 81, no. 325 (1982): 557. This is also the view in Mahmood Mamdani, *Citizen and Subject: Contemporary Africa and the Legacy of Late Colonialism* (Princeton, NJ: Princeton University Press, 1996), 172–77.

24. Philip Raikes, "Ujamaa and Rural Socialism," *Review of African Political Economy* 2 (1975): 49.

25. Julius Nyerere, "After the Arusha Declaration," in *Freedom and Socialism*, 407.

26. The Communist experience in Bengal provides the best of the cultural-political approach toward land reform rather than the administrative-bureaucratic approach. As Hari Krishna Konar, the Communist minister of Land and Land Revenue, put it, "The primary task is abolition of large-scale landholding and the distribution of land to the landless. The next step would be for the Government to explain to the peasants the disadvantages of cultivating smallholdings. The peasants will then voluntarily take to collective farming. Private ownership of land will then be done away with. . . . It is impossible for the Government to solve the land problem under the present social system. The Constitution stands in the way." Nevertheless, forcible removal would be equally unproductive as would forcible collectivization. If "land and liberty" was the

slogan of the multitude, then there could be no solution to the land question without liberty. Hari Krishna Konar, *Mainstream*, June 29, 1967.

27. Bryceson, "Peasant," 558; Louise Fortmann, *Peasants, Officials, and Participation in Rural Tanzania: Experience with Villagization and Decentralization* (Ithaca, NY: Center for International Studies, Cornell University, 1980).

28. Quoted in Government of India, *Problems of the Third Plan: A Critical Miscellany* (New Delhi: Ministry of Information and Broadcasting, 1961), 49–50.

29. UN General Assembly Resolution 1526 (15), "Land Reform," December 15, 1960; UN Department of Economic Affairs, *Land Reform: Defects in Agrarian Structure as Obstacles to Economic Development* (New York: United Nations, 1951).

30. Thomas Anderson, *Matanza: El Salvador's Communist Revolt of 1932* (Lincoln: University of Nebraska Press, 1971).

31. Purshotamdas Thakurdas, J.R.D. Tata, G.D. Birla, and Shri Ram, *A Brief Memorandum Outlining a Plan for Economic Development of India* (London: Penguin, 1944), 30–31.

32. Sunil Khilnani, *The Idea of India* (New York: Farrar, Straus and Giroux, 1999), 79.

33. Arvind N. Das, "Agrarian Change from Above and Below: Bihar, 1947–78," in *Subaltern Studies II*, ed. Ranajit Guha (New Delhi: Oxford University Press, 1983), 194.

34. Renato Constantino, *The Making of a Filipino* (Quezon City, Philippines: Malaya Books, 1969), 23–24.

35. Samuel P. Huntington, *Political Order in Changing Societies* (New Haven, CT: Yale University Press, 1968), 385.

36. An informative critical history is available in Harry M. Cleaver, "The Contradictions of the Green Revolution," *American Economic Review* 62, nos. 1–2 (1972): 177–86.

37. Solon L. Barraclough, "The Legacy of Latin American Land Reform," *NACLA Report on the Americas* 28, no. 3 (November–December 1994): 19.

38. Andrew Pearse, *Seeds of Plenty, Seeds of Want: Social and Economic Implications of the Green Revolution* (Oxford: Clarendon, 1980); John Perkins, *Geopolitics and the Green Revolution: Wheat, Genes, and the Cold War* (Oxford: Oxford University Press, 1997). These transnational agricultural firms that spanned the Atlantic Ocean grew from the 1930s onward largely because of a combination of import tariffs and export subsidies—a formula that the Atlantic powers denied to the Third World. The large farmlands of the U.S. Midwest thrived on public inputs and the agglomeration of land in the hands of factory farms. The vast production of food grains allowed U.S. firms to "dump" them at cheap prices in the darker nations, whose own farmers felt pressured to move to cultivate other raw materials (misnamed as cash crops) for industrial production. The farmers in the Third World faced incredible competition for food grains, and because of a lack of import tariffs in their countries, large numbers of them shifted their cultivation away from food—which tended to make the Third World dependent on food grain export from the advanced industrial states. Or if sufficient food grains could be produced, their prices remained outside the reach of the domestic markets. Harriet Friedman, "The Political Economy of Food: A Global Crisis," *New Left Review* 197 (1993): 29–57; Harriet Friedman and Philip McMichael, "Agriculture and the State System: The Rise and Decline of National Agricultures, 1870 to the Present," *Sociologica Ruralis* 29, no. 2 (1989): 93–117.

39. These thoughts are elaborated in V.K. Ramakrishnan and Madhura Swaminathan, eds., *Financial Liberalization and Rural Credit in India* (New Delhi: Tulika, 2005).

40. Ralph Phillips, *FAO: Its Origins, Formation, and Evolution, 1945–1981* (Rome: Food and Agriculture Organization, 1981).

41. World Bank, *Poverty and Hunger: Issue and Options for Food Security in Developing Countries* (Washington, DC: World Bank, 1986).

42. Alan Rake, "Collapse of African Agriculture," *African Development* 9 (February 1975): 18.

43. For the crisis after ujamaa, see Marjorie Mbilinyi, *Big Slavery: Agribusiness and the Crisis in Women's Employment in Tanzania* (Dar es Salaam: University of Dar es Salaam, 1991).

44. Kjekshus, "The Tanzanian Villagization Policy," 281.

New Delhi

1. Tariq Ali, *The Nehrus and the Gandhis: An Indian Dynasty* (London: Picador, 1991), 226.

2. David Ottaway and Marina Ottaway, *Afrocommunism* (New York: Africana Publishing House, 1981).

3. Quoted in José U.M. Carreras, "La Sextas Conferencias de los Paises no Alienadoes, La Habana, septiembre 1979," *Revisita de Estudios Internacionales* 3 (1980).

4. The book originally appeared as Fidel Castro, *La crisis económica y social del mundo: sus repercusiones en los paises subdesarrollados* (Havana: Ediciones del Consejo de Estado, 1983), and *The World Economic and Social Crisis: Its Impact on the Underdeveloped Countries, Its Somber Prospects, and the Need to Struggle If We Are to Survive* (Havana: Publishing Office of the Council of State, 1983).

5. "Speech by Mr. S. Rajaratnam, Minister for Foreign Affairs, at the 34th Session of the United Nations General Assembly on 24th September 1979," Acc. No. 79, 0051, National Archives and Records Centre, Singapore, 2.

6. "Speech by Mr. S. Rajaratnam, Minister for Foreign Affairs, at the Opening Session of the Tenth ASEAN Ministerial Meeting Held at the Shangri-La Hotel on Wednesday, 6th July 1977," Acc. No. 77, 0057, National Archives and Records Centre, Singapore, 4.

7. "Speech by Mr. S. Rajaratnam, Minister for Foreign Affairs, at the 34th Session of the United Nations," 9.

8. Ibid., 10.

9. Quoted in A.W. Singham and Shirley Hune, *Non-Alignment in an Age of Alignments* (Chicago: Lawrence Hill, 1986), 306–7. The rest of the quote reads, "It stands for peace and the avoidance of confrontation. It aims at keeping away from military alliances. It means equality among nations, and the democratization of international relations, economic and political. It wants global cooperation for development on the basis of mutual benefit. It is a strategy for the recognition and preservation of the world's diversity."

10. NIEO, which passed in the UN General Assembly on December 12, 1974, read:

    1. Raw material producers' associations to give the primary commodity states control over the market, and therefore over prices. The terms of trade, as UNCTAD had found, favored the buyers of raw materials. This had to be reversed through the creation of buffer stocks, a generalized system of preferences for primary commodities, the reduction of tariffs in the G-7, and the reduction of the cost of transportation and insurance of these goods to their eventual markets.

    2. Creation of an international monetary policy that did not penalize the less powerful states, who had to hold their foreign exchange reserves in dollars or other "hard currency" and thereby suffered from the wiles of US monetary policy. Since the dollar had become the de facto currency of trade and reserve, US monetary policy deeply affected the Third

World. The use of devaluation to increase trade, and the growth of inflation in the G-7, particularly the US, had devastating consequences for the rest of the world. The IMF needed to review its policies to ensure that it did not operate largely or only as the insurance policy for G-7 states and their commercial banks.

3. Increased industrialization in the Third World.

4. Transfer of technology from the advanced industrial states to the rest of the world, at minimal cost.

5. Regulation and Control over the activities of global conglomerates or transnational corporations. The UN had created the UN Centre on Transnational Corporations (UNCTC) in 1974 to study the growth of these firms, to secure international treaties to regulate them, and to strengthen the capacity of the Third World to negotiate with them.

6. Promotion of cooperation among the Third World states to enable these policies to make an impact.

7. Finally, the NIEO could not be successful without a strong UN presence and with a genuine global commitment to the Charter of Economic Rights and Duties of States.

11. "The Seventh Summit opposed the intervention of ideology and politics into global economy policy." Quoted in Singham and Hune, *Non-Alignment*, 329.

12. Rajiv Gandhi, "An Overview of Non-Alignment," *Black Scholar* (March–April 1987): 39.

13. Castro, *The World Economic and Social Crisis*, p. 73.

14. Ibid., 126–28.

15. For a general treatment of the ferment before the Emergency, see Bipan Chandra, *In the Name of Democracy: JP Movement and the Emergency* (New Delhi: Penguin, 2003). For a specific study of one part of the movement, see Nandita Gandhi, *When the Rolling Pins Hit the Streets: Women in the Anti-Price Rise Movement in Maharashtra* (New Delhi: Kali for Women, 1996). For a fuller treatment of what follows in this section, see Vijay Prashad, "Emergency Assessments," *Social Scientist* 24, nos. 9–10 (September–October 1996): 36–68.

16. For more on the Emergency, see Chandra, *In the Name of Democracy*, 156–245; Emma Tarlo, *Unsettling Memories: Narratives of the Emergency in Delhi* (Berkeley: University of California Press, 2003).

17. Hubert van Wersch, *The Bombay Textile Strike, 1982–83* (New Delhi: Oxford University Press, 1992).

18. "Speech by Mr. S. Rajaratnam, Minister for Foreign Affairs, at the 34th Session of the United Nations," 5.

19. John H. Jackson, Jean-Victor Louis, and Mitsuo Matsushita, eds., *Implementing the Tokyo Round: National Constitutions and International Economic Rules* (Ann Arbor: University of Michigan Press, 1984); T.E. Ibrahim, "Developing Countries and the Tokyo Round," *Journal of World Trade Law* 12 (1978): 1–26.

20. Carol Geldart and Peter Lyon, "The Group of 77: A Perspective View," *International Affairs* 57, no. 1 (Winter 1980–81): 95–96.

21. Singham and Hune, *Non-Alignment*, 154.

22. On the role of NAM in West Asia, see my *Namaste Sharon: Sharonism and Hindutva under US Hegemony* (New Delhi: LeftWord, 2003). Even Reagan's assistant secretary of state for African affairs, Chester Crocker, opposed apartheid. Sanford Ungar and Peter Vale, "South Africa: Why Constructive Engagement Failed," *Foreign Affairs* 64, no. 2 (Winter 1985–86): 234–58.

23. Chandra Kumar, "The Indian Ocean: Arc of Crisis or Zone of Peace?" *International Affairs* 60, no. 2 (Spring 1984): 233–46.

Kingston

1. For a detailed study of the rebellions of the Jamaican working class from the abolition of slavery to the labor rebellion of 1938, see Thomas Holt, *The Problem of Freedom: Race, Labor, and Politics in Jamaica and Britain, 1832–1938* (Baltimore, MD: Johns Hopkins University Press, 1992). For a study that takes the story along, see Abigail Bakan, *Ideology and Class Conflict in Jamaica: The Politics of Rebellion* (Montreal: McGill-Queen's University Press, 1990).

2. W. Arthur Lewis's point was that given the choice of foreign and domestic capital, the latter is always better, but if there is none, then the state should control the entry of foreign capital as much as possible. W. Arthur Lewis, *The Theory of Economic Growth* (London: Allen and Unwin, 1955), is the classic text that makes the case, but it is repeated to good effect in his *The Evolution of Foreign Aid* (Cardiff: University College, 1971).

3. For all the details, see Carlton E. Davis, *Jamaica in the World Aluminum Industry, 1938–1973*, vol. 1 (Kingston: Jamaica Bauxite Institute, 1989).

4. Norman Girvan, "The Development of Dependency Economics in the Caribbean and Latin America: Review and Comparison," *Social and Economic Studies* 22, no. 1 (1973): 1–33, and *Foreign Capital and Economic Underdevelopment in Jamaica* (Kingston: Institute for Social and Economic Research, 1971). For the excellent point about the export of labor, see Paget Henry, *Caliban's Reason: Introducing Afro-Caribbean Philosophy* (New York: Routledge, 2000), 228.

5. Efrayim Ahiram, "Income Distribution in Jamaica, 1958," *Social and Economic Studies* 13, no. 3 (1964): 333–69.

6. Susanne Soederberg, "Grafting Stability onto Globalisation? Deconstructing the IMF's Recent Bid for Transparency," *Third World Quarterly* 22, no. 5 (2001): 851.

7. For two reasonable assessments, see Evelyne Huber Stephens and John Stephens, *Democratic Socialism in Jamaica: The Political Movement and Social Transformation in Dependent Capitalism* (Princeton, NJ: Princeton University Press, 1986); Fitzroy Ambursley, "Jamaica: The Demise of 'Democratic Socialism,'" *New Left Review*, no. 128 (July–August 1981): 76–87.

8. "Agreement Establishing the International Bauxite Association," Conakry, March 8, 1974, preamble and Article 3 (b).

9. Evelyne Huber Stephens and John Stephens, "Bauxite and Democratic Socialism in Jamaica," in *States versus Markets in the World System*, ed. Peter B. Evans, Dietrich Rueschemeyer, and Evelyne Huber Stephens (Beverly Hills, CA: Sage, 1985).

10. The story is detailed in Faysal Yachir, *Mining in Africa Today: Strategies and Prospects* (Tokyo: United Nations University, 1988), chap. 4. I have concentrated on bauxite, but I should at least mention the myriad of other strategies adopted by the Manley government, including the expansion of land to the landless, the creation of free secondary education, and the nationalization of much of the economic commanding heights. As Manley put it, these measures sought to move "power away from the wealthy apex towards the democratic base." Michael Manley, *Jamaica: Struggle in the Periphery* (London: Third World Media, 1982), 87.

11. Alfred Maizels, *Commodities in Crisis: The Commodity Crisis of the 1980s and the Political Economy of International Commodity Policies* (Oxford: Clarendon Press, 1992), and "The Continuing Commodity Crisis of Developing Countries," *World Development* 22, no. 11 (November 1994): 1685–95.

12. Ibrahim Elbadawi and Francis Mwega, "Can Africa's Savings Collapse Be Reverted?" in *The Economics of Savings and Growth*, ed. Klaus Schmidt-Hebbel and Luis Servén

(Cambridge: Cambridge University Press, 1999); Pierre-Richard Agénor and Joshua Aizenman, "Savings and the Terms of Trade under Borrowing Constraints" (Washington, DC: World Bank Institute, 2000).

13. Although there remains a debate over its persistence. John Cuddington, "Long-Run Trends in 26 Primary Commodity Prices: A Disaggregated Look at the Prebisch-Singer Hypothesis," *Journal of Development Economics* 39 (1992): 207–27 Paul Cashin, Hong Liang, and C. John McDermott, "How Persistent Are Shocks to World Commodity Prices?" *IMF Working Paper*, WP/99/80, 1999.

14. W. Marvin Will, "A Nation Divided: The Quest for Caribbean Integration," *Latin American Research Review* 26, no. 2 (1991): 3–37; William Demas, "The Caribbean and the New International Economic Order," *Journal of Interamerican Studies and World Affairs* 20, no. 3 (August 1978): 229–63.

15. At the Master Lecture in Venezuela (1999), Castro recalled the early decades of the Cuban Revolution: "The Soviets sold us oil. At world price, yes, to be paid in sugar, yes; at the world price of sugar, yes, but we exported our sugar to the USSR and received oil, raw materials, food, and many other things. It gave us time to build a consciousness; it gave us time to sow ideas; it gave us time to create a political culture. It gave us time! Enough time to build the strength that enabled us later to resist the most incredibly hard times." Fidel Castro, *On Imperialist Globalization* (New Delhi: Left-Word Books, 1999), 66. Janette Habel's overview of Cuban economics in the 1970s and 1980s shows that the USSR and Comecon provided insufficient assistance, and that the Warsaw states might even have bilked Cuba on the price it offered for sugar. In 1987, Castro harangued the leadership of the Soviet bloc: "A socialist country in the Third World must develop; it must not only postpone indefinitely—or even eternally—the payment of its debt, but also receive new credits and resources for its development." Quoted in Janette Habel, *Cuba: The Revolution in Peril* (London: Verso, 1991), 29.

16. Timothy White, *Catch a Fire: The Life of Bob Marley* (New York: Holt, Rinehart and Winston, 1983).

17. I'm relying on the excellent summary on the bank loans in Emma Rothschild, "Bank: The Coming Crisis," *New York Review of Books* 23, no. 9 (May 27, 1976): 16–21.

18. The roots of this go back to the IMF loan to Chile in 1956. The U.S. banks insisted on an IMF agreement so that they could not be accused of "dollar imperialism."

19. Rothschild, "Bank."

20. The first director of the IMF, the Belgian Camille Gutt, noted that devaluation "is a form of confiscation." Quoted in Anthony Sampson, *The Money Lenders* (London: Hodder and Staughton, 1981), 112.

21. Rothschild, "Bank"; United Nations, "World Exports," *Monthly Bureau of Statistics*, December 1975.

22. Atif Kubursi and Salim Mansur, "The Political Economy of Middle Eastern Oil," in *Political Economy and the Changing Global Order*, ed. Richard Stubbs and Geoffrey Underhill (Toronto: M and S, 1994); Atif Kubursi, *Oil, Industrialization, and Development in the Arab Gulf States* (London: Croom Helm, 1984).

23. Peter Körner, Gero Maass, Thomas Siebold, and Rainer Tetzlaff, *The IMF and the Debt Crisis: A Guide to the Third World's Dilemma* (London: Zed, 1986), 43.

24. For the analysis of Jamaica's accession to the IMF, I have relied on Richard Bernal, "The IMF and Class Struggle in Jamaica, 1977–1980," *Latin American Perspectives* vol. 11, no. 3 (Summer 1984): 53–82; Norman Girvan, Robert Bernal, and Wesley Hughes, "The IMF and the Third World: The Case of Jamaica, 1974–1980," *Development Dialogue* 2 (1980): 113–65.

25. For the case of Zaire, see Andrew Schoenholtz, "The IMF in Africa: Unnecessary and Undesirable Western Restraints on Development," *Journal of Modern African Studies* 25, no. 3 (1987): 420–27.

26. Körner, Maass, Siebold, and Tetzlaff, *The IMF and the Debt Crisis*, 110; Bernal, "The IMF and Class Struggle," 70.

27. Derek Gordon, "Women, Work, and Social Mobility in Post-war Jamaica," in *Women and the Sexual Division of Labour in the Caribbean* (Kingston: Consortium Graduate School of Social Sciences, 1985).

28. Joan Ross Frankson, "Higglers, Hagglers, and Empty Stomachs," *New Internationalist* 214 (December 1990); Elise LeFranc, "Petty Trading and Labour Mobility: Hagglers in the Kingston Metropolitan Area of Jamaica," in *Women and the Sexual Division of Labour in the Caribbean*, 99–132.

29. "The IMF has exerted a strong influence over developing countries by setting stiff conditions on the loans it offers. This conditionality has generally been monetarist and deflationary, obliging governments to reduce their demand for imports by curtailing overall demand—cutting back on both private and public spending. These cutbacks have often reduced consumption, investment and employment—and stifled economic growth." UN Development Program, *Human Development Report* (New York: UN Development Program, 1992), 75.

30. Mohsin Khan, "The Macroeconomic Effects of Fund-Supported Adjustment Programs," *IMF Staff Papers* 37, no. 2 (June 1990): 215.

31. Quoted in Körner, Maass, Siebold, and Tetzlaff, *The IMF and the Debt Crisis*, 129.

32. Quoted in *IMF Survey*, February 9, 1981.

33. Willy Brandt, *North-South: A Program for Survival* (Cambridge, MA: MIT Press, 1980), 216.

34. Bernal, "The IMF and Class Struggle," 71.

35. Ibid.

36. Anita M. Waters, *Race, Class, and Political Symbols: Rastafari and Reggae in Jamaican Politics* (New Brunswick, NJ: Transaction Books, 1985), 203.

37. Jamaican Labour Party, *Change without Chaos: A National Programme for Reconstruction* (Kingston: Jamaican Labour Party, 1980).

38. Cheryl Payer, *The Debt Trap* (New York: Monthly Review Press, 1974), 79.

39. Albert F. Celoza, *Ferdinand Marcos and the Philippines: The Political Economy of Authoritarianism* (Westport, CT: Praeger, 1997); Payer, *The Debt Trap*, 79.

40. William Stief, "Seaga under Siege," *Multinational Monitor* 6, no. 6 (May 31, 1985).

41. Payer, *The Debt Trap*, 217–19; Ismail-Sabri Abdala, "The Inadequacy and Loss of Legitimacy of the International Monetary Fund," *Development Dialogue* 2 (1980): 25–53.

42. Judy L. Baker, *Poverty Reduction and Human Resource Development in the Caribbean: A Cross-Country Study* (Washington, DC: World Bank, 1997), 95.

43. A Nobel laureate (Douglass North, *Institutions, Institutional Change, and Economic Performance* [Cambridge: Cambridge University Press, 1990]) and the World Bank (*Governance and Development* [Washington, DC: World Bank, 1992]) argued that the state is an integral institution for development. The World Bank report offers a justification for the adjustment of the state, but nonetheless exclaims great anxiety about the destruction of the state form itself.

44. The neoliberal state does not spell the demise of the state form, as expected by many postmodern theorists. Arjun Appadurai, *Modernity at Large: Cultural Dimensions of Globalization* (Minneapolis: University of Minnesota Press, 1996).

45. *Gleaner*, December 5, 1980.

46. Americas Watch, *Human Rights in Jamaica* (New York: Americas Watch Committee, 1986).

47. This is the assessment of both the World Bank and Jamaican sociologists. Caroline Moser and Jeremy Holland, *Urban Poverty and Violence in Jamaica* (Washington, DC: World Bank, 1997); Centre for Population, Community, and Social Change, *They Cry "Respect!": Urban Violence and Poverty in Jamaica* (Kingston: Centre for Population, Community, and Social Change, 1996).

48. Horace Campbell, *Rasta and Resistance* (Trenton, NJ: Africa World Press, 1987), 88.

49. Stephen J. Kobrin, "Sovereignty@Bay: Globalization, Multinational Enterprise, and the International Political System," and Mira Wilkins, "The History of Multinational Enterprise," *Oxford Handbook of International Business*, ed. Alan Rugman and Thoma Brewer (Oxford: Oxford University Press, 2001).

50. R.J. Barnet and R.E. Miller, *Global Reach: The Power of Multinational Corporations* (New York: Simon & Schuster, 1974), 16.

51. The problem was identified by Raymond Vernon, *Sovereignty at Bay* (New York: Basic Books, 1971).

52. In addition, institutions such as GATT and the WTO moved the state to protect the property rights and interests of foreign business. Much of this was anticipated in Samuel Huntington, "Transnational Organizations in World Politics," *World Politics* 25 no. 3 (1973): 333–68.

53. I am guided by Charles-Albert Michalet, *Le Capitalisme mondial* (Paris: PUF, 1976), and *L'enterprise plurinationale* (Paris: Dunod, 1969).

54. L.S. Stavrianos, *Global Rift: The Third World Comes of Age* (New York: Morrow, 1981), 446.

55. This is not strictly true. In 1999, UN secretary general Kofi Annan revived the idea as the UN Global Compact Program. In Davos, during the World Economic Forum, Annan announced, "I want to challenge you to join me in taking our relationship to a still higher level. I propose that you, the business leaders gathered in Davos, and we, the United Nations, initiate a global compact of shared values and principles, which will give a human face to the global market." In 2003, the United Nations produced the Draft Norms on the Responsibilities of Transnational Corporations and Other Business Enterprises, but it took much of its "values and principles" from the rather lukewarm 2000 Organization for Economic Cooperation and Development's Revised Global Codes of Conduct for multinational corporations. The main point is that the United Nations would cease to be an independent arbiter of international rules crafted by the UN General Assembly, but that it would become a "partner" with global conglomerates to "work together" to create a "platform" for "a human face to the global market." All this relies on bonhomie and good intentions. For that reason, I argue that the UNCTC's Code of Conduct is dead. What we have is something quite different.

56. Vijay Prashad, *Fat Cats and Running Dogs: The Enron Stage of Capitalism* (Monroe, ME: Common Courage Press, 2002).

57. "The ICC and Corporate Cooptation of the UN," factsheet produced by Corporate Europe for the ICC World Congress Meeting in Budapest, May 3–5, 2000.

58. Ibid.

59. Quoted in Larry Elliot, "A Bridge to Fairer World Trade," *Guardian Weekly*, June 4–10, 2004, 29.

60. Rhoda Reddock, "Women's Organizations and Movements in the Commonwealth Caribbean: The Response to Global Economic Crisis in the 1980s," *Feminist Review*, no. 59 (Summer 1998): 66–67; Beverley Anderson-Manley, "Gender and the State: A Caribbean Perspective," *Women Transforming Society* (Cambridge, MA: Radcliffe College

Press, 1991); Maxine Henry, "Women's Participation in the Social and Political Process in Jamaica in the 1970s" (Mona: University of the West Indies, 1986).

61. The World Bank heralded this sector independent of the government that works "for humanitarian or cooperative rather than commercial ends, and to relieve suffering, promote the interests of the poor, protect the environment, provide basic social services or undertake community development." "Involving Non-Governmental Organizations in the Bank-Sponsored Activities," Operational Manual Statement 14.70 of the World Bank, 1989, quoted in Paul Nelson, *The World Bank and the Non-Governmental Organizations* (New York: St. Martin's Press, 1995), 37.

62. Honor Ford-Smith, "Ring Ding in a Tight Corner: Sistren, Collective Democracy, and the Organization of Cultural Production," in *Feminist Genealogies, Colonial Legacies, Democratic Futures*, ed. M. Jacqui Alexander and Chandra Talpade Mohanty (New York: Routledge, 1997), 231. This is not an isolated example: see, on Latin America, James Petras, "Imperialism and NGOs in Latin America," *Monthly Review* 49, no. 7 (December 1997): 10–27; on Asia, Sangeeta Kamat, "The Structural Adjustment of Grassroots Politics," *Sanskriti* 7, no. 1 (October 1996); also on Asia, Ahmed Nimer, "From Mobilizers to Service Providers: NGOs and the Left in Palestine," *News from Within* 13, no. 11 (December 1997); on Africa, Patrick Bond, *Against Global Apartheid: South Africa Meets the World Bank, IMF, and International Finance* (London: Zed, 2004), 201–2. For a broad theoretical take on the political assault on this grain, see Elisabeth Armstrong, "Globalization from Below: AIDWA, Foreign Funding, and Gendering Anti-Violence Campaigns," *Journal of Developing Societies* 20, nos. 1–2 (2004): 39–55.

63. The UN efforts on the women's question gained traction from the mid-1970s onward, just when the state form, the main institution to put reforms into practice, ceased to be able to do this job. The International Research and Training Institute for the Advancement of Women, the Division for Women within the UN Development Program, and eventually the UN Development Fund for Women emerged by 1975. By Beijing, the fourth UN conference in 1995, the agenda of the interstate meeting was far from that of the nongovernmental organizations.

64. "The Terra Nova Statement on the International Monetary System and the Third World," *Development Dialogue*, no. 2 (1980): 30.

65. U.S. Department of the Treasury, *United States Participation in the Multilateral Development Banks in the 1980s* (Washington, DC: U.S. Department of the Treasury, 1982), 47.

66. "The Terra Nova Statement," 30.

67. "The Arusha Initiative: A Call for a United Nations Conference on International Money and Finance," *Development Dialogue*, no. 2 (1980): 18.

68. "The Terra Nova Statement," 33.

Singapore

1. World Bank, *The East Asian Miracle: Economic Growth and Public Policy* (New York: Oxford University Press, 1993), table 1.5, 38. The political intrigue behind the drafting of this report is well documented in Robert Wade, "Japan, the World Bank, and the Art of Paradigm Maintenance: 'The East Asian Miracle' in Political Perspective," *New Left Review* 217 (May–June 1996): 3–36. For a close analysis of its ahistorical claims, see Sanjaya Lall, "The East Asian Miracle Study: Does the Bell Toll for Industrial Strategy?" *World Development* 22, no. 4 (1994): 645–54.

2. World Bank, *The East Asian Miracle*, fig. 1.3, 31.

3. If you don't want to read the original, see Kenneth Surin, "Hostage to an Unaccountable Planetary Executive: The Flawed 'Washington Consensus' and Two World Bank Reports," in *World Bank Literature*, ed. Amitava Kumar (Minneapolis: University of Minnesota Press, 2003). The second book was on Africa and structural adjustment: World Bank, *Adjustment in Africa: Reforms, Results, and the Road Ahead* (New York: Oxford University Press, 1994).

4. World Bank, *World Development Report 1992* (New York: Oxford University Press, 1992), table 1.

5. Chua Beng Huat and Tan Joo Ean, "Singapore: Where the New Middle Class Sets the Standard," in *Culture and Privilege in Capitalist Asia*, ed. Michael Pinches (London: Routledge, 1999), 151.

6. Sinnathamby Rajaratnam, "Singapore: Global City," in *The Prophetic and the Political: Selected Speeches and Writings of S. Rajaratnam*, ed. Chan Heng Chee and Obaid ul Haq (Singapore: Graham Brash, 1987). The sociologist Saskia Sassen follows Rajaratnam on this. The "global city" functions as a nodal point in the world economy. But for her the main cities are New York, London, and Tokyo. Saskia Sassen, *The Global City: New York, London, Tokyo* (Princeton, NJ: Princeton University Press, 1991).

7. Peter Schoppert, "Displacing Singapore," in *Singapore: Views on the Urban Landscape* (Antwerp, Belgium: Pandora, 1998), 98.

8. Walden Bello and Stephanie Rosenfeld, *Dragons in Distress: Asia's Miracle Economies in Crisis* (San Francisco: Institute for Food and Development Policy, 1990).

9. World Bank, *The East Asian Miracle*, 26.

10. Ibid.

11. The best two "revisionist" books are Alice Amsden, *Asia's Next Giant: South Korea and Late Industrialization* (Oxford: Oxford University Press, 1989); Robert Wade, *Governing the Market: Economic Theory and the Role of Government in East Asian Industrialization* (Princeton, NJ: Princeton University Press, 1990). The literature on Singapore is not so well developed. The most learned account is W.C. Huff, *The Economic Growth of Singapore: Trade and Development in the Twentieth Century* (Cambridge: Cambridge University Press, 1995). A clear-sighted reassessment of its development is presented in Chao-Wei Lan, "Singapore's Export Promotion Strategy and Economic Growth (1965–1984)" (working paper no. 116, Development Planning Unit, University College London, 2001); Garry Rodan, *The Political Economy of Singapore's Industrialization: National State and International Capital* (Petaling Java: Forum, 1991).

12. Glenn Melancon, *Britain's China Policy and the Opium Crisis: Balancing Drugs, Violence, and National Honour, 1833–1840* (Aldershot, UK: Ashgate, 2003); Tan Chung, *China and the Brave New World: A Study of the Origins of the Opium War (1840–42)* (Durham, NC: Carolina Academic Press, 1978); Carl Trocki, *Opium and Empire: Chinese Society in Colonial Singapore, 1800–1910* (Ithaca, NY: Cornell University Press, 1990).

13. The literature is vast. On Japan, see W.G. Beasley, *Japanese Imperialism, 1894–1945* (New York: Oxford University Press, 1991); W. Dean Kinzley, *Industrial Harmony in Modern Japan: The Invention of a Tradition* (London: Routledge, 1991); Carol Gluck, *Japan's Modern Myths: Ideology in the Late Meiji Period* (Princeton, NJ: Princeton University Press, 1985); Jon Halliday, *A Political History of Japanese Capitalism* (New York: Monthly Review Press, 1975). On Korea, see Dennis McNamara, *The Colonial Origins of Korean Enterprise, 1910–1945* (Cambridge: Cambridge University Press, 1990); Martin Hart-Landsberg, *The Rush to Development: Economic Change and Political Struggle in South Korea* (New York: Monthly Review Press, 1993; Chong-Sik Lee, *The Politics of Korean Nationalism* (Berkeley: University of California Press, 1963); Gi-Wook Shin,

Peasant Protest and Social Change in Colonial Korea (Seattle: University of Washington Press, 1996). For a useful summary, see Bruce Cumings, "The Origins and Development of the Northeast Asian Political Economy: Industrial Sectors, Product Cycles, and Political Consequences," *International Organization* 38, no. 1 (1984): 1–40.

14. On Singapore, see Lee Kuan Yew (the British left behind "an administration that worked"), *Social Revolution in Singapore* (Singapore: Government Printing Office, 1967), 2. For Taiwan and Korea, see the assessment of Adrian Leftwich, "Bringing Politics Back In: Towards a Model of the Developmental State," *Journal of Development Studies* 31, no. 3 (1995): 410.

15. The Pacific Rim story is a far better database for Bill Warren's theories than the rest of Asia or Africa. Bill Warren, *Imperialism: Pioneer of Capitalism* (London: Verso, 1980).

16. People's Action Party, *The Tasks Ahead: PAP's Five-Year Plan, 1959–1964* (Singapore: Petir, Organ of the PAP, 1959).

17. Rodan, *The Political Economy of Singapore's Industrialization*, 71–72.

18. Goh Keng Swee's theory is laid out in *The Economics of Modernization and Other Essays* (Singapore: Asia Pacific Press, 1972), and *The Practice of Economic Growth* (Singapore: Federal Publications, 1977). See also Robert Wade, *Governing the Market: Economic Theory and the Role of Government in East Asian Industrialization* (Princeton, NJ: Princeton University Press, 1990).

19. "Transcript of a Press Conference Given by the Prime Minister of Singapore, Mr. Lee Kuan Yew, at Broadcasting House, Singapore, at 1200 hours on Monday, 9th August 1965," Acc. No. 1ky/1965/1ky0809b.doc, National Archives and Records Centre, Singapore, 21.

20. Lee continued, "Singapore does not have a Malay Raja, nor a Chinese Raja nor an Indian Raja. Although Inche Khir Johari has insinuated that PAP has a Raja, Rajaratnam." "Press Conference of the Singapore Prime Minister, Mr. Lee Kwan Yew, with Malay Journalists at the Studio of TV Singapura on Wednesday, 11th August 1965," Acc. No. 1ky/1965/1ky0811a.doc, National Archives and Records Centre, Singapore, 2.

21. "The Jodidi Lecture: Addess by Singapore's Prime Minister Mr. Lee Kuan Yew at Lowell Lecture Hall, Harvard University, Wednesday, 4th December 1968," Acc. No. 1ky/1968/1ky1204.doc, National Archives and Records Centre, Singapore, 15, 16, 24.

22. "Transcript of Speech Made by Prime Minister Mr. Lee Kuan Yew at the Kampong Glam Branch of the PAP on 2nd January 1966," Acc. No. 1ky/1966/1ky0102a.doc, National Archives and Records Centre, Singapore, 1.

23. "National Day Message from the Minister for Foreign Affairs, Mr. S. Rajaratnam," Acc. No. 66.0026.281, National Archives and Records Centre, Singapore, August 8, 1966.

24. For more analysis on this dampened middle class, see David Martin Jones and David Brown, "Singapore and the Myth of the Liberalizing Middle Class," *Pacific Review* 7, no. 1 (1994): 79–88.

25. Saw Swee-Hock and Aline K. Wong, *Adolescents in Singapore: Sexuality, Courtship, and Family Values* (Singapore: Singapore University Press, 1981); Lily Kong, Martin Perry, and Brenda Yeoh, *Singapore: A Developmental City* (New York: Wiley, 1997), 6.

26. Fareed Zakaria, "Culture Is Destiny: A Conversation with Lee Kuan Yew," *Foreign Affairs* 73, no. 2 (March–April 1994): 109–26.

27. "Transcript of a Press Conference Given by the Prime Minister of Singapore, Mr. Lee Kuan Yew, at Broadcasting House, Singapore, at 1200 hours on Monday, 9th August 1965," Acc. No. 1ky/1965/1ky0809b.doc, National Archives and Records Centre, Singapore, 27–28.

28. M. Rajendran, *ASEAN's Foreign Relations: The Shift to Collective Action* (Kuala Lumpur: Arenabuku sdn. bhd., 1985), 156. At a G-77 meeting in Arusha, in February

1979, Singapore's senior minister of state Suppiah Dhanabalan told the Third World, "Although Singapore itself is a resource-scarce, net-importing developing country, we join our fellow developing countries in wanting the early establishment of the Integrated Programme for Commodities. As a developing country itself, Singapore shares the needs and aspirations of other developing countries and we realize that the Common Fund is a proposal which will benefit immensely all developing countries." Rajendran, *ASEAN's Foreign Relations*, 159.

29. Lee Kuan Yew, *From Third World to First: The Singapore Story, 1965–2000* (New York: HarperCollins, 2000), 174.

30. Economic Intelligence Unit, *Quarterly Economic Review: Malaysia, Singapore, and Brunei* (London: Economic Intelligence Unit, 1970), 11; Soon Teck-Wong and C. Suan Tan, *The Lessons of East Asia; Singapore: Public Policy and Economic Development* (Washington, DC: World Bank, 1993), xi.

31. Taiwan (Kaohsiung) and South Korea (Masan) led the way in the creation of EPZs.

32. George T. Crane, *The Political Economy of China's Special Economic Zones* (Armonk, NY: Sharpe, 1990); Won Sun Oh, *Export Processing Zones in the Republic of Korea: Economic Impact and Social Issues* (Geneva: International Labor Organization, 1993); Sébastien Dessus, Jia-Dong Shea, and Mau-Shah Shi, *Chinese Taipei: The Origins of the Economic "Miracle"* (Paris: Development Centre of the Organisation for Economic Cooperation and Development, 1995).

33. For a broader theoretical analysis of the role of gender and the New International Division of Labor, see Maria Mies, *Patriarchy and Accumulation on a World Scale: Women in the International Division of Labor* (London: Zed, 1986); June Nash and Maria Patricia Fernandez-Kelly, eds., *Women, Men, and the International Division of Labor* (Albany: State University of New York Press, 1983).

34. Sociologist Immanuel Wallerstein argues that "East Asia has been the great beneficiary of the geographical restructuring of this Kondratieff B-phase" in *The End of the World as We Know It* (Minneapolis: University of Minnesota Press, 1999), 37.

35. Linda Lim and Eng Fong, *Trade, Employment, and Industrialization in Singapore* (Singapore: International Labor Organization, 1986), 17–18.

36. This is what economist Alice Amsden calls "late industrialization." Alice Amsden, "Third World Industrialization: 'Global Fordism' or a New Model?" *New Left Review* 182 (1990): 5–31; and *Asia's Next Giant: South Korea and Late Industrialization* (New York: Oxford University Press, 1989).

37. Ichiro Numazaki, "The Export-Oriented Industrialisation of Pacific Rim Nations and Their Presence in the Global Market," in *The Four Asian Tigers: Economic Development and Global Political Economy*, ed. Eun Kim (New York: Academic Press, 1998), 80.

38. Japan had performed this role most enthusiastically for ASEAN. Rajendran, *ASEAN's Foreign Relations*, 194–95.

39. "National Day Message from the Minister for Foreign Affairs, Mr. S. Rajaratnam," Acc. No. 66.0026.281, National Archives and Records Centre, Singapore, August 8, 1966.

40. Steven Radlet, Jeffrey D. Sachs, Richard Cooper, and Barry Bosworth, "The East Asian Financial Crisis: Diagnosis, Remedies, Prospects," *Brookings Papers on Economic Activity* 1 (1998): 7.

41. The logic of this had already been identified in Naomi Katz and David Kemnitzner, "Fast Forward: The Internationalization of the Silicon Valley," in *Women, Men, and the International Division of Labor*. See also the *Silicon Run* series of videos by Ruth Carranza (1986, 1993).

42. It should be pointed out that China's rust belt in its interior is home to high rates of unemployment; that those industrial centers, if they function, do so because of the iron

rice bowl set out by the military; and that China's resilience obscures these long-term problems for its economic fundamentals. Liu Yingqiu, *Chinese Economy Is in the Second-Highest Growth Period* (Beijing: Chinese Social Sciences Publishing House, 2002); Meng Xianfan, *Chinese Women and Reform* (Beijing: Chinese Academy of Social Sciences and Chinese Women's Press, 1995).

43. Robert Wade and Frank Veneroso, "The Asian Crisis: The High Debt Model versus the Wall Street-Treasury-IMF Complex," *New Left Review* 228 (March–April 1998): 9.

44. The work of Fred Bergsten is at the center of this: "APEC and World Trade: A Force for Worldwide Liberalization," *Foreign Affairs* 73, no. 3 (May–June 1994): 20–26;"The Case for APEC: An Asian Push for World-Wide Free Trade," *The Economist*, January 6, 1996, 41; and "Globalizing Free Trade," *Foreign Affairs* 75, no. 3 (May–June 1996): 105–20. The work of Bagong Alyansang Makabayan (BAYAN) is a direct contradiction to Bergsten, and BAYAN's protests in Manila made it clear that trade liberalization would be a disaster for the nations and peoples of East Asia. The collapse came as no surprise to them. See Bello and Rosenfeld, *Dragons in Distress*.

45. François Godement, *The Downsizing of Asia* (London: Routledge, 1999), 93–94. The best analyst of the Asian financial flu is Kwame Sundaram Jomo, *Tigers in Trouble: Financial Governance, Liberalisation, and Crises in East Asia* (London: Zed, 1998), and his useful edited collection *Paper Tigers in Southeast Asia? Behind Miracle and Debacle* (Basingstoke, UK: Macmillan, 2001).

46. Kuan-Hsing Chen, "America in East Asia: The Club 51 Syndrome," *New Left Review* 12 (November–December 2001): 75.

47. The tendency toward an "Americanization" of the elite vision is detected in Singapore as well. Michael Barr, "Beyond Technocracy: The Culture of Elite Governance in Lee Hsien Loong's Singapore," *Asian Studies Review* 30, no. 1 (2006): 1–18.

48. "Speech by Prime Minister Lee Hsien Loong at the NUS Society Lecture, 19th March 2005," National Archives and Record Centre, Singapore.

49. See Lionel Jospin, *Le monde comme je le vois* (Paris: Gallimard, 2005).

50. In this regard, I found Benjamin Barber's suggestions for "a civic nexus across all boundaries" and the creation of a "civic bulletin board across national boundaries" to be truly naive; those who can access such technologies have little interest in the type of global democratic institutions that he imagines. Without an engagement with the state, which remains the mainstay of local democracy, such fantasies will be deeply elitist. Benjamin Barker, *McWorld vs. Jihad: Terrorism's Challenge to Democracy* (New York: Ballantine, 1995), 277, 287.

51. Quoted in Godement, *The Downsizing of Asia*, 107. See also Syed Hussein Alatas, *Corruption and the Destiny of Asia* (Selangor Darul Ehsan, Malaysia: Prentice Hall, 1999), 112–13. "Asian society never puts the individual values above the societal values. Societies are always more important than individuals. I think that this value will save Asia from the greatest calamities." Lee Kuan Yew, *40 Nian Zhenglun Zuan: Selections from 40 Years of Political Writings* (Singapore: Lianhe Zaobao Press, 1993), 502. The South Korean democrat who would become president three years later, Kim Dae Jung, replied to Lee Kuan Yew in terms of the need for political reform in East Asia as a value that was not inimical to East Asian society but necessary to its democratic modernity. Kim Dae Jung, "Is Culture Destiny? The Myth of Anti-Democratic Values: A Response to Lee Kuan Yew," *Foreign Affairs* 73, no. 6 (November–December 1994): 189–94. The discussion of Asian values is fairly widespread in Singapore. See Seong Chee Tham, "Values and National Development in Singapore," *Asian Journal of Political Science* 3, no. 2 (December 1995): 1–14. In Asia broadly, see Khoo Boo Teik, "The Value(s) of a Miracle: Malaysian and Singaporean Elite Constructions of Asia," *Asian Studies Review* 23, no. 2 (June 1999): 181–92.

52. One could argue, as Michael Backman suggests, that these value are not ancient Singaporean but actually Victorian. Michael Backman, "Asians and Victorian Values," *Far Eastern Economic Review*, March 30, 2000, 32.

Mecca

1. Quoted in "Islam against Nationalism," *The Economist*, June 2, 1962, 903; Abdullah M. Sindi, "King Faisal and Pan-Islamism," in *King Faisal and the Modernization of Saudi Arabia*, ed. Willard Beling (London: Croom Helm, 1980), 186.

2. Sindhi, "King Faisal," 191.

3. I am mindful of Natana J. Delong-Bas's detailed account of the complexity of Sheikh Muhammed ibn 'Abd al-Wahhab and how she shows that only after his death did his interpretation of Islam become reactionary. My own interest in Wahhabi Islam is not in its original state but in what it becomes by the 1950s and onward. Natana J. Delong-Bas, *Wahhabi Islam: From Revival and Reform to Global Jihad* (New York: Oxford University Press, 2004).

4. Gerald de Gaury, *Faisal: King of Saudi Arabia* (London: Barker, 1966), 166.

5. Philip Jenkins, *The Next Christendom: The Coming of Global Christianity* (New York: Oxford University Press, 2002); Harvey Cox, *Fire from Heaven: The Rise of Pentecostal Spirituality and the Reshaping of Religion in the Twenty-First Century* (Reading, MA: Addison-Wesley, 1996); Toyin Falola, *Violence in Nigeria: The Crisis of Religious Politics and Secular Ideologies* (Rochester, NY: University of Rochester Press, 1998); David Laitin, "The Shari'ah Debate and the Origins of Nigeria's Second Republic," *Journal of Modern African Studies* 20, no. 3 (1982): 411–30. Less dramatic, because of the lack of an effective world Jewish or world Hindu population, has been the rise of settler Judaism (for Israel) and Hindutva (for India). I am interested in Juan Sepulveda's notion of "indigenous pentecostalism," where Chilean *indigenistas* threw off the elitist Catholic and Methodist clergy for a spiritual experience that they could define and control. Whereas this is perhaps true in an institutional sense, my analysis follows the promotion of religious thought in opposition to, rather than in conversation with, secular anticolonial thought. Juan Sepulveda, *De peregrinos a ciudadanos: breve história del cristianismo evangélico en Chile* (Santiago: Fundación Konrad Adenauer, Facultad Evangélica de Teologia, Comunidad Teologia Evangélica, 1999).

6. The basic facts are in Georges Nzongola-Ntalaja, *The Congo from Leopold to Kabila: A People's History* (London: Zed, 2002).

7. Madawi al-Rasheed, *A History of Saudi Arabia* (Cambridge: Cambridge University Press, 2002), 114–16.

8. Sarah Yizraeli, *The Remaking of Saudi Arabia* (Tel Aviv: Tel Aviv University Press, 1997), 169.

9. Mustafa Mahmud, *Marxism and Islam* (Cairo: n.p., 1984), 21. The Iranian sociologist Ali Shariati is equally disposed toward an engagement with Marxism, even as he vehemently opposes Communism. Ali Shariati, *Marxism and Other Western Fallacies* (Berkeley: Mizan Press, 1980). Shariati's populism is stark, for instance, when he notes, "Whenever in the Qur'an social matters are mentioned, Allah and *al-nas* [the people] are virtually synonymous." Ali Shariati, *Islam and Revolution* (Berkeley: Mizan Press, 1981), 55.

10. Nasser was not averse to the incorporation of Islam into his agenda. "Our religion is a socialist religion," he said. "In the Middle Ages, Islam successfully implemented the first socialist experience in the world." Quoted in Paul Balta and Claudine Rulleau, *La vision Nassérienne* (Paris: Sindbad, 1982), 131.

11. David Long, *The Hajj Today* (Albany: State University of New York Press, 1979), 76.

12. al-Rasheed, *A History of Saudi Arabia*, 107.

13. Saïd K. Aburish, *Nasser: The Last Arab* (New York: Thomas Dunne Books, 2004), 146; Alexei Vassiliev, *The History of Saudi Arabia* (London: Saqi Books, 1998), 336–37; Saïd K. Aburish, *The Rise, Corruption, and Coming Fall of the House of Saud* (New York: St. Martin's Press, 1994).

14. Quoted in Vassiliev, *The History of Saudi Arabia*, 357.

15. Aburish, *The Rise*, 130.

16. Quoted in Douglas Little, *American Orientalism: The United States and the Middle East since 1945* (Chapel Hill, NC: University of North Carolina Press, 2002), 61, 63–65.

17. In 1953, the CIA returned the Shah to the Peacock Throne. In Jordan, the CIA assisted King Hussein in 1957 to overthrew his country's popular cabinet (filled with Arab socialists and Communists, many of whom were Nasserites). When Lebanon fell to the nationalist tsunami, the CIA gave support and eventually the U.S. Marines landed to take charge of Beirut. All this was the outcome of the Eisenhower Doctrine. Salim Yaqub, *Containing Arab Nationalism: The Eisenhower Doctrine and the Middle East* (Chapel Hill: University of North Carolina Press, 2004); John Badeau, *The American Approach to the Arab World* (New York: Harper and Row, 1968).

18. Wilbur Crane Eveland, *Ropes of Sand: America's Failure in the Middle East* (London: W.W. Norton, 1980), 244; Aburish, *The Rise*, 161.

19. Ethan Nadelmann is quite possibly right to suggest that the Saudis and the Jordanian monarchy conjured up the WML to circumvent a U.S. overture to the Egyptian government. Ethan Nadelmann, "Setting the Stage: American Policy toward the Middle East, 1961–1966," *International Journal of Middle East Studies* 14 (1982): 448.

20. Georges de Bouteiller, "Le Ligue Islamique mondiale: une institution tentaculaire," *Défense Nationale* 37 (February 1981): 73–80; Jacob Landau, *The Politics of Pan-Islam: Ideology and Organization* (Oxford: Clarendon Press, 1990); Mushirul Haq, "The Rabitah: A New Tradition in Panislamism," *Islam and the Modern Age* 9, no. 3 (1978): 55–66; and Reinhard Schulze, *Islamisher Internationalismus im 20. Jahrhundert: untersuchungen zur geschichte der Islamischen Weltliga (Mekka)* (Leiden, Netherlands: Brill, 1990).

21. For the story of the first congress, see Arnold J. Toynbee, "The Proclamation of Sultan Abdul-Aziz bin Sa'ud as King of the Hijaz and the Islamic Congress at Mecca (1926)," in *Islam and International Relations*, ed. J. Harris Proctor (New York: Frederick Praeger, 1965).

22. James P. Piscatori, "Islamic Values and National Interest: The Foreign Policy of Saudi Arabia," in *Islam in Foreign Policy*, ed. Adeed Dawisha (Cambridge: Cambridge University Press, 1983), 40.

23. Benedict Anderson, *Imagined Communities: Reflections on the Origin and Spread of Nationalism* (London: Verso, 1991), 36.

24. Quoted in Sindhi, "King Faisal," 188.

25. The ibn Saud clan posed as chiefs of Islam at home, as they became famously mischief men abroad: the Saudi royals "should have more fear of God," said one of the Islamists. "On the one hand they pray but in the other they pick up the bottle." Mai Yamani, *Changed Identities: The Challenge of the New Generation in Saudi Arabia* (London: Royal Institute for International Affairs, 2000), 39.

26. Vassiliev, *The History of Saudi Arabia*, 396.

27. Ibid., 454; Fareed Mohamedi, "The Saudi Economy: A Few Years till Doomsday," *Middle East Report* 185 (November–December 1993): 14–17.

28. For the roots of the religious police, see al-Rasheed, *A History of Saudi Arabia*, 49–58.

For their modern manifestation and links to the radical Islamist rhetoric and institutions, see ibid., 153–55; Ayman al-Yassini, *Religion and State in the Kingdom of Saudi Arabia* (Boulder, CO: Westview Press, 1985), 70.

29. Quoted in Sindhi, "King Faisal," 193.

30. Quoted in *Kabul Times*, May 28, 1978.

31. The story of the formation of this alliance is in Steve Coll, *Ghost Wars: The Secret History of the CIA, Afghanistan, and Bin Laden, from the Soviet Invasion to September 10, 2001* (New York: Penguin, 2004).

32. Quoted in "Oui, la CIA est entreé en Afghanistan avant les Russes," *Le Nouvel Observateur*, January 15–21, 1998.

33. For an excellent appraisal, see Stephen Kotkin, *Steeltown USSR: Soviet Society in the Gorbachev Era* (Berkeley: University of California Press, 1991).

34. Thane Gustafson, *Crisis amid Plenty: The Politics of Soviet Energy under Brezhnev and Gorbachev* (Princeton, NJ: Princeton University Press, 1989).

35. Abdul Hameed Nayyar, "Madrasa Education," in *Education and the State: Fifty Years of Pakistan*, ed. Pervez Hoodbhoy (Karachi, Pakistan: Oxford University Press, 1998), 226.

36. Quoted in Owen Bennett-Jones, *Pakistan: Eye of the Storm* (New Delhi: Penguin, 2002), 260.

37. In Sudan, for instance, the WML enabled the establishment of the Islamic Charter Front (1964) of Hasan al-Turabi, later the leader of the Sudanese Muslim Brotherhood. John Voll, "The Evolution of Islamic Fundamentalism in Twentieth-Century Sudan," in *Islam, Nationalism, and Radicalism in Egypt and Sudan*, ed. Gabriel Warburg and Uri Kupferschmidt (New York: Praeger, 1983).

Conclusion

1. "Address by Mwalimu Julius K. Nyerere, Chairman of the South Commission, at the Commission's Inauguration Ceremony, 2nd October 1987" (Geneva: South Centre, 1987).

2. World Bank, *World Development Report 2000/2001: Attacking Poverty* (New York: Oxford University Press, 2001), 51.

3. *The Challenge of the South: The Report of the South Commission* (New York: Oxford University Press, 1990), 148.

4. The fifteen are Algeria, Argentina, Brazil, Egypt, Indonesia, India, Jamaica, Malaysia, Mexico, Nigeria, Peru, Senegal, Venezuela, Yugoslavia, and Zimbabwe.

5. Quoted in Kripa Sridharan, "G-15 and South-South Cooperation: Promise and Performance," *Third World Quarterly* 19, no. 3 (September 1998): 357–74.

6. Quoted in ibid.

7. *The Challenge of the South*, 274–75.

INDEX

Note: Page numbers in *italics* refer to illustrations.

Aadha Gaon (*Half a Village*) (Raza), 174–75

Abbas, Ferhat, 124, 292n4

Abd al-Aziz, Prince Nawwaf ibn, 265

Abdulaziz, Prince Talal bin "Red Prince," 265–66

Abdul-Rahman, Aisha, 53–55, 58, 60

Aborigines Protection Society, 18

Acheson, Dean, 48, 71–72

Advani, L.K., 218

Afghanistan, 170, 274; CIA in, 272, 273; jihadist groups in, 273; land reform in, 272; Marxist control of, 209, 271–72; Soviet invasion of, 210, 272–73

'Aflaq, Michel, 159

Africa: colonialization of, 3–4, 9, 13, 17–19, 82, 324n19; guerrilla warfare in, 111, 112, 309n32; independent states in, 33; Marxism-Leninism in, 209; military coups in, 138, 144–45, 147; and *négritude*, 81, 82; NEPAD, 280–81; postcolonial nation-building in, 128–29, 145; single-commodity nations in, 227; unity for, 18, 23–24. *See also specific nations*; Third World

African National Congress, 144

Afro-Asian Conference, Bandung (1955). *See* Bandung conference

Afro-Asian movement, formation of, 15

Afro-Asian People's Solidarity Conference (1957), 52–53, 87

Afro-Asian Women's Conference, Cairo (1961), xvi, 50, 57–61, 304–5n43

Afro-Malagasy Union, 70

Ahluwalia, Montek, 212

Aidit, Dipa Nusantara, 152–54, 162

Ait Ahmed, Hocine, 124

Alawi, Mortesa, 21

Al-e Ahmad, Jalal, 78–81, 88–89, 90–92, 303n20

Algeria: Amis du Manifeste et de la Liberté, 4–5; boundary wars, 167; Charter of Algiers (1964), 123, 126, 128, 131; Communist Party in, 120–21, 123, 130, 158, 315n38; Constitution of (1963), 123; Front de Libération Nationale (FLN) in, 5, 52, 98, 119–27, 130, 315n35; independence of, 112, 119–21; March Decrees in, 125; military coup in, 130–32, 147;

Algeria *(cont.)*
Mouvement pour le Triomphe des
Libertés Démocratiques in (MTLD),
119; NAM summit meeting in (1973),
132, 219, 254; nation-building in,
122–29; oil in, 131, 189; as one-party
nation, 123–27, 128, 131, 132; social
unrest in, 130; at war with France, 5, 6,
43, 110, 119–21
Ali, Mohammad (Albania), 319n51
Ali, Mohammed (Pakistan), 38
Ali, Tariq, 208
Allende, Salvador, 147, 240
Alliance for Progress, 134, 137, 142
Amer, Hussein Sirri, 51
Americas Watch, 238
Amin, Idi, 83
Andean Pact (1969), 70
Anderson, Benedict, 268
Anderson, Robert, 266
Anglo-Iranian Oil Company, 75
Angola: Cuban aid to, 112, 209;
independence of, 112, 210; Movimento
Popular de Libertação de (MPLA),
103; as Portuguese colony, 18
Annan, Kofi, 240–41, 339n55
Antarctic Treaty (1959), 221
APRA (Alianza Popular Revolucionaria
Americana), 26, 88
Arab League, 25, 265
Arab nations: anti-British sentiment in,
98–99; anti-nationalism in, 267–68;
armed revolutions in, 51–52, 262–63;
and Cold War, 98–100; disunity of,
24–25; Eisenhower Doctrine in, 266;
vs. Israel, 167, 188; nuclear reactors in,
160; oil in, 179–88, 263–64, 266,
269–70; and OPEC, 184–90. *See also*
Islam; *specific nations*
Arab Revolt (1916–37), 25
Arab Socialism, 52, 148, 158, 184
Aramco (Arab-American Oil Company),
183, 264, 266, 269
Arbenz Guzmán, Jacobo, 106, 137, 142
Argentina, 62–63, 66, 156, 215
'Arriyah, Rawiyah, 60
Arusha Declaration (1967), 191–93, 195, 199
Arusha Initiative (1980), 243–44

ASEAN (Association of Southeast Asian
Nations), 211, 252
Asia: colonialization of, 9, 13, 249;
culturalism in, 258–59; economic
crisis in, 255–59; global cities of,
247–48, 249, 252, 253; guerrilla
warfare in, 112–13; independent states
in, 33, 48; liberalization of financial
markets in, 256–57; military coups in,
138; "new Asia," 165–66;
technological development in, 254,
255; "Tiger" economies of, 215, 222,
245–49, 252–56; unity in, 27, 211, 252,
256; World War II in, 249. *See also*
specific nations; Third World
Asian Relations Conference (1947), 27
Asia-Pacific Economic Cooperation
meeting (1996), 256
Assadoff, Ahmed, 21
Ataturk, Kemal, 51, 84
Australia, 38, 40, 155, 280
Awan, Mohammed Akram, 273
Azam, Abdullah, 273
Azhari, Ismail el, 37
Azikiwe, Nnamdi, 23

Baghdad Pact (Central Treaty
Organization), 38, 40, 98, 99
Bailey, Frederick Markham, 169, 170
Baku, First Congress of the Peoples of
the East in (1920), 21, 156
Baldwin, Roger, 22, 29
Bali, 153, 154–56, 163, 164
Bandarnaike, Srimavo, 100
Bandung Conference (1955), 32–38,
40–50; arguments taken to UN from,
xvi; "Bandung Spirit," 45–46, 48, 50,
165; and Cold War, 39–40, 42–45,
46–47; on cultural cooperation, 45,
87–88; divided opinions in, 40–41; on
economic cooperation, 44–45, 69;
ideology crafted in, xv, xvii, 14–15, 163;
legacy of, 32, 41–42, 46, 48–49, 50, 95,
107, 162, 167, 263; non-alignment idea
born in, 46–50, 213; pro–First World
states at, 38–41, 47; Sukarno's opening
speech, 30, 33–34; U.S. attitude toward,
47–48; Zhou En-lai in, 36–37

Bangladesh, 174

Baraka, Ben, 163

Baran, Paul, 73

Barger, Thomas, 266

Barkatullah, Mohamed, 21–22

Barracks, James Russell, 266–67

Barraclough, Solon, 201

Barrientos, René, 134, 143

The Barrel of a Gun (First), 144–46

Baruch, Bernard, 7

Baruch Plan (1946), 308n22

Batista y Zaldívar, Fulgencio, 105, 108, 284n23

Bauer, Lord Peter T., 12–13

Bay of Pigs, 101, 139, 142

Baz, Shaykh 'Abd al-'Aziz ibn, 269

Belgium, colonies of, 16–19, 23

Belgrade conference (1961), xvi, *4*, 95–97, 167, 185, 308n20

Ben Bella, Ahmed, xvii, 119, *120*, 123–26, 130–31, 132, 306n6

Bendjedid, Chadli, 132

Berlin Conference (1884–85), 17, 324n19

Berlin Wall, 101

Bernal, Richard, 236

Bernardino, Minerva, 55

Bhagat Singh, Shaheed, 43

Bhava, Vinoba, 200

Biafra, 327n39

Bin Laden, Osama, 267, 273

Bismarck, Otto von, 17

Black, Eugene, 9, 71

Bolivia: Alliance for Progress in, 134, 137; Communist Party in, 109; elections in, 279; lack of central authority in, 136; land reforms in, 135, 136; military coup (golpe) in, 137–39, 140; Movimiento Nacionalista Revolucionario (MNR) in, 134–38; oil war of, 178; Spanish invasion of, 134–35; tin industry in, 135, 137; universal suffrage in, 135

Bonaparte, Napoléon, 3

Boudiaf, Mohammed, 123, 124

Boumédienne, Houari, 108, 123, 130–32, 158, 189, 315n35

Bourdet, Claude, 6

Bouteiller, Georges de, 267

Boutros-Ghali, Boutros, 49–50

Bowes, Wilbert, 238

Brady Plan (1989), 230

Brandt, Willy, 235

Brandt Report (1980), 235

Brazil: bauxite industry in, 226, 227; industrial output of, 215, 230; loans to, 230; military coup in, 140; women activists in, 55, 56

Bretton Woods Conference, 44–45, 68

Brijuni, Yugoslavia, 1956 conference, 95–97, 100–101, *277*

Britain: and Baghdad Pact, 38; Canton bombarded by, 41; colonies of, 9, 18–19, 23, 33, 42, 43, 66, 224, 249, 251, 324n19; Commonwealth of, 98, 100; continued imperial power sought by, 47; and Indonesia, 155; international investments by, 63; and Middle East, 25, 98–99, 263; nuclear weapons of, 42, 101; and SEATO, 38; and UN Security Council, 102; as U.S. satellite, 10, 47

Brussels, 1927 conference in. *See* League against Imperialism

Brzezinski, Zbigniew, 272

Budiardjo, Carmel, 156

Bulganin, Nicolay Aleksandrovich, 46, 97, 300n43

Bundy, McGeorge, 140, 291n54

Burma: borders of, 166–67, 169; Communist Party in, 158, 162, 323n8; independence of, 33, 49; military coup in, 162

Caballero de Castillo Ledón, Amalia, 55

Cabral, Amilcar, 103, 104, 111, 115, 129

Cairo: Afro-Asian Women's Conference in (1961), xvi, 51, 57–61, 304–5n43; Second NAM Conference in (1964), 44, 110, 221

"Call to Arms" (Farrokhzad), 77–78

Calles, Plutarco Elías, 20

Cambodia, 140, 210

Cameroon, 18

Camus, Albert, 89

Cantos General (Neruda), 149–50

Cape Verde, independence of, 112

Cárdenas, Lázaro del Rio, 14, 179–80, 313–14n21

Caribbean Community and Common Market (Caricom), 228

Carter, Jimmy, 210

Casement, Roger, 18

Castro, Fidel, xv, 105, 106, 108, 139, *206*, 210, 212–13, 221–22, 248

Castroism, 162

Central America. *See* Latin America

Césaire, Aimé, 3, 5, 6, 81, 82–84, 85, 87, 90–91

Ceylon, independence of, 33

Chad, military coup in, 147

Chapultepec Conference, Mexico City (1945), 26–27

Chasteen, John, 25

Chatterjee, Partha, 295n36

Chattopadhyaya, Virendranath, 20, 21

Chávez, Hugo, 148

Chen, Ivan, 170

Chile: Communist Party in, 151, 156; copper mines nationalized in, 240; military coup in, 140, 141, 147–48, 174; U.S. intervention in, 147

China: armed struggle as tactic of, 107; border wars of, 165–75; and Cold War, 109; Communist Party in, 9, 10, 29, 37, 153, 156, 157–58, 172; Cultural Revolution in, 37; and foreign aid, 72, 158; foreign policy changing in, 174; and Formosa/Taiwan, 37, 109, 167, 172; independence of, 33; and India, 165–75, 215; influence of, 47, 255–56; and Japan, 107, 167; Kuomintang in, 29, 35, 156, 167; nuclear weapons of, 44, 308n25; People's Liberation Army (PLA) of, 165–68; population shifts in, 197; represented at Bandung conference, 34, 36–37; represented at Brussels conference, 22; Shanghai massacre in (1928), 156; Silk Road, 87; and United Nations, 37, 102; and USSR, 10, 37, 47, 110, 166

Chinese, Maoism in, 113

Chun Doo-hwan, 251

Churchill, Winston, 7, 95

Chu Tu-nan, 87

CIA (Central Intelligence Agency): in Afghanistan, 272, 273; in Africa, 110;

anticommunism of, 164; in Cold War, 7, 133, 157; in Indonesia, 153; in Iran, 75, 76, 140, 346n17; in Latin America, 140, 142; in military coups, 140–43; and political economies, 143; in Saudi Arabia, 266–67

Cold War: arms race in, 173–74, 220; and Bandung Conference, 39–40, 42–45, 46–50; Berlin Wall in, 101; CIA in, 7, 133, 157; and disarmament, 41–44, 101, 114; East vs. West in, 7–11, 156, 278; end of, 278; foreign aid in, 72; Iron Curtain in, 7; non-aligned states in, 13, 15, 46–50, 99, 210, 213; nuclear threat in, xv–xvi, 42–44, 101, 110, 113; peaceful coexistence in, 95–96, 97, 99, 103–4, 106–7, 109; proxy armies in, 210, 211, 212, 220; regional conflicts in, 43–44, 110; and Third World, 8–11, 13, 42, 98–100, 105, 106–7, 113–14, 278, 327n37; transition of, 213; two-camp theory of, 46–49, 97, 99; and USSR, 7–8, 9–10, 37, 46–48, 109, 113, 156, 278

Colombia, 322n36

colonialism: anticolonialism, xvii, 9, 11, 12–13, 24, 29–30, 31, 33, 34, 36, 43, 127, 146, 218, 222; and cultural transformation, 91–92; economic impact of, 66, 125; end of, 85–86; and illiteracy, 89; legacy of, 8, 44, 324n19; nationalism vs., 82, 83–86, 163, 217; and nativism, 82; neocolonialism, 10, 110–11; reparations for, 66

Columbus, Christopher, 224

Communism: absolutism of, 144; adherents drawn to, 151; and anticolonialism, 9, 29–30; and Baku conference, 21; and Bandung Conference, 46–49; and Cold War, 7, 8–11, 97, 156, 210, 278; and cultural imperialism, 81; development theories of, 157–59; Marxism-Leninism, 209, 289n19, 314n30; opponents of, 151, 154, 156, 159–60, 163–64, 262; rise to power of, 37, 151, 153, 156, 157, 279

Confucianism, 258

Congo: as Belgian colony, 17–18, 23; Cuban intervention in, 108; military coup in, 140, 141, 262; postcolonial, 128, 161, 163; U.S. intervention in, 141; as Zaire, 262

Congo Free State, 17–19

Congo Reform Association, 18–19

Congress of Black Writers and Artists, 82

Congress of Democratic and Political Parties of America (1940), 26

Corrieri Hernández, Sergio, 94

Council for Mutual Economic Assistance, 185

The Crisis of Democracy (Trilateral Commission), 141

Cuba: and African nations, 108, 112, 113, 209, 310n6; armed struggle as tactic in, 107; Bay of Pigs in, 101, 139, 142; Communist Party in, 129; Constitution of, 105; debt crisis of, 210–11, 212; independence of, 211, 215, 237; popular mobilization in, 139; Revolution in, 43, 105–7, 337n15; in Soviet orbit, 72–73, 106, 210, 228; U.S. intervention in, 101, 106, 109, 236

Cuban Missile Crisis, 308n22

cultural nationalism. *See* nationalism

Cummings, Hugh S. Jr., 47

Dahomey, military coup in, 147

Dalai Lama, 170

Dalvi, John S., 165

Daneshvar, Simin, 92

Daniels, Josephus, 180

D'Arcy, William Knox, 80

Debray, Régis, 162

de Gaulle, Charles, 119

Dia, Mamadou, 302n17

Ding Ling, 88

Diop, Alioune, 3, 81–82, 83, 332n22

Discourse on Colonialism (Césaire), 3, 81

Djebar, Assia, 88

Dominican Republic, U.S. intervention in, 106, 140

Dorticós Torrado, Osvaldo, 100–101

Dostoyevsky, Fyodor Mikhaylovich, 89, 198

Dow Chemicals, 239

Draper Committee study (1959), 140

DuBois, W.E.B., 23

Dulles, John Foster, 48, 52, 98–100

Dumont, René, 195

Dutt, R.C., 297n21

Duvalier, François "Papa Doc," 106

economics: accelerated growth as goal in, 73–74; agriculture sector in, 194–96, 197, 199, 200–203, 227, 239; Asian "Tiger" nations, 215, 222, 245–49; asset stripping, 234; balance of payments deficits, 241; Brandt Report, 235; capital investment transfer, 299n35; comparative advantage in, 67; Cuban model, 225; currency markets, 256; cycle of dependency in, 68, 71, 72–74, 280; EPZs (export processing zones), 237, 248, 253, 254, 255; export-oriented, 233, 237, 240; free-market competition, 211–12, 232, 236, 299n35; G-7 and, 214–15, 219, 220, 227–29, 231, 240, 243, 244; global (*see* globalization); IMF policies (*see* IMF); import-substitution industrialization, 68, 73, 211–12, 218, 225, 233, 240, 251, 252; Keynesian development model of, 212; liberalization of financial markets, 256–57; marketing cooperative movement, 197; military power and, 141; modernization theory, 65–66, 67, 71; monetarism, 212; NAM Common Fund, 220, 280; neoliberal, 215; NIEO, 132, 163, 189, 214, 229; outsourcing jobs, 240; and politics, 213, 214, 220, 237, 242–43, 255; privatization, 281; Puerto Rican model, 225; sovereignty and cooperation in, 214; tariffs and trade barriers, 69–71, 215, 219, 232, 256, 333n38; technical issues of, 214, 239–40, 255; transnational firms, 147–48, 185, 189, 193, 201–2, 215, 227, 239–41, 252–53; wealth gap, 79–80, 209, 277

Ecuador, 140, 142–43

Eden, Anthony, 47, 52

Egypt: Anglo-French-Israeli assault on (1956), 43, 47, 52, 100; Aswan Dam in, 52, 99–100; in Cold War, 98–100; Communist Party in, 162; cultural nationalism in, 54, 87; farmers in, 200;

Egypt *(cont.)*
   Free Officers coup in, 51–52, 148, 261;
   IMF influence in, 271; military
   dictatorship in, 149; Muslim
   Brotherhood in, 148–49; Nasser in *(see*
   Nasser, Gamal Abdel); Revolution
   (1952), 148, 262; and Saudi border pact,
   263; and Suez Canal, 52, 100, 263;
   USSR aid to, 52, 149, 158; welfarism of,
   148, 183; women's rights in, 54–55,
   56–57, 60
Ehrlich, Paul, 8
Einstein, Albert, 22
Eisenhower, Dwight D., 76, 106, 140, 186,
   290n41, 310n9
Eisenhower Doctrine, 266
Enlightenment, 3, 79, 90
Erem, M., 21
Esso/Exxon, 178, 179, 184
Ethiopia, 112, 209, 212; Marxist revolution
   in, 209
Europe: capitalism in, 66; colonialization
   by, 9, 17–19, 26, 324n19; cultural
   development in, 90–91; fascism in, 157;
   and global economy, 63, 66, 68, 192;
   Marshall Plan in, 64–65; nationalism in,
   12, 84–89, 168, 170–71, 219;
   rationalism in, 90–91; relative peace in
   (1815–1914), 41. *See also specific
   nations*
Eytan, Walter, 289n33

Fanon, Frantz, 81, 82, 85, 86, 107, 121–22,
   123, 130, 138–39
Farid, Ahmed, 79
Farouk, king of Egypt, 51
Farrokhzad, Forugh, 77–78, 93
Faysal, king of Saudi Arabia, 37, 260–61,
   263, 264, 267, 268
First, Ruth, 144–46, 149
First World: and Bretton Woods, 44–45,
   68; and Cold War *(see* Cold War);
   G-7, 214–15, 219, 220, 221, 227–28,
   231, 240, 243, 244, 248, 270; and global
   economy, 63, 66–69, 70, 71–72, 192,
   213–15, 243; hegemony of, 213,
   237–38, 278–80; market capitalism in,
   7, 8, 39, 66, 69, 71; materialism of, 79;

and negritude, 81, 82; presentation of
   the idea of, 6–7; resistance to, 109–10;
   transnationals of, 147–48, 185, 189,
   193, 201–2, 215, 227, 239–41, 252–53,
   257, 270, 278
Ford-Smith, Honor, 242
Formosa (Taiwan): China's threat to, 109,
   167, 172; Club 51 in, 257; information
   technology in, 212; land reform in, 200,
   249; and military pacts, 40; "Tiger"
   economy of, 245, 252, 254; and United
   Nations, 37, 102; U.S. aid to, 252
Fox, Edward, 138
France: ancien régime of, 11; colonies of,
   3–6, 19, 25, 28, 29, 52, 110, 125, 126,
   324n19; in Indochina, 4, 29, 119;
   nuclear weapons of, 101; and SEATO,
   38; as U.S. satellite, 10
Frankson, Joan Ross, 234
Freire, Paolo, 129
French Revolution, 3, 11, 79, 325n22
Friedman, Milton, 147
Fürer-Haimendorf, Christoph von, 169

Gandhi, Indira, 158, 207–9, *208*, 211,
   212–13, 215–16, 221, 317n20
Gandhi, Mohandas K. "Mahatma," 33, 35,
   167
Gandhi, Rajiv, 214, 218
Garang, Joseph, 161
GATT (General Agreement on Trade and
   Tariffs), 69–71, 219
Geertz, Clifford, 303n26
Germany: Berlin Wall in, 101; colonies of,
   19; Nazi Party in, 6, 157, 325n22
Gerstacker, Carl, 239
Ghana: African unity conferences in, 24;
   Convention People's Party, 12; cultural
   nationalism in, 87; independence of, 24,
   33; military coups in, 143, 147, 162; and
   nonviolence, 43; one-party state of, 110
Gide, André, 89
globalization: adoption of, 215; and
   cosmopolitan extranational sentiments,
   257–58; G-7 dominance of, 220;
   IMF-led *(see* IMF); vs. nationalism,
   217–19, 258, 274–75
Goh Keng Swee, 250, 251

Gomes, Leonard, 297n25

Gomes, Teodora Ignacia, 60

Gómez, Juan Vincente, 176

Gramsci, Antonio, 315n30

Great Britain. *See* Britain

Greece, 7, 140, 174

Green Revolution, 201–2

Grenada, New Jewel Movement in, 209, 237

Group of 7 (G-7), 214–15, 219, 220, 221, 227–29, 231, 240, 243, 244, 248, 270

Group of 15 (G-15), 280–81

Group of 77 (G-77), 13, 70, 72, 221, 243, 277

Gryseels, Guido, 285n5

Guatemala: Communist Party in, 164; guerrilla warfare in, 113; military dictatorship in, 142; U.S. intervention in, 106, 137, 142

Guevara, Che, 104, 108–9, 129, 290n43

Guinea-Bissau: Communist Party in, 158; independence of, 112, 128, 129; popular mobilization in, 139

Gumeda, Josiah, 21

Gutiérrez Alea, Tomás, 94

Hadj, Messali, 119

Haiti, 3, 106

Hajj, 'Aziz al-, 160

Hanum, Najiye, 295n34

Harbi, Mohammed, 312n3

Hassan, Sayeda, 54

Hassan, Seifel Islam, 37

Hatem, Mervat, 60

Hatta, Mohammad, 21, 29, 36

Havana: 1928 Conference in, 26; 1948 UN Conference on Trade and Employment, 68–69; 1966 Conference in (*see* Tricontinental Conference); 1979 NAM Summit in, 113, 209–12

Haya de la Torre, Víctor Raúl, 22, 26, 88

Hearne, R.P., 41–42

Heikal, Mohammad, 53, 329n37

Hendryk, Franck, 183

Hirohito, emperor of Japan, 27

Hitler, Adolf, 6

Hobsbawm, Eric, 325n22

Ho Chi Minh, xvii, 4, 5–6, 35, 129

Hochschild, Adam, 19

Holocaust, 6

Honduras, U.S. intervention in, 106

Hong Kong: as British colony, 249, 251; as global city, 249; "Tiger" economy of, 245, 247–48, 254

Hoxha, Enver, 291n51

Hungary, Soviet invasion of, 109, 309n31

Huntington, Samuel P., 140–41, 143–44, 145, 146, 200

Husayni, Jamal al-, 21

Hussein, king of Jordan, 260, 346n17

Hussein, Saddam, 160

IAEA (International Atomic Energy Agency), 42, 101

IMF (International Monetary Fund): and debt crisis, 222, 256; G-7 and, 243; globalization driven by, 209–15, 217, 219, 222, 236, 238, 239, 241, 243, 244, 247, 258, 271, 273–75, 277, 279, 280; inequality perpetuated by, 242–44; influence of, 243, 271; loans with conditions attached, xviii, 71, 216, 222, 226, 230–39, 234; Terra Nova Statement on, 242–44; and UNCTAD, 233, 234

imperialism: cultural, 81–84; European, 19, 80–81; fight against, xvii, 20–21, 27, 34, 45, 105–7, 111–12, 217; and neocolonialism, 111; and women's rights, 57–58

India, 207–23, 317n20; arms buildup of, 174, 215; banks nationalized in, 215–16; Bharatiya Janata Party (BJP) in, 218; border wars of, 165–75; in British Commonwealth, 98, 100; British goods unloaded in, 73, 84, 167; British rule in, 66, 207; and China, 165–75, 215; in Cold War, 98; Communist Party in, 158, 161–62, 208; Congress Party in, 208, 209, 215–18; cultural nationalism in, 87, 88, 218; economic concerns in, 199, 215–16, 218, 232; freedom movement in, 12, 29–30, 43; Green Revolution in, 201; independence of, 33, 36, 200, 293n31; industrial output of, 215; information technology in, 212, 218; and Kashmir, 167; mass

India (cont.)
    protests in, 54; and military pacts, 40,
    215; National Congress Party in, 33,
    35; Nellie, Assam, massacre in, 208–9;
    and nonviolence, 43, 167; nuclear tests
    by, 221, 302n14; and Pakistan, 167, 168,
    207, 215; Partition of, 207; population
    shifts in, 196–97; social problems in,
    199, 200, 215–17, 218; and United
    Nations, 42, 43, 174; welfarism of, 193,
    202; women's rights in, 84
Indian Ocean, zone of peace in, 221
Indochina: Dien Bien Phu in, 119; French
    colony of, 4, 29. See also Vietnam;
    Vietnam War
Indonesia, 31–33, 163; Communist Party
    (PKI), 35, 36, 152–56, 158–59, 162;
    freedom movement in, 29–30, 152–54;
    independence of, 33, 34, 36; military
    coup in, 141, 152–54; NASAKOM,
    152–54; nationalism in, 35; PNI (Partai
    Nasional Indonesia), 35, 36; and United
    Nations, 156; U.S. intervention in, 106,
    108, 140, 155, 237; welfarism in, 202
Industrial Revolution, 79
Inter-American Conference (1889), 25
International Alliance of Women (1939),
    55
International Chamber of Commerce,
    240–41
International Conference for Women,
    Rome (1924), 54–55
International Women's Year (1975), 56
Ionesco, Eugène, 89
Iran, 75–80; and Baghdad Pact, 38; CIA
    intervention in, 75, 76, 140, 346n17;
    Communist Party in, 76; cultural
    development in, 90–91; Niru-ye Sevum
    (Third Force) in, 77; oil in, 75, 76, 80,
    179, 184; Revolution in, 76, 269; Shah
    of, 75, 76–77, 78, 266; Tudeh Party in,
    76–77, 78; women's protests in, 54
Iraq: Baath Party in, 159–60; and
    Baghdad Pact, 38; Communist Party in
    (ICP), 39, 149, 158, 159–60, 161;
    military coup in, 148, 262, 264; and
    NAM, 163; and OPEC, 184; U.S.
    invasion of, 278

Iron Curtain, 7
Irredentist Party, 325n22
Islam: Communism vs., 267–68;
    community in, 268; Jihad Fund,
    270–71; Mecca, 263–64, 267; Movement
    of Muslim Revolutionaries of the
    Arabian Peninsula, 269; Muslim
    Brotherhood, 148–49, 267, 273; and
    nationalism, 263; Organization of the
    Islamic Conference (OIC), 260–61,
    268; and Saudi royal family, 260–61,
    268–69; and Third World, 268–69;
    Wahhabism, 261, 263, 264; World
    Muslim League (WML), 260–62,
    267–68, 270–73
Israel: Arab wars with, 167, 188; denial of,
    289–90n33; Likud regime in, 221; and
    military pacts, 40
Italy, 19, 41, 42, 306n3, 325n22
Ivory Coast, 128

Jamaica: Arawak population of, 224;
    bauxite industry in, 225, 226–28, 237,
    239; as British colony, 224; democratic
    socialism in, 226, 228, 236, 241;
    economic problems of, 229, 233–39; fall
    of government in, 235–36; foreign
    investment in, 225–26, 239;
    independence of, 224; People's National
    Party in, 224–25; reconstruction
    program for, 236–37, 238; social unrest
    in, 238–39; sugarcane grown on, 224,
    227; women's movement in, 241–42
Japan: and China, 107, 167; economic
    success of, 245, 280; imperialism of, 27,
    35, 49, 249; land reform in, 200;
    surrender of, 35–36
Johnson, Lyndon B., 140
Justo, Juan Bautista, 28, 63

Kahin, George, 35
Kalecki, Michal, 64
Kalinin, Mikhail, 97
Karam, Bahia, 294n25
Kardelj, Edvard, 102, 103, 307n11
Kashmir, 167, 273
Kaunda, Kenneth, 108
Kaur, Rajkumari Amrit, 10–11, 88

Keita, Mobido, 100, 101, 158
Keita, Sundiata, 324n19
Kennedy, John F., 101, 137, 140
Kenya, 9, 128
Kenyatta, Jomo, 23, 312n10
Kerton, Sudjana, xvii
Keynes, John Maynard, 68, 212, 328n16
Khalil, Hamida, 54
Khan, Abdul Rahman, king of
   Afghanistan, 170
Khan, Ayub, 98, 147, 158
Khan, Yahya, 147
Khrushchev, Nikita, 46, 77, 97, 101,
   300n43
Kim Dae Jung, 344n51
Kissinger, Henry A., 189, 318n48
Konar, Hari Krishna, 332
Korea, independence of, 33
Korean War, 28, 37
Kotelawala, John, 36, 38, 40, 48
Krieg, Bill, 164
Kripalani, Acharya, 11, 167
Kulthum, Umm, xvii, 52
Kuwait, 184, 186–87

La Guma, James, 21
Lansky, Meyer, 105
Latin America: Alliance for Progress in,
   134, 137, 142; anti-imperialist
   movements in, 105–6; Casa de Las
   Americas, 88; Castroism in, 162; CIA
   in, 140, 142; colonialization of, 4, 13,
   28, 66; Communist Party in, 109, 138,
   156, 262; economic problems of, 28,
   62–64, 66–68; Free Trade Organization, 70; guerrilla warfare in, 113, 279,
   322n36; military coups in, 138, 140–44,
   145, 148; and NAM meetings, 310n6;
   Prebisch's writings on, 62–64; Punta
   Del Este Conference (1967), 201; social
   upheavals in, 200, 279; Spanish
   invasion of, 134–35; transnational firms
   in, 147–48; and United Nations, 10,
   26–27, 102; U.S. interventions in,
   25–27, 101, 105–6, 109, 136–38, 140,
   142–43, 147, 236; women's rights in,
   55–56, 293n24. See also specific nations
Lavosiere, Jacques de, 235

League against Imperialism: Brussels
   conference (1927), 12, 14, 16, 19–20,
   21–23, 25, 26, 156; Communist funding
   of, 19–20; formation of, 21; inflexibility
   of, 29–30; legacy of, 29, 30, 32
League of Nations, 21, 25, 28, 102
Lechín, Juan, 138
Leclerc, Victor, 3
Lee Hsien Loong, 257
Lee Kuan Yew, 211, 250–53, 258–59
Leiris, Michel, 6
Lenin, Vladimir Ilyich, 20, 287–88n39,
   314n30
Leopold II, king of Belgium, 16–18, 19
Lévi-Strauss, Claude, 6, 45
Lewis, W. Arthur, 225
Libya: independence of, 33; military coup
   in, 148, 262; and OPEC, 187, 188;
   Popular Resistance Force in, 139
Lin Biao, 107, 158
Lippmann, Walter, 7
Locke, John, 5
Lui Shao-Ch'i, 158, 171
Lumumba, Patrice, 161, 163, 262, 285n5
Luther, Martin, 79
Lutyens, Edwin, 207
Lutz, Bertha, 55
Lu Xun, 88

MacArthur, Douglas, 48
Machel, Samora, 220
MacMillan, Harold, 307n12
Madagascar, 4, 5
Madani, Tawfiz al-, 292n4
Magsaysay, Ramon, 38
Mahdi, Sadiq al-, 161
Mahgoub, Mohamed Ahmed, 89
Mahjub, Abdel al-Khaliq, 161
Mahsas, Ali, 125
Makhluf, Shakyh Hasanayn, 56–57
Malawi, postcolonial, 128
Malaysia: anti-Chinese riots in, 83, 250;
   Communist rebellion in, 38;
   independence of, 33, 249
Maleki, Khalil, 77, 78
Mali, 158, 167, 324n19
Malik, Charles, 92
Mandela, Nelson, xvii, 144

Manila Pact (SEATO), 38, 40

Manley, Michael, 108, 209, 226–28, 232, 235–36, 241

Manley, Nelson, 224–26

Mao Tse-tung, 37, 107, 109

Maoism, 113, 161, 162, 215

Marcos, Ferdinand, 237

Marcuse, Herbert, 91

Marley, Bob, 224, 228–29, 232, 233

Marshall, Alfred, 296–97n16

Marshall Plan, 64–65

Marx, Karl, 146

Marxism. *See* Communism

Matango, R.R., 196

Mattei, Enrico, 186

Mauritania, boundary wars, 167

Maxwell, Kenneth, 318n48

McKinsey and Co., 197

McNamara, Robert S., 141, 144, 173, 235

Memories of Underdevelopment (Gutiérrez Alea), 94

Merak Lama (Lodre Gyaltso), 169–70

Messali, Hadj-Ahmed, 21

Mexican Eagle, 179

Mexico: agrarian solutions in, 200–201; economic concerns of, 217, 230; industrial output of, 215; oil in, 179–80, 217; PEMEX, 180, 313–14n21; Revolution, 294n35, 313–14n21

Miin Wu, 212

military coups, 130–32, 133, 138–49; colonels' coups, 146, 148–49; generals' coups, 146–48; political process frozen by, 149, 203; reasons and logic for, 145–46, 318n32; social reforms rolled back in, 147, 148, 172–73

Miranda, Miguel, 63

Mobutu Sese Seko (Joseph Désiré), 141, 161, 262

Mohamed, Mahathir, 276

Mohamed, Shafika, 54

Monje, Mario, 109

Moore, Richard, 22

Morel, E.D., 18

Morocco: boundary wars, 167; Communist Party in, 163; Spanish bombardment of, 41, 42

Morrison, William, 18

Morshead, Henry T., 169, 170

Mosaddeq, Muhammed, 75–78, 80

Moscono, Teodoro, 134

Mozambique, 103, 112

Mulele, Pierre, 161

Mulk Raj Anand, 88

Muntasser, Mahmud, 37

Münzenberg, Willi, 20, 21

Musa, Nabawiya, 54

Musharraf, Pervez, 147

Muslim Brotherhood (Ikhwan al-Muslimin), 148–49, 267, 273

Nabaraoui, Ceza, 54, 55

Naguib, Mohamed, 148

Naim, Moisés, 212

Naim, Sardar Mohammed, 36

NAM. *See* Non-Aligned Movement

Namboodripad, E.M.S., 301n49

Naoroji, Dadabhai, 66

NASAKOM, xvii, 152–54, 158

Nassar, Shaykh Allam, 57

Nasser, Gamal Abdel, xv, xvii, 4, 13, 108; at Bandung Conference, 39, 46, 48, 50, 52, 263; at Brijuni conference, 95, 96–97, 100; and Cold War, 98–100, 158; and Free Officers coup, 51–52, 261; influence of, 184, 264; and Islam, 345n10; and oil, 181, 182; power amassed by, 148–49; and UAR, 162, 264; and women's rights, 56–57, 60

Nasserism, 264–65, 266, 267, 270

nationalism: anticolonial, 82, 83–86, 163, 217; and borders, 168–72; concepts of, 268; cultural, xviii, 82–91, 115; degradation of idea of, xviii, 219, 258–59, 262–63, 274; and economic autarky, 217; ethno-, 163–64, 172, 219, 262; globalization vs., 217–19, 258, 274–75, 279; internationalist, 12, 163, 197; multinationalism, 85–89; national identity sought in, 86, 105, 115; political illusion of, 237, 279; populist, 26, 35; progressive, 45; sectarian, 219; and secular democracy, 217, 274; transformations in, 91–92, 217–19; Wahhibism as, 261, 263 national liberation movements: achievements of, 221; alternative national theory of, 12; anticolonialism of, 13, 30, 83; armed struggle as tactic of, 107, 122; and Cold War, 10, 105; and Communist Party, 22, 29–30, 97, 209; economic targets of, 66, 192–93, 217–18; IMF vs., 236, 238; and military coups, 146, 149; nostalgia in, 131–32; and one-party states, 145, 146; political power centralized in, 123–24; post-revolution nation-building, 122–30; and socialism, 123–24, 130, 191–99; and women's rights, 54, 57, 59–61

National Security Council (NSC), 141

National Women's Congress of Workers and Peasants (1931), 56

nativism vs. colonialism, 82

NATO (North Atlantic Treaty Organization), 7, 10, 96, 173

Nazi party, 6, 157, 325n22

Nehru, Jawaharlal, xv, xvii, 4, 11–12, 27, 29, 34; at Bandung conference, 36, 39, 46, 48, 165–66, 213; and border problems, 165–66, 167, 171–72; at Brijuni conference, 95, 96–97, 100; at Brussels conference, 21, 22; and Cold War, 98, 99, 100; and Communist Party, 110, 162; death of, 108, 162; and Indian independence, 33, 36, 293n31; and military pacts, 40; and NAM, 13, 14, 29; on nonviolence, 43, 167; on nuclear weapons, 101; and United Nations, 41; and USSR, 46, 98

Nehru, Rameshwari, 53

Neish, Robert, 238

neocolonialism, use of term, 10

Neocolonialism (Nkrumah), 110

Neopatriarchy, use of term, 14

NEPAD (New Partnership for Africa's Development), 280–81

Neruda, Pablo, xvii, 88, 108–9, 147, 149–50, 151–52

New Delhi, 207–8; NAM meeting in (1977), 163; NAM Summit in (1983), 208–14

Ne Win, 158

New Zealand, and SEATO, 38, 40

Nguyen Thi Binh, xvii

Nguyen Van Tien, 108

Nicaragua: guerrilla warfare in, 113, 209, 210, 237; U.S. interventions in, 26, 42, 106, 236

Nigeria, civil war in, 327n39

Nimeiri, Jaafar al-, 148, 159, 160–61, 174

Nixon, Richard M., 147, 188

Nkrumah, Kwame, xv, 4, 14, 23, 24; in Brijuni conference, 100; on neocolonialism, 10, 110–11; on nuclear threat, 101; one-party state of, 110; removal of, 162

Non-Aligned Movement (NAM): achievement of, 103; Algeria summit (1973), 132, 219, 254; in Bandung (see Bandung Conference); Belgrade meeting (1961), 185, 308n20; Brijuni conference, 95–97, 100–101, 277; Cairo conference (1964), 44, 110, 221; Common Fund of, 220, 280; creation of, xvi, 4, 13–15, 49, 95–97, 100, 163, 221; decline of, 220, 277; economic concerns of, 132, 220, 254–55; G-15, 280–81; G-77, 13, 70, 72, 221, 243, 277; Harare Summit (1986), 276–78; in Havana (1966) (see Tricontinental Conference); Havana conference (1979), 113, 209–12; Head of State Conferences, 307n18; and IMF-driven globalization, 209–15; New Delhi meetings, 163, 208–14; New International Economic Order (NIEO) of, 132, 163, 189, 214, 219, 229, 252, 255; peaceful coexistence as challenge of, 96, 101, 103–4, 106–7; political issues involving, 101, 104, 107, 110, 222; South Commission of, 276–78; split in, 209, 213; and USSR, 210–11

nostalgia, political purpose of, 131–32

Nyerere, Julius, 113, 191–99, 202, 276, 304n40

oil: in Algeria, 131, 189; in Arab nations, 179–88, 263–64, 266, 269–70; Bolivia-Paraguay war, 178; control of, 177–81, 183, 184, 186–87, 215; embargo (1973), 188–89, 229, 231; exploration for, 186;

oil *(cont.)*
    and global economy, 231; Maadi Pact, 184; in Mexico, 179–80, 217; nationalization of, 186–87, 189; as nonrenewable resource, 184; OPEC, 184–90, 229; as political weapon, 266; prices, 180, 181, 182, 184–86, 188–89, 229, 270; profits from, 179, 185–86, 188, 270; Seven Sisters of, 178–85, 186–87; in Venezuela, 176–90
Omar, Aisha, 54
OPEC, 184–90, 229
Organization of African Unity, 113
Ottoman Empire, 24, 25, 39

Padmore, George, 23
Pakistan: and Baghdad Pact, 38; and Bangladesh, 174; and China, 166; CIA in, 272; Communist Party in, 38, 149, 158; IMF influence in, 271; independence of, 33; and India, 167, 168, 207, 215; Islamization of, 271, 272, 273; and Kashmir, 167; military coup in, 147; Partition of, 207; and SEATO, 38; U.S. deals with, 98
Palestine, 25, 221
Palestine Liberation Organization (PLO), 311n24
Pan-African Conference, London (1900), 23–24
Panama, U.S. intervention in, 106, 278
Pan-American Union, 25, 26
Pan-Asian People's Conferences, 27
Paraguay, 138, 178
Park Chung-hee, 251
Patiño, Simón Ituri, 135
Pavicevic, Miso, 308n20
Paz, Octavio, 79
Paz Estenssoro, Víctor, 135, 138
Pellegrini, Carlos, 63
Pentagon, U.S., military modernization theory of, 140–44
Peralta Azurdia, Enrique, 142
Perez, Luis, 85
Pérez Alfonzo, Juan Pablo, 182–83, 184, 185, 189–90
Pérez Cisneros, Guy, 10
Pérez Jiménez, Marcos, 177

Péron, Juan, 63
Peru, IMF loan to, 232–33
Philippines: dictatorship of, 237; Huk Rebellion (1946–54), 38; independence of, 33; industrial output of, 230; land reform in, 200; and SEATO, 38
The Philosophy of the Revolution (Nasser), 184
Pinochet Ugarte, Augusto, 141, 147–48, 174
Pitroda, Sam, 212
The Political Economy of Growth (Baran), 73
The Population Bomb (Ehrlich), 8
Portal, Magda, 88
Portugal: colonies of, 18, 53, 82, 103, 108, 110, 111, 112, 113, 209, 324n19; coup in, 112, 209; Methuen Treaty, 297n25; PAIGC in, 103, 111–12
Powell, Adam Clayton Jr., 47–48
Prebisch, Raúl, 225; on public commodity cartels, 180, 183, 185; on Third World economic problems, 62–64, 66–68, 69, 71, 72, 73–74; and UNCTAD, 70
Présence Africaine, 3, 81–82, 121
Punta Del Este Conference (1967), 201

Qaddafi, Muammar, 148
Qasim, 'Abd al-Karim, 148, 158, 159–60, 182

Radi, Husain ar-, 160, 161
Raikes, Philip, 198
Rajaratnam, Sinnathamby, 211–13, 219, *246*, 247, 251–54
Ramabai, Pandita, 293n13
Ramarao, N.T., 208
RAND Corporation, 140
Rao, V.K.R.V., 70
Ratebzad, Anahita, 272
Raza, Rahi Masoom, 174–75
Reagan Doctrine, 210
"Recabarren" (Neruda), 151–52
Recabarren, Luis Emilio, 151
Reed, John, 21
Reformation, 79
Renascent Africa (Azikiwe), 23
Riad, Fahima, 54

Ricardo, David, 67
Ricupero, Rubens, 241
Robinson, Geoffrey, 155, 164
Rockefeller Foundation, 200
Rodriquez, Miguel, 212
Rogers, William D., 318n48
Rolland, Romain, 22
Romulo, Carlos, 36, 38, 39, 44, 48
Roosevelt, Eleanor, 10
Roosevelt, Franklin D., 95
Roosevelt, Kermit "Kim," 75
Rostow, W.W., 65
Rothschild, Emma, 230
Roxas, Manuel, 38
Rushkanfekri, 90–91
Russell, Bertrand, 156
Russia. *See* USSR

Saadawi, Nawal El-, 54
Sadat, Anwar es-, 52–53, 149
Said, Karima El, 57
Salah, Walid, 37
Salam 'Arif, 'Abd al-, 148
Sampson, Anthony, 9
Santamaría, Haydée, 88
São Tomé, independence of, 112
Sarraut, Albert, 5
Sartre, Jean-Paul, 89, 121
Sarvodaya, xvii
Saudi Arabia: and Communist Party,
    264–65, 266, 267, 270, 274; Nasserism
    in, 264–65, 267, 270; oil in, 179,
    183–84, 186–87, 263–64, 269–70; royal
    family of, 178, 260–61, 263–66, 268–69,
    270, 274; and Soviet bloc, 263; U.S.
    influence in, 266–67, 274; U.S. military
    base in, 264
Sauvy, Albert, 6, 10, 11, 13, 32
Savushun (Daneshvar), 92
Schoppert, Peter, 247
Scott, James, 332n18
Seaga, Edward, 236, 237–38
SEATO (South East Asian Treaty
    Organization), 38, 40, 46
Second World: collapse of, 219, 258, 278,
    279; presentation of the idea of, 6–7;
    socialism in, 7; and zone of peace, 46.
    See also USSR

Selassie, Haile, 100, 112
Semaun, 21
Senegal, 324n19
Senghor, Lamine, 23
Senghor, Léopold, 81
Sharabi, Hisham, 14
Sha'rawi, Huda, 54–55
Shariati, Ali, 91–92
Sheikh, Ahmed El, 161
Sheppard, William, 18
Shukri, Aminah, 60
Sihanouk, Prince Norodom, 100
Singapore, 245–59; as British colony,
    249; Communist Party in, 211,
    249–50; Development Plan (1960–64),
    251; and economic crisis, 256, 258;
    Economic Expansion Incentives Act
    (1967), 253; free-trade port of, 211,
    253; independence of, 247; People's
    Action Party (PAP) in, 250–51, 252,
    254; professional flight to, 254;
    technology in, 254; "Tiger" economy
    of, 245–49, 252–55; trade unions in,
    253
Singer, H.W., 64, 294n1
Singh, Manmohan, 212
Slovo, Joe, 144
socialism: abandoned goals of, xviii;
    Arusha Declaration, 191–93;
    bureaucratism in, 196, 198; in Cold
    War, 8; commandism in, 196, 197; and
    Communist Party, 156–57, 158, 306n3;
    of consumption not production, 199;
    economic autarky as, 217; in former
    colonial states, 191–99; in a hurry, 191,
    196, 197; in mixed economy, 199,
    306n6; as new democracy, 158; in
    Second World, 7; as Third World goal,
    xvii, 24, 123–24, 130, 148, 191, 262;
    transitional stages toward, 20–21, 193,
    195, 197; ujamaa (villagization), 192,
    194–98
Soederberg, Susanne, 226
Solh, Riad as-, 265
Solh, Sami, 37
Somalia, armed struggle in, 112
"Someone Who Is Not Like Anyone"
    (Farrokhzad), 93–94

Sorel, George, 311n23

South Africa: apartheid in, 40, 144, 221; Communist Party in, 156; Defiance Campaign (1952), 12; NEPAD in, 280–81; Umkhonto we Sizwe in, 111

South America. *See* Latin America

South Korea: financial crisis in, 256; industrial output of, 215, 230; land reform in, 200, 249; "Tiger" economy of, 245, 252, 254; U.S. aid to, 252

South Yemen, Marxism in, 271

Soviet Union. *See* USSR

Spain, colonies of, 66

Spaulding, Winston, 238

Stalin, Joseph, 37, 46, 95, 97

Stanley, Henry, 17

Stanovnik, Janez, 299n35

Stone, I.F., 39

Stroessner, Alfredo, 138

Sudan: Communist Party in, 149, 159, 160–61; famine in, 212; IMF loan to, 233; independence of, 33; military coup in, 148; and NAM, 163; and Saudi Arabia, 274

Suez Canal, 52, 100, 263, 292n62

Suharto, Haji Mohammed, 141, 143, 154, 155–56, 163, 237

Sukarno, Ahmed, *4*, 33–36, 48, 156; in Bandung conference, xvii, 30, 33–34, 39; in Belgrade conference, 306–7n11; in Brijuni conference, 100; in Brussels conference, 21; and Communist Party, 110, 152–54, 159, 162; and independence, 36; national theory of, 12, 13, 14; on nuclear threat, 101; overthrow of, 108, 154, 310n9; rise to power of, 152–54, 162

SUNFED (Special UN Fund for Economic Development), 44, 70

Sun Yat-sen, 27

Sun Yat-sen, Madame (Soong Ch'ingling), 22, 171

Syria, 161, 264

Taiwan. *See* Formosa

Tanarat, Sarit, 138

Tanganyika African National Union (TANU), 191–94

Tanzania: agriculture in, 192, 194–96, 197, 202; armed struggle in, 113; and Arusha Declaration (1967), 191–93, 195, 199; and Arusha Initiative (1980), 243–44; *Mwongozo* (Leadership Code) in, 191; National Service in, 139; postcolonial, 128, 133, 194–98; socialism as goal in, 191–98, 202; ujamaa program in, 194, 195–98, 202

Tariqi, 'Abdullah al- "Red Sheikh," 183–84, 265–66

Teresa, Mother, 9

"Terra Nova Statement on the International Monetary System and the Third World," 242–44

Thailand, 38, 138

Therborn, Göran, 7, 8

Third World: absolutism in, 144; anticolonialism in (*see* colonialism); armed struggle as tactic of, 106–7, 110, 111–13, 122, 162; arms expenditures of, 220; character of governance in, 128; and civil rights, 89–90, 135; and Cold War, 8–11, 13, 42, 98–100, 105, 106–7, 113–14, 278, 327n37; Communist Parties in, 133, 161–63; community in, 70, 268; cultural nationalism in, xviii, 82–91, 105, 115, 217–18; demise of, xviii–xix, 14, 15, 133, 162, 209, 219–22, 240, 258, 276–79; dissent in, 140, 174; on economic development, 45, 91–92; economic problems of, 34, 62–64, 69–70, 114–15, 173, 197, 210–11, 212, 214–17, 229–39, 247, 258, 276, 280; education and literacy in, 88–90, 115; food security in, 201–2; foreign aid to, 64–65, 71–73; goals of, 11, 163; guerrilla wars in, 57, 162; idea of, xvii, 6–7, 11, 13, 15, 30, 32, 221; internationalist nationalism of, 12, 163, 197; land reform in, 74, 127, 142, 147, 198–201, 202; and League against Imperialism, 16, 22; military coups in, 130–32, 133, 138–49, 159, 162, 203; multiplicity (diversity) in, 84–87; nationalization of industries in, 186–87; and non-alignment, 99 (*see also* Non-Aligned Movement);

one-commodity nations of, 181, 182, 227, 233, 270; one-party states of, 123, 128–29, 139–40, 145, 312n10; and peaceful coexistence, 106–7, 109; political platform developed in, 14, 113–14, 162; popular mobilization in, 122, 133, 139–40; post-revolution nation-building in, 122–30; as project, xv, xvii, 231, 258; proxy wars in, 210, 211, 212, 220; racialism opposed by, 45; reconstruction in, 64, 127–28; separatist movements in, 84; social hierarchies maintained in, xvii–xviii, 14, 36, 45, 73, 91, 110, 115, 122–24, 129–30, 199, 212, 217–18, 219; socialized democracy lacking in, 123–26, 130; social unrest in, 198; structural adjustment of, 258; teachers in, 78–79, 80; technological development in, 91–92; ujamaa (villagization), 192, 194–98; and United Nations, xvi, 10, 11, 13, 15, 27–28, 41, 49, 73–74, 103; unity in, xvii–xviii, 11, 34, 217; and Vietnam War, 107–10; welfarist nations of, 193, 202, 242, 248; xenophobia in, 217, 218–19; in zone of peace, 46. *See also specific nations*

Tibet, 167, 168, 169, 170, 172

Tidjani, Hashemi, 126

Tito, Marshall, *4*; African tour of, 307n17; at Brijuni conference, 95, 96–97, 100; and Cold War, 46, 97–98, 100, 162

Tlatelelco Treaty (1963), 221

Togo, military coup in, 147

Touré, Sékou, 158

Tran Danh Tuyen, 108

tribalism, 262

Tricontinental Conference, Havana (1966), 209; arguments taken to UN from, xvi; ideology crafted in, xv, 104, 107, 111–13, 122; on struggle against Third World's own weakness, 114–15; on Vietnam War, 107–9

Trilateral Commission, 141

Truman, Harry S., 7, 38, 290n42

Tunisia, nationalism in, 84

Turkey, 7, 38, 84–85

Uganda, military coup in, 147

UNCTAD (UN Conference on Trade and Development): creation of, xvi, 45, 299n35; decline of, 277, 280; and G-77, 70, 72; and IMF, 233, 234; Nairobi meeting of (1976), 220; and NIEO, 189; on one-commodity nations, 181, 185; and Third World economic development, 70–74, 189, 222; and transnationals, 241

UNCTC (UN Centre on Transnational Corporations), 240, 241

UNESCO (UN Educational, Scientific, and Cultural Organization), 6, 10–11, 45, 85, 87, 89–90

United Arab Republic (UAR), 162, 264

United Fruit Company, 18, 106, 137

United Kingdom. *See* Britain

United Nations (UN): Charter of, 48; and Cold War, 44, 109, 173–74; Convention on the Law of the Sea, 219; demo-cratization of, 96, 101, 102–4, 163; Development Programs, 44, 70, 234; diminishing influence of, 49; Food and Agriculture Organization, 70, 74, 201–2; founding of, 10, 102; Global Compact Program, 339n55; and global economy, 64, 68–69, 70–74; and IAEA, 42; and land reform, 74; and Latin America, 26–27, 102; membership in, 41; and NAM, 96, 100, 102–3, 163; and NIEO, 163, 189, 214, 219; and nuclear threat, 101, 173, 221; reform urged for, 280; roles of, xvi, 44, 167; Security Council of, 102, 221; successes of, 28; and Third World, xvi, 10, 11, 13, 15, 27–28, 41, 49, 73–74, 103; and transnational corporations, 240–41; and women's rights, 56

United States: arms sales by, 71–72, 98, 99; and Baghdad Pact, 38; and Bandung Conference, 47–48; and Bay of Pigs, 101, 142; deficit spending of, 231, 270; deindustrialization of, 188; foreign aid from, 71–72, 192, 252, 267; and global economy, 63, 66, 68, 243; hegemony of, 213, 237–38, 278–80; interventions in Latin America by, 25–27, 105–6, 109,

United States *(cont.)*
136–38, 140, 142–44, 147, 236; Marshall Plan of, 64–65; military umbrella of, 38–39; nuclear weapons of, 42–43, 221; and SEATO, 38, 46; and UN Security Council, 102; and World War II, 8

Universal Declaration on Eradication of Hunger and Malnutrition (1974), 202

U Nu, 34, 36, 39, 46, 48–49, 100, 101, 108, 162, 166–67

Uruguay, Communist Party in, 156

Uslar-Pietri, Arturo, 176, 178

USSR: and African nations, 112; and Arab nations, 98–100, 160, 263; arms sales by, 46, 50, 99; Bolshevik Revolution in, 97; and China, 10, 37, 47, 110, 166; and Cold War, 7–8, 9–10, 37, 46–48, 109, 113, 156, 278; Comecon of, 72; Cominform in, 9, 97–98; Cominterm of, 20–21, 22, 29–30, 156, 157; Communist Party in, 8, 46, 97, 153, 156, 157–58, 278; decline of, 210–11, 212, 213, 219, 228, 272–73, 278; Eastern European states in orbit of, 7, 72–73; economic aid from, 46, 52, 72–73, 149, 156, 158, 192; Karakhan Manifesto, 166; and Latin America, 72–73, 106, 143; nuclear weapons of, 42–43, 101; October Revolution in, 210; oil in, 180, 186; Stalinist purges in, 286n12; and Third World, 9–10, 20–21, 46, 106–7, 133, 156, 209; and UN Security Council, 102; and World War II, 8, 72; and zone of peace, 46

Vandervelde, Émile, 19

Vasconcelias, José, 22

Venezuela: foreign investment in, 177; military coup in, 148; oil in, 176–90; social upheaval in, 177, 279

Vietnam, 4, 33, 35, 129

Vietnam War, 4, 5, 106, 107–10, 112–13, 209

Wahhab, Muhammed ibn 'Abd al-, 261

Wahhabism, 261, 263, 264

Wallace, W.T., 176

Warsaw Pact, 10, 37, 72, 96, 173

Wilcox, Clair, 69

Williams, Henry Sylvester, 23

Wilson, Woodrow, 21

women: in guerrilla warfare, 57; programs for, 242; rights of, 53–61, 84, 241–42, 293n24

World Bank: on agriculture sector, 194, 201; and Asian "Tiger" economies, 248–49; Brandt Report of, 235; and global debt, 229; and land reform, 202; loans with conditions attached, xviii, 9, 71, 216, 222, 232, 235, 276, 338n43; on military vs. social spending, 173; and wealth gap, 277

World Muslim League (WML), 260–62, 267–68, 270–73

World Trade Organization (WTO), 228

World War II: alliances in, 157; economic impact of, 72, 249; horrors of, 6; populations lost in, 8

The Wretched of the Earth (Fanon), 121–22

Wright, Richard, 81

Yalta Conference (1945), 95, 96

Ydígoras Fuentes, Miguel, 142

Yemen, in UAR, 264, 265

Youssef, Ben, 100

Yugoslavia: Belgrade conference (1961), xvi, *4*, 95–97, 167, 185, 308n20; Brijuni conference (1956), 95–97, 100–101, *277*; in Cold War, 97–98; and Communist Party, 97–98; dismemberment of, 278; and Third World, 46, 306n5; and USSR, 46, 98, 162; U.S. violation of airspace of, 98

Zaire, 233, 262

Zakaria, Fareed, 251

Zaki, Khalid Ahmed, 161

Zhdanov, Andrei, 10, 97, 99

Zhou En-lai, 36–37, 165–67, 171–72

Zia ul-Haq, Muhammad, 271, 272, 273

Zimbabwe, 111, 112